THE GREAT BOOK OF
DETROIT SPORTS LISTS

THE GREAT BOOK OF
DETROIT
SPORTS LISTS

BY MIKE "STONEY" STONE AND ART REGNER

Running Press
PHILADELPHIA · LONDON

9 8 7 6 5 4 3 2 1

Digit on the right indicates the number of this printing

Library of Congress Control Number: 2008926940

ISBN 978-0-7624-3354-4

Cover and Interior Designed by Matthew Goodman

Running Press Book Publishers
2300 Chestnut Street
Philadelphia, PA 19103-4371
Visit us on the web!

www.runningpress.com

Dedication

Dedicated to my parents Lewis and Sandra Stone, and my sister Lisa Stone Falasco, for supporting my obsession with sports from an early age (although my mom wanted me to be a doctor or lawyer). To my lovely and talented wife Cyndi for putting up with me, my job, and my Bruce Springsteen obsession; I love you very much. To my darling, beautiful twin daughters Jessica and Marissa, who give me more happiness than they know. I also want to thank Bernie Smilovitz for bringing me to Detroit in 1986, Mitch Albom for allowing me to co-host "The Sunday Sports Albom" from 1988-1994, and Bob "Wojo" Wojonowski for being the best radio partner a guy could have. And thanks to the listeners of WDFN for over 14 years of support.

—Stoney

This book is dedicated to the people of Detroit and Michigan. Without their support and enthusiasm we could not have written The Great Book of Detroit Sports Lists.

—Art

CONTENTS

Acknowledgements

Thanks to our many media friends for their lists and contributions. Special thanks to Jeff Moss and Mike Regan for their many uncredited contributions to this book and for helping us in a bind. We also were aided by many friends, public relations people and fans, including Harry Glanz, Jay Levine, Alan Borsen, Mike O'Hara, Mickey Rosner, Ken Droz, Tom "Governor" Milliken, Gordy Leff, Robert Brown, Brian Cohen, Rona Danziger, Ron Wolf, Matt Fiorito, Bill Keenist, Kevin Grigg, Matt Dobek, readers of the Detroit Sports Rag, our WDFN listeners and coworkers, and publisher Greg Jones.

—Stoney

There are so many people to thank that trying to name them all would be the longest list in this book. I am grateful to everyone that contributed a list; your commitment to this book was overwhelming. I must also let my family, friends, and colleagues know that you're all part of this project. I have learned so much from all of you that without your guidance and friendship, my life would be empty. Most of all I am greatly indebted to two people. Greg Jones of Running Press who really helped me navigate through a difficult time. You're a rare human being, Greg. The other one is my friend Chris Saucier. Without Chris this book would never have been completed. Being able to bounce lists and ideas off a younger fan allowed me to understand the scope of this project. It's about all of us. Thanks Chris, I never had a little brother until now.

—Art

Introduction

Stoney

I moved to Michigan in 1986, and since my arrival I have witnessed many incredible sports moments. In that time, the area has experienced multiple Stanley Cups, NBA titles, collegiate championships, a surprising trip to the World Series and Barry Sanders. I have been blessed by world-class events such as a Super Bowl, Ryder Cup and even a Wrestlemania. After spending the first 28 years of my life on the East Coast before moving here, I am convinced Detroit is the most well-rounded sports area in the country. I was asked to find a co-author for this book. I chose Art Regner. The choice was easy. He is a lifelong Michgander, he is passionate and he is a helluva writer. Although as our editor Mike Regan, publisher Greg Jones, and many of Art's radio co-hosts throughout the years will attest, punctuality is not his greatest strength. That aside, we hope you will find this book both informative and somewhat humorous.

The lists cover the obvious, from the best players for each team to the worst draft choices of our teams. The lists also delve a bit into non-sports as well. (We had to have a list of best Coneys, for example). Thanks to many friends in the media, front office, and the athletes themselves. We have lists ranging from Matt Millen's favorite Three Stooges episodes and Joe Dumars' favorite Sanford and Son episodes to Chris Osgood's hardest shots to face.

These lists are obviously not definitive. Yes, there are omissions (sorry Wayne County, Macomb County, Port Huron, Kalamazoo and the Upper Peninsula, among others). And they are debatable. And it is with debate in mind that we bring to you The Great Book of Detroit Sports Lists.

Art

As you read this book, there is one thing to keep in mind: this is a launching pad. Let the debate, and hopefully the not-too-heated discussions, begin. When Michael Stone (Stoney) first asked me if I was interested in this project, I immediately flashed back to the first time I met Stoney. It was after Gary Moeller's Monday media luncheon that Michigan has during the football season. I was working for Channel 2 and Stoney was at Channel 4. He introduced himself and told me if there was anything he could do for me just ask. I was stunned. Working at Channel 2 was the worst experience of my professional career. I was extremely turned off by television, but Stoney changed that by a simple act of kindness. Michael Stone is a true friend. It was easy to say "yes" to him, however, this was a difficult book to write.

Detroit has been a "Sportstown" for so long that trying to include all of the great athletes, moments, personalities, and traditions was more than we ever imagined. There is so much sports history in the Motor City that we tried to create a tapestry of why Detroit and the state of Michigan are completely devoted to their teams, city, and state. It was a daunting task and one that will forever remain incomplete. That is the true beauty and attraction of sports. It is a constant. Each era is uniquely defined and each era can make a case of why it had the best teams and athletes. In the end, we're all from the same sports melting pot. It doesn't really matter about the era you identify with, the teams you root for, or your favorite athletes. It's about a city and state that can lay claim to some of the greatest teams, athletes, traditions and athletic achievements to ever be chronicled in the annals of athletic competition.

Making a good pick in the draft is not the easiest thing in the sports world to do, even if you have one of the top selections—as Matt Millen and Randy Smith have proved so often. But Detroit sports teams have found some great players with picks from almost every round in drafts. So many, that cutting this list to 10 proved extremely difficult. As a result, obvious ones like Barry Sanders and Isiah Thomas were not included, because, let's face it, any jackass could have made those picks. This list is limited to diamond-in-the-rough picks from later rounds or guys who were brought in from unlikely places to play a big role in Detroit sports.

10. Lou Whitaker, Tigers, 1975, fifth round, 99th overall. The Tigers first three picks of the 1975 draft were Les Filkins, John Murphy and Bob Grandas. A free copy of the sequel to this book will go to anyone who knows who those guys were. But the club's fifth rounder became the 1978 Rookie of the Year. He went on to play 19 seasons with the Tigers, gaining five All-Star game selections and three Gold Gloves while combining with Alan Trammell to form the longest-running double-play combination in MLB history.

9. Henrik Zetterberg, Red Wings, 1999, seventh round, 210th overall. The Red Wings waited three years for the Swede to join the team, but the wait was worth it. Zetterberg was runner up for 2002-03 Rookie of the Year, with 22 goals and 22 assists. For the 2005-06 campaign, he took a giant step up to 39 goals and 46 assists. Zetterberg has remained at about that level since, establishing himself as one of the best players in the world. He usually comes up big in the playoffs as well.

8. Vladimir Konstantinov, Red Wings, 1989, 11th round, 221st overall. Former scout Neil Smith fell in love with Konstantinov during the 1987 World Junior Championships when he noted that Vlad was the only Russian not to back down from Canada in a bench-clearing brawl. The Vladinator's crushing hits and aggressiveness quickly made him a fan favorite here as he helped the Wings pick up a pair of Stanley Cups. Unfortunately, he is best remembered for the limousine accident that ended his career in 1997. But he enjoyed an amazing career before that, especially for an 11th-round pick.

7. Jack Morris, Tigers, 1976, fifth round, 98th overall. He may have been an a-hole to many, but there is no disputing the fact that Jack Morris was the best Tigers starting pitcher since Mickey Lolich. Morris owned the 80s, winning 111 games between 1982-87. In the 1984 championship year, he went 19-11 and threw a no-hitter in Chicago. He won all three of his starts in the postseason, giving up just five runs and 18 hits. He left the Tigers as a free agent after the 1990 season.

6. Joe Dumars, Pistons, 1985, first round, 18th overall. With Isiah Thomas and Vinnie Johnson already on the team, many wondered why GM Jack McCloskey would select another guard in the first round, especially one from a small school named McNeese State. Few wondered after seeing him play. Joe was a six-time All-Star, a four-time All-NBA Defensive Team member and the NBA Finals MVP in 1989. He finished his career as the Pistons' second all-time leading scorer and second in assists. He gained entry into the Basketball Hall of Fame in 2006.

5. Lem Barney, Lions, 1968, second round, 34th overall. The unknown cornerback from Jackson State turned into one of the greatest Lions of all time. In his first game, he picked off a Bart Starr pass and returned it for a touchdown. He went on to win Defensive Rookie of the Year after finishing with a spectacular 10 interceptions, including three in one quarter of the last game of the season. Over the course of his great career, Barney gained seven Pro Bowl selections and snagged 56 interceptions, seven of which he returned for touchdowns. He was enshrined into the Pro Football Hall of Fame in 1992.

4. Sergei Fedorov, Red Wings, 1989, fourth round, 74th overall. The Wings basically helped smuggle him away from Russia while he was playing for his country at the 1990 Goodwill Games in Seattle. Sergei became an immediate hit in Detroit, scoring 31 goals and 79 points as a rookie. He would score at least 30 goals every year through the 1996-97 season, except for one season cut short by a work stoppage. He won the Hart Trophy as the NHL's Most Valuable Player with 56 goals and 120 points for the 1993-94 season. He is currently the Wings' fourth leading goal and points scorer and second all time in playoff scoring.

3. Dennis Rodman, Pistons, 1986, second round, 27th overall. A key part of the Bad Boys two championship teams, "The Worm" was named to five straight NBA All-Defensive first teams and led the league in rebounding with a staggering 18.7 a game in 1992 and then again in 1993 by averaging 18.3 per. He started acting strange after he left the next season. But he still played well in San Antonio and Chicago, where he averaged at least 15 rebounds per game in three seasons and picked up three rings. He belongs in the Basketball Hall of Fame.

2. Joe Schmidt, Lions, 1953, seventh round, 85th overall. He revolutionized defensive football, becoming one of the first players to play middle linebacker and the first to star as one. His career totals: 13 seasons, 10 Pro Bowls, 10 All Pro selections, two NFL titles and a co-MVP award in 1960. Schmidt also became a member of the 1950s All-Decade Team and the Pro Football Hall of Fame.

1. Nicklas Lidstrom, Red Wings, 1989, third round, 53rd overall. No argument—this is the best draft pick in Detroit sports history. Lidstrom ranks as the best defenseman in team history and, some might argue, the best player in Wings history after Gordie Howe. He made All Rookie in 1991-92 and just kept getting better. The accolades tell the story: five Norris Trophies, nine All-star selections, three Stanley Cups and a Conn Smythe Trophy as NHL Finals MVP (the only European to claim that award). His leadership and skill are so respected that he was named as the Wings' captain after Steve Yzerman.

Drafting players is certainly not a science, or many of Detroit's general managers would have flunked the course. Even great GMs like Joe Dumars and Jimmy Devellano occasionally fail. But here are the nine worst picks by all the city's pro GMs. Why nine? Well, to be fair, we gave the Tigers, Pistons and Red Wings three slots each. Why no Lions? Because, as in most "Worst" categories, they deserve their own list. To be considered awful enough to gain entry onto this list, a pick had to be a first-rounder (with non-first-rounders relegated to Dishonorable Mentions). Also, since baseball had multiple drafts from 1966-1987, the Tigers got a reprieve until the 1987 draft. Other than that, the main criterion for making the list is per-formance, or rather lack thereof—and the quality players still available on the draft board when the lousy selection was made.

Dishonorable Mentions: Tigers—Bill Henderson in 1987 (with Craig Biggio still available), Matt Wheatland in 2000 (with Chase Utley still available), Greg Gohr in 1989 (Mo Vaughn and Chuck Knoblauch were still on the board); Red Wings—Yves Racine in 1987 (with Joe Sakic still available), Terry Richardson in 1973 (Rick Middleton was still on the board); Pistons—Antoine Carr in 1983 (could have had Clyde Drexler), Greg Kelser in 1979 (with Sidney Moncrief still on the board).

9. Keith Primeau, Red Wings, 1990, third overall.
Primeau eventually became a very good player. But his playoff failures frustrated the club and he was never as physical as Detroit fans wanted. Some even thought he was soft because he owned an extensive collection of Mickey Mouse artifacts. He was traded right before the 1997 season.

Still on the board: The choice of Primeau was not horrific, until you consider that Jaromir Jagr and Mike Ricci were still available.

8. Leon Douglas, Pistons, 1977, fourth overall pick.
The 6-foot-10 center was a dominant player and consensus All-American at Alabama. His NBA career was a bit different. He averaged just nine points and seven rebounds per game as a Piston, then finished out his NBA career with three forgettable years as a Kansas City King.

Still on the board: Adrian Dantley and a guard from Baylor named Vinnie Johnson. But at least we ended up getting both later through trades.

7. Mike Foligno, Red Wings, 1979, third overall.
He scored 36 goals in his rookie year and had another year-and-a-half of very good play for the Red Wings before being sent to Buffalo. He finished his career with a very respectable 355 goals. So why is he on this list? Check it out.

Still on the board: Mike Gartner and Ray Bourque. Gartner scored 708 goals in his illustrious career and Bourque turned out to be one of the greatest defensemen of all time, winning five Norris Trophies.

6. Rodney White, Pistons, 2001, ninth overall. After only playing one year at UNC-Charlotte, the 6-foot-9 forward just was not mature enough to handle the grind of the NBA. White played in only 16 games and rarely showed anything before being shipped to Denver.

Still on the board: Joe Johnson, Richard Jefferson, Tony Parker or Gilbert Arenas.

5. Fred Williams, Red Wings, 1976, fourth overall. You expect results when you have the fourth overall pick in a draft. The Red Wings got Fred Williams instead. He played in just 44 games, scoring two goals, as a rookie and never got another sniff of the NHL. To put it kindly, Fred Williams was a colossal bust.

Still on the board: Not the greatest crop of draft eligible players in 1976, but St. Louis got Bernie Federko and Brian Sutter, who combined to score 692 goals in their NHL careers—or 690 more goals than Fred Williams scored.

4. Scott Moore, Tigers, 2001, eighth overall. Drafting a shortstop right out of high school is pretty much a crapshoot. And the Tigers certainly got themselves some crap with Scott Moore. In his first three years of minor league baseball, Moore offered zero reminders of his schoolboy greatness, then was traded to the Cubs.

Still on the board: Cole Hamels, Jeff Francis, Kahalil Greene, Jeff Francouer, Scott Kazmir, Nick Swisher, Joe Blanton and Matt Cain, just to name a few. Oh, and to make matters worse, the Milwaukee Brewers had the pick right before the Tigers and chose Prince Fielder.

3. Matt Brunson, Tigers, 1993, ninth overall. Another fine high school shortstop, Brunson never even got a chance to suck in Detroit because he sucked so thoroughly in the low minor leagues. The only thing that Brunson showed he could do was run, stealing 50 bases for Fayetteville in 1994, which was fitting since he essentially stole the signing bonus money he got from the Tigers.

Still on the board: Billy Wagner, Tori Hunter, Derek Lee and Jason Varitek all would have looked good in the Olde English D.

2. Matt Anderson, Tigers, 1997, first overall. The Tigers had a rare first overall draft pick and needed everything, including starting pitching. But they were right in the middle of their penny-pinching era and must have figured that a relief pitcher would sign for less than a starter. So they chose Rice University closer Anderson. He did become a fan favorite with his 100-mph fastball. But he never lived up to the hype. Then in May of 1992, Anderson injured his arm in, I kid you not, an octopus-throwing contest.

Still on the board: Lance Berkman and Tory Glaus, among others.

1. Darko Milicic, Pistons, 2003, second overall. The ultimate "what if" pick. The ultimate reach. The one major negative on Joe Dumars' record during his reign as General Manager. The ultimate bust. The Darko pick remains extraordinary in a number of ways, all of them bad.

Still on the board: This is where the full horror of the Darko pick becomes apparent. Instead of Darko, the Pistons could have chosen Carmelo Anthony, Chris Bosh, Kirk Hinrich, David West, Josh Howard, Boris Diaw, Leandro Barbosa or, oh, yeah, some guy named Dwayne Wade.

Throughout their pathetic history, the Detroit Lions have consistently made lousy draft picks. In fact, they've made some of the worst picks of any team in any league. To keep this list from filling up the rest of the book, it's been limited to the worst 10 picks from the first two rounds.

Honorable Mentions: Nick Eddy (1966, second round, 24th overall); Walt Williams (1977, second round, 42nd overall); David Lewis (1984, first round, 20th overall); Pat Carter (1988, second round, 32nd overall); Terry Fair (1998, first round, 20th overall); Bob Bell (1971, first round, 21st overall); Ernest Price (1973, first round, 17th overall); Mark Nichols (1981, first round, 16th overall.); Stockar McDougle (2000, first round, 20th overall); Chuck Long (1986, first round, 12th overall).

10. John Ford, 1989, second round, 30th overall. The wide receiver told the Detroit media that he modeled his game after Jerry Rice, but he was more like Donna Rice—politician Gary Hart's infamous bottle-blonde mistress. At least he was honest. Ford had five catches in his first and only year in the NFL, then followed Donna Rice into oblivion.

Could have picked instead: Darryl "Moose" Johnston or Wesley Walls.

9. Juan Roque, 1997, second round, 35th overall. Roque was the first of Bobby Ross's many poor offensive line picks. Yeah, injuries hampered him. But Roque was just a bad player. He only managed to get into 17 games before being cut, much to the relief of the quarterbacks he was supposed to be protecting.

Could have picked instead: Tiki Barber, Sam Madison, Marcellus Wiley or Darren Sharper.

8. Kalimba Edwards, second round, 35th overall, 2002. A disappointment to say the least, the DE boasted great speed and did pile up 6? sacks his rookie year. But Kalimba was basically a non-factor for the rest of his six years here.

Could have picked instead: Antwaan Randle-El, Andre Gurode, LeCharles Bentley or, oh, yeah, some guy named CLINTON PORTIS. *Oy!*

7. Lynn Boden, 1975, first round, 13th overall. Although he started in 49 games in his four seasons as a Lion, the o-lineman was mediocre at best on a team already overloaded with mediocrity. He became the 1970s symbol of Lion draft futility.

Could have picked instead: something tells me Russ Francis, Louie Wright or Hollywood Henderson would have worked out better.

6. Aaron Gibson, 1999, first round, 29th overall. Bobby Ross had a good plan: use the draft to build an offensive line for Barry Sanders. But trading up to get this guy was a colossal mistake. Gibson was fat, lazy and injury-riddled. His only impact came at the training camp buffet line.

Could have picked instead: Michigan's Jon Janzen or Virginia defensive lineman Patrick Kearney.

5. Joey Harrington, 2002, first round, third overall. Some rank him as the Lions' worst all-time pick because of how far back he set the organization. But at the time, Joey Harrington filled a general need for a new quarterback. Problem was he did not meet the specific need for a West Coast offense quarterback for coach Marty Mornhinweg's West Coast offense. In fact, GM Matt Millen made the pick against the wishes of the coaching staff. Harrington's chronic inaccuracy, perceived lack of toughness and perpetual optimism made him an easy target for disgruntled fans.

Could have picked instead: Quentin Jammer or Dwight Freeney.

4. Charles Rogers, 2003, first round, second overall. Fans were cautiously optimistic when the Lions took Rogers. Optimistic because they had seen Rogers' dynamic receiving ability when he played up the road at Michigan State. Cautious because they were also familiar with all of the off-field issues that came with the temperamental wide receiver. Rogers did catch two TDs in his rookie season opener against Arizona. Then strange injuries and strange, drug-fueled behavior took over his career. This wasted waste of talent was such a malcontent during the 2006 training camp that the Lions released him. He tried to earn a tryout in 2007, but could not even motivate himself to get in shape to run a decent 40 time. To the end, he blamed everyone but himself for his failures.

Could have picked instead: Andre Johnson.

3. Andre Ware, 1990, first round, seventh overall. Wayne Fontes was so wowed by this Heisman Trophy winner's pre-draft workout that he used his top pick in the draft to get him, even though the Lions already had a QB in Rodney Peete. Ware connected with guys on the other team for INTs more often than with his teammates for TDs. Appropriately, when owner William Clay Ford called to congratulate Ware for his first start, he accidentally dialed Erik Kramer instead.

Could have picked instead: Richmond Webb, Emmitt Smith or Shannon Sharpe.

2. Mike Williams, 2005, first round, 10th overall. A senseless pick, even by the Lions' standards. Matt Millen ignored the fact that he had taken WRs with early picks in the previous two drafts, that Williams had not played football in a year and that he was perpetually overweight. But after two seasons that featured as many drops as catches, even Millen could no longer ignore that Mike Williams was a flat-out bust. He traded him to Oakland before the 2007 season for a fourth-round pick—and had to add Josh McCown to the deal to get that much.

Could have picked instead: Shawne Merriman two picks later.

1. Reggie Rogers, 1987, first round, seventh overall. A great player in college, Rogers was a bust for the Lions both on and off the field. He played in just 11 games as a Lion, recording one sack. He is best remembered, unfortunately, as a murderer. In October of 1988, a drunken Rogers drove through a red light and slammed into another car, killing three local teenagers. After being sentenced to prison, he returned to the NFL with Buffalo in 1991 and finished out his putrid career with Tampa Bay in 1992.

Could have picked instead: Jerome Brown and Rod Woodson.

Years before Matt Millen was even born, the Lions mastered another way to screw up the NFL draft. Instead of applying their current strategy of wasting high picks on head cases and drop cases, the team drafted budding superstars, then let them go to other teams. Employing this strategy, the Lions stocked the rosters of their rivals with some of the best players in NFL history. Here are ten of the great ones that got away.

10. Jack Kemp. The QB out of southern California spurned the Lions in favor of Pittsburgh, then Buffalo. He made seven Pro Bowls in the 1960s. He almost became Vice President, too.

9. Gerry Philbin. The Lions didn't put in much of an effort into signing the defensive end after drafting him in 1964. But, what the heck, he was just their third-round pick and an imminent Pro Bowler. Insulted by the Lions lowball tactics, Philbin went to New York, where he anchored the left side of the Jets' d-line for a decade and helped them win the Super Bowl four years later, gaining the first of his two All-Pro selections in the process.

8. John Hadl. The Lions first-round pick in 1962 was more impressed that the AFL's San Diego Chargers had designated him as their third-rounder. The QB made the first of his six Pro Bowls two years later and would go on to throw for over 33,000 yards and 244 TDs in his fine 16-year career.

7. Pete Retzlaff. The Lions drafted the combination receiver/back in 1953, then cut him. But, hey, who needs a guy who would go on to win five Pro Bowls selections, an NFL title and the 1965 Bert Bell Award as the NFL's top player? And just remember: cutting Retzlaff freed up space on the roster for Gene Gedman and Jug Girard.

6. Mac Speedie. The aptly-named wideout got chosen by Detroit in the 1942 draft. But World War II detoured his career into the army, where he was spotted playing in an exhibition game by Paul Brown. After the war, Brown took over as head coach of the Cleveland franchise in the AAFC and lured Speedie from the Lions with a few thousand extra dollars. Speedie made a nice return on Brown's investment, gaining All-Pro status in six of his seven seasons in Cleveland.

5. Grady Alderman. A Detroit native, Alderman came to the Lions in the 1960 draft, then spent his rookie season on the bench. But the coaches from the Minnesota Vikings saw something in the offensive lineman that the Lions' staff missed. The Vikings grabbed Alderman from their rivals and made him their starting left tackle for the next 13 seasons, six of which ended with Alderman in the Pro Bowl. Alderman's stellar career in Minnesota is particularly annoying when you consider how often he kept Lions pass rushers from blindsiding Fran Tarkenton.

4. Fred Biletnikoff. After drafting the Florida State grad in 1965, the Lions didn't pony up enough cash to keep the All-American from bolting to Oakland and the AFL. The wily, little receiver came up huge for the Raiders, making six Pro Bowls and helping coach John Madden establish Oakland as one of pro football's dominant franchises. Biletnikoff claimed MVP honors for the Raiders' 1977 Super Bowl triumph over the Vikings. Meanwhile back in Detroit, the Lions failed to place a single wide receiver in the Pro Bowl during Biletnikoff's stellar 14-year career.

3. Johnny Robinson. The third overall pick out of LSU by Detroit, the fleet defensive back ran as fast as he could to the Dallas Texans, an expansion team in the AFL. He played in seven Pro Bowls and made six All-Pro first teams during his brilliant 12-year career. Robinson revolutionized the safety position and played a key role in the Kansas City Chiefs' Super Bowl IV win. He remains in the league's all-time top ten for career interceptions with 57 picks.

2. Y.A. Tittle. The Lions drafted the LSU standout with the sixth overall pick in the 1948 NFL draft, then let him walk to the AAFC's Baltimore Colts. Tittle taunted the Lions from afar by going on to play in seven Pro Bowls and claim five MVP awards while passing for over 33,000 yards and 240 TDs during his Hall of Fame career.

1. Otto Graham. Who's the greatest quarterback in the history of pro football? Johnny Unitas? Not quite. Marino? Put on a pair of those gloves you used to hawk on TV and try to get a grip, Dan. Joe Montana? Well, at least you got a little town in the Big Sky state named after you. And sorry, Michigan alum Tom Brady, but you have another half-dozen Super Bowls to get to before you catch up to Otto Graham. Graham was drafted in 1944—by the Lions, of course. But military obligations took him away for a year, during which time he was spotted and then courted by our old friend Paul Brown—who ranks right up there with Matt Millen as a nemesis to the Lions' fortunes. After signing with Brown's Cleveland Browns, Graham took over as the team's QB and led them to four straight AAFC championships in his first four seasons while winning the league's MVP award twice. Graham kept right on going when Cleveland joined the NFL in 1950, leading the Browns to the NFL title in their first year in the league. Behind Graham, the Browns returned to the NFL title game each of the next five seasons, winning two while their quarterback claimed three more MVP awards. Graham retired after only a decade. He made All Pro and guided his team to the league title game in each of his ten seasons as a pro. He was elected to the Pro Football Hall of Fame in 1965. What could have been?

Let's start with a few parameters, before anybody gets confused or PO'd about some of the names that did and did not make this list. An athlete must have played his or her first full year of professional sports on a Michigan-based team to qualify, or have been a Michigan-based athlete who competed in an individual sport, like boxing. Going to college, high school or being born in Michigan, then playing your first year of pro ball somewhere else, disqualifies you from this list (sorry, Magic, but you did become a Laker). Also, a player's impact on the team or sport weighed as heavily as individual stats (so don't go looking for anybody named Tripucka).

Honorable Mentions: Lou Whitaker, 1978 Tigers; Justin Verlander, 2006 Tigers; Dave Bing, 1966-67 Pistons; Lem Barney, 1967 Lions.

10. (Tie) Jim David and Yale Lary, 1952, Lions. They didn't gain the first of
their combined 15 Pro Bowl selections until the following season. But the Lions started winning NFL titles the first year Jim David and Yale Lary showed up in Detroit's secondary. The young defensive backs registered 11 interceptions and countless bone-crunching hits. Sure, Lem Barney had a better individual season 15 years later, but his impact on the team's overall fortunes was negligible. David and Lary helped transform the Lions into the league's top-rated defensive team—and NFL champions.

9. Cheryl Ford, 2003, Shock. The Louisiana Tech star came to a Shock team
that finished the previous season in last place with a 9-23 record. By the end of the year, Ford had helped Detroit gain the best record in the WNBA and the league title. Along the way, Ford averaged a double-double, claimed Rookie of the Year honors and won a spot on the All-WNBA second team.

8. Joe Louis, 1934-35, boxing. He earned $50 for his first pro fight in 1934 at a
small venue in Chicago. But the Detroit heavyweight became so popular, so quickly that less than a year later, he claimed a purse of over $60,000 for knocking out former champ Primo Carnera in Yankee Stadium. Louis' totals for his first year of pro boxing: 22 fights, 22 wins, 18 knockouts.

6. (Tie) Barry Sanders and Billy Sims, 1989 and 1980, Lions. Sanders
stands head and shoulders above every other Lions running back in just about any category imaginable. But his fellow Heisman Trophy winner and Oklahoma collegian Sims pretty much equaled him in terms of rookie season achievement. The Sanders/Sims comparison: 1470/1303 rushing yards; 1870/1924 all purpose yards; 14/16 touchdowns. Sims may actually get the slight nod due to impact. The Lions won three more games with Sanders than they had the previous season; Sims' arrival helped improve Detroit by a whopping seven wins. Both made the Pro Bowl and picked up Rookie of the Year honors.

5. Dan Severn, 1994, UFC. "The Beast" had a beauty of a first year in mixed martial arts, reaching the finals of his first one-night, eight-man, single-elimination Ultimate Fighting Championship tournament. He lost the final, despite dominating undefeated, two-time tourney winner Royce Gracie, who caught him in a triangle choke. Severn learned from the mistake and won the following UFC tourney five months later. Next time out, he bested the most prestigious MMA tournament field yet gathered to win the Ultimate Ultimate, a tournament of former UFC tourney winners. The success of Severn, the first world-class, traditional wrestler to enter the UFC, changed the sport, showing other wrestlers, like future champions Mark Coleman and Randy Couture, how to compete and thrive in mixed martial arts.

4. Steve Yzerman, 1983-84, Red Wings. He scored 39 goals, added 48 assists and became, at age 18, the youngest player to appear in an NHL All-Star game. Most importantly, he began leading the franchise out of its dark ages, taking the Wings to their first playoffs in six seasons. Yzerman's arrival marked the start of a new, glorious era for the team.

3. Mark Fidrych, 1976, Tigers. A roster afterthought, the young hurler didn't even start a game until six weeks into the season. He went on to win 19, post the league's best ERA and start for the AL in the All-Star game while leading the Tigers to jump 17 wins in the standings from the previous season. More significantly, "Big Bird" revived a franchise that had suffered over 100 losses and dwindling attendance the previous season. His winning ways and lovable antics packed Tiger Stadium every time he pitched and made Fidrych a national media sensation. A series of injuries the following spring undermined his career and his rookie year turned out to be his one and only full season in the Major Leagues. But few ever made more of their time in the bigs than Mark Fidrych.

2. Al "Bubba" Baker, 1978, Lions. The NFL didn't keep official sack records back then. But Bubba racked up 23 of them during his 1980 rookie season. (Let us pause a moment to ponder the sheer awesomeness of that stat.) Baker would still hold the season sack record if the league recognized his effort. Can't somebody from the NFL stat office just go back and watch tapes of all the Lions games that season and make it official? It wouldn't be that much trouble. Or even that painful. The Lions were actually pretty good that season, improving from 2-14 the previous year to 9-7 and winning their division—due in no small part due to Bubba turning the opposition's backfield into his backyard.

1. Terry Sawchuk, 1950-51, Red Wings. A 20-year-old, "Uke" played every minute of every game for the Wings in the crease, allowing an average of less than two goals a game while posting 11 shutouts. He played a huge role in Detroit becoming the first team in the league to exceed 100 points in a season. And, oh, yeah: Sawchuk revolutionized his position in the process. Bending from the waist instead of at the knees like other goaltenders, Sawchuk gained a better view of the puck and a big advantage over other netminders. Every other goalie in the NHL soon copied him. They still do.

If you take a completely objective look at the all-time rosters of Detroit's sports teams, you would come to the conclusion that the Red Wings have had more super-stars than any other franchise. Here are the best of them.

10. John "Black Jack" Stewart, defenseman (1938-43, '45-50). A five-time All-Star with the Wings, Stewart was nicknamed "Black Jack" because he was one of the most ferocious body checkers of his generation. He played on two cup-winning teams in 1943 and 1950, with his inspired leadership and grit proving instrumental to Detroit's success.

9. Sid Abel, center/left wing (1938-43, '45-52). A great playmaker and leader (in 1943 he was named Detroit's captain at age 24), Abel centered the Wings' famed "Production Line" with Gordie Howe and Ted Lindsay. Inducted into the Hockey Hall of Fame in 1969, he won three Stanley Cups in Detroit. For a good portion of his broadcasting career, the Red Wings struggled and Sid couldn't mask his disgust. I remember the last TV telecast of one really long season and the Wings were getting hammered. As the final seconds ticked away, Sid told his play-by-play man Bruce Martyn, "You know Bruce, it used to mean something to wear that Red Wing sweater. Now it means nothing at 'toll Bruce, nothing at 'toll!" Once you put on the 'C' it never comes off.

8. Alex Delvecchio, center and left wing (1950-74). Is it just me, or is Delvecchio the forgotten Red Wing? I'm not sure why that is, but you hardly ever hear his name come up. When he retired after 24 seasons, he was second to only Gordie Howe in goals (456), assists (825) and points (1,281). "Fats" Delvecchio was captain of the Wings from 1962-74 and served as coach and general manager when he hung up the blades. Although his front office career never came close to matching his play-ing accomplishments, he's still considered one of the classiest and most talented men to ever don the Winged Wheel.

7. Sergei Fedorov, center (1990-2003). If Alex Delvecchio is the forgotten Red Wing, then Sergei Fedorov has to be the most misunderstood. It didn't take long for the Russian defector to establish himself as one of the most gifted two-way players in NHL history. I have always called him "Flake Boy" because he's just a little off in a good way. Years ago, I interviewed Chris Osgood in the Wings' dressing room during the first peri-od of a game against Phoenix. All the injured and scratched Red Wings were working out while they were watching the game on TV. All except Sergei. He was sitting in the assistant coaches' office reading the newspaper and watching the Cartoon Network. A winner of three Stanley Cups with Detroit, he has twice won the Selke Trophy as the NHL's best defensive forward (in 1994 and 1996) and the Hart Trophy as the NHL's MVP (in 1994). He also snagged the 1993-94 Lester B. Pearson Award as the NHL's outstanding performer. His departure and a highly publicized romance with Anna Kournikova clouded his career and mood, but you can't deny him his place among Detroit's greatest hockey stars.

6. Red Kelly, defenseman (1947-60). Red Kelly was one of the NHL's most versatile players. An all-round talent, his skill on the blue line led to a deadly transition game which solidified Detroit's dominance of the NHL during the 1950s. He was an All-star for eight consecutive seasons and in 1954 became the first recipient of the Norris Trophy as the league's top defenseman. A riff with management led to a trade to the Leafs—which is why, I believe, his #4 has never been retired by the Wings. It should be.

5. Ted Lindsay, left wing (1944-57; 1964-65). "Terrible Ted" was the toughest Red Wing ever! The ultimate team player, Lindsay would do anything to get the win, even if it meant bending the rules a bit. But he wasn't a goon. Lindsay was a natural goal scorer who was just as comfortable lighting the lamp or pounding the opposition. At 5-foot-8 and 160 pounds, Lindsay amazed fans with the way he handled himself against larger players. He didn't back down and won more battles than he lost. Lindsay is the heart and soul of the Red Wings, he cared that much, he sacrificed that much. Just look at his face.

4. Terry Sawchuk, goalie (1949-55; 1957-64; 1968-69). Sawchuk is still considered in many hockey circles as the greatest goalie ever. When he was 12, he broke his right arm playing rugby and never told anybody. It wasn't until two years later that doctors discovered the break. The injury caused his right arm to be two inches shorter than his left arm. It's truly amazing that he made it to the NHL at all, let alone became the league's leader in victories with 447 and shutouts with 103 (a record he still holds today). Sawchuk was a conflicted man whose presence in Detroit's goal will never be surpassed.

3. Nicklas Lidstrom, defenseman (1991-). When the Red Wings won the Stanley Cup in 2002, Steve Yzerman told me that Lidstrom was not only their best player during the playoffs (he won the Conn Smythe Trophy as the playoffs MVP), but that Nick was their best player for the last several years. Called "Mr. Perfect" because he never seems to make a mistake, Lidstrom will go down as the best defenseman of his generation.

2. Steve Yzerman, center (1983-2006). Yzerman's ability to play through pain was remarkable. A strong will and a burning desire to win enabled him to reinvent himself into a two-way player when Scotty Bowman took over as Wings coach. The NHL's longest-serving captain and the Red Wings second-leading career scorer (1755 points in 1514 games), Yzerman is the face of modern day Detroit sports.

1. Gordie Howe, right wing (1946-71). "Mr. Hockey." "Number 9." Or plain old "Gordie." We all know whom these monikers refer to: hockey's greatest player and one of the greatest in the annals of athletic competition.

If you're a hockey fan, you'll recognize the guys on this list. You just may not remember that they played for Detroit at one point in their fine careers—even if you're a big Red Wings fan.

Honorable Mentions: Carl Brewer, Tiger Williams, Ted Harris, Wendel Clark.

5. Eric Vail. The 1974-75 NHL Rookie of the Year with the Flames, the left wing scored 25 goals in five of his NHL seasons. Still, not too many Red Wing fans probably remember that Vail played here for 52 games and scored 10 goals in the 1981-82 season—and was one of the last players to wear #19 before Steve Yzerman took it over. By the following season, Vail was skating for the Wings farm team in Adirondack.

4. Reggie Leach. He once scored 61 goals in a season for Philly and 19 in a post-season to become the only non-goalie to win the Conn Smythe trophy for a losing team in the Stanley Cup playoffs. Leach was 32 when he came here in 1982 and still managed to score 15 goals. But it was his one and only season in Detroit, and his last season in the NHL.

3. Dennis Hull. His slap shot was never as good as his older brother Bobby's. But Dennis could still light the lamp on a regular basis. He scored 303 goals in his career, but only the last five came while he was a Red Wing during the 1977-78 season.

2. Darryl Sittler. What a difference a decade makes. Today, most NHLers would give anything to end their careers with the Red Wings. But not back in Darryl Sittler's day. Sittler began his Hall of Fame career in Toronto. But like many other Leafs, he bickered with owner Harold Ballard over money and the way the team was run. After nearly 400 goals in Toronto, he was dealt to Philadelphia during the 1981-82 season. He scored 70 goals the next two years, then was sent to Detroit. A pissed-off Sittler contemplated retirement, then reported and struggled here under coach Nick Polano, scoring just 11 goals in 61 games for his worst goals-per-game average of his career. The Wings bought out his contract after the season and Sittler retired.

1. Borje Salming. The first Swede enshrined in the Hockey Hall of Fame closed out his magnificent NHL career as a Red Wing under Jacques Demers in 1990. He scored just two goals in his 49 games, although his low productivity was not Salming's fault. The team just wasn't very good; the 1989-90 season was the last time the Red Wings failed to make the playoffs. It was also, unfortunately, the last season Salming would play in the NHL. Two years later, another Swedish defenseman made his NHL debut with the Red Wings. Five Norris trophies later, Nicklas Lidstrom has arguably taken over Salming's spot as the greatest Swede in NHL history.

My Top Ten Favorite Things About Tiger Stadium :: Ernie Harwell

Note: Ernie Harwell is the most beloved broadcaster in the history of Detroit. He came to the Tigers in 1960 after previous stints with the New York Giants, Brooklyn Dodgers and Baltimore Orioles. Harwell's voice quickly became a staple of Michigan summers, as thousands listened to him announce Tigers games as they drove or relaxed in their hammocks. Ernie Harwell was baseball in Michigan and the state was shocked in 1991 when Tiger President Bo Schembechler announced that it would be Ernie's last season. Ernie Harwell fired? Blasphemy! People went crazy. In fairness, the decision came at the request of WJR, but Schembechler was willing to take the heat. Mike Ilitch bought the club in 1992 and one of the first things he did was re-hire Ernie Harwell. Ernie stayed on through the 2002 season before retiring at the age 84. He was elected to the Baseball Hall of Fame in 1981 and the Radio Hall of Fame in 1998. He is also an accomplished musician, has authored eight books, made numerous CDs featuring his work and continues to write a baseball column for the *Detroit Free Press*. Ernie also ranks as one of the kindest people you will ever meet. Ernie Harwell is a treasure to Detroit, Michigan and the country. Here are the memories he treasures most of Tiger Stadium.

10. Home clubhouse. Where Cobb, Greenberg, Kaline and other greats dressed. Featured an old bone that Cobb used to rub down his bats.

9. Left-field roof. Only four players (Harmon Killebrew, Frank Howard, Cecil Fielder, and Mark McGwire) hit home runs over it. I saw them all.

8. Third-deck seats in right field. I sat there the night of the 1971 All-Star game and watched Reggie Jackson's line drive home run hit the transformer. The hardest hit ball I've ever seen.

7. Smell of the stadium. It smelled like traditional baseball, with the hot dogs, beer, popcorn, etc. all blending.

6. Forest green seats. Great background for hitters. They loved it. Jim Campbell made a huge mistake when he replaced the green with Howard Johnson blue. Ugh!

5. Press room. Great post–game conversations with managers, coaches, executives and media types. More information here than in any press conference.

4. Center-field flagpole. Highest obstacle in fair territory in any ballpark in America, this unique feature reached 125 feet and provided an interesting hazard to fielders chasing down long fly balls.

3. Bleachers in center field. The only double-decked bleachers in the Majors. In 1985 Jim Campbell closed them for nearly a month when the language became too rough.

2. The ten-foot overhang in right field. Only other overhang I can remember was leftfield at the Polo Grounds in New York. That one cut the distance from home plate to leftfield by 250 feet.

1. Radio booth. We were so close that we could hear the players cuss and see them sweat. Often, players would tell me that when they were on the field, they could hear our broadcast.

Note: For 42 years, Ernie Harwell was the voice of the Detroit Tigers, calling balls, strikes, and home runs on radio and television to the great benefit of the greater Detroit area. Here are his favorite memories, all of which are shared by the fans.

10. My first broadcast at Briggs Stadium in 1954. I was announcing for Baltimore. It was the Orioles' first game in modern big league history. Steve Gromek blanked the Orioles, 3-0.

9. First home opener as Tiger announcer. It was in 1960. A warm, sunny afternoon. The Tigers played Chicago. George Kell and I had to re-tape a TV interview with Nellie Fox three times because of technical glitches.

8. Willie Horton's throw in the 1968 World Series. He nipped Lou Brock at home plate and turned the Series completely around after the Tigers had looked miserable against the Cardinals.

7. The 22-inning game in 1962. Longest game I ever broadcast. Jackie Reed won it for the Yankees with the only home run in his big league career. In the last inning, when Rocky Colavito went through his stretching at home plate, Yankee pitcher Whitey Ford yelled, "Hey, Rocky, ain't you loose yet?"

6. Kirk Gibson's home run in 1984 World Series. He hit it off his old nemesis, Goose Gossage. Gibby's around-the-bases tour was caught by Mary Schroeder in one of the best sports photos of all time.

5. José Feliciano's rendition of the national anthem, prior to the fifth game of the 1968 World Series. He was my pick to sing and I faced a lot of critical flack. José gave a beautiful and soulful version, which many thought too radical. Compared to the renditions we hear now, it seems exceedingly tame.

4. Nolan Ryan's 1973 no-hitter. This was the one featuring Norman Cash batting with a table leg from the clubhouse. Ryan struck out 17 in the most dominating pitching performance I have ever seen.

3. Filming the movie _Tigertown_. Ray Lane and I appeared as ourselves in this Disney production, directed by former Detroiter Alan Shapiro. The stars were Roy Scheider, best known for _Jaws_, and the kid actor Justin Henry, who had starred in _Kramer vs. Kramer_.

2. Closing Tiger Stadium. A long-anticipated event that came off in beautiful fashion because of the capacity crowd's reverence for the stadium. It was a distinct thrill to say goodbye to the treasured old Corner.

1. Comerica Park statue. I was overwhelmed when the Tigers designated a day in my honor in 2002. The highlight was Mike Ilitch's unveiling a statue for me. It was realistic with wrinkles in my trousers. I was hollow and weighed over 300 pounds.

In 1960, a new convention facility and adjacent arena opened in the Motor City. Originally called Convention Center, the complex was eventually renamed in honor of former Detroit Mayor Alfred Cobo, who had died in office of a heart attack in 1957. In 1989, Cobo expanded to 2.4 million square feet. The complex's ability to host numerous types of events allowed Cobo to serve as the site of everything from rock concerts to car shows to NBA basketball games.

12. The Super Bowl XL NFL Experience, February 1–5, 2006. Throughout the hall, giant displays and game areas allowed fans to catch seminars, peruse memorabilia, compete against each other for prizes and obtain autographs from players. Roger Penske, Detroit's Super Bowl committee chairman, pulled off the unlikely feat of convincing the NFL to let Detroit host the Super Bowl, then organized a heck of a great Super Bowl week.

11. Dancing Gus Sinaris' performances during home Pistons games in the 1960s and 70s. On many nights, the Pistons played to a packed house, even during the many seasons they stunk. One reason for the enthusiasm was fans could always count on a generous show from "Dancing" Gus Sinaris, a legendary vendor at Cobo, Olympia, and Tiger Stadium. A former boxer with a flat nose, Gus would perform silly dances for the onlookers. His popularity rivaled that of most Pistons' players.

10. Floyd Mayweather, Jr. vs. Emanuel "Burton" Augustus, October 21, 2000. Floyd fought "Burton" as a tune-up for his upcoming bout with the then-undefeated Diego Corrales. The overmatched but spirited Burton pushed the bout to nine rounds, before his trainer finally threw in the towel. A Grand Rapids native, Mayweather went on to beat Corrales and join the long line of great Michigan boxers.

9. The annual North American International Auto Show, since 1965. The Motor City has hosted auto shows in various locales around the city for over a century. Of all the annual public shows at Cobo, the NAIAS ranks as their signature event. The premiere show for all automakers, the annual January event kicks off with a black-tie affair, followed by days of exhibitions by automakers from around the world unveiling their new concept vehicles and production cars.

8. Pistons vs. Bulls, Game I, NBA Playoffs, March 30, 1974. Bob Lanier scored 27 as Detroit stunned Chicago, 97-88. The Pistons dropped all four road games to lose the series in seven games. Still, 1973-74 marked a rare season of success for the Pistons during their largely forgettable Cobo era (1961-78).

7. Sugar Ray Robinson vs. Wilf Greaves, September 25, 1961. One of boxing's all-time greats, Sugar Ray treated his hometown fans to what would be his last fight in Michigan. Coming off a title loss in Nevada, Robinson decided to face Greaves as a "tune-up." The split-decision win by Robinson felt more like a win for Greaves, considering that he went the distance with a legend. Greaves would fight Robinson again in Pittsburgh, but Robinson showed him the floor with a KO in the rematch.

6. KISS Alive! concert, March 27, 1975. Gene Simmons, Paul Stanley, Ace Frehley and Peter Criss rolled into Detroit on their "Dressed to Kill" tour, armed with audio engineer Eddie Kramer. KISS had a plan. While the band's studio albums sold anemically, KISS routinely packed arenas for their stunning live shows that played better in Detroit than anywhere else. So they decided to record a live album here that went on to rave reviews and huge sales. KISS melted many faces that night, and they continue to entertain audiences worldwide, with much of their success attributed to the live album they recorded that night at Cobo. The tune "Detroit Rock City" was the band's way of paying homage to the fans, the arena and the city that put them on the rock-and-roll map.

5. Roberto Durán vs. Kirkland Laing, September 4, 1982. Roberto came out on the losing end of what was later voted *Ring Magazine*'s 1982 Upset of the Year. A top British boxer, Laing went the distance with the legendary "Hands of Stone" and scored a split decision. The loss proved another tough blow to Durán, who was looking to atone for his infamous "no más" loss to Sugar Ray Leonard in 1980.

4. The Doors concert, May 8, 1970. The Doors played what was probably the band's longest and best show—as well as the most lucid performance in Morrison's career. They also recorded it, preserving a very unique moment in the band's oft-troubled history. The show was later released as a great record: The Doors Live in Detroit. Cobo officials banned The Doors from ever playing there again after the band played past the arena's time limit by over an hour.

3. Joe Frazier vs. Bob Foster, November 18, 1970. Scheduled for 15 rounds, "Smokin' Joe" ended it in the second with a series of devastating left hooks. Frazier's KO of Foster marked his first successful defense of his WBC and WBA heavyweight titles. His next fight was his epic win over Muhammad Ali at Madison Square in NY.

2. Bob Seger and the Silver Bullet Band concerts, September 4-5, 1975. Seger, an Ann Arbor native, was a local legend, but he and his band received little regard in other markets. The fine *Live Bullet* album recorded at these shows and the enthusiasm of the devoted Cobo crowd turned heads outside of Detroit, propelling Seger on the way to international rock stardom.

1. Thomas Hearns vs. Dennis "The Hackney Rock" Andries, March 7, 1987. One of boxing's all-time greats, Hearns fought a number of matches in this area, none better than this one. Hearns knocked down "The Hackney Rock" three times in the 10th to claim the Brit's WBC Light Heavyweight title and to become only the 12th man to win three world championships in three weight classes. That he did it in front of his hometown crowd made the moment extra-special. Making it even better, Detroit's "Queen of Soul" Aretha Franklin sang the national anthem to start the night.

Top Ten Athletes from Oakland County
:: Pat "The Book" Caputo

Note: Caputo has covered all the major sports for *The Oakland Press* since 1984. Now an award-winning columnist for the Press, "The Book" is also a talk show host on 97.1 FM, The Ticket in Detroit.

10. Steve Howe, Clarkston. Threw as hard as any left-handed pitcher in the Major Leagues during the 1980s. Was the National League Rookie of the Year with the Dodgers. Off-the-field problems marred his career, but couldn't totally dull his brilliance.

9. Ted Simmons, Southfield. His career statistics for the St. Louis Cardinals and Milwaukee Brewers rank with most of the all-time great catchers. One of the best switch hitters in baseball history. Also a brilliant prep football player at Southfield High School as a running back.

8. Alexi Lalas, Bloomfield Hills. A true pioneer in soccer. A big, rugged defender who did his best work on the international stage for the U.S. national team. Also an All-American at Rutgers.

7. Micki King, Pontiac. Won the gold medal in springboard diving at the 1972 Olympics in Munich. It was redemption for her after she hit the board during the 1968 Mexico City Olympics, costing her a medal. One of the greatest divers in U.S. history.

6. Campy Russell, Pontiac. A true schoolboy legend at Pontiac Central High School. A brilliant player at the University of Michigan, winning Big Ten Player of the Year and All-American honors. One of the best players in the history of the Cleveland Cavaliers.

5. Meg Mallon, Farmington Mercy. One of the greatest golfers in the history of the LPGA Tour. Has won four major championships, including two U.S. Women's Opens.

4. Pete Dawkins, Royal Oak. The graduate of Bloomfield Hills Cranbrook High School won the 1958 Heisman Trophy while at Army. A triple-threat running back, Dawkins was also a Rhodes Scholar who advanced to the rank of Brigadier General during his military career.

3. Hayes Jones, Pontiac. One of the greatest track hurdlers of all-time. Unbeaten for several years in his specialty. Won the gold medal in the high hurdles at Tokyo Olympics in 1964 and a bronze at Rome in 1960. Also a brilliant sprinter. Was part of a world record 400-meter relay team. Won several national championships while at Eastern Michigan.

2. Pat LaFontaine, Waterford. Arguably the greatest U.S. hockey player of all-time. Concussions cut short his career, but not his brilliance. A pioneer in the way he went to the Canadian junior ranks and dominated, opening the door for others. Very skilled, yet tough. Special on the power play. One of the nicest people ever in sports, too.

1. Kirk Gibson, Waterford. Never one to worry about his statistics or individual accolades. Had one of the most memorable home runs in baseball history off Goose Goosage in the 1984 World Series for the Tigers. And his homer off Dennis Eckersley in the 1988 World Series for the Dodgers was one for the ages. A rare combination of size and speed. A better football player than baseball player at Michigan State.

Note: The three-time Michigan Sportswriter of the Year winner spent more than 24 years at the *Lansing State Journal* before moving to talk radio, television and freelance writing. Ebling has authored five sports books and contributed to *Sports Illustrated* and *The Sporting News*.

10. Dean Look. The Everett High standout was an All-American quarterback at Michigan State and a sixth-place Heisman finisher in 1959. Played pro baseball with the Chicago White Sox and football with the New York Titans.

9. Sam Vincent. Was named Michigan's first Mr. Basketball. Won a Big Ten scoring championship and was a first-team All-American and a first-round draft pick. Played seven seasons in the NBA.

8. Jay Vincent. Lansing Eastern star was one of the best players never to win a state title. Scored 25 points in his first college game at Michigan State. Started for two Big Ten titlists and the 1979 NCAA champs. Won Big Ten scoring titles the next two years. Made the NBA All-Rookie team and played nine years in the league.

7. Todd Martin. East Lansing native was a fixture on the ATP Tour and a title contender for more than a decade. Runner-up in several Grand Slam events. Won eight professional singles titles.

6. Ryan Miller. Best performer from the most important family in Big Ten history. Set collegiate hockey records for shutouts at Michigan State and was one of the five best goalies in NCAA history. Second member of his family to win the Hobey Baker Award.

5. Muhsin Muhammad. Superior all-around athlete at Lansing Waverly and excellent wide receiver at Michigan State. Could finish among the NFL's all-time top ten in receptions.

4. Judi Brown. Dominant sprinter/hurdler at East Lansing High and Michigan State. Was the first female named Big Ten Athlete of the Year. Won a silver medal in the 400 hurdles in the 1984 L.A. Olympics. Shared *Sports Illustrated*'s "Sportsperson of the Year" award in 1987 in an "Athletes Who Care" montage.

3. John Smoltz. Starred in two sports at Lansing Waverly after transferring from Lansing Catholic Central. Signed to play baseball at Michigan State. Drafted by the Tigers, but won the Cy Young Award and World Series with the pitching-rich Braves. Excelled as a starter, as a closer and again as a starter. Still making his case for Cooperstown.

2. Kevin Jackson. Won two Class A state championships at Lansing Eastern. Was a four-time All-American at two schools—LSU and Iowa State. Earned an Olympic gold medal in 1992 in Barcelona and was a two-time freestyle world champion. Wrestling Hall of Famer who became the USA national freestyle coach.

1. Earvin Johnson, basketball. Won a Michigan Class A title at Lansing Everett, two Big Ten crowns in two years at Michigan State and an NCAA championship in a 1979 classic against Larry Bird and Indiana State. Hall of Famer was an Olympic gold medalist, five-time NBA champion, three-time league MVP and one of the top five players in basketball history.

Over the years, the Detroit area has served as home to more than its share of doomed franchises in every sport from roller derby to arena football to team tennis. Some lasted years, some lasted no longer than a typical Lions' winning streak. We feel blessed and, in some instances, not-so-blessed, to have witnessed the efforts and gotten to know the characters of these "classic" area sports franchises.

13. Detroit Dogs. The Dogs played in the American Basketball Association (ABA), but not the fun one from the 1960s and 1970s with Dr. J and George Gervin. This is the minor league ABA that started in 2000 and will be lucky to make it out of the decade. The Dogs weren't so lucky, getting put to sleep after the 2002 season. George Gervin actually coached the Dogs in their inaugural 2000-01 season and guided them to the ABA title. There was no parade.

12. Motor City Mustangs. Co-owners Sean Burr and Dino Ciccarelli thought that ice hockey's spike in local popularity from the Red Wings' 1995 trip to the Stanley Cup Finals that spring would naturally inspire hockey fans to pack Cobo to see the game played on wheels by this Roller Hockey International league franchise. It never happened. The team was so comical that only a fledgling radio station called *WDFN* would broadcast their games. One of their play-by-play guys was a doofus named Mike Stone, who would yell "MUSTANG MANIA!!" to the accompaniment of a neighing horse sound effect when they scored. They lost to the St. Louis Vipers in the first round of the playoffs. The Mustangs and the neighing horse sound effect were never heard from again.

11. Detroit Loves. Professional mixed team tennis (yes, professional mixed team tennis) hit Cobo in 1974. Led by Rosie Casals, the Loves won their division, but got taken out by Evonne Goolagong, Vitas Gerulaitis and the Pittsburgh Triangles in the first round of the playoffs. The Loves found none here and moved to Indiana the following season.

10. Michigan Stags. The World Hockey Association (WHA) transferred the Los Angeles Sharks to Cobo and renamed them the Michigan Stags for the 1974-75 season. The Wings were struggling, so the owners thought the Stags could offer a popular alternative. But they were wrong. Their games averaged only about 3000 fans. The WHA was counting on the return of Gordie Howe to spark more interest in the Stags when he came back to Detroit with his Houston Aeros for a game in February. Unfortunately, the Stags folded in mid-January.

9. Detroit Turbos. Men's indoor lacrosse is a fast-paced, exciting game and few played it better than the Turbos . . . at least for a little while. The Turbos won the Major Indoor Lacrosse league title in their third season in 1991, but left Joe Louis Arena just three years later. Twin brothers Paul and Gary Gait powered the team's offense, scoring 79 goals between them during the championship season. But when the future United States Lacrosse Hall of Famers left for Philadelphia in 1993, the Turbos' fortunes went with them.

8. Detroit Rockers. Across 11 seasons and four venues, the Rockers *were* professional soccer in the area. They started downtown and ended up playing games at the Compuware Sports Arena in Plymouth Township. English import Andy Chapman served as the main attraction for their first five seasons before giving way to a bald wizard and scoring machine named Drago. The Rockers won the National Professional Soccer League title in 1992, but never repeated as champs. They failed to qualify for the playoffs the last five years of their existence, which ended when the league went under in 2001.

7. Detroit Wheels. Against all odds, the World Football League's Detroit Wheels actually managed to be worse than the NFL's Lions. Debuting in 1974, they played their games at Eastern Michigan University's Rynearson Stadium. A syndicate of 33 people, including Marvin Gaye, owned the team. But by the middle of their first and only season, the Wheels' players were the ones wondering "What's Going On?" The team was 1-13 before going on out of business.

6. Detroit Spirits. Attempting to fill the pro basketball void left by the Pistons' move to Pontiac, the Continental Basketball Association inserted the Detroit Spirits into downtown Motown in 1982. One of the first minority-owned sports franchises, the club was led by General Manager Sam Washington, the man who ran the city's legendary St. Cecelia's summer basketball league. The Spirits won the title their first year with a thrilling, seven-game finals win over George Karl's Montana Golden Nuggets. But the Spirits floated off to Savannah after the 1985-86 season.

5. Detroit Vipers. Minor league hockey came to the Palace in 1994 to offer an alternative to the NHL, which was stalled by a labor lockout. The Vipers broke International Hockey League attendance records as coach Rick Dudley guided the team to the Central Division crown in their debut season. They lost in the first round of the playoffs. But the Vipers went all the way two years later, capturing the league's Turner Cup. Many future and former NHL stars laced up their skates for the Vipers, including Sergei Samsonov, Petr Sykora, Miroslav Satan, Peter Bondra, Mike Hartman, Mike Donnelly, Jimmy Carson, Daniel Shank and Brent Fedyk. Gordie Howe skated a shift for them in a 1997 game to become the only man to play professional hockey in six different decades. It was an embarrassing publicity stunt for all involved and things went downhill from there. The league and the Vipers folded after the 2000-01 season.

4. Detroit Express. A soccer team that actually made a bit of a splash, Detroit's entry in the North American Soccer League (NASL) played at the Silverdome for three seasons beginning in 1978. The Express boasted a bona fide superstar in Trevor Francis. Averaging more than a goal per game, the English forward finished his NASL career with more points than Pele. Manager Ken Furphy guided the Express to the playoffs their first year. But they failed to qualify in their last two seasons and folded one year after moving to Washington D.C.

3. Detroit Stars. One of the original members of baseball's legendary Negro Leagues, the Stars had some superstars, led by Norman "Turkey" Stearnes. "Turkey" topped the league in home runs in seven seasons and batted over .400 three times. He is still considered one of the greatest players in baseball history and was inducted into Cooperstown in 2000, over two decades after his death. Andy Cooper ranked as the Stars' best pitcher and also won a place in the Hall of Fame. At times, the Stars outdrew the Tigers. But interest in the team waned when the MLB integrated in the 1940s and 1950s. In a desperate effort to increase attendance, the Stars renamed themselves Goose Tatum's Detroit Clowns in 1958. They folded two years later.

2. Detroit Drive. They set the standard for success in the Arena Football League (AFL). Debuting in 1988, the Drive reached the Arena Bowl in each of its six seasons, winning the title four times. The property of Tigers and Red Wings owner Mike Ilitch, the Drive regularly packed Joe Louis Arena, thanks to an abundance of free and discounted tickets. Tim Marcum coached the team for five seasons and proved the perfect personality for guiding a roster full of AFL legends like George LaFrance and ex-USFL players like Novo Bojovic. The team's most famous and infamous player was former Ohio State QB Art Schlichter. Attempting to comeback from gambling problems that drove him out of the NFL and into bankruptcy court, Schlichter proved he was still a better quarterback than a gambler, winning the league MVP in 1990. The Ilitch organization made a bad bet of its own after the 1993 season, opting to hold onto the faltering Rockers and sell the successful Drive, which moved to Boston and became the Massachusetts Marauders.

1. Michigan Panthers. The United States Football League (USFL) Panthers were everything the NFL Lions were not: a joy to watch and a champion team. After a 1-4 start to their first season, the Panthers rallied under coach Jim Stanley to finish 12-6. Cajun quarterback Bobby Hebert led the offense, getting a lot of help from running backs Ken Lacy and John Williams, plus a certain former University of Michigan wide receiver named Anthony Carter. The three-time All-American became nearly as good a Panther as he was a Wolverine. The Panthers scored an unforgettable Western Conference title victory over the Oakland Invaders before 60,237 frenzied hometown fans at the Silverdome, then defeated Jim Mora, Sr.'s Philadelphia Stars 24-22 to win the USFL championship. The following year, they started 6-0 before Carter broke his arm. They were never the same. The Panthers merged with the Oakland Invaders in 1985 and advanced to the championship game. But they lost to the Stars, who had moved from Philly to Baltimore by then. It proved to be the USFL's last game as the league went out of business in the offseason.

Local and national businesses have used Detroit-area sports figures to hawk everything from roofs to Lasik eye surgery. These are not necessarily the best or worst ads featuring area athletes, just ones that we couldn't forget—in some cases, no matter how hard we tried.

Honorable Mentions: Jacques Demers for Ford, Chuck Daly for Kozins Clothing Store; Alan Trammell and Ernie Harwell for Mr. Roof; and who can forget the scintillating Larry Brown ad for Jack's Place for Men's Clothes.

10. Bob Probert, Metro 25 Tire. I wonder what former Michigan backup quarterback turned entrepreneur Duane Rao was thinking when he decided to hire Probert to appear in his old Metro 25 Tire Centers commercials. *Now who would be the perfect pitchman? Hmmm, how about a guy who is a habitual drunk driver, got caught at the Windsor-Detroit border with a half-ounce of cocaine and who shuttles back and forth between deportation and incarceration hearings? PERFECT!!!* You know how some movies are so bad that they are actually entertaining? Well, that would be a good way to sum up the Rao-Probert-Metro 25 ads.

9. Steve Mariucci, Local Ford Dealers. In hiring ex-49ers head coach Steve Mariucci in 2003, not only did the Ford family believe they tabbed the right man to lead their floundering football team to the Promised Land, but also the perfect spokesman for their floundering automobile business. With his shiny white teeth, big blue eyes and nice tan, Mariucci did look like he was born to play the role of an automobile huckster. He was so right for the part, the Fords whisked Mariucci away to begin filming commercials for the local Ford dealers before he even had the chance to size up his new team. While this wasn't a great commercial, its value as comic relief cannot be underestimated and earned it a spot here. Listening to Mariucci recite, "We're building something good here," during a commercial break while the Lions were getting hammered by 20 points was about the only entertainment Detroit fans were treated to during the dark days of Mooch's tenure.

8. Barry Sanders, Cadillac. Over the years, Ford Motor utilized many of their Lions' players and coaches, no matter how bad they were, to sell the company's Escort, Explorer and Taurus. So when the Ford family finally secured the services of one of the best running backs to ever play the game in Barry Sanders, they naturally hired him to also represent the FOMOCO? Uh . . . no. In typical blundering Ford fashion, they sat by while Sanders associated himself with their rival, General Motors. The people at GM were smart because they didn't ask the introverted Sanders to do any acting for the Cadillac ad. Instead they produced a commercial featuring a montage of #20 working his magic on the field, intertwined with shots of speeding Caddies. It might not been as bad as retiring on the eve of training camp with a fax to *The Wichita Eagle*. But Sanders clearly meant plugging for GM as a slap in the face to the man who signed his paychecks.

7. Ben Wallace, Local Ford Dealers. Ben Wallace was the face of the Pistons when they won the NBA title in 2004. Well, actually he wasn't the face of the franchise so much as the hair. Big Ben's huge, retro 'fro attracted national attention and earned him commercials with T-Mobile and *ESPN*'s basketball video game. Yeah, the T-Mobile and video game spots sucked. But not as much as Chauncey Billups' Adidas commercial where the floor started attacking him, or Tayshaun Prince's Wallside Windows ad or Rip Hamilton's shilling for Dr. Roumani. Ben's Metro Detroit Ford dealers made clever use of Ben's most prominent feature by having crap keep popping out of his hair. The climax: a Ford truck sped out of Ben's 'fro.

6. Sergei Fedorov, Nike Campaign. In 1994, Nike decided to get into the hockey skate business and sign up Red Wings star and reigning NHL MVP Sergei Fedorov for the marketing campaign. The centerpiece was an ad showing Fedorov taking on virtually the rest of the league in one end-to-end rush. After lighting the lamp, a victorious Fedorov skated backwards with his arms raised as a goalie riding a Zamboni machine moved in to flatten him.

5. Cecil Fielder, McDonald's. In the early 1990s, McDonald's took advantage of Fielder's 51-home run season (that many dingers was a big deal before the Steroid Era) by placing the Tigers' Super-Sized Slugger in an ad promoting the chain's cheeseburgers. The spot also starred Cecil's young, portly son Prince, who grew up to become the Milwaukee Brewers All-Star first baseman. But McDonald's shouldn't expect any sequel to the successful commercial. Prince no longer speaks to Cecil due to the old man taking a portion of Prince's signing bonus, as well as the animosity he still feels toward his father over Cecil's ugly divorce from his mother. And Prince became a vegetarian during spring training in 2008.

4. Grant Hill, *ESPN Sportscenter* and Sprite. The station's "This is *Sportscenter*" campaign got a dose of Detroit flavor when Hill starred in one spot in his Pistons uniform as the piano player in the *ESPN* headquarters lobby. The ad also co-starred a dejected Dan Patrick (then the co-anchor of *Sportscenter*) walking out of the building, only to be cheered up by Hill's rendition of sports arena anthem "Charge." The hilarious ad ends with Patrick putting a dollar bill in Hill's tip jar. A more realistic ending would have seen the piano collapsing on Hill's ankle, requiring the small forward to undergo season-ending surgery. Hill's Sprite commercial centered on the theme of "Image is Nothing" and featured a little kid drinking a Sprite and thinking the soft drink would assist him in beating a professional basketball player. The pudgy adolescent proceeded to get thrashed by Hill in a game of one-on-one.

(Note: Just in case you're counting, that is two commercials on this list for Hill, which is two more commercials than Pistons playoff series victories during Hill's tenure in the Motor City.)

3. Petr Klima, Vernors. Local soft drink vendor, Vernors, thought it would be a good idea to make the Red Wings star and teen hearthrob Klima a spokesman for their brand of ginger ale, even though the Czech barely spoke a word of English. In the spot, Klima listed all of the things he loved about his new home in Detroit (including Vernors, of course) before getting to the punch line. At the end of the commercial, Klima tried to show where he currently lived. The only problem: the left-winger pointed to Kalamazoo instead of Detroit.

2. Isiah Thomas, Detroit Edison. "Oh Isiah." While "Where's the Beef?" and "Time to Make the Doughnuts" became iconic commercial catchphrases across America during the 1980s, "Oh, Isiah" established itself as the Motor City equivalent. In a series of ads for Detroit Edison (now known as DTE Energy), the Pistons captain and his mother, Mary, educated children on how to avoid getting electrocuted. At the end of each spot, Isiah's mother would turn to her point guard son and say, "Oh, Isiah." The commercials permeated the airwaves and Detroit culture; for a time you might have thought that Thomas' first name was actually "Ohisiah." To this day, anyone who was old enough to remember the ads still utters the catchphrase when Zeke effs some-thing up. Thomas traded away a lottery pick to the Bulls for a center with a heart con-dition? Oh, Isiah. Zeke acquired noted team cancers, Stephon Marbury and Steve Francis and their horrid contracts? Oh, Isiah. Isiah sexually harassed a female team executive and cost the New York Knicks over $11 million in a court judgment? Oh, Isiah. To his credit, Isiah has never taken a bath with a plugged–in toaster. Although a bunch of Knicks fans probably wish he would.

1. Mel Farr, Mel Farr Automotive Group. Mel Farr was the Detroit Lions first-round pick in the 1967 NFL Draft, won the NFL Offensive Rookie of the Year, went to two Pro Bowls and played his entire career in Detroit. But if you went up to the aver-age Detroiter on the street today and asked him who Mel Farr was, you would almost assuredly get the following response: "Mel Farr Superstar, for a Farr better deal." Between 1975 and 2002, the former running back owned several successful car deal-erships in the Motor City. You couldn't turn on your television without seeing his ads, which always included the "Mel Farr Superstar, for a Farr better deal" catchphrase. In the ads, Farr would dress up like Superman and dub himself the "Superstar Dealer." With the help of low quality CGI effects, Farr would fly around his Oak Park location to come to the rescue of confused car shoppers. But by 2002 the "Superstar Dealer" had closed all of his locations. According to Ward's Business Dealer, Farr's kryptonite was "bad press and class-action lawsuits for allegedly charging high interest rates and sell-ing used cars of low quality to people of low means."

Note: Joe Dumars is a six-time NBA All-star, two-time league champion, a highly successful front office executive and a Basketball Hall of Fame member. Joe D. is also a *Sanford and Son* freak who owns copies of every episode, many of which he knows line-by-line. Starring Redd Foxx as junkyard owner Fred Sanford and Demond Wilson as his son Lamont, the hit sitcom ran on NBC from 1972–1977. Here are Joe's favorite episodes.

10. "A Guest In The Yard." A homeless man hurts his back in Fred's junkyard and threatens to sue. Fred, the mark instead of the con for once, has to take care of him and prove he is not really injured.

9. "Whiplash." After getting in a truck accident, Fred thinks he has whiplash, or just pretends he has it because his friend Bubba thinks Fred can make big money in court. Foxx is even funnier than usual, crying "whiplash" every chance he gets.

8. "Presenting The 3 Degrees." Lamont and his friend Rollo manage a female singing group called The 3 Degrees. The band has to stay at the house, which angers Fred until he sees the sexy trio with his own eyes.

7. "Mama's Baby, Papa's Maybe," Season Three. Fred's pal Grady tells Fred that his friend "Big Money Grip" dated Fred's deceased wife Elizabeth and that Lamont may actually be the son of "Big Money." Fred sets out to prove that Grip is just a jive turkey.

6. "The Copper Caper." Fred and Lamont buy a load of copper, then find out the copper was stolen from their own plumbing pipes. Fred's catchphrase "Big Dummy" premiered in this episode.

5. "The Dowry." Fred's cousin arrives with her not-so-good-looking stepdaughter Betty Jean. After finding out that Betty Jean will inherit ten thousand dollars when she gets married, Fred tries to convince Lamont to propose to her. This episode was written by none other than Richard Pryor.

4. "Fred Sanford: Legal Eagle." After Lamont gets a traffic ticket, Fred shows up in court to serve as his lawyer. The great character actor Antonio Fargas (Huggy Bear from *Starsky and Hutch*) guest stars.

3. "The Shootout." While using an antique gun to re-enact his old war stories, Fred accidentally fires a bullet into the house of his neighbor Goldstein. When Goldstein drops out of sight, Fred thinks he's killed him.

2. "Here Comes the Bride, There Goes the Bride." Lamont's bride leaves him standing at the altar. The wedding guests all want their gifts back. Fred has other ideas.

1. "A House Is Not A Poolroom." Lamont buys Fred a pool table for his birthday. But things get out of hand when Fred's friends come over to play. They proceed to eat and drink to their hearts' content, leaving the Sanfords with an empty refrigerator and Lamont with a serious case of buyer's remorse. Lamont has to try to convince his dad that "that the house is not a pool room." My all-time favorite episode.

Top 22 Old-School Lions Names and Nicknames

Back in the days before Chris Berman, players had to get by on their own names and nicknames. Here's a starting lineup worth of the Lions' most entertaining old-school handles.

22. Showboat Boykin, 1952.

21. Bryan Bumthorne, 1956.

20. Clem Crabtree, 1940-41.

19. Bob DeFruiter, 1947.

18. Dorne Dibble, 1951-57.

17. Father Lumpkin, 1934.

16. Slok Gill, 1942.

15. O.K. Ferguson, 1956.

14. Dom Fucci, 1955.

13. Huel Hamm, 1943.

12. Bob "Hunchy" Hoernschemeyer, 1950-55.

11. Monk Moscrip, 1938-39.

10. Garvin Mugg, 1945.

9. Garth Ten Napel, 1976-77.

8. Dunc Obee, 1941.

7. Gerry Perry, 1954-59.

6. Moroni Schwab, 1948.

5. Zealand Thigpen, 1949.

4. Bob "Choo Choo" Train, 1936.

3. Pug Vaughn, Lions, 1935-36.

2. Socko Wiethe, 1939-42.

1. Jules Yakapovich, 1944.

Honorable Mentions: Les Bingaman, Jim David, Alex Wojciechowicz, Yale Lary, Lou Creekmur, Billy Sims, Chris Spielman, Wayne Walker, Robert Porcher, Dick LeBeau, Roger Brown, Herman Moore, Dick "Night Train" Lane.

10. Lomas Brown. The seven-time Pro Bowler was the best Lions offensive lineman in recent memory. Drafted sixth overall by Detroit in the 1985 NFL Draft, the Florida native played 11 seasons in Detroit, becoming a top offensive tackle. After playing for the Lions, Lomas spent seven more seasons with the Cardinals, Browns, Giants, and Buccaneers. Upon his retirement, Lomas returned to the area. He is a local radio show host, and he occasionally does work for The NFL Network and *ESPN*.

9. Jack Christiansen. The five-time Pro Bowl defensive back led the Lions legendary Chris's Crew secondary that terrorized opposing offenses for years. Christiansen also dominated on special teams. A member of all three Lions championship squads in the 1950s, Jack was inducted into the Pro Football Hall of Fame in 1970.

8. Earl "Dutch" Clark. A throwback to the early era of the sport when QBs were tailbacks who called the plays in the huddle, "Dutch" was a triple-threat player (he passed, ran and dropkicked field goals). The three-time NFL scoring leader made six All-Pro squads while leading the Lions' famous "Infantry Attack" of the 1930s. Clark helped Detroit win its first championship in 1935. He made the NFL's 1930s All-Decade Team and the Pro Football Hall of Fame.

7. Alex Karras. The nine-time All-Pro was the most decorated member of the Lions "Fearsome Foursome" defensive lines of the 1960s. A gambling scandal put him out of the game for a year and probably kept him out of the Hall of Fame. But Karras made the NFL's 1960s All-Decade Team.

6. Doak Walker. The 1948 Heisman winner entered the league amid doubts about whether he would thrive in the NFL due to his relatively slight, 5-foot-11 frame. But Doak quickly put them to rest by winning Rookie of the Year in 1950. Reunited in Detroit with his good buddy Bobby Layne, Doak won two championships in 1952 and 1953. He did almost everything for the Lions, playing halfback, flanker and subbing as a situational defensive back. He also returned kickoffs and punts, and served as the Lions' primary kicker and field goal specialist. Doak led the NFL in points in 1950 and 1955 and scored the winning TD in the 1952 NFL championship game on a 67-yard run—one of the many clutch plays he delivered during his time in Detroit. He was inducted into the Pro Football Hall of Fame in 1986.

5. Charlie Sanders. The seven-time Pro Bowler revolutionized the tight end position with his excellent leaping ability, soft hands, and speed. Prior to Charlie's arrival in the league, the tight end was used primarily as an extra blocker. At 6-foot-4 and 225 pounds, Charlie was undersized for that traditional role, but proved just as exceptional a blocker as receiver. He made the NFL's 1970s All-Decade Team and was inducted into the Pro Football Hall of Fame in 2007.

4. Lem Barney. When the Lions selected Lem in the second round of the 1967 NFL Draft, they weren't sure whether Lem was going to play offense or defense. After a handful of games, the Lions realized they possessed one of the best defensive backs ever. The Mississippi native racked up 10 interceptions his first year, earning the Associated Press Defensive Rookie of the Year award. In addition to playing DB, Lem returned kicks and punts. Lem also performed two seasons of punting duty. The seven-time All-Pro played 11 seasons for the Lions, finishing with 56 interceptions and seven defensive touchdowns from those snags. A member of the NFL's 1960s All-Decade Team, Lem was inducted into the Pro Football Hall of Fame in 1992.

3. Joe Schmidt. Due to his injury history in college, Schmidt lasted until the seventh round of the 1953 draft. He ended up practically inventing the position of middle line-backer and becoming the best defender the Lions ever employed. Joe was a ten-time Pro Bowler and ten-time All-Pro, dominating teams with his uncanny positioning and defensive playcalling. Opponents feared him because he seemed to know their strategy better than they did. He was the Lions team captain for nine years, helping the team to two championships. He also served as the Lions head coach after his playing career was finished. He was inducted into the Pro Football Hall of Fame in 1973.

2. Bobby Layne. The six-time Pro Bowl QB may not have been flashy, but he got the job done. Layne practically invented the two-minute drill when he engineered a late, 80-yard drive to get the Lions the win in the 1953 championship game. He was a grand leader who cultivated a fierce loyalty among his peers. A legendary drinker, Bobby's partying would sometimes show up as throw-up in the Lions huddle. Despite such wild behavior, he never let his off-field exploits affect his game and led the Lions to three titles. He was inducted into the Pro Football Hall of Fame in 1967.

1. Barry Sanders. Shortly after arriving in Detroit in 1989, the running back began to exceed all expectations, rushing for 1,470 yards and 14 touchdowns that rookie season. Barry would play 10 seasons for the Lions, earning All-Pro and Pro Bowl honors every year. His low center of gravity, blazing speed, exceptional leaping ability and instinctual, jackrabbit running style, made him almost impossible to tackle one-on-one. People will remember him most for his epic 1997 season when Barry rushed for 2,053 yards and racked up 14 straight games of 100-plus yards, an NFL record. His 1997 performance earned Barry the AP, Pro Football Writers, and NFL MVP awards. Barry rushed for 15,269 rushing yards in his career, placing him third overall among NFL running backs. In 2004, Barry was inducted into the Pro Football Hall of Fame.

Top Seven Barry Sanders Memories :: Mark Champion

Note: Champion served as the Lions' radio play-by-play voice from 1989-2004, calling every one of Barry Sanders' runs. He currently is the Pistons' radio voice.

7. Which way did he go? September 25, 1994. The Lions lost at home to the Patriots 23-17. But the day belonged to #20. In one of my favorite plays, Sanders juked and practically corkscrewed New England's Harlon Barnett into the ground on an amazing run. He finished with 131 yards and two touchdowns.

6. Dismantling the Bucs, October 12, 1997. Sanders scored twice from 80 and 82 yards on his way to 215 for the day. If memory serves, Barry ran out of his shoe during the 82-yard scamper. The Lions won, 27-9.

5. Emmitt vs. Barry, September 19, 1994. The biggest debate in Detroit during the 1990s was who is better: Barry Sanders or Emmit Smith? Barry won this duel in Dallas, rushing for 194 yards on a career high 40 carries. The Lions won the game in OT, 20-17.

4. How did he get free? September 6, 1992. The Lions lost at Chicago, 27-24, with Barry rushing for 109 yards on 19 carries. But it was his unbelievable touchdown that I will always remember. Barry got stuffed at the line, but somehow escaped and motored 43 yards to the end zone.

3. Playoff win, January 5, 1992. The Lions won a resounding 38-6 victory over Dallas. The Silverdome exploded when Barry sealed the game with an exhilarating 47-yard touchdown. Who knew it would be the last playoff win I would ever call as a Lions announcer?

2. Two thousand yards, December 28, 1997. What a scene and bizarre game. The host Lions and Jets both needed a win to make the playoffs, while Barry was trying to become just the third player to rush for 2,000 yards in a season. For much of the game, it looked grim for Barry. But in the third quarter, he uncorked a 47-yarder, then a 15-yard touchdown run. He reached the magic 2000 mark on a ho-hum, two-yard run. But then after the wild celebration, he sealed it by busting one for 53 yards. It was a surreal day as Reggie Brown sustained the career-ending neck injury and a man died of a heart attack in the stands right in front of our booth.

1. The first of many, September 10, 1989. He signed his contract just days before. He didn't know many plays. But the Lions were doing nothing offensively. So in the third quarter, Wayne Fontes decided to give the kid a shot. On his first NFL carry, Barry gave us a taste of what would come over the next 10 seasons. Sanders gained 18 yards and finished with 71 yards and a touchdown. I will never forget most of Barry Sanders' runs, but I remember his first one best of all.

Some players' jersey numbers become as famous as the players themselves. Here are 10 local sports icons next to the numbers they turned into icons as well, plus honorable mentions of some other guys who did their digits proud.

#10. Alex Delvecchio. The third-leading scorer in Wings history, he played in 13 All-Star games and won three Lady Byng Trophies. The NHL Hall of Famer was also the Wings' captain, coach and general manager.

Honorable Mention: Dennis Rodman.

#9. Gordie Howe. When you say "number nine" around here, everyone knows you're talking about Gordie Howe. "Mr. Hockey" played 26 seasons with the Red Wings, leading four Stanley Cup teams. Most of the records the Hall of Famer held have been broken since the game opened up offensively in recent decades. But many experts still rate #9 as the #1 hockey player of all time.

Honorable Mentions: Sorry, no one can compare.

#8. Igor Larionov. A member of the 1997, 1998 and 2002 Red Wings' Stanley Cup teams, "The Professor" was part of the Russian 5 and one of the greatest players in the history of the Soviet Union.

Honorable Mentions: Syd Howe, Johnny Wilson.

#7. Ted Lindsay. One of the toughest guys in NHL history, he captained the Wings to back-to-back Cups in 1954 and 1955. The Hall of Famer was a vital member of the club's famed "Production Line."

Honorable Mentions: Dutch Clark, Harvey Kuenn, Rick Leach.

#6. Al Kaline. A 10-time Gold Glover and 15-time All-Star, Kaline won the AL batting title at age 20. The rightfielder batted .379 with two home runs in the Tigers' 1968 World Series win over St. Louis. He became a first-ballot Hall of Famer in 1980.

Honorable Mention: Larry Aurie.

#5. Nicklas Lidstrom. One of the greatest defenseman in NHL history, Lidstrom won five Norris trophies and a Finals MVP award in 2002. He played on three Stanley Cup winning teams.

Honorable Mention: Hank Greenberg.

#4. Joe Dumars. The Hall of Fame Pistons guard claimed MVP honors for the 1989 NBA Finals. He played in six All-Star games before becoming the Pistons' General Manager and rebuilding the club's 2004 title team from scratch.

Honorable Mentions: Leonard "Red" Kelly, Scott Skiles, Jason Hanson.

#3. Alan Trammell. The great Tiger shortstop won the MVP for the 1984 World Series, along with four Gold Gloves. Trammell hit .300 or more in seven seasons.

Honorable Mentions: Ben Wallace, Mickey Cochrane, Eddie Murray.

#2. Charlie Gehringer. The greatest second baseman in Tigers history hit .320 over his career and claimed the American League MVP award in 1937 on his way to winning entry into the Baseball Hall of Fame.

Honorable Mentions: "Black "Jack Stewart, Gary Bergman, Charles Woodson.

#1. Terry Sawchuk. Considered by some as the best goalie of all-time, the Hall of Famer led the Wings to three Stanley Cups and still holds the NHL record for shutouts with 103.

Honorable Mentions: Lou Whitaker, Chauncey Billups, Anthony Carter, Braylon Edwards.

Art's Seven Favorite Uniforms in Michigan Sports History :: Art

Our teams have some of the most recognizable and traditional uniforms in the sporting world that uniquely state who we are and what we're all about.

7. Michigan Wolverines basketball (Fab Five era). The baggy shorts forever changed the look of basketball uniforms. Michigan may try and erase that the Fab Five ever existed, however their legacy lives on because of the shorts. That's the long and not so short of it in a nutshell.

6. Detroit Express, home orange. All orange with two blue stripes on the shoulders and shorts, with a blue collar, blue numbers on the right leg, left arm and on the front of the jersey below the word "Express" made this uniform colorful and sleek without being gaudy. Well done, mate!

5. Michigan Panthers, home plum. Champagne, plum and light blue may not sound too appealing, yet the Panthers pulled it off. A plum jersey, with a light blue stripe on the sleeve highlighted in white, the numbers were white on the shoulders and in the front and back of the jersey highlighted in light blue. Champagne pants with a light blue stripe on the side highlighted in plum. But, it was the helmet that really sets the uniform apart. A color called "champagne-silver" was the main hue with a snarling plum panther on the sides highlighted with light blue accents.

4. Detroit Lions, home uniform without black accents. Look, the Lions may lack a competent direction but, their home uni, sans the black, was a classic. Top it off with 'Bubbles the Lion' on the side of the helmet and you have a pretty uniform for a pretty awful franchise.

3. Detroit Red Wings, home red. It's basic, all red with a white stripe on the sleeve, bottom of the sweater, on the side of the pants, and stockings covering the shin pad. Throw in the winged wheel logo and it ranks up there with the very best in all of sports. Yet, it's the color of red that makes this simple uniform a masterpiece. As the late Joe Falls told me years ago, "the blood red color makes that uniform more intimidating than any other color, including black." You're so right Joe!

2. Detroit Tigers, home white. You can take your Yankee pinstripes, but it's the Olde English "D" for me. All white with blue piping and "D" over the heart. For over a hundred years the Tigers have worn (with some slight variations) their current home uniform. And why not! It's one of the most distinctive looks in all of sports.

1. Michigan Wolverines, home football. I could go on about how simple it is: blue jersey with maize numbers, maize pants and black shoes. But, let's keep it real! Whether you love or hate the winged football helmet, Michigan's headgear makes this otherwise plain basic uniform flashy, intimidating, and the most recognizable uniform in the country, if not the entire world.

There is that old expression that "clothes make the man." Unfortunately that wasn't the case in these athletic abominations.

7. Detroit Vipers. Aqua and Eggplant with a splash of red doesn't sound all that bad. However, it was all too big. Gigantic logo, not a bad logo, just gigantic with over-sized numbers, letters and stripes; in true Palace fashion, it was a bit overdone.

6. Detroit Pistons, Silver Anniversary home uniform. The standard uniform of the Bad Boys during their championship years and the uniform of today's Pistons team, except the lettering style is different. The only problem with the Silver anniversary edition? It was silver! You could see every speck of Piston perspiration. There's something unsettling about seeing someone's crotch and butt sweat.

5. Detroit Tigers, road uniform (1993-94). New owner Mike Ilitch tried to bring Tigers baseball out of the Dark Ages by creating a new logo: a tiger entwined in the Olde English "D." The logo was all right, but the new road uni was putrid. It was way too busy! Script Detroit along with a number on the front, with a blue shoulder stripe accented with orange. The baseball cap was the real topper. A blue cap, an orange bill, with the new logo and an orange button on top . . . ugly!

4. Michigan State's green. Okay, I can hear all of you Spartans already: "You just hate MSU—green isn't a uniform!" And that's my point: there isn't a uniformed shade of green that every athletic team wears. Until there is, Sparty, your uniforms are way too inconsistent.

3. Detroit Lions, black accents addition home and away. The Lions added subtle black accents to their pants, jerseys and helmets in 2003. Why? Unless you're up close you can't really see them. Maybe they thought the black would make the Honolulu blue and silver more menacing. What a stretch, it's the Lions we're talking about!

2. Detroit Lions, alternate black home uniform. When the Lions unveiled this hideous gem for the 2005 campaign, the subtle black accents started to make some sense. It about the marketing, essentially the Lions are saying, "We can't produce a competitive team so, here's our new black uniform because we haven't fleeced you enough. Make sure you're the first one on the block to own one!" The only problem is, IT DOESN'T GO WITH THEIR PANTS OR HELMETS, even with their subtle black accents. It was slapped together, like the team.

1. Detroit Pistons, teal home (1996-2000). The Pistons changed their colors to teal, black, yellow and red to keep up with Detroit's internationally known hip fashion crowd. All right, I'm being a bit of a jackass, but this uniform is the worst! First and foremost it's teal. Then there's the horse's head with the flaming mane and the exhaust pipes spitting out flames to represent horsepower. It looks like somebody put some five-alarm chili in the horse's feedbag and he's letting it rip!

Beginning with the Ancient Olympic Games, one of the many fringe benefits of being a sports star has been the poonage. Loads of Motor City athletes have nailed hot chicks. But only the elite have been able to hook up with famous hot babes.

10. Grant Hill (Detroit Pistons forward) and Tamia (Singer).

You have to give Grant Hill's wife credit for one thing—chutzpah. Most singers who go by one name (Madonna, Prince) are actually, like, known by the people outside of their families. But despite her lack of fame, this "singer" makes this list for two reasons: she is undoubtedly attractive; and, most importantly, she gets credit for assisting the Pistons in avoiding signing Hill to a max contract that would have crippled the organization for years. You see, rumor has it that Tamia felt it would be easier to pursue her singing career in Orlando than in Detroit and made Grant sign with the Magic instead of the Pistons when Hill was a free agent during the summer of 2000. So Hill forced the Pistons into a sign-and-trade that netted the team Ben Wallace instead of Tamia's chronically injured hubby. So thanks, Tamia, we could never have achieved that 2004 title without you. It almost makes me want to listen to one of your songs in gratitude.

9. Luc Robitaille (Red Wings) and Stacia Robataille (singer).

Robitaille scored 30 goals in 2001-02 and helped bring the Stanley Cup back to Detroit. But his greatest gift to Motown might have been bringing his prototypical MILF wife to Detroit. And I always thought that Luc got his nickname "Lucky" because he had a propensity for fortuitous goals.

8. Garry Unger (Red Wings) and Pam Eldred (Miss America).

In the history of sports and broads, one of the more typical stories is an athlete going into the tank after getting some new trim. But one coupling here had the opposite effect. Around Christmas of 1969, Unger was in a rut, having only scored seven goals all season. At about that time, the Wings invited Bloomfield native and reigning Miss America Pam Eldred to drop the ceremonial first puck before a game. Unger told the beauty queen that he would score a goal that night for her. He didn't. But after the game, Unger gave Eldred a stick, a puck and a guarantee to fulfill his goal promise for the rest of that season. He ended up with 42 goals and Miss America as his girlfriend. With the 40-year anniversary of this monumental meeting approaching, current Miss America and Farmington Hills native Kirsten Haglund should take one for the city and turn Valtteri Filppula or Jiri Hudler into a 40-goal scorer.

7. Henrik Zetterberg (Red Wings) and Emma Andersson (reality TV Star, singer, model).

Zetterberg has been shacked up with Andersson for a while now. A couple years ago, Emma was voted Sweden's hottest chick by *Café Magazine*. Not the hottest skirt in River Rouge or Waterford. THE #1 FREAKING HOTTIE IN SWEDEN!!!! I mean, we are talking about Sweden here. That is the equivalent of being the smartest guy at Harvard or the fattest customer at Pizza Hut.

6. Rodney Peete (Lions) and Holly Robinson (actress). The Lions quarter-

back somehow got 21 *Jump Street* star Robinson to marry him. (Not sure if that was meant as an indictment of Lions' QBs or a compliment to Robinson . . . probably a little of both.) While the oft-injured former USC star Peete didn't transfer his collegiate success to the NFL, he did parlay his L.A. background into a successful marriage with Robinson. Which beats the hell out of a Pro Bowl selection.

5. Chris Webber (Pistons) and Tyra Banks (model/TV). Before Banks lost

her mind, admitted to a fear of dolphins and ballooned up to 160 pounds, the *Sports Illustrated* swimsuit cover girl dated Detroit native Chris Webber for three years. The pairing became an ugly public spectacle. After *The Sacramento Bee* first reported the relationship, the then-Kings power forward unleashed the following diatribe: "You can repeat this to the editor of the [expletive] Bee or whatever the [expletive] you want to do. Since the first [expletive] day I came here I gave you all interviews, I've done every [expletive] thing you've wanted . . . and you are going to violate me like that? And I know everybody didn't do it, but everybody's got to pay for it . . . stay out of my [expletive] business. I play basketball for you all. I don't live for you all."

Why the hell was C-Webb so upset? The *Bee* said that he'd hooked up with a Victoria's Secret model. It's not like they told everyone he'd married Whoppi Goldberg.

4. Mike Modano (NHL star, Michigan native) and Willa Ford (actress, model). Mike Modano netted 528 goals in the NHL, but none of his scores was as

impressive as Willa Ford. She dated the UFC superstar Chuck Lidell and might have had a relationship with her *Dancing with the Stars* partner Maksim Chemerkovskiy. But the actress, model and singer ended up married to the greatest hockey player from the state of Michigan. The Dallas Stars forward certainly put his biscuit in one of the hottest baskets out there.

3. Joe Louis (heavyweight boxing champ) and numerous hotties. Louis

could have dominated this list on his conquests alone. Even though the champ was married to three different women (twice to his first wife), he still had time to date actress Lena Horne. Not only was Miss Horne a multiple Grammy winner, but she was also considered one of the hottest dames of her time. Louis was also romantically linked with Norwegian figure skater and three-time gold medalist Sonja Henie. But maybe the most impressive notch on the champ's bedpost was blonde bombshell Lana Turner. The star of *The Postman Always Rings Twice* and *Peyton Place* somehow squeezed Louis into her schedule between Tyrone Power and Judge Wapner. (I couldn't make this stuff up. And hopefully Wikipedia didn't either.) Maybe they bronzed the wrong part of Joe's anatomy for that sculpture on Woodward?

2. Sergei Fedorov (Red Wings) and Anna Kournikova (tennis player, model).

Make no mistake about it: there was absolutely nothing normal about the Fedorov-Kournikova relationship. Seriously, how many other Detroit athletes have ever been a major component of an *E! True Hollywood Story*? My research tells me NONE. The two never admitted that they were romantically involved when a 16-year-old Kournikova showed up at the Red Wings 1997 Stanley Cup parade wearing a skin-tight leopard print outfit. They were just "friends." Kournikova made four appearances on *People*'s "50 Most Beautiful People" list and was named "Sexiest Woman in the World" in 2002 by *FHM* magazine. Unfortunately for Fedorov, it wasn't easy dating the most wanted chick in the world. It was rumored that Kournikova was caught having sex on the beach in Miami with Sergei's former Russian linemate (and friend), Pavel Bure. But through it all, Fedorov tried to keep the relationship together. At one point, things got so bad that Wings owner Mike Ilitch allegedly let Fedorov borrow the team's plane in the middle of the season so he could try to win back Anna's heart. Kournikova finally shacked up with Latin lothario Enrique Iglesias and left Fedorov for good. A few months before Fedorov exited Detroit to sign with Anaheim, he opened up to *Hockey News* about his doomed romance. "This love was worse than a bout of flu," he said. "It lasted longer and hit me harder." Sergei tried to get over the "flu" by banging actress Tara Reid for a while. But Bunny Lebowski and her horrid fake boobs couldn't replace the void left by Sergei's one true love.

1. Jeff Garcia (Lions) and Carmella DeCesare (*Playboy* Playmate).

Shortly after his former 49ers teammate Terrell Owens told *Playboy* magazine that Garcia was gay, Garcia affirmed his heterosexuality by banging the 2004 "Playmate of the Year" DeCesare. His case became even stronger a few weeks later when DeCesare opened up a can of whoopass on fellow Playmate Kristen Hine at a Cleveland bar—which led to the public revelation that Garcia was having an affair with Hine WHILE dating DeCesare. And not only is DeCesare an incredibly hot badass, she is also very loyal. Never was this more evident than when she called a Detroit sports radio talk show to defend her man against attacks by Lions fans. Yep, she pulled a play out of the Brenda Warner playbook. But that play works a lot better when the bitching wife is a Playmate of the Year, not a butchy lookalike of Alice, the maid from *The Brady Bunch*. Congratulations Carmela, on being named the hottest girlfriend/wife in the history of Detroit athletics. We miss you more than we miss your husband.

Top 25 Tigers Names and Nicknames

Maybe it's the sport's long history. Or how it accommodates players of all shapes and sizes from around the globe. Or just all the spare time it allows players, fans and broadcasters to think during games. But baseball has always boasted the best nicknames and names of any major sport. Here's a roster of some of the Tigers best.

25. Yorman Bazardo, 2007-

24. Lu Blue, 1921-27.

23. Fred "The Great Stone Face" Hutchinson, 1939-40, 1946-53.

22. Exavier Prente "Nook" Logan, 2004-05.

21. Slim Love, 1919-20.

20. Firpo Marberry, 1933-35.

19. Scat Metha, 1940.

18. Roscoe "Rubberlegs" Miller, 1901-02.

17. Pepper Pepolski, 1913.

16. Hub "Piano Legs" Pernoll, 1910, 1912.

15. Herman Polycarp "Old Folks" Pillette, 1922-23.

14. Cletus Elwood "Boots" Poffenberger, 1937-38.

13. Emory Elmo "Topper" Rigney, 1922-25.

12. Heine Schulbe, 1929-35.

11. Ivey Shiver, 1931.

10. Larry Sherry, 1964-67.

9. Chick Shorten, 1919-21.

8. Vic "The Philosopher" Sorrell, 1928-37.

7. Doug Strange, 1989.

6. Dizzy Trout, 1939-52.

5. Bun Troy, 1905.

4. Orville Inman "Coot" Veal, 1958-63.

3. Jim Walkup, 1927.

2. Ed "Satchelfoot" Wells, 1923-27.

1. Squanto Wilson, 1911.

A charter member of the American League in 1901, the Detroit Tigers have fielded some of baseball's greatest players in their long history. Here are the top Tigers of all time by position. Instead of numbering them in terms of their relative quality, we've used the old baseball scoring system in which each fielding position is designated by a number 1-9.

9. (Right Field) Al Kaline. Kaline joined Ty Cobb as one of only two Tigers to achieve 3,000 hits and holds the club's records for games played (2,834), HRs (399) and walks (1,277). He also won 10 Gold Gloves and selections to 15 All-Star Games. By the time he played his last game in 1974, Al Kaline had become the most beloved Tiger of all. In 1980, Kaline's #6 was retired by the Tigers, the same year he won induction into the Baseball Hall of Fame on his first ballot.

Backup: Sam Crawford.

8. (Centerfield) Ty Cobb. He was one of the greatest players ever to play the game, certainly one of the most feared, and probably the least liked. He would literally do anything to win, practicing such methods as sharpening his spikes in preparation for meeting the shins of opposing fielders while on the base paths. Despite multiple cases of ill regard, no one can dispute his extraordinary play. During his 24 seasons, Cobb hit over .400 three times. He won the 1909 Triple Crown and the 1911 AL MVP when he hit .420, with 127 RBIs, and 83 stolen bases. Ironically, one of baseball's best players never won a World Series. Cobb still holds the record for highest career batting average (.367), as well as the record for 54 steals of home. In 1936, Cobb was one of the inaugural inductees into the Baseball Hall of Fame. *The Sporting News* ranked him #3 on their 100 Greatest Baseball Players, behind only Willie Mays and Babe Ruth.

Backup: Harry Heilmann.

7. (Left Field) Heinie Manush. The Alabama native played his first five years of a 17-year career in Detroit. Heinie won the AL batting title in 1926 when he hit .378 and was inducted as a Tiger into the Baseball Hall of Fame in 1964.

Backup: Willie Horton.

6. (Shortstop) Alan Trammell. "Tram" was the team leader throughout the 1980s and 90s, often speaking the way he played, with unselfishness and modesty. He will be most remembered for his 1984 World Series performance, going 9 of 20 at the plate, while slugging two home runs and six RBI. Trammell played 1,918 games with his infield mate Lou Whitaker. This ranks as the most games played together by a duo in the American League. The two also turned the most double plays together in MLB history. Trammell earned four Gold Gloves, six All-Star selections and three Silver Slugger awards and hit at least .300 in seven seasons.

Backup: Harvey Kuenn.

5. (Third Base) George Kell. Younger generations knew George as part of a long-time television broadcasting pair with Al Kaline. In his playing days, Kell was a ten-time All-Star and batted over .300 in six of his seven seasons with the Tigers. He won a batting championship in 1949, hitting .343 while striking out only 13 times (still a record low among the batting champs). George was inducted into the Hall of Fame as a Tiger.

Backup: Aurelio Rodriguez—as a late-inning fielding replacement.

4. (Second Base) Charlie Gehringer. "The Mechanical Man" was given his nick-name by Lefty Gomez in reference to his consistency as a hitter and fielder. He was born in Fowlerville and attended the University of Michigan before he signed with the Tigers in 1924. He was a pleasant man with a sense of humor, albeit a man who was well known as one of a most quiet nature. Charlie believed that "rabble-rousing" did-n't do much good, so he chose to lead with his bat and his glove. The six-time All-Star had a career year in 1937, winning the AL MVP with 209 hits, 40 doubles, 133 runs scored and a .371 batting average. Charlie was an excellent contact hitter, notching batting averages over .300 in 13 different full seasons. His career batting average is .320, ranking him sixth among all-time Tigers.

Backup: Lou Whitaker.

3. (First Base) Hank Greenberg. "Hammerin' Hank" was one of the most feared sluggers of his day..Despite missing several years while serving in World War II and playing only nine full seasons, Hank still won two AL MVP Awards and two champi-onships with Detroit. Hank's 306 home runs rank him third among all-time Tigers and his 58 home runs in 1938 remains a Tigers single-season record. Hank was inducted as a Tiger into the Hall of Fame in 1956. In 2006, the United States Postal Service hon-ored Hank with a postage stamp.

Backup: Norm Cash.

2. (Catcher) Mickey Cochrane. He was the best Tiger catcher of all-time and one of the game's best catchers ever. Mickey was a player/manager for the Tigers, and he led them to their first world championship in 1935, scoring the winning run in the decid-ing Game 6 of the Series. Despite playing a majority of his career for the Philadelphia A's, Mickey was inducted into the Hall of Fame in 1947 as a Tiger.

Backup: Bill Freehan.

1. (Pitcher) Hal Newhouser. The Detroit native made his debut with the Tigers in 1939 at the age of 18. In 1944, Hal had his breakout year, winning 29 games with a 2.22 ERA. "Prince Hal" is the only pitcher in AL history to win back-to-back MVP awards, doing so in 1944 and 1945. Critics argued that Hal's numbers would decline when the great players returned from duty in WWII. But he silenced his critics, having a third magnificent year, winning 26, striking out 275, and notching a 1.94 ERA. Hal fin-ished second in the MVP voting in 1946, just missing out on his third consecutive MVP. He was inducted into the Hall of Fame in 1992.

Long Relief: Mickey Lolich.

The numbers on this list are not a ranking, but relate directly to the list items they introduce. If you don't understand, don't worry—you'll get the hang of it after a couple.

20. World boxing champions to come out of Detroit's Kronk Gym; Al Kaline's age when he won the 1955 batting title.

19. Earvin "Magic" Johnson's age when he led Michigan State basketball to a national title in 1979, then became the first overall pick in the NBA draft.

18. National championships won by Michigan college hockey teams.

17. Age of Ann Arbor native Aaron Krickstein when he broke into the top ten of ATP's men's rankings.

16. Points scored by Isiah Thomas in the final 91 seconds of a 1984 game vs. the Knicks.

15. Times Al Kaline was selected to play in the All-Star Game.

14. Major tournaments held at Oakland Hills Country Club in Bloomfield Hills.

13. Big Ten titles won by Bo Schembechler; number of consecutive three-pointers made without a miss by Piston Terry Mills in 1996 to set an NBA record.

12. Number of players offered by Pistons GM Jack McCloskey to the Lakers in exchange for Magic Johnson in 1979; teams Larry Brown has coached.

11. Current streak of consecutive NCAA Men's Basketball appearances by Michigan State; national championships won by UM football.

10. NHL All-Star teams made by Steve Yzerman; number of runs scored by the Tigers in the ninth inning for a 14-13 win in their first game as a Major League franchise in 1901.

9. Shutouts pitched by Tigers' Denny McLain during the 1969 season.

8. Films former Tigers' announcer Ernie Harwell has appeared in.

7. Interceptions thrown by Ty Detmer in his first start as Lions QB in 2001.

6. Weight classes in which boxer Thomas Hearns won world title belts.

5. Total points scored by the Detroit Lions and Dallas Cowboys in their 1970 playoff game.

4. Final Four appearances by Michigan State men's basketball in the last decade; consecutive undefeated seasons for Michigan football teams coached by Fielding Yost.

3. Interceptions snared by Lions cornerback Lem Barney in one quarter during a 1968 game; grand slams hit by Tigers outfielder Jim Northrup during one week in the 1968 season.

2. Number of baskets Pistons Hall of Fame guard Dave Bing saw during his frequent bouts with double vision; number of bases (including home for the winning run) stolen by Ty Cobb while Yankees fielders argued a call with umpires in a 1911 game.

1. All-time rank of Michigan's football program in wins and winning percentage; playoff wins by Detroit Lions over the last 50 years.

0. Losses suffered by Michigan State during the 1951 and 1952 college football seasons.

The tensions and competitive spirit of sports occasionally blow up in ugly ways. Screaming matches between players and coaches. Rash comments blurted out to the media. Obscene gestures flashed by players at fans, and vice versa. They are all a semi-regular part of sports. But sometimes, players, management and/or fans blow up in big, ugly, nuclear kinds of ways, like these:

Dishonorable Mentions: Red Wings assistant coach Joe Kocur imitates Bobby Knight and hurls a chair onto the ice during a 2003 Red Wings–Blues brawl; Mickey Cochrane gets so upset after a 1934 World Series loss, he needs to be hospitalized; the Tigers-White Sox Brawl (Parts I and II) on April 22, 2000; Willie Hernandez douses Mitch Albom in 1988; Wings' coach Jacques Demers tries to oblige Leafs coach John Brophy after he gives him the "choke" sign during a 1987 playoff game; Stack Puts the Smack on Jerome Williams in 2000, Wings coach Scotty Bowman curses out Claude Lemiuex in front of his family in 1996 (buy, hey, it was Claude Lemiuex).

Honorable Ommisions: Billy Martin, Rasheed Wallace and Dennis Rodman— despite their infamous reputations, they all were relatively well-behaved in Detroit (though Rasheed still has time).

12. Dick Vitale shows his dark side. In 1978, Dick Vitale, then the coach of a lousy Pistons team, had to be hospitalized for complications due to excessive stress. The first game he returned to the bench, Vitale got ejected by refs for going ballistic about a bad call. Then the future college basketball TV analyst had to be restrained and carried off the court by security guards. It was the first month of the season.

11. Matt Millen drops another kind of "F" bomb. In 2003, the Lions CEO showed how versatile he could be in finding ways to embarrass the franchise when he got into a public shouting match with Kansas City Chiefs receiver Johnnie Morton, calling Morton a "faggot." The ugly incident seemed to provide William Clay Ford with the perfect opportunity to fire Millen, who had guided the team to an 8-36 record up to that point. But he remained calm and stood by his man. Proving that sometimes losing your temper and doing something drastic can be the best course of action.

10. Cobb washes Suds down the drain. Suds Sutherland's career got off to a dream start in the first two months of the 1921 season as the rookie starting pitcher posted a 6-2 record for the Tigers, while also batting over .400. But then he ran into the nightmare that was Tiger player-manager Ty Cobb's temper. Outraged that his young pitcher had just given up a long home run to his superstar rival Babe Ruth in a June 22 game, Cobb ran in from centerfield and not only yanked Sutherland from the game, he threw him off the team. The Tigers could have used Suds' arm and his .400 bat the rest of the season. Despite posting a team batting average of .321 (an American League record that still stands), Cobb's Tigers finished 71-82, well out of the pennant race. The young pitcher fared even worse than the team after Cobb ran him off. Despite his great start with the Tigers, Suds Sutherland never played again for Detroit or any other MLB team.

9. Gary Moeller loses it, and his job. Five years into his tenure as Michigan's head football coach, Moeller over-imbibed at a fancy Southfield restaurant, got loud and out of control, then threw a punch at a cop trying to calm him down. Soon after, the Bo Schembechler disciple was fired from the job he planned to hold the rest of his career. Moeller does deserve credit for keeping his cool six years later, in 2000, while serving as the Detroit Lions' interim coach. He led the team on an unlikely late run. But he lost the final game, the final playoff spot and probably his final shot at career redemption on the last play of the season—a 54-yard field goal by the Bears' Paul Edinger.

8. Alvin Robertson chokes. The former NBA Defensive Player of the Year took offense to Pistons GM Jack McKinney questioning his back injury at a 1993 team practice. Robertson then attacked McKinney and choked him until teammates pulled him away. Somewhere, a young Latrell Sprewell was taking notes.

7. The Bobby Layne trade. In the second game of the 1958 season, Lions QB Layne refused to let Detroit's kicker convert a 17-yard field goal with 40 seconds remaining in a tie game. He insisted on trying a TD pass instead and threw an incompletion, costing Detroit the win. According to some of his fellow players, Layne, a heavy gambler, had bet on the Lions and needed the six points from the TD to cover the point spread. Whatever the reason for Layne's move, Lions management was furious. The next day, Layne, who had led the Lions to three NFL titles in nine years and was wildly popular with fans, was on his way out of town. The Lions haven't won a title since.

6. The Brawl in Hockeytown, March 26, 1997. Ah, but you know, it was fun. Maybe not good, clean fun. But good, dirty, bloody fun. And it had to happen. There was just too much ill will built up from Claude Lemieux's criminal hit on Kris Draper the previous season and the simmering Avs-Wings rivalry for it not to explode in the first period. Then explode again four seconds into the next period. Then again the next season. Watching replays of the original battle royale, with Lemieux and Patrick Roy getting smacked around by Darren McCarty and Mike Vernon, is almost enough to make you nostalgic for the days when the Avs were good enough to piss you off on a consistent basis.

5. Malice in the Palace, 2004. Too ugly, senseless and fresh in the memory to recount here. How bad was it? So bad that Rasheed Wallace had to act as a peacemaker. So bad that it wiped the original Malice in the Palace brawl in 1989 between Charles Barkley, Bill Laimbeer and a few dozen Detroit fans, off the books. This is the one we remember now, much as we'd like to forget it.

4. Tigers Fans in Game 7 of 1934 World Series. Considering its context, this ugly outburst during Game 7 of the 1934 World Series probably tops the Malice in the Palace. With the Tigers coming home to Navin Field with a 3-2 Series lead, Detroit fans saw their team lose late in Game 6, then fall behind 7-0 early in Game 7. In the sixth inning, the Cards' leftfielder Ducky Medwick slid hard into Tigers third baseman Marv Owen, injuring him. When Medwick took the field for the bottom half of the inning, Tiger fans in the leftfield bleachers pelted him with fruit, bottles, seat cushions and anything else they could get their hands on. Fearing a riot was about to break out, baseball commissioner Kenesaw Landis ordered the Cards to take Medwick out of the game. With debris continuing to fly around them, the Cards closed out the 11-0 rout to win the Series.

3. Woody Hayes punches out ABC sideline cameraman. Everybody remembers "The Punch" that the Ohio State coach delivered to the Clemson player at the 1978 Gator Bowl. But few recall that he did something even worse a few weeks before when he decked an ABC sideline cameraman during the Buckeyes' annual showdown with Michigan. The poor guy was only doing his job, approaching Woody to get a reaction shot after a late Buckeyes' turnover. Woody spotted him, reared back and knocked the cameraman to the ground in front of over 100,000 fans at the Big House and millions on national TV.

2. Terry Sawchuk's death. The four-time winner of the Vezina Trophy as the NHL's best goalie had been gone from Detroit for six years by then. But the Hall of Famer would always be a Red Wing in the hearts of the Detroit faithful. And nobody dreamed he'd be gone in the larger sense so soon. In 1970, a drunken Sawchuk, who battled violent mood swings throughout his career, got into a fight with Rangers teammate Ron Stewart. During the scuffle, Sawchuk suffered a lacerated liver and other internal injuries, including blood clots that led to his death a short time later. Sawchuk, who started in goal for four of the Red Wings' Stanley Cup champion teams in the 1950s, was only 40 years old.

1. Ugueth Urbina imitates Charles Manson. The closer gave hints of his potential for random acts of violence during his time with the Tigers. Popular with some teammates, he got into fights and shouting matches with others. The Tigers traded him in 2005 shortly after Urbina started a fight during an airplane flight. Two years later down on his farm in his native Venezuela, Urbina assaulted five of his employees with a machete, then poured gasoline on them. He was sent to prison for 14 years.

Note: Jo-Ann Barnas works as a sports feature writer and Olympics beat reporter at the *Detroit Free Press*. The Livonia native and Michigan State grad has covered five Winter and Summer Games. Barnas has won numerous state and national writing awards, including being named Michigan Sportswriter of the Year in 2005 by the National Sportscasters and Sportswriters Association. Her list includes Olympians who were born in Michigan or spent the majority of their athletic careers training here (which is why you won't find Tara Lipinski or Michael Phelps on it). The 2008 Beijing Games were held after this list was produced, so there could be some changes to it before the book's next edition.

10. Hayes Jones. Born in Mississippi, Jones grew up in Pontiac and graduated from Eastern Michigan. He won the Olympic bronze medal 110-meter hurdles in 1960 at the Rome Olympics. Jones, who won 52 consecutive indoor hurdle races between 1959 and 1964, came back four years later at the 1964 Tokyo Games to win the gold medal in a close race against American teammate Blaine Lindgren.

9. Steve Fraser. The Ann Arbor resident became the first U.S. athlete to ever win an Olympic medal in Greco-Roman wrestling—and he made it gold. At the 1984 Los Angeles Games he rallied to beat Romanian Ilie Matei in the final 50 seconds for the victory.

8. Greg Barton. The Homer native became the first U.S. kayaker to win an Olympic gold medal at the 1988 Seoul Games. With four Olympic medals from 1984 to 1992 (two gold and two bronze), Barton has won more medals than any other American in the sport.

7. Shelia Taormina. A Livonia native, she became an Olympic swimming relay gold medalist at the 1996 Atlanta Olympics. She then made the inaugural U.S. Olympic team in women's triathlon, finishing sixth in the 2000 Sydney Games. She won the world title in the event in 2004 before turning to modern pentathlon two years ago in an effort to become the first athlete to compete in three different Olympic sports.

6. Karch Kiraly. The only player to win Olympic medals in both indoor and beach volleyball, Kiraly was born in Jackson and grew up in Ann Arbor. He took indoor gold in 1984 and 1988, and an Olympic beach gold medal in 1996.

5. Angela Ruggiero. The three-time U.S. Olympic women's ice hockey medalist from Harper Woods was the youngest member of the 1998 squad that won the inaugural gold medal against Canada at Nagano (where Shelly Looney of Trenton scored the winning goal). A Harvard grad, Ruggiero is considered the finest women's ice hockey defender in the world.

4. Micki King. The Pontiac native was in first place in women's springboard diving at the 1968 Mexico City Olympics when she broke her left forearm during her ninth dive. She completed her final dive, but placed fourth. Four years later, at the 1972 Munich Games, King won the gold medal on the same dive she had tried four years earlier with a broken arm—a reverse 1-1/2 somersault with 1 1/2 twists.

3. Shelia Young Ochowicz. The Birmingham native became the first U.S. athlete to win three medals at a single Winter Olympics in 1976 in Innsbruck, where she took gold, silver and bronze in speedskating. In 1973, Young won world sprint titles in both speedskating and cycling.

2. Eddie Tolan. The former Cass Tech High football player and University of Michigan sprinter became the first black athlete to win two Olympic gold medals. At the 1932 Los Angeles Games, Tolan defeated American teammate Ralph Metcalfe in an Olympic record 10.3 seconds in the 100 meters. Then he was victorious in 200 meters in the same Games, also in Olympic record time.

1. Norbert Schemansky. The Detroit native won four Olympic medals in four Games over a 16-year period in men's weightlifting. He captured a heavyweight silver medal at the 1948 London Olympics; middle-heavyweight gold in Helsinki in 1952; heavyweight bronze in Rome in 1960; and another heavyweight bronze, in Tokyo in 1964. In 2005, he was recognized as "Best Weightlifter of 100 years" by the International Weightlifting Federation.

In the early days of WDFN, we used to goof around and have lots of fun doing absurd things. One day, we pulled out the All Body Parts Team. Legends like Rollie Fingers and Toe Blake were no-brainers. As the show went along the conversation headed into the gutter with names from listeners like Aubrey Beavers and Randy Bush. Here is area sports' All Body Parts Team . . . and yes this will head to the gutter as well. Almost right off the bat. Homonyms are eligible and names appear in alphabetical order.

16. Steve Baack, Lions, DE, 1984–87.

15. Jerry Ball, Lions, DT, 1987–92.

14. Cloyce Box, Lions, WR, 1949–50 52–54.

13. Dan Bunz, Lions, LB, 1985.

12. Donie Bush, Tigers, SS, 1908–21.

11. Harry Colon, Lions, S, 1992–94 1997.

10. Red Cox, Tigers, RHP, 1920.

9. Roy Face, Tigers, RHP, 1968.

8. Larry Foote, Michigan Football, LB, 1998–2001.

7. Larry Hand, Lions, DE, 1964–77.

6. Shawn Hare, Tigers, OF, 1991–92.

5. Leon Hart, Lions, E, 1950–57.

4. Galen Head, Red Wings, 1967–68.

3. Rusty Kuntz, Tigers, OF/IF/DH, 1984–85.

2. Heinie Manush, Tigers, OF, 1923–27.

1. Chris Pusey, Red Wings, G, 1985–86.

Note: A 1993 graduate of CMU, Rob Otto has reported on every team in town, helmed his own weekend show and sung sports updates to the tune of the Styx classic "Mr. Roboto" on WDFN. For this list, he considered a candidate's impact on the national scene, as well as his efforts in Mt. Pleasant.

10. Jim Meyers. He used the ring name George "The Animal" Steele as a WWE Hall of Fame pro wrestler for 40 years after earning his master's at CMU. The Detroit native was also inducted into the Michigan Coaches Hall of Fame after leading his Madison High School team to top rankings in both wrestling and football.

9. Chris Kaman. Carried CMU to the 2003 NCAA Men's Basketball tourney then became the sixth overall pick in the NBA Draft. In 2006, Kaman helped the L.A. Clippers claim the franchise's first NBA playoff series win since 1978.

8. Tom Crean. Head men's hoops coach at Marquette for a decade, Crean lead the Golden Eagles to five NCAA Tournament berths and the Final Four in 2003 before becoming head coach at Indiana in 2008.

7. Ray Bentley. The linebacker played 10 seasons in the USFL and NFL, winning a championship with the Michigan Panthers and playing in two Super Bowls with Buffalo.

6. Dan Roundfield. The 6-foot-8 forward and center was twice named All-MAC. A first-round pick of the Pacers, the Detroit native played three seasons with Indiana before moving to Atlanta, where he became a three-time All-star.

5. Curt Young. The southpaw spent 10 years in the Majors, primarily in Oakland. He won two World Series and pitched a pair of one-hitters.

4. Tom Tresh. Led Chippewas to conference baseball title in 1957, then played nine years in the Majors. The 1962 AL Rookie of the Year played in three World Series with the Yankees, was a two-time All-Star and won a Gold Glove.

3. Dan Majerle. A surprise member of the 1988 U.S. Olympic basketball team, the Traverse City product went on to play 14 seasons in NBA. A three-time All-star, Majerle played in the 1993 NBA Finals and co-holds the record for most treys in a playoff series (17).

2. Kevin Tapani. Helped CMU baseball win three MAC Titles and tossed a 1986 no-hitter against EMU. Pitched 13 seasons in Majors, winning 143 games. Started two games in 1991 World Series, helping Twins take the title. Finished seventh in Cy Young voting that year.

1. Dick Enberg. A broadcaster, not a player, Enberg still had a bigger impact on sports than any other Chippewa. He's won (as of this printing) 13 Emmys (including a Lifetime Achievement award), nine National Sportscaster of the Year awards, the NFL's Pete Rozelle Trophy and the Basketball Hall of Fame's Curt Gowdy Award for outstanding work in media. The Mount Clemens native has broadcast Super Bowls, Olympics, Final Fours, World Series and Rose Bowls.

Note: Shepard has worked many years as a TV and radio announcer for a variety of networks and sporting events, calling everything from the Pistons basketball to Eastern Michigan football.

10. The No-Names (Marcus Kennedy, Carl and Cal Thomas, Kory Hallas and Lorenzo Neely). During EMU's contentious nickname change from Hurons to Eagles, this squad won the MAC regular-season and tourney titles, then upset Mississippi State and Penn State in the NCAA tourney to advance to the school's first Sweet Sixteen.

9. Grant Long. The forward played in over 1,000 games and averaged 9.5 points and 6.1 rebounds during his 15-year NBA career.

8. Dave Pureifory. Defensive lineman played 11 years in the NFL with the Packers, Bengals and Lions.

7. Charlie Batch. Owns pretty much every EMU quarterback record worth having. Passed for over 10,000 yards in eight seasons in the NFL and picked up a Super Bowl ring with the Steelers. Still, his greatest achievement may be taking over as Lions starting quarterback as a rookie 1998, thus ending the Scott Michell era in Detroit.

6. Chris Hoiles. Enjoyed a distinguished, 10-year career with the Baltimore Orioles, hitting .262 with 151 home runs and 449 RBI. Hit 29 homers and had 82 RBI in 1993. Later inducted into both the Eastern Michigan Athletics and the Baltimore Orioles Hall of Fames.

5. Earl Boykins. The 5-foot-5 and 133-pound point guard led EMU to two NCAA tournaments and averaged 26.8 points per game in 1997-98. Established himself as the school's all-time assists leader. Averaged at least 10 points a game between 2003-07 for the NBA's Denver Nuggets. Earned the nickname, "The Double Digit Midget."

4. John Banaszak. Defensive lineman started on the legendary Steel Curtain defense during four of his seven seasons (1975-81) with the Pittsburgh Steelers, picking up three Super Bowl wins.

3. Ron Johnson. A four-year starter at EMU, the defensive back was a third-team AP All-American and first-round pick in 1978 NFL draft. Played seven seasons for the Pittsburgh Steelers, winning two Super Bowls. Member of both the EMU and MAC Halls of Fame.

2. Bob Welch. EMU hurler enjoyed exceptional Major League career, winning 211 games and posting a 3.47 ERA. Compiled a spectacular 27-6 record for Oakland on his way to winning the 1990 AL Cy Young award. No MLB pitcher since has posted more than 25 victories in a season.

1. George Gervin. During his sophomore season of 1971-72, the forward averaged a shocking 29.5 points per game. But after slugging an opposing player, he was suspended and eventually dismissed from team. "Ice" took his smooth scoring repertoire to the ABA, where he averaged 21.9 points per game over a four-year period. After moving to the NBA in 1976, Gervin won four scoring titles for the Spurs. He ended up playing in 12 All-Star games and being named to the NBA's Top 50 All-Time Team and the Pro Basketball Hall of Fame.

When the Pontiac Silverdome opened in 1975, many people heralded it as a state-of-the-art venue. After a few years, those people realized they were wrong. The Silverdome was not the most aesthetically pleasing structure, nor was it the most stunning achievement of engineering. What the Silverdome did, however, was provide a site for amazing events with record crowds. The following is a list of the top moments experienced at the Pontiac Silverdome.

12. The NBA All-Star Game, February 4, 1979. The 31,745 fans were treated to the NBA's mid-season classic. Philadelphia's Julius Erving had 29 points and Detroit native George Gervin, representing the San Antonio Spurs, tallied 26. The West held off the East, winning the game 134-129. Denver's David Thompson was voted the game's MVP for his 25-point effort. But West Bloomfield's "The Great Impostor," Barry Bremen, stole the show. Bremen disguised himself in a Kansas City Kings uniform and walked right past security to take part in the pregame warm-ups.

11. Leon the Barber, many occasions. On many Pistons game nights in the Silverdome, superfan Leon "The Barber" Bradley gave players a memorable piece or two of his mind. Leon's tongue-lashings were the stuff of legend. Anyone and everyone (including some Pistons) were subjected to The Barber's verbal taunts. He was the consummate heckler, one who stayed within the boundaries of decency while letting his target know that their performance was less than acceptable. He made games a lot more fun to watch, even when the Pistons were getting crushed.

10. The Who concert, December 6, 1975. Over 75,000 attended a great performance by the original lineup of the legendary English rock band. Townshend, Daltrey, Entwistle and Moon opened their show with an inspired rendition of "Pinball Wizard," and continued for two hours, attacking other hits, such as "My Generation" and "Won't Get Fooled Again."

9. Game 5 of the 1988 NBA Finals, June 16, 1988. The Pistons defeated the Lakers, 104-94, in front of 41,732 raucous fans—one of the largest NBA crowds ever. Detroit took a 3-2 lead in the Finals, ultimately losing the next two in Los Angeles. It was the last game the Detroit Pistons played in the Silverdome.

8. Elvis concert, December 31, 1975. "The King" performed a special New Year's Eve concert for 60,500 of his fans. Elvis Presley was known at this time for the stunning array of jumpsuits that he would wear onstage. For this concert, he donned both a White Stud and a Rainfall Suit. He ripped the seat of the pants of his first outfit in mid-performance. After informing the crowd of his wardrobe malfunction, he went to change into the other suit, and then returned to finish his epic set.

7. FIFA World Cup 1994, U.S. vs. Switzerland. The first indoor World Cup soccer match in history was played in front of 63,425. Real grass was grown by Michigan State University agronomists, then shipped in modules and assembled under the gray dome.

6. Barry Sanders Hits 2,000 Yards, December 21, 1997. Fans turned out 77,624 strong to witness Barry Sanders reach his season milestone on a two-yard run with 2:15 to go in the fourth quarter. Barry became only the third running back in NFL history to reach 2,000 yards in a single season. That same game, young Lions linebacker Reggie Brown broke his neck and almost died on the field, ending his career prematurely. The Lions would win, 13-10, propelling themselves into the playoffs.

5. Led Zeppelin concert, April 30, 1977. Over 77,000 fans packed the Silverdome for a rock concert of religious proportions. At the time, this concert exceeded the legendary band's previous attendance records, becoming the largest audience for a single-act concert. The band played their epics, including "The Song Remains the Same," "No Quarter," "Kashmir," and "Stairway to Heaven." Many consider this concert as Led Zeppelin's zenith of live performances.

4. Pope John Paul II Mass, September 19, 1987. Over 93,682 set a Silverdome indoor attendance record, receiving Catholic mass from the world-famous religious leader. The Pope made an 11-day visit to North America—stopping in Detroit, Hamtramck and Pontiac to spread a message of peace. The arena was converted into a temporary church, making use of the game floor for extra seating. The mass culminated in a full sharing of bread and wine with the entire congregation.

3. Detroit Lions 1991 Divisional Playoffs, January 5, 1992. The Lions hosted their first home playoff game since 1957 and 79,835 were treated to the Lions only playoff victory since that '57 championship season as Detroit beat Dallas, 38-6. Lions QB Erik Kramer completed 29 of 38 passes for 341 yards and 3 touchdowns.

2. Super Bowl XVI, January 24, 1982. Over 81,000 attended the first Super Bowl in a cold-weather city. The Silverdome served as an oasis from icy roads and the sub-zero wind-chill outside. On this evening, the San Francisco 49ers defeated the Cincinnati Bengals, 26-21. Forty million people also watched the game on *CBS* and it remains the fourth highest-rated TV program in history. Pat Summerall and John Madden did the play-by-play. There was a Lions' presence on the field that day when Detroit's legendary QB Bobby Layne participated in the pre-game coin toss.

1. Wrestlemania III, March 29, 1987. A crowd of 93,173 set a reported world indoor attendance record. We Metro Detroiters, after all, love our pro wrestling. Of all the Wrestlemanias before and since, this event is consistently rated as one of the best of the bunch. The main event featured Hulk Hogan against Andre the Giant for the WWF Championship belt in the culmination of a storyline that had been building for years. Hulk won the belt, after picking up and bodyslamming the 500-plus-pound giant. Multiple celebrities attended the event. Aretha Franklin rocked the house with her rendition of "America the Beautiful." Bob Uecker was a guest announcer, bringing extra comic relief to the booth. Alice Cooper was a special celebrity manager for Jake "The Snake" Roberts.

Note: Don Shane has been a fixture on Detroit television for 25 years. He was the first anchor for *Sports Final Edition* from 1978-83 at WDVI. After stints in Chicago and Boston, Don came back to Detroit to become sports director at WXYZ in 1989. Besides anchoring the station's 5 p.m., 6 p.m. and 11 p.m. sportscasts, Don co-hosted the *Big Ten Ticket* with Bo Schembechler for 13 years. They were very good friends and Don was probably the last person to see him alive as Bo died of a heart attack at the WXYZ studios right before the taping of a Big Ten Ticket episode on the day before the 2006 Michigan-Ohio State game. But mostly, Don remembers how Bo lived and made his life better through their friendship. Here are the fondest of those memories.

10. Bo interviews USC coach Pete Carroll at the 2004 Rose Bowl. I saw an aspect of Bo that day that I never saw before—nervousness. It was the first time he ever interviewed someone as co-host of our pre-game show. When he was done, he wanted input and criticism, repeatedly asking me, "How did I do?" He did great! And Carroll, who said he wouldn't do any one-on-one interviews that day, was thrilled to talk to Bo.

9. Painting at the 1998 Rose Bowl. We were taping pre-game show segments in the stands a few days before the Michigan-Washington State game when Bo was asked to come down and paint the block "M" in the Michigan end zone. He was thrilled that they asked and was proud to do it. He acted like a little kid, laughing and smiling as he was painting.

8. Getting his make-up put on before our TV shows. Bo says he hated it, but trust me, he loved the attention and enjoyed being pampered. For a guy who had the reputation of being gruff and tough on the outside, he could be a real softie in a setting like that. I enjoyed hearing the sweet conversations he had with the women who were helping him look good on TV. But when the show was over, he couldn't wait to get the face paint off.

7. Enduring terrible fans at Ohio State. Bo and I were doing a "live" pre-game Michigan-Ohio State show in the end zone in Columbus when some Buckeyes fans recognized Bo and started throwing bottles, food, and almost anything else they had at us. The Ohio State cops were no help at all. We dodged a lot of junk for an hour and Bo vowed that we would never do the Ohio State pre-game show "live" again. And we didn't. All future Columbus shows were taped either very early in the morning on the field or in our studio. As usual, Bo stuck to his promise.

6. Bo's last temper tantrum. His final game as Michigan's coach came at the 1990 Rose Bowl against USC. The Wolverines got hit with just a terrible, crucial call made very late by an official 25 yards from the play. It cost Michigan a chance to win the game and Bo went crazy on the sidelines, throwing down his headset and ripping into the officials. It was his last classic tirade and it was hilarious. We rarely see coaches get that angry anymore.

5. Football Saturdays in his Big House box. Bo liked to arrive at home games very early with his friends and he obviously enjoyed talking football. It was a privilege to sit by him, to listen and learn from him, even about things as simple as players warming up and the band practicing. (You might not know it, but he loved watching the bands perform at halftime.) He said a lot in those moments and I learned a lot and I couldn't repeat any of it on TV because the Michigan people would know exactly where the information came from.

4. Football Saturdays when Michigan was on the road. Bo would gather with some friends at his home or watch games all day by himself. No distractions, just football. His wife Cathy would provide all the terrific food. I once asked him if Cathy was okay with this arrangement. He replied, "This is one time Cathy has nothing to say about it."

3. Bo's aura. Bo was like a rock star—people wanted to touch him, wanted to hear his words of wisdom, wanted to get his autograph. He was always thoughtful and accommodating. When Bo met people, he made them feel as if they were the most important people in his life at that moment. That's a special gift few have.

2. "Get the heat turned on." Bo once visited a recruit in Detroit in the middle of the winter. The house was freezing. The family had no heat on because they couldn't pay the bill. When Bo got back on campus, he told his staff to "get the heat turned on" in that house and pay for it for the rest of the winter. Bo had an unreal compassion for people and the tough times they might have been going through. He said it was the only time that he knowingly broke NCAA rules. By the way, that recruit went to Michigan and had a very nice college football career.

1. Bo on Cathy. When Bo met Cathy, she had no idea he was Michigan's football coach. He fell for her immediately. Cathy is an absolutely beautiful woman, inside and out. I attended a number of charity functions and events with Bo and Cathy and he would frequently nudge me, point to Cathy and say, "I can still recruit, can't I? I mean, can you believe that I'm with her?" I would always laugh with him, but you could tell it was no joke—he loved her dearly. Knowing Bo the way I did, I can answer his question now. Yes, Bo, I could always believe that you were with her.

Note: A 2002 graduate of Michigan State, Valenti worked at 92.7 The Ticket from 2000-2003 in Lansing before moving to Detroit's 97.1 The Ticket, where he currently co-hosts "The Valenti and Foster Show." If you had any doubts about his feelings toward his alma mater's hated rival, this list should lay them to rest.

10. False Bravado. It's not like it's a Michigan exclusive. Fans from places like Tuscaloosa, Los Angeles and Austin share the same annoying trait with one exception—those places actually accomplish things. No school has done less on the national scene while believing they are God's gift to Earth than Michigan.

9. Back in 1903. Look, I love history, stats, legendary games, myths, etc. But Wolverine fans don't just honor the past, they live in it. Only at Michigan would the response to a 7-5 season or another bowl loss be, "We are the leader in wins in history" or "We won a national title in 1903." Nobody cares, good Lord, the sport was filled with 100-pound tackles and no cups then.

8. Wal-Mart Wolverines. Yes, you know exactly who I'm talking about—the guy who doesn't even have a GED but will attack the value of an MSU degree. Now, look, you don't have to go to a school to be a fan. But you might want to at least have a degree, much less one from Michigan, to enter that argument.

7. Mascot. Sorry but if your mascot is so lame that you don't put him on ANY team uniforms, no flags, not even a mascot at the games, you have issues. Then again, you did name your school after a giant rat.

6. We are Michigan. From the ludicrous assertion of being the "Harvard of the West" to the end-all, be-all defense of "We are Michigan, we don't do that," this university subscribes to a level of hypocrisy never to be duplicated.

5. The Big Hole. Many schools name their stadiums. But at least places like "Death Valley" and "The Shoe" are worth going to. "The Big House" is a flat-out dump. You get six inches of seat, one bathroom and an atmosphere more reflective of a Barnes and Noble cappuccino café than that of a football cathedral.

4. Football Rules. How convenient that at a place where they haven't hung a "clean" banner since Gibby was pasting the Pads, they would simply stop recognizing basketball as a sport. Basketball doesn't matter and nobody cares and we are a football school. Yet, let's go back to the Fab Five days. Funny how many people cared then, right? Hell you had white guys from Bloomfield Hills rocking a high-top fade like Juwan and Grandma Ethel wearing yellow shorts to her calves. Yeah, nobody cared.

3. Bo. Now understand this. I respect the hell outta the man. He did things the right way, valued people, was clean, etc. But that doesn't mean I cannot hate him. May he rest in peace, the guy was a pain in the ass to Spartan fans. From his "proper perspective" comment to those aviators and ultra tight pants, nothing annoyed me more than his gritting teeth while spitting that tired "Michigan Man" line as if he were chewing the words. Easily one of the most beloved/hated men in the history of the game, he also goes down as one of the most overrated. Bo had a losing record in bowls, no national titles and a refusal to change that ended up costing him and his beloved program a ton. Did I mention he owned MSU? Ugh.

2. Excuse Factory. They've never lost, they've just run out of time. You may as well tattoo that on any Wolverine coach, player and fan, as the go-to line for all losses. From blaming the refs (common) to the crown on the field (I'm serious), this school simply has no limits on how far they will go to defend the fact that they lost. Bad calls, bad Gatorade (see Washington game), bad clocks, heck, an international conspiracy against Michigan—it's all fair game when they lose.

1. The Helmet. Nothing, and I mean NOTHING, bothers me more than those ridiculous helmets. First of all, they copied what MSU had years before. Secondly, they make no sense whatsoever. They are impossible to look at. They make the kids look more like members of some space club than a proud football team. Looks like they handed a baby a Sharpie and said, "Be creative son."

Note: A native of Troy, Michigan, Gregg Henson is a multi-state radio veteran. He has worked at WCSX and WDFN, helping launch the station by co-hosting both "The Sunday Afternoon Sit-In" and "The Jamie and Gregg Show." The creative Henson has always loved the Maize and Blue—and making fun of Michigan State.

10. Sparty. Easily the dumbest mascot in sports. Class schools don't even bother with mascots. I know he was voted the best, but he really is the worst. The whole concept of a grown man running around in a loin cloth is scary. Even Charlton Heston was embarrassed by "Sparty."

9. Spartan yapping. This started back in the Scott Skiles era and has never stopped. Michigan State athletes are notorious for their "yapping" even when they are down by 30 points. Doesn't matter the sport or the player. Skiles or Ezor, doesn't matter. The celebration rarely matches the accomplishment. Skiles is famous for calling Antoine Joubert "fatboy." But has Skiles ever looked in the mirror? He was bald even before I was sporting the dome.

8. We recruited the pants off Michigan. Michigan State football coach George Perles was so proud to have recruited a good class in his early days that he took a shot at Michigan Head Coach Bo Schembechler by saying, "We recruited the pants off Michigan." Too bad he didn't have much success to go with those "pants." Bo followed up the comments by whipping Perles and his Spartans 42-0 in East Lansing. Perles went 4-8 against the "pantsless" Wolverines in 13 seasons.

7. Spartan Insecurity. Easily the loudest guy in the room is a Spartan fan after any win against Michigan. Sparty has a chip on his shoulder because he is so insecure about his place in the Michigan college athletic pecking order. Can't they just accept the fact that MSU will always be inferior on the football field. No, they need to be the loudest Michigan basher in the building.

6. Johnny Spirit. Please lose this guy once and for all; he isn't enhancing MSU's image at all. A grown man in tights and satin shorts NEVER reflects well on anybody.

5. Spartan Riots. MSU fans really need to learn how to hold their booze. The constant torturing of couches in the name of a good time reflects poorly on us all. Maybe Sparties need a committee to study the party habits of Central Michigan University, after all, we've never seen the "End of the World Party" on CNN.

4. Spartan Bob. The clock operator at Spartan stadium just couldn't take another loss fair and square; he had to cheat the clock for the 2001 win. The sad part is that most Sparties can't even admit that they cheated to win the game.

3. Whaaaaaaa. Michigan did recruit me. The MSU athletes "I hate Michigan" mantra. Get a grip Sparties, they didn't recruit ANY of you. Why? Because you weren't the cream of the crop. Don't take it personally.

2. Changing the uniform every year. Part of being a "traditional power" is selecting a classic uniform and sticking with it. Michigan State doesn't know what they want. Do they want the block S or is it a cartoonish Spartan on the helmet. Make a decision and stick too it. (I have to give them credit, the color green they are using now is the best yet).

1. Spartan Fan. Always the most insecure guy in the room, always hateful of anybody who isn't an MSU fan. The Spartan fan is a unique animal, insecure, drunk and irrational. Usually a Spartan fan is a middle child, kinda like Jan Brady, who didn't get enough love from mommy and daddy. They truly are "little brother."

Note: Michigan native Turk Regan thinks the intrastate feud between UM and MSU can sometimes make us forget the real enemy: Ohio State. The author of *The Sports Fan Voodoo Kit* began cataloguing reasons to Hate the State early in life and found it impossible to limit this list to 10 items. So to paraphrase *Spinal Tap's* Nigel Tufnel, "This one goes to 11."

11. They call themselves "Buckeyes." Have any other schools named their sports teams after stinking, poisonous tree droppings? Tasty and nutritious tree products like apples, limes and bananas haven't gained that honor. So why the buckeye? It has no use but to create more stinking, poisonous buckeyes . . . .Well, come to think of it, the name does fit.

10. They burn couches. Everyone thought Florida State fans had locked down the top spot for most obnoxious tradition with their tomahawk chopping. But you should never count out the Buckeyes' faithful. Somewhere along the line, a 10-watt light bulb flickered over the head of an OSU fanatic, giving him the idea to celebrate a win by dragging his couch outside and setting it on fire. It being Columbus, instead of getting arrested, the idiot was mimicked. Now ritual couch torchings erupt around Cbus whenever the Buckeyes score a big win. Given all the spilled grain alcohol and jelly doughnut farts soaked into those Buckeye couch cushions, the demented revelers probably don't even need lighter fluid to get the blazes going. West Virginia football fans also practice the couch-burning victory ritual. Though they probably won't be celebrating too often now that Rich Rodriguez is gone.

9. Their "O-H-I-O" Chant. It sounds like 70,000 kindergartners showing off that they just learned how to spell their first word. And sometimes, they get it wrong.

8. The "The." They put a "the" in front of the school name in their logo. "The Ohio State University." What? Were they afraid some impostor Ohio State University was going to set up shop and trick their students into enrolling there instead? That, right there, should tell you something about OSU's admission standards.

7. They go the extra mile to be classless, and are proud of it. The Buckeyes are so desperate to gain an advantage in "The Game" that they recruit their campus cops to harass Michigan players on the way to the Horseshoe. And local journalists to plant stories that Michigan players will be arrested when they show up in Columbus. Despicable and pathetic.

6. Jim Tressel. It's not just that he's had great success against Michigan and Michigan Sate, it's the way he hasn't done it. At least when you lost to Woody, the man got excited. But The Vest just stands there, blank-faced, looking like a Stepford Husband figuring out the most efficient way to mow the lawn.

5. Art Schlichter's damage to the regional economy. The former Buckeye quarterback conned millions from area people with investment scams to cover his gambling debts, undermining investor confidence throughout the Midwest. And he cost the government millions more to prosecute and incarcerate him for 10 years. Economists should stop harping about the decline of the auto industry and pay more attention to the crippling Schlichter Effect. The Buckeyes' former BMOC serves as a true icon for Ohio State's motto: Disciplina in Civitatem ("Education for Citizenship"). Other distinguished OSU alumni: David Boston, George Steinbrenner and Judith Miller.

4. The big toe on my right foot. I broke it when I was a kid kicking the TV after a Buckeyes' score against Michigan. It still hurts every time it rains.

3. Their 2007 and 2008 BCS title game fiascoes. With CBS shilling for the SEC all season and NBC serving as Notre Dame's own Bagdhad Bob, it's gotten hard enough for a Big Ten team to gain a spot in the BCS title game. Hell, the conference can't even be sure to get a team in the Rose Bowl anymore. History stinks with examples of Big Ten teams getting the national-title shaft, including undefeated Penn State and Michigan teams in recent decades. And now, thanks to the Buckeyes filling their pants against Florida and LSU, the future stinks even worse.

2. They unleashed Maurice Clarett on a blameless world. The hero of the BCS title game that OSU did win, Clarett wasn't exactly a model citizen when he showed up in Columbus, where young thugs tend to blend right in. But his Ohio State education developed Clarett from a simple juvenile delinquent into a multi-faceted felon, capable of perpetrating insurance fraud, armed robbery and witness tampering. And of loading himself up like Rambo for an assault that might have turned Columbus into Columbine if the cops hadn't intervened in time. (You know, Mr. Tressel, like responsible authority figures are supposed to do when they spot warning signs in a troubled young person?) Maurice is now continuing his studies in solitary confinement at the Toledo Correctional Institution. Chances are, he'll come out of there a better person than when he emerged from Ohio State University.

1. Their Woody Whitewash. Has any coach ever done more to embarrass college football than Ohio State "legend" Woody Hayes? "The Punch" thrown at the opposing player in his final game against Clemson in 1978 wasn't the act of a demented old man. It was the latest chapter in his long, bizarre history of violence. Woody started physically assaulting people early in his career. He attacked a TV cameraman after a 1956 loss to Iowa, then beat up a journalist and an innocent bystander a couple years later after a loss to USC. He sucker punched an ABC sideline cameraman during a loss to Michigan in 1977. Ohio State officials brushed off the incidents as misunderstandings—begging the question: what part of "dangerous, unhinged lunatic" didn't they understand? They let Woody keep coaching. (Until he stopped competing for national titles, anyway). Hell, they made him an icon. So what does it say about a program when the likes of Woody Hayes ranks as its greatest hero?

America's greatest sports rivalry has always been a part of my life. Some of my earliest childhood memories are of my father going absolutely crazy during the Michigan–Ohio State game. When you grow up in that kind of environment (a whacked-out dad during Michigan/Ohio State week) it's just not about a football game. You become aware of everything that surrounds this spectacle of the Wolverines vs. the Buckeyes.

10. Jim Tressel's Declaration. This is not a fond memory. "The Vest" was introduced as the Buckeyes new coach during halftime of a basketball game between Michigan and Ohio State on January 18, 2001 in Columbus. Tressel vowed, "I can assure you that you will be proud of your young people in the classroom, in the community and most especially in 310 days in Ann Arbor, Michigan." He may be a bit grammatically challenged, but you have to give it up to "The Vest" for backing up his words. Ohio State upset Michigan 26 to 20 exactly 310 days later and have been dominating the rivalry ever since.

9. Michigan 31, Ohio State 23, November 25, 1995. I was too hungover from my high school reunion the night before to attend the game. I watched from my couch with barely one eye opened as Tshimanga Biakabutuka rushed for 313 yards, leading Michigan to the upset of the undefeated and second-ranked Buckeyes. Soon after that game, I curtailed my drinking significantly.

8. The Savages in Columbus. Buckeyes fans are the vilest in sports. If you're an opposing fan attending a game in Columbus, good luck. If you're a Michigan fan attending a game in Columbus, make sure your will is updated.

7. Woody Hayes Toilet Paper. During the heyday of "The Ten-Year War" between Woody and Bo, people were hawking everything. One item that caught my eye was a roll of toilet paper where each sheet had a portrait of Woody Hayes. My dad asked me if I wanted a roll and I recoiled at the thought of buying something that gross. He told me that one day I'd regret not having a roll of Woody Hayes toilet paper and he was right.

6. Michigan 20, Ohio State 14, November 22, 1997. This game had many unforgettable moments. David Boston ripping off Charles Woodson's helmet during a feisty confrontation. Woodson returning a punt 78 yards for a TD. Ian Gold's pass breakup on fourth down to seal the Buckeyes' fate. The Wolverines celebrating with the crowd after the game. Most of all, it was the feeling I had walking out of Michigan Stadium that day because they had finally pulled it off! Michigan was undefeated and the national championship was within their reach.

5. The Snow Bowl. I may not have been born yet, but I've heard so much about this game it seems like I was there. A blizzard was pelting Columbus for two days before the 1950 UM-OSU clash. Over 50,000 people showed up and Michigan won 9 to 3 without gaining a first down or completing a pass and punting 24 times. Former Michigan linebacker Roger Zatkoff told me that the visibility was so bad that the Michigan bench couldn't see Ohio State's bench across the field. How renowned is this game? The state of Michigan has a road named, "Snow Bowl Road."

4. Woody Hayes tearing up the Sideline Marker. In 1971, the Wolverines defeated Ohio State 10 to 7. Late in the game, the Buckeyes were mounting a comeback when All-American DB Thom Darden intercepted a pass going over the back of an Ohio State receiver. Woody was incensed. He believed Darden interfered. As the Michigan crowd booed, Hayes went after the refs, then ripped up a first-down marker and the orange yard markers before flinging them on to the field. A classic moment from Dr. Strange Hayes.

3. "The Vote." In 1973, undefeated and #4-ranked Michigan met undefeated and #1-ranked Ohio State. The Wolverines fought back from a 10-point deficit to tie the Buckeyes in the fourth quarter, then just missed on a couple of late field goals. With the game ending in a tie and both teams sporting identical records, the decision on who would represent the Big Ten in the Rose Bowl was left to a vote among conference athletic directors the next day. Nearly everyone assumed that since Michigan looked like the better team and because Ohio State had gotten the trip to Pasadena the year before, the Wolverines would get the nod. But the vote ended up 6-4 in favor of the Buckeyes. Bo Schembechler never forgave the Big Ten for slighting his team. The only good to come from "The Vote" was the conference changed its rules so more than one team could participate in postseason play.

2. "The Pose." In 1991, Michigan defeated the Buckeyes, 31 to 3 for their fourth-straight victory over OSU. With the Maize and Blue comfortably ahead, Heisman Trophy candidate Desmond Howard returned a punt 93 yards for a touchdown. After he crossed the goal line, the Ohio native struck the pose of college football's legendary trophy.

1. Michigan 24, Ohio State 12, November 22, 1969. The greatest upset in the history of college football (except for that Appalachian State thing. Who did they beat again?). Defending national champions OSU entered the game riding a 22-game winning streak. The year before, the Buckeyes throttled Michigan 50 to 14, but that didn't seem to deter Michigan's first year coach Bo Schembechler, a Woody Hayes' disciple. The Maize and Blue forced seven turnovers and put a lid on the Buckeye offense in the second half. Barry Pierson's 60-yard punt return set up the game's deciding score and the rivalry's greatest upset was born. The 1969 Ohio State game revived a Michigan program that had lapsed into mediocrity. That one victory launched the current era of Michigan Football.

Owning a professional sports team is, in many people's minds, basically a great way to inflate your ego. The person is obviously filthy rich and uses the franchise as a hobby or as a tax write-off. Some feel that running a team also gets you a home on Easy Street. You draft players, trade them like you would your fantasy football team guys, sit in a luxury box and occasionally fire a coach. But neither job is that easy. Because if they were, there would be a lot more names on this list, and a lot less on the next list.

Honorable Mentions: Bill Laimbeer, GM of Detroit Shock; Alfred Taubman, owner of the Michigan Panthers; Dave Dombrowski, president and CEO of the Detroit Tigers.

7. Jim Campbell, Tigers. Jim Campbell may have been cheap. He may have been a bit prejudiced. And he may have been a curmudgeon. But nobody could dispute that Jim Campbell was a baseball man and a loyal one at that. He began his Tiger career as their scouting director in 1960, before taking over the role of General Manager in 1963. Under his leadership the Tigers won the World Series in 1968 and the division title in 1972. He made the bold move to hire Sparky Anderson during the 1979 season. His scouting department led by Bill Lajoie put together the 1984 championship team. He was vilified by many players for being too frugal and by fans for closing the bleachers when they got a bit too lively for his liking. He was let go shortly after Tom Monaghan sold the team to Mike Ilitch. The succeeding years showed us just how good he had been as Tigers GM.

6. Joe Dumars, Pistons. What can you say about a guy who took a franchise from the outhouse to the penthouse? Joe Dumars did just that after taking over as Pistons President of Basketball Operations in 2000. He loses Grant Hill to free agency, but somehow gets Ben Wallace and Chucky Atkins out of it. He gets Jon Barry and a number-one pick for Mateen Cleaves. He dumps the salaries of Jud Buechler, Christian Laettner and Loy Vaught. He signs Chauncey Billups. He trades for Rasheed Wallace and Rip Hamilton. He drafts Tayshaun Prince and Rodney Stuckey. All that adds up to a GM who knows what he's doing. Oh, yes, there have been failures: drafting Cleaves, Rodney White and some guy named Darko. But the bottom line is the Pistons are considered an elite franchise again and Joe Dumars deserves a lot of the credit.

5. Ken Holland, Red Wings. Considered one of the best general managers in the NHL, Holland has been able to work his magic in different ways under different rules over the last decade. It was not as hard to win using an unlimited payroll as the Wings did in the 90s. But, Holland has been able to keep this franchise elite even in the current salary cap era. He has been willing to sacrifice first-round picks in order to pick up key veterans like Chris Chelios, Dominik Hasek and Matthieu Schneider. His scouting skills are second to none as he and his staff have been able to find great players from all over the world. He has made a few misses along the way, such as Uwe Krupp, Wendel Clark and Todd Bertuzzi, and the Hasek-Curtis Joseph situation could have been handled better. But the record shows that Ken Holland is one of the top front office guys in his, or any other, sport.

4. Jack McCloskey, Pistons. The most positive thing coach Dick Vitale did for the Pistons was recommend Jack McCloskey as general manager to owner Bill Davidson in 1980. McCloskey came to be called "Trader Jack" and with good reason. He made 30 trades as the Pistons GM. Many of them helped turn the Pistons from jokes to champions. He got Bill Laimbeer for Phil Hubbard and Paul Mokeski: Vinnie Johnson for Greg Kelser; Adrian Dantley for Kelly Tripucka; Rick Mahorn for Dan Roundfied; and James Edwards for Ron Moore. He also drafted Joe Dumars when many wanted Sam Vincent. He found Dennis Rodman in the second round. And, of course, he hired Chuck Daly as coach. Everything he touched did not turn to gold. But McCloskey helped keep the Pistons on top with his fire. He was as competitive a guy as you could find and a brilliant GM.

3. Jimmy Devellano, Red Wings. Mike Ilitch did the right thing when he made the New York Islander's assistant general manger his first hire after buying the club in 1982. Devellano was responsible for securing the players and scouts that made the Red Wings the hockey dynasty it is today. His first Red Wings draft consisted of, in order, Steve Yzerman, Lane Lambert, Bob Probert, Dave Korel, Petr Klima and Joe Kocur. Only Korel failed to become a productive member of the Red Wings. Under his watch, the Wings became the first team to consistently go after European players. Lidstrom, Fedorov, Konstantinov, etc. would probably not be household names if it were not for Jimmy D. He also convinced Mike Ilitch to go after Scotty Bowman, who guided the Wings from good to great. The Red Wings success would not be possible without the contributions of Jimmy Devellano.

2. William Davidson, Pistons. Davidson bought the Pistons in 1974 and struggled in his early years as owner. He went through the Dick Vitale debacle before hiring Jack McCloskey to run the show. The Pistons then turned into the model franchise of professional sports, buying their own team plane and building their own arena with their own money. Mr. D. is not perfect. He did move the team from the city, refuses to go over the luxury tax and has fired coaches for non-basketball matters. But under his tutelage, the Pistons and the Palace Empire have been the classiest in town (at least publicly). And let's not forget the championships won by his Detroit Shock, as well. The basketball world will never forget Bill Davidson, as he was selected to the Basketball Hall of Fame in 2008.

1. Mike Ilitch, Red Wings and Tigers. One of the all-time greats for the city of Detroit, Mike Ilitch bought the Detroit Red Wings in 1982 and turned the struggling team into one of sports' greatest franchises. Whatever the team needed, they got it, as Ilitch's Wings built a dynasty, making the playoffs 17 straight seasons and winning four Stanley Cups (so far). Some called his Wings, "the Yankees of hockey," because of the big money that the pizza tycoon paid his players. But the Wings sustained their greatness by investing in scouting, helping them bring in a steady stream of the world's best players. Call it a marketing ploy, but the name "Hockeytown" became synonomous with Detroit under Ilitch. He purchased the Tigers in 1992 and by his own admission was clueless early on. He had trouble sorting out his front office and how much money to spend. The awful showing of the Tigers throughout the early years of his ownership almost prevented him from being #1 on this list. But the hiring of Dave Dombrowski in 2002 helped turn the franchise around and win the American League pennant in 2006. With a good product, Ilitch kept his promise to spend more money and now the Tigers have one of the highest payrolls in baseball. He also owned the Detroit Drive when they won four Arena Football titles in the late 1980s and early 1990s. And although it does not count in the criteria for this list, he should be saluted for moving his business from the suburbs into Detroit, not to mention for his amazing support of youth hockey over the last three decades. Mike Ilitch gained a deserved place in the Hockey Hall of Fame in 2003.

Detroit has endured some of the most incompetent management and ownership in the history of not only sports, but mankind. Here are the worst of the worst.

Dishonorable Mention: Billy McKinney (Pistons), Rick Sund (Pistons), John McHale (Tigers), Joe Klein-Jerry Walker-Joe McDonald (Tigers).

7. Ned Harkness, Red Wings. They called his tenure "Darkness with Harkness." After failing in half-a-season as the Red Wings' head coach, Harkness was promoted to general manager in 1971. Harkness didn't get the Wings into the playoffs during his four years in charge. He traded Garry Unger, who had led the team with 42 goals the previous season, because he thought his hair was too long. The former college lacrosse coach was completely out of his element in the NHL.

6. Dick Vitale, Pistons. It was a short, but not so sweet tenure for the former University of Detroit head coach. He had three of the first 15 picks in the 1979 NBA draft and didn't get a single good player. He got Bob McAdoo from Boston for M.L Carr and two future first rounders (one a first overall). The Celtics used those picks to acquire Kevin McHale and Robert Parrish. Vitale was also a lousy coach. His 2008 induction into the Basketball Hall of Fame had nothing to do with his work with the Pistons.

5. Russ Thomas, Lions. "The Architect of Crap." At least that's what this guy should have been called. He took over as general manager in 1967 and established the Lions as the league's symbol of futility. They played in a whopping total of three playoff games in his 24 years as GM. He constantly low-balled players and pissed off coaches. Joe Schmidt quit as coach because of Thomas. He also allegedly tried to finagle Don Shula out of more than they'd agreed to in a deal for Anthony Carter, causing Shula to ship A.C. to Minnesota, where the former Wolverine gained three Pro Bowl selections. This may seem crass, but the best year that the Lions had since 1957 was the 12-4 1991 season—the first after Russ Thomas' death. Nobody could figure out why William Clay Ford failed to fire this guy. Unfortunately, we are asking the same question about a different guy some 15 years later.

4. Bruce Norris, Red Wings. His father gave him the Red Wings to run. Norris' first year of ownership brought Detroit the Stanley Cup in 1955. They would go 42 years without winning another. Other "highlights" of Mr. Norris' tenure: he traded Ted Lindsay because he wanted to start a union; he hired Ned Harkness; he called down to his coaches during games to question their decisions; he threatened to move the team to Oakland County; the Red Wings failed to make the playoffs in 14 of the last 16 seasons he owned the team. In other words, the guy was a horrible owner. How he gained a place in the Hockey Hall of Fame is a mystery, unless his dad bought him that, too.

3. Randy Smith, Tigers. Where do we begin? A quarter of his trades were with Houston or San Diego. He actually thought Jose Macias was a Gold Glove player. He drafted Matt Anderson with the first overall pick. He traded Luis Gonzalez for Karim Garcia, He signed Craig Poquette. . . . Shall we go on? Can you say, "Juan Gonzalez," or is it still too painful? How about huge contracts for Bobby Higginson, Tony Clark and Damien Easley. ENOUGH! Let's just make it simple. Randy Smith's record as Tigers General Manager: 253-566.

2. Matt Millen, Lions. When the Lions hired Matt Millen out of the broadcast booth, many applauded the team's outside-of-the-box thinking. Millen was a good football player and a good football analyst, so even without any front office experience he would probably prove a good guy to run a football team. But that thinking just ended up getting us the worst sports GM in Detroit history. The Millen file is gruesome: Marty Mornhinweg, Joey Harrington, drafting three wide receivers with top-ten picks in four years, Bill Schroeder, a fourth rounder for Ty Detmer, Steve Mariucci, breaking the Rooney Rule, calling Johnnie Morton "faggot" in public, questioning a player by saying, "Where are your testicles?" and so much more. "FIRE MILLEN" has become the most popular chant in Detroit. How many front office guys can say they had fans march to the game in their "honor"? And, oh, yes, let's end with his record over his first seven seasons: 31-81.

1. William Clay Ford, Sr., Lions. A nice man. A loyal man. A stupid man. Yes, "stupid." How else can one explain his owning a team for 44 years and enjoying only one playoff win. He refused to fire Russ Thomas when it was obvious the guy was a wreck, inspiring Darryl Rogers to ask, "What does it take to get fired around here?" He refuses to hold Matt Millen accountable for his 31-81 record. Maybe the reason for this is loyalty or maybe it's because he knows the only one accountable for the awful state of the franchise is himself. After all, he is the ONE CONSTANT. Mr. Ford does get cred-it for never threatening to move the team to another city (although some fans would love for that to happen). We appreciate that he's kept the traditional Thanksgiving Day game here. But we'd also appreciate a championship—or just a burning desire to win a championship in our team's front office. Yes, the team spends money now. But, please, Mr. Ford: GIVE YOUR FANS SOMETHING TO BE PROUD OF BESIDES A FRICKING STADIUM. PLEASE! We are sorry to bestow this honor on you, Mr. Ford. But as you know, it's all about titles and it all-starts at the top, and that's why you are, by far, the worst owner/executive in Detroit sports history.

Randy Smith Trades with San Diego and Houston
:: Stoney

Randy Smith became General Manager of the Detroit Tigers on October 30, 1995 and somehow held onto the job until April 8, 2002. During that time, he established a record of failure that rivals Matt Millen's decimation of the Lions, a mind-boggling "achievement." Prior to coming to Detroit, he served as General Manager of the San Diego Padres. Randy's father Tal Smith has been President of the Houston Astros since 1994 and worked as the club's GM. Randy Smith made a lot of bad trades during his time with Detroit. What's amazing is how many of those deals involved his dad in Houston and his old club in San Diego. A quarter of Smith's deals (15 in all) involved those two teams and often saw the same players being shuffled from one club to another, then back again. We present the trades in chronological order and without comment, because they speak volumes on their own on why the Tigers were stuck in a rerun of futility during Randy Smith's tenure as GM.

15. 3/22/96: Acquired Raul Casanova, Melvin Nieves and Richie Lewis from Padres for Sean Bergman, Todd Steverson and Cade Gaspar.

14. 6/18/96: Acquired Brad Ausmus, Andujar Cedeno and Russell Spear from Padres for Chris Gomez and John Flaherty.

13. 8/26/96: Acquired Kevin Gallaher and Pedro Santana (as "players to be named later") from Astros for Gregg Olson.

12. 9/11/96: Acquired cash from Astros for Andjuar Cedeno.

11. 9/20/96: Acquired Fernando Hernandez from Padres for Justin Mashore.

10. 12/10/96: Acquired Brian Hunter, Todd Jones, Doug Brocail, Orlando Miller and cash from the Astros for Brad Ausmus, Jose Lima, Daryle Ward, Trever Miller and C.J. Nitkowski.

9. 12/17/96: Acquired Willie Blair and Brian Johnson from Padres for Joey Eischen and Cam Smith.

8. 3/22/97: Acquired Jody Reed from Padres for Mike Darr and Matt Skrmetta.

7. 7/16/97: Acquired Earl Johnson from Padres for Dave Hajek.

6. 11/18/97: Acquired Tim Worrell and Trey Beamon from Padres for Dan Miceli, Donnie Wall and Ryan Balfe.

(Much to everyone's amazement, Smith didn't make any trades with San Diego or Houston in 1998.)

5. 1/14/99: Acquired Brad Ausmus and C.J. Nitkowski from Astros for Dean Crow, Brian Powell, Mark Persalis, Paul Bako and Carlos Villalobos.

4. 7/17/00: Acquired Dusty Allen from Padres for Gabe Alvarez.

3. 12/11/00: Acquired Roger Cedeno, Chris Holt and Mitch Meluskey from Astros for Doug Brocail, Nelson Cruz and Brad Ausmus (do you think Randy Smith had a Brad Ausmus fetish?).

2. 6/23/01: Acquired Jose Lima and cash from Astros for Dave Milicki.

1. 3/23/02: Acquired Matt Walbeck and Damian Jackson from Padres for Javier Cardona and Rich Gomez.

Note: A terrific linebacker in both the NFL and college, Millen played at Penn State (Linebacker U), where he was a three-year starter and first team All-American in 1979. A second-round pick by Oakland in 1980, Millen played nine seasons with the Raiders, two with San Francisco and one in Washington. He retired in 1991 with four Super Bowl rings. He went to the broadcast booth, where he shined for both CBS and Fox. He was hired as Lions General Manager and President in 2001. But things have not worked out quite as well in that aspect of his career. Still, Millen is a good guy who has donated over $30,000 to the Stoney and Wojo Radiothon for the Leukemia and Lymphoma Society. His great sense of humor makes you want to hang out with him for hours. The *Three Stooges* show was constantly on television from the mid-1960s to the late 70s while Millen was growing up in Pennsylvania. Millen, like many guys in his generation, became a big fan of Larry, Moe, Curly, Shemp and, yes, even Joe.

10. "Dizzy Doctors" (1937). The Stooges get new jobs selling the medicine Brighto, but think it's a cleaning fluid. Demonstrating the product, they ruin a guy's car and people's clothing. After figuring out what Brighto really is, they try to peddle it at the local hospital. But they have to escape when they realize the hospital superintendent owns the car they trashed with Brighto.

9. "Men in Black" (1934). While working at a hospital, Larry, Moe and Curly try to perform surgery on their boss to recover the combination to the safe that he swallowed.

8. "Uncivil Warriors" (1935). The Stooges work as spies for the Union in the Civil War, impersonating Confederate officers to gain valuable information. When they are found out, they hide in a cannon and get blown back to their headquarters in the north.

7. "A Plumbing We Will Go" (1940). On the lam from the cops, the Stooges pose as plumbers and are hired to fix a leak in a mansion. They wind up crossing the electrical system with the plumbing pipes and trashing the place. The lady of the house tunes into a television broadcast from Niagara Falls just before water pours from her TV.

6. "Three Little Pigskins" (1934). Larry, Moe and Curly are mistaken for three football players called "The Three Horsemen." Lucille Ball guest stars as a gun moll.

5. "Malice In The Palace" (1949). The list's only Shemp episode finds the Stooges out to recover the stolen Rootin' Tootin' diamond from the Emir of Shmo. After traveling to the Emir's fortress, they disguise themselves as Santa Clauses to scare the ruler into giving them the diamond.

4. "You Nazty Spy" (1940). In this satire on the Nazi takeover of Germany, the Stooges play paperhangers in the country of Moronica. When evil cabinet ministers overthrow the king, they name Moe as Dictator, Curly as Field Marshall and Larry as Minister of Propaganda, thinking they'll be stupid enough to follow their orders. But the boys are quickly routed from office by a mob and eaten by lions.

3. "Disorder In The Court" (1936). The Stooges go to court to clear an accused murderer. But are flustered by a talking bird who keeps repeating, "find the letter." The title says it all.

2. "Punch Drunks" (1934). Moe is a boxing promoter looking for a good fighter. Curly is a mild-mannered waiter who goes crazy whenever he hears the song "Pop Goes the Weasel." Larry is a violinist recruited to play the tune during Curly's fights. Curly gets a championship match, but things look bad when Larry's violin is smashed. But he saves the day driving a truck through the arena wall.

1. "Hoi Polloi" (1935). My absolute favorite. A professor bets that he can turn the Stooges into gentlemen. After schooling them in proper etiquette, he brings them to a fancy society party, where the Stooges rile up the other guests so badly, they begin behaving like violent idiots. The Stooges leave in disgust as proper gentlemen.

Royal Names

These guys' names suggested they should be sitting on a throne somewhere. They are listed in approximate order of their royal rank.

14. Chuck Noble, Pistons, 1956-62.

13. Count Campau, Detroit Wolverines, 1888.

12. Steve "Duke" Duchesne, Red Wings, 1999-2002.

11. Royal Lohry, Lions, 1943.

10. Earl "The Earl" Whitehill, Tigers, 1923-32.

9. Charles "Lady" Baldwin, Wolverines, 1885-88.

8. Earl "The Duke" Wilson, Tigers, 1966-70.

7. Prince Oana, Tigers, 1943-45.

6. Tayshaun Prince, Pistons, 2002-

5. "Prince Hal" Newhouser, Tigers, 1939-53.

4. Chief Zimmer, Detroit Wolverines, 1884.

3. King Block, Lions, 1951.

2. Cozell McQueen, Pistons, 1987.

1. Guy "King Tut" Tutwiler, Tigers, 1911, 1913.

My Top Ten Red Wing Draft Picks :: Jimmy Devellano

Note: When Mike Ilitch purchased the Red Wings in June of 1982, the first person he hired was Jimmy Devellano as the Red Wings' General Manager. He was named to his current position of Senior Vice-President in 1990. Devellano built modern-day Detroit Red Wings hockey. The day he was hired, Devellano pledged that he would never trade a first-round draft pick and he didn't until the 2006 Brendan Shanahan deal. Jimmy D. gives us his top ten reasons why Wings fans should be glad he hung onto all those picks. He focuses on the period from his hire to the mid-1990s when one of his main responsibilities was the NHL Entry Draft.

10. Adam Graves, 1986 second rounder (22nd overall). A great leader and a wonderful hockey player. He was tough to trade. But we made the deal with the Oilers to bring in a local kid. That kid was Jimmy Carson.

9. Joey Kocur, 1983 fifth rounder (91st overall). Joey was a tough player who became one-half of the Bruise Brothers with Bob Probert. They really packed the seats for us when we were still building. When we brought him back from the beer leagues, I was a bit skeptical. But Scotty saw something and he was right.

8. Mike Sillinger, 1989 first rounder (11th overall). A good hockey player, he got caught up in a numbers game with our team. I knew he would have long career, I just didn't know it would be with 12 teams—an NHL record.

7. Chris Osgood, 1991 third rounder (54th overall). This was Ken Holland's pick. When you draft a player, it's not just one person doing the picking. You have to trust your scouts and I have total trust in Kenny. He wanted Ozzie, I listened and now he's only behind Terry Sawchuk in Red Wing career victories.

6. Keith Primeau, 1990 first rounder (third overall). Primeau wanted out of Detroit and I don't understand why. He turned into a very good hockey player with his combination of skill and size. I wish he stayed with the Red Wings. His advisors gave him some bad advice.

5. Bob Probert, 1983 third rounder (46th overall). I wanted Bob to be my Clark Gillies. He was that good. It's a shame that he couldn't control his addiction problems with drugs and alcohol. A lot of potential just wasted.

4. Vladimir Konstantinov, 1989 eleventh rounder (221st overall). A tragedy, especially because it wasn't his fault—a terrible, terrible, terrible thing. If Vlady wasn't hurt in that limo accident, there would have been no need for Uwe Krupp or Chris Chelios here in Detroit. I'm not knocking Chelios, he's been fantastic for us. It's just that Vlady was that good.

3. Sergei Fedorov, 1989 fourth rounder (74th overall). We won three Cups with Sergei and for whatever reason he wanted to leave Detroit. He tried leaving us twice, the first time when he signed that offer sheet with Carolina and then successfully as a free agent with Anaheim. He should have played his entire career here in Detroit. If he would have, Sergei's number would one day been hanging in the rafters at Joe Louis Arena.

2. Nicklas Lidstrom, 1989 third rounder (53rd overall). We had a scout in Sweden named Christer Rockstrom who's responsible for Nick. The original report said he was small and weak and we should let him develop in Sweden for a couple of years. He's going to keep winning Norris Trophies until the day he retires. I hope that day is many, many days away. Nick will be the next Red Wing to have his jersey hung at the Joe.

1. Steve Yzerman, 1983 first rounder (fourth overall). If the Islanders didn't take Pat LaFontaine just before us, we would have because he's from Detroit. Yzerman would have starred somewhere else, which is now kind of hard to imagine. Steve's the cornerstone of what we were able to build. It took us a little longer than we thought, but eventually we were able to surround him with talent and win three Stanley Cups. Everything good for the Red Wings began on the day we drafted Steve Yzerman. We were extremely fortunate.

Note: If you were to play a game of word association with a metro Detroiter and you said to them "The Captain," they would immediately respond "Steve Yzerman." It doesn't matter if they're a hockey fan or not, everybody knows The Captain. Yzerman ranks as not only the longest-serving captain in NHL history (19 seasons); he's the longest-serving captain of any team in North American sports history. An athlete that defines class, Yzerman will live forever in the annals of great Michigan/Detroit athletes. Here's The Captain's list of his favorite captains.

10. Captain Morgan. Once in a while you need to take the edge off. When done in a responsible way, Captain Morgan is the right call, especially after a tough loss or a big win.

9. Captain Horatio McCallister. The sea captain from *The Simpsons*, he hates everything to do with the sea. YARRR!

8. Captain Benjamin Franklin "Hawkeye" Pierce. The way he enjoyed himself, pulled pranks and buckled down when there was a job to do, he would've been a great hockey player.

7. Captain Ahab. I'll be the first to admit this guy is nuts! However, his quest for the great white whale, Moby Dick, is something I could identify with chasing the great silver chalice—the Stanley Cup.

6. Captain Canuck. Anybody who wears red and white and upholds the honor, tradition, and the maple-leafed way of life is a hero.

5. Captain America. He was just an ordinary guy caught in some extraordinary circumstances. He never carried a gun, but his shield let freedom ring.

4. Captain Jack Sparrow. Captain Jack is way ahead of the game. Eccentric and flamboyant, he'd rather use his brain than force. In an odd kind of way, if Scotty Bowman were a . . . oh, forget it!

3. Captain James T. Kirk. The youngest captain in Starfleet, he's Canadian, he overacts and he has the best interest of his crew in mind—the traits of a great captain.

2. Cap'n Crunch. Anybody that can make a cereal that stays crunchy even when you add milk is not only one of the greatest captains of all time; his contribution to mankind is almost unmatched.

1. Alex Delvecchio. If there is a Red Wing player who I would want to be identified with, it would be Alex Delvecchio. His commitment to excellence and tradition paved the way for me to understand what being a captain and a Red Wing were all about. I thank Alex for leaving an inspiring legacy.

Sporting contests can sometimes get so intense and divisive it's easy for fans to forget that we're watching a form of entertainment. But that was impossible to forget when these guys were playing. Here's a list of the top local oddballs, flakes, weirdos and comedians of the local sporting world.

12. Gee Walker. The Mississippi native became a favorite with Tigers fans in the 1930s for his hard play and great hitting. But Walker's wandering mind and overly aggressive tactics got him in trouble with management. The eccentric outfielder once tried to steal a base during an intentional walk, and was picked off first during the 1934 World Series while arguing with players on the opponent's bench. When "The Madman from Mississippi" got picked off base twice in the same inning in 1934, manager Mickey Cochrane suspended him for 10 days. After his best season in 1937—when he hit .335 and collected 118 RBI—Walker was traded to the White Sox. Detroit fans were so upset about the beloved Walker's departure, Tigers owner Walter Briggs had to issue a public statement endorsing the deal from his winter home in Florida.

11. Barry Bremen. The West Bloomfield native and marketing executive enjoyed a stellar athletic career, of sorts. Known as "The Great Impostor," Bremen dressed like players and snuck into major sporting events to warm up with the pros. He played practice rounds with the likes of Fred Couples and Jack Nicklaus at three different U.S. Opens, participated in lay-up drills at two NBA All-Star Games, and performed pregame warm-ups on the field with the stars at a pair of MLB All-Star Games. Bremen also got onto the field for a 1980 World Series game disguised as an umpire and once celebrated on the sidelines as a member of the Dallas Cowboys cheerleaders. Bremen, who went onstage at the 1985 Emmy Awards to accept a best supporting actress statue for Betty Thomas, finally got too famous for his own good and had to retire in the late 1980s.

10. Marvin Barnes. He did more drugs than anyone this side of Hunter S. Thompson. He served long suspensions and jail sentences. He once got caught burglarizing a porn shop. Yet a lot of people still love former Detroit Spirit and Piston Marvin "Bad News" Barnes—nice, regular people, not just his fellow criminals. Which is a tribute, of sorts, to Barnes' "character." The former Providence power forward and All-American wins affection for his upbeat personality, sense of humor and years of working to help urban youth avoid the temptation of drug use—though Barnes still sometimes gives in to the temptation himself. The American Basketball Association even named one of its divisions after him. Without being familiar with all the details of Conn Smythe's bio, I doubt he took a similar route to winning the same honor for a while from the NHL.

9. John L. Smith. With his hobbies of skydiving, paragliding and mountain climbing, the Idaho native always seemed more like an eccentric summer camp counselor than a major college football coach. Though John L. could coach—at least for the first half of a season when his Michigan State teams tended to win a lot of games and score a lot of points. The second half of seasons and games were not so kind to Smith, who was fired after losing eight of his last nine in 2006. Still, John L. did provide plenty of comic relief. At a 2006 post-game press conference, he demonstrated how he felt about blowing a big, second half lead to Notre Dame by slapping himself across the face. Not too often you see that.

5. (Tie) The Carlson Brothers and Dave Hanson. Few athletes are so outrageous that they become movie characters—particularly guys who never made it out of the minor leagues for longer than a couple cups of coffee. Starting their pro careers in Michigan for the minor league Marquette Iron Rangers, Jeff, Jack and Steve Carlson quickly established reputations as fearsome brawlers. Their violent antics captured the imaginations of the people making the 1977 film *Slap Shot*. The Carlsons were called in to play the Hanson Brothers, a trio of entertaining thugs who revive the struggling minor league hockey team's fortunes. When Jack Carlson got called up to the Edmonton Oilers just before filming began, he was replaced in the movie by Dave Hanson (who actually played 11 games for the Detroit Red Wings the following season). *Slap Shot* became a hit, in no small part due to the hilarious scenes involving the Hanson Brothers. Over three decades after the film's release, Dave Hanson, Jeff Carlson and Steve Carlson continue to play the Hanson Brothers characters on the minor league hockey circuit, skating out between periods to beat up refs, mascots and Zamboni drivers. Fans still love them.

4. Alex Karras. A huge and strangely lovable malcontent, the star defensive tackle often battled with coaches and management. While playing in college, he threw a shoe at his Iowa head coach and refused to return to the team until the coach agreed not to talk to him anymore. After leading Iowa to the 1957 Rose Bowl, the All-American and Heisman runner-up complained to the media that he couldn't find a date in Pasadena because all its female residents were senior citizens. Karras starred for the Lions for five seasons before being forced to work as a pro wrestler while serving a year-long suspension from the NFL in 1963 for betting on games. When he came back, he refused to call "heads or tails" on a pre-game coin toss, telling the head official, "I'm sorry, sir, but I'm not permitted to gamble." A six-time Pro Bowler, he went into acting after retiring from football, gaining roles in Mel Brooks' *Blazing Saddles*, *Victor/Victoria* and even hosting *Saturday Night Live*. Karras also served as a color analyst for a couple years on *Monday Night Football* in the 1970s and as a regular on the sitcom *Webster* the following decade. How many guys can say they've co-starred with Howard Cossell and Emmanuel Lewis? Only Alex Karras. But "only Alex Karras" serves as the answer to a lot of questions.

3. Joe Don Looney. He never lived up to the expectations generated by his vast potential as a running back. But Joe Don Looney did live down to the expectations generated by his cartoon name. A Texas native, Looney played for and was thrown off four different college teams, then five NFL teams during his three-season pro career. He finally found a home in Detroit, where he had a productive 1965 season. But he fell out of favor after refusing coach Harry Gilmer's order to take a play into the huddle from the sideline. "If you want a messenger boy, call Western Union," Looney told him. After retiring from football, Joe Don converted to Hinduism and became a follower of Swami Muktanada. The Swami reportedly employed Looney as a henchman to violently keep followers in line who dared to question his teachings of peace and compassion. (Meditate on that awhile.) Looney died at the age of 45 in a motorcycle accident.

2. Mark Fidrych. The rookie righthander entertained fans by getting on his knees to manicure the mound with his bare hands and talking to baseballs—then discarding the ones that he thought "had hits in them." Fidrych also won 19 games and led the league in ERA. The wildly popular hurler drew over 900,000 fans, or about 40 percent of that season's home gate, to Tiger Stadium for games he started in 1976. Injuries the following year kept him from ever pitching a full season in the bigs again.

1. Bobby Layne. The Lions QB became nearly as famous for his partying exploits the night before games as for his on-field accomplishments, which were legendary. A national magazine reporter who traveled to Texas to see Layne play in college got lost and stopped at a fraternity to ask directions from a guy who had a martini in one hand and beautiful coed in his other. The reporter realized that the boozing frat guy was Bobby Layne when he saw the Longhorns QB trot onto the field less than an hour later. With liquor on his breath and a beer belly hanging over his belt, the Texas native established himself as an NFL icon and perhaps the league's most popular player in the 1950s. Fans saw Layne as one of their own and cheered him on as he led the Lions to three NFL titles. Layne employed unusual motivational techniques on his teammates, sometimes kicking an offensive linemen in the butt on his way back to the huddle after he gave up a sack. Though not a superstitious guy (unless you count his pregame ritual of going out and getting loaded), Layne pronounced a curse on the Lions when they traded him in 1958, declaring that they wouldn't win another NFL title for 50 years. It worked. And considering the current state of the team, it looks like Bobby Layne's curse comes with a hangover. Just like Bobby Layne himself.

A Twelve Pack of Party Names

Being a professional athlete offers numerous opportunities to overindulge in the nightlife of wine, women, song and drugs of the non-performance-enhancing variety. Here are a dozen Detroit players whose names and nicknames made them prime candidates for early curfews and urine tests. The list is ordered alphabetically, not by their suspected levels of intoxication.

12. Tom Beer, Lions, 1994-96.

11. Jug Girard, 1952-56.

10. Hugh High, Tigers, 1913-14.

9. Brandon "Binge" Inge, Tigers, 2001-

8. Major Jones, Pistons, 1985.

7. Chick King, Tigers, 1954-56.

6. Kirk "Malts" Maltby, Red Wings, 1995-

5. Matt Snorton, Lions, 1962.

4. Lil' Stoner, Tigers, 1922-28.

3. Suds Sutherland, Tigers, 1921.

2. Frank Tanana "Daiquiri", Tigers 1985-92.

1. Buzz Trebotich, Lions, 1944-45.

Top Ten Classic Piston Names

The names of NBA players became more varied and amusing with the recent infusion of foreigners into the league. But as this list shows, the old-school Pistons also featured some guys with pretty great names.

10. Cornelius Cash, Pistons, 1977.

9. Dillard Crocker, Pistons, 1949.

8. Fennis Dembo, Pistons, 1989.

7. Happy Hairston, Pistons, 1968–70.

6. Tree Rollins, Pistons, 1991.

5. Zeke Sinicola, Pistons, 1952–54.

4. Odie Spears, Pistons, 1956.

3. Justus Thigpen, Pistons, 1973.

2. Blackie Towery, Pistons, 1949.

1. Dick Triptow, Pistons, 1949.

Note: Chris McCosky has been covering sports in Detroit for close to 29 years. He has been the Pistons beat writer for the *Detroit News* the last 13 seasons, which means coaches Doug Collins, Alvin Gentry, George Irvine, Rick Carlisle, Larry Brown and Flip Saunders had to put up with him on a daily basis. It's no wonder none of them lasted very long. All kidding aside, McCosky who also dabbles as WDFN's Pistons Insider, is considered a pro's pro. He is the dean of basketball writers in Detroit.

Honorable Mention: Pistons head coach Doug Collins crying in 1997 after he finally beat his former team, the Chicago Bulls, in the playoffs.

12. The 1989 brawl vs. the Sixers. Bill Laimbeer went at it with Charles Barkley and former teammate Rick Mahorn. After the game Barkley said that Chuck Daly could "suck his *****."

11. The roof at the Silverdome falling apart. It happened a few times, forcing the Pistons to play some playoff games at Joe Louis Arena, including the one in 1985 in which Vinnie scored 22 in the fourth quarter to beat the Celtics, and the one a year earlier when Isiah scored 16 in the final 65 seconds against Bernard King and the Knicks. King had 44 and Thomas 35 in the Pistons' loss.

10. The walk-off. After winning the two previous championships in 1989 and 1990 (and after ousting Michael Jordan's Bulls from the playoffs the previous three years), the Pistons' Bad Boys team finally walked off into the sunset. And they did so in typical Bad Boys fashion. On May 27, 1991, while losing Game 4 on their way to being swept by the Bulls, Isiah Thomas led the Pistons starters off The Palace floor before the final seconds ticked off, walking right past the Bulls bench without saying a word or shaking a hand. Thomas masterminded the move in response to Jordan having spent the previous couple of seasons disparaging the Pistons and their rough-housing style of basketball. Only Joe Dumars and John Salley stayed on the floor to congratulate the Bulls.

9. They called him "Bison." When the Pistons signed him as a free agent in 1997, he was known as Brian Williams and he had just helped the Bulls win the NBA title. A free spirit the likes of which the Pistons hadn't known since Dennis Rodman, he could be seen skateboarding (he was 6-foot-10, if you can picture it) around the Pistons practice facility, or engaging reporters in mystic conversations about Eastern religions. When he came back the next season, he announced that he had legally changed his name to Bison Dele. He said he did it for spiritual reasons, to honor both his African (Dele, he said, is the early form of Williams in Nigerian tribal speak) and Indian (Cherokee) heritage. The oddest thing he ever did though was abruptly retire after the 1998-99 season, leaving $36.5 million on the table. Three years later, Dele was killed on his boat outside of Tahiti, shot by his mentally-disturbed brother.

8. No choke. For days, then-general manager Billy McKinney had been stewing about highly-paid guard Alvin Robertson's unwillingness to play. Robertson was complaining of a sore back, though the Pistons' medical people couldn't pinpoint any specific problem. Finally, during an open practice on November 4, 1993, McKinney challenged Robertson. He told him that if he didn't return to practice that day, he would start fining him. Robertson, with television cameras rolling, lunged at McKinney and had both hands around his neck before players intervened and pulled them apart. Robertson was traded to Denver 15 days later—and the back injury prevented him from playing that season.

7. Stack's Fraudulent 57. Well, fraudulent is probably strong, but Jerry Stackhouse's franchise-record, 57-point performance against the Bulls on April 3, 2001 should at least come with an explanation. The Bulls were on their way to a 15-67 season and the Pistons were going to miss the playoffs for the first time in this millennium. Both teams were just playing out the string. But Stack was on fire. And the more he scored, the more odd the game became. The Bulls stopped defending, for one thing. They were almost rooting for Stackhouse to score. In fact, Ron Artest, then a reserve for the Bulls, was applauding every Stackhouse basket. Point guard Mateen Cleaves, on several occasions, would have an unimpeded path to the basket but would stop, wait for Stackhouse to catch up and give him the ball for the lay-up. Kelly Tripucka, who held the previous single-game record with 55 points, also against the Bulls, was doing the television broadcast for the Pistons. He was a good sport about it, but he knew that his record was broken under dubious circumstances.

6. Just keep it close. The Doug Collins era—the Doughouse, as it was known—was as volatile and manic as Collins himself. It is only fitting that the team was breaking apart even during its greatest regular season—the 54-win, 1996-97 campaign. The center of the split was Collins' relationship with Otis Thorpe. It got so bad that Thorpe refused to speak to Collins, literally. Collins had to send his messages through his assistant coaches. When pulled from a game, Thorpe would walk all the way around the court to avoid walking past Collins on his way to the bench. The worst came in the first round of the playoffs, the deciding Game 5 at Atlanta. At halftime, Collins told the team, "Guys, if you can keep it close, I will find a way to win it for you down the stretch." Thorpe was incensed. "What are you going to do, check in?" Then, with about two minutes left and the score tied, Thorpe came to the bench during a timeout and said, "Okay, Doug, now go and win it." Final score: Hawks 84, Pistons 79.

5. Bogus Bowie. This may have been Doug Collins' finest moment as the Pistons' head coach. It was March 14, 1996 and the Pistons were getting blown out by the Magic in Orlando. The Magic had the final possession with four seconds left and the Pistons expected them to simply hold the ball and let the clock run out. Nope. Magic journeyman Anthony Bowie, against the protestations of his coach Brian Hill, called a timeout. Seems he needed one more assist to complete his first (and only) triple-double. The Magic, with Hill leaving the huddle in disgust, drew up a play where Bowie would feed David Vaughn for a basket. Collins was beyond incensed. He ordered his team to stand at the far end of the arena, opposite the basket the Magic were attacking, and not even contest the play. Bowie got his dubious triple-double, and Collins' got a $5,000 fine, but his point was registered loud and clear.

4. Bashing the Junkyard Dog.

Jerome Williams was popular with the fans and media in Detroit, but not so much with his teammates. His non-stop self-promotion grated on the other players, especially since his production on the court never seemed to live up to his chatter off it. This all came to a head on April 27, 2000. The Pistons were down 2-0 in a best-of-five series against Miami. On the eve of Game 3, Williams was addressing the media after practice and he was being very critical of his teammates' work ethic and commitment to winning. When Jerry Stackhouse was apprised of Williams' comments, he stormed away from his interview and raced into the locker room to confront Williams. Confront is the wrong word. He pummeled Williams. And the rest of the players, already annoyed at Williams, let Stackhouse pound away for several minutes. Terry Mills finally stepped in to break it up, but the damage was done. Williams walked out of the locker room several hours later, bandaged up like a mummy.

3. When "The Worm" turned.

Dennis Rodman was a shy, lovable, hard-working, glad-to-be-here guy for his first six seasons in Detroit. Then came the 1992-93 season. Nobody knows for sure what turned him, but there have been numerous theories—it was a contract dispute, he hated that the team was losing, he felt disrespected and most famously, that Vinnie Johnson had slept with his then-wife Annie. Those who were there insist that while Rodman may have caught Johnson and Annie together, they never, in fact, slept together. Rodman, to this day, doesn't believe that. In any case, the situation reached its bizarre peak late in February. Rodman had been trying to force a trade all season and when the trade deadline passed and he was still in Detroit, he became despondent. Early one morning, employees of The Palace found Rodman asleep in his truck in The Palace parking lot. Reports surfaced that there was a loaded gun in the truck. The natural assumption was that Rodman was contemplating suicide. Those who were closest to Rodman insisted that he never would have done that, and that he was just seeking attention. In fact, the gun was actually in the trunk, not under the seat. In any case, Rodman eventually was traded to San Antonio where his weirdness escalated and continued to, unabated, for the rest of his career.

2. Not-so-great Scott.

Ray Scott was a pretty popular cat in Detroit in the mid-1970s. In 1974, he was the league's coach of the year, after he'd gotten the Pistons to the playoffs for the first time in six seasons. He got them there again the following season, and even though the 1975-76 team was struggling through its first 42 games, he was still the winningest coach in franchise history at the time and there was no hint of discord. All of which made the afternoon of Jan. 26, 1976, such a shock. Scott was in the middle of a practice when general manager Oscar Feldman walked into the gym. He was flanked by a couple of security personnel. With the players looking on in disbelief, Feldman announced that Scott had been fired and then escorted him out of the building. Later, it came out that Scott had been having a romantic dalliance with the wife of a high-ranking Pistons official.

1. They called it a brawl. It was November 19, 2004 and it started with a blue plastic beer cup, tossed by fan John Green onto the chest of Pacers forward Ron Artest, who was lying atop the scorer's table. Artest, who moments earlier had been in a tussle with the Pistons' Ben Wallace, got up and stormed into the stands, looking for Green. He roughed up a couple of fans, none of them Green, while his teammates—most notably Stephen Jackson and Jermaine O'Neal—followed him and the whole arena erupted into one of the nastiest player-fan brawls ever. The funny thing about it was—as Wallace later pointed out—Artest had ample opportunity to fight on the court. Wallace had offered to settle the dispute right then and there. But Artest refused. Yet, he didn't even hesitate to go after the fans. Nine spectators were injured, though none seriously. Criminal charges were brought against several Pacers. Artest drew a record 86-game suspension, while Jackson got 30 games and O'Neal 25. The Pacers, the No. 1 team in the East at the time, were never the same that season.

Note: Kirk Gibson grew up in Waterford and went on to football and baseball stardom at Michigan State. Despite being an All-American wide receiver, "Gibby" chose baseball as his career path. Drafted by the Tigers in 1978, he made his MLB debut the following year. He helped bring the World Series home to Detroit in 1984, punctuating the season with two home runs in the clinching Game 5. In 1988, he left the Tigers and signed with the Dodgers. He enjoyed an amazing first season in L.A., winning the National League MVP award and rising to legend status during the playoffs. With his knees ravaged from injuries sustained in the NLCS, he only made one appearance in the '88 World Series. But he made it count. A hobbling Gibby's pinch-hit, ninth-inning, game-winning home run off Dennis Eckersely is considered one of the most dramatic moments in sports history. After stops in Kansas City and Pittsburgh, Gibby returned to Detroit in 1993 and retired a Tiger in 1995. He later became a broadcaster and a coach with the team. Gibby currently works as the bench coach of the Arizona Diamondbacks.

5. Wrigley Field, Chicago. The second-oldest park in the Major Leagues, Wrigley has hosted more than its share of history, including Babe Ruth pointing to centerfield with his bat to call his home-run shot in the 1932 World Series. It's a hitter-friendly park with the ivy walls at just 365 feet in the alleys. But Wrigley presents a challenge to visiting outfielders in dealing with the fans sitting beyond those walls. I remember one time when I argued a called third strike with umpire Jerry Crawford and I thought he was about to eject me. Instead, he said, "What inning is it?" I replied, "The first" "OK," he said, "now get your ass out there in left field and let those lunatics bury you for nine innings!" I told him that was a good one.

4. Yankee Stadium, The Bronx. This stadium has the most history of all. Ruth, Gehrig, DiMaggio, Berra, Maris, Munson, Jackson and so many other all-time greats played there. One of the stadium's coolest features is Monument Park, a collection of monuments, plaques, and retired numbers from Yankee history out in left field. I put this in my Top 5 not because I enjoyed playing there, but because it was a real test of character as a team and a person. I always thought the playing surface was one of the league's worst, but right field was very short and pull-friendly for a lefty like me. I hit one of my longest home runs of my career off Bob Shirley on a muggy Sunday afternoon into right field. When I touched home plate and ran toward our dugout, a fan yelled to me, "YOU SUCK!" Yes, only in Yankee Stadium.

3. Fenway Park, Boston. Fenway stands as the oldest park in the bigs and looks much like it did the day it opened in 1912. The Green Monster in left field adds so much to the game. It makes LHH pull hitters like me try to go Oppo, and average outfielders beg to play left field. The fans are right on top of you everywhere on the field, hawking you with, "Gimme a baaawl." You better bring a ton of mental toughness and be ready to slug it out. No lead is safe at Fenway until the final out!

2. Dodger Stadium, Los Angeles. For obvious reasons. It's a beautiful park that set the perfect stage for my home run off Dennis Eckersley in the 1988 World Series. To this day, it amazes me how a stadium built in the late 1950s can still look so clean and new. Every time I walk into Dodger Stadium, I look at the seat my home-run ball landed in and get chills.

1. Tiger Stadium, Detroit. A no-brainer because it's a great, old park that perfectly fit my game. Being a pull hitter, the 315 feet to the right-field upper deck was rewarding, and that short distance also served my weak arm well, making my throws to Lou Whitaker and Alan Trammell easier. I muffed a home-run ball hit by Carl Yastrzemski as a kid sitting in the right-centerfield bleachers. It was always a real thrill playing in the ballpark when I grew up.

Our Least Favorite Places to Play :: Todd Jones, Chauncey Billups, Richard Hamilton, Rasheed Wallace, Isiah Thomas, Lou Whitaker and Kirk Gibson

Note: We surveyed some top Detroit's athletes about their least favorite place to play on the road. They offered a lot of different answers, and some surprising ones.

7. Todd Jones, Philadelphia. "Because of their fans. They love to hate on you. They get whipped into a frenzy by shock jocks and they get to the park with their beer and hate on you cause they realize their life sucks. No other city is close. Just ask J.D. Drew, Scott Rolen, Allen Iverson and Donovan McNabb."

6. Chauncey Billups, Salt Lake City. "The altitude and the noise in that building makes it tough. Plus, we can't seem to win there."

5. Richard Hamilton, Salt Lake City. "The altitude gives me problems and there is nothing to do there. Very boring."

4. Rasheed Wallace, Denver. "The altitude sucks."

3. Isiah Thomas, the old Chicago Stadium. "It got so loud, you could hardly hear. Plus, I am from Chicago, so emotionally, it was hard and it was so damn loud."

2. Lou Whitaker, Milwaukee County Stadium. "I don't know what it was, but I never played well there. I always had problems hitting and the worst thing was I was a good fielder and it seemed I always made errors there."

1. Kirk Gibson, the old stadium in Cleveland. "There were no fans!"

Note: *The Detroit News'* longtime golf writer has covered over 60 majors, including all of Tiger Woods' wins. The current vice-president of the Golf Writers Association of America, Kupelian will serve as president of the 950-member organization beginning in 2009.

10. Western Golf & Country Club, Redford. A gem from designer Donald Ross, Western is land-locked. Very little has been done to it over nearly 100 years to change its nature and character. In other words, the course is almost 100 percent true to Ross. How do you top that?

9. High Pointe, Williamsburg. It was a toss-up between two Tom Doak designs—High Pointe and Black Forest. The edge, barely, goes to High Pointe because it's his first in Michigan and because I became attached to it before Black Forest came along. There are so many good holes at High Pointe. Here's another reason it's on this list: it's a contemporary course with classic instincts.

8. Country Club of Detroit. Once again, the secret is its simplicity. This design by British architect Harry S. Colt is a prime example of a course that dates back to the early 1900s. It may be the finest course in America set on a perfectly flat parcel of land.

7. The Heather at Boyne Highlands, Harbor Springs. This Robert Trent Jones' beauty is long, difficult and always a pleasure to play. That's a rare combination.

6. Bay Harbor, Bay Harbor. The first "modern" layout on my list offers sensational views and some of the finest holes Arthur Hills has ever designed.

5. Indianwood Old Course, Lake Orion. I much prefer the older, classic designs to modern architectural concepts. The Old Course, designed by Wilfrid Reid, is a classic gem.

4. Belvedere Golf Club, Charlevoix. This Willie Watson course designed back in the 1920s isn't about trappings or modern amenities. It's about classic instincts and beautiful, uncomplicated golf. What you see is what you get. It's not a jigsaw puzzle. It's pure golf at the highest level.

3. Franklin Hills Country Club, Franklin. This wonderful course dates back to the golden era of architecture in American golf, the 1920s. Like Oakland Hills, it's a Donald Ross design and that says all I need to know. A recent renovation restored many of the original Ross bunkers and instincts.

2. Crystal Downs, Frankfort. A masterpiece by Alister MacKenzie, the man who designed Augusta National, this course is extraordinary in so many ways. It offers brilliant design, unique greens, breathtaking views and tremendous balance in the look and feel of the holes.

1. Oakland Hills Country Club/South Course, Bloomfield Hills. "The Monster" ranks as one of America's great courses and remains a regular on the major championship rotation. For the rest of us, it's not only about terrific golf, it's also about tradition. Just thinking about walking down the same fairways as Hogan, Snead, Jones, Nicklaus, Palmer, Woods and putting on the same greens is enough to elevate an already majestic club.

Note: A Grosse Pointe native and alum of the University Ligget School, Krickstein enjoyed a brilliant run in the junior ranks, winning the US 18-and-unders at age 16. He then burst onto the national professional scene in 1983, becoming the youngest player to win a pro title and be ranked in the Association of Tennis Professionals (ATP) top ten. He scored dramatic, five-set set wins over Vitas Gerulaitis and Stefan Edberg in his first US Open later that year. He went on to claim nine pro titles in his 13-year career and was once ranked as high as sixth in the world. He competed as a member of the U.S. Davis Cup team on several occasions and became known as the "Marathon Man" for his uncanny ability to win five-set matches, especially when coming from behind. Unfortunately, his most famous match was a five-set, heartbreaking loss to Jimmy Connors at the 1991 U.S. Open. His career would have been even more successful if he hadn't been plagued by injuries, including stress fractures in his feet. There must be something in his genes, because his three sisters—Renee, Rachel and the late Kathy—were all excellent junior players as well. His niece Morgan Pressel is one of the best players on the LPGA tour. On a personal note, all the Kr021icksteins are some of the nicest, down-to-earth people you will ever meet. I have the pleasure of spending New Year's Day with them every year and the only downer is that they are all rabid fans of Michigan football and January 1 has not been kind to the Wolverines. Aaron currently works as the tennis professional at St. Andrews Country Club in Boca Raton, Florida and is a participant on the Outback Champions Series for former top players now over 30. He is married with one daughter named Jade.

10. Andres Gomez. The man from Ecuador was my worst nightmare for the first eight times we played. His big serve, heavy groundstrokes and underrated net game made him a very tough opponent for me. The 1990 French Open champion took three titles away from me in Rome, Washington and Hong Kong, but at least I beat him three of our last four matches to salvage a little pride. Gomez was one of the best clay court players I faced in my career.

9. Stefan Edberg. This rare Swedish serve-and-volley specialist had one of the best one-handed backhands and the best backhand volley I ever had to play against. His court coverage was excellent and his pressure on you was constant. Somehow, Stefan was on the losing end to me in four classic matches, although he did beat me seven times. A great champion who's playing style has unfortunately vanished from today's game.

8. Mats Wilander. Mats was the heir to fellow Swede Bjorn Borg and he certainly filled his shoes quite nicely. I beat Mats the first time we played when I was just 17 and the last time we played when I was 26. But he won the six times in between. He was one of the fastest players I played against and one of the smartest, as well. His groundstrokes were like a backboard and his mental toughness was envied by all players. One of the few to win three Grand Slam titles in one year.

7. Jim Courier. Jim "Rock" Courier had the best inside-out forehand around. His power and placement from the left side of the court was incredible and he was probably in the best shape of any player on tour. Jim beat me once in Basel, Switzerland and it was one of the few times I ever walked off the court and said I couldn't play any better. His three-year run from 1991-93 when he won four Grand Slam titles was quite remarkable.

6. Andre Agassi. The "King" was perhaps the best pure ball striker to ever pick up a racket. When you played Andre Agassi, you knew you didn't want to get too far behind, as he was also the best front-runner in the game. I had some good success against Andre with three wins, but I always knew I could play really well and still go down. He just took the ball so early and really used his great two-handed backhand to set up his big forehand. Andre had a lot of amazing achievements in his career, but I believe winning Wimbledon had to be his greatest.

5. Boris Becker. The kid nicknamed "Boom Boom" was definitely not kind to this kid from Grosse Pointe. Boris beat me in more big matches than anyone I ever played. First one was in Hamburg in a deciding fifth match Davis Cup Tie. Then came the semis and quarters of the U.S. Open. Then the fourth round of Wimbledon. All losses! I did get a little redemption and beat Becker on the red clay in Monte Carlo. I think his powerful groundstrokes, big serve and all-court game made him one of the best. I still cannot believe to this day he won Wimbledon at just 17. Incredible.

4. John McEnroe. Mac was by far the most talented and unique player I ever played against. Putting aside his sometimes atrocious and obnoxious on-court behavior, John could do more with the ball on certain shots than anyone I have ever seen. His anticipation was amazing and his touch from all areas of the court, especially at the net, was downright scary. Mac's serve was not the biggest by any means, but he had great disguise and placement, which made it difficult for me to break his serve. I never beat him in our days on the ATP Tour, but I have gotten him a few times since then on the Champions Tour. Of course, Mac got a bit angry, to say the least!

3. Jimmy Connors. For whatever reason, I just could not beat this guy. Maybe it was because he kept the ball so darn low to my forehand or maybe I was just plain psyched out! My 0-7 record against him speaks for itself. Heck, I couldn't even beat him when he was 39! Possibly growing up and watching Jimbo win all those Wimbledons and U.S. Open titles on TV carried over somehow to our matches. Ironically, two of my seven losses to Connors were famous for different reasons. Everyone remembers the 7-6 in the fifth Flushing Meadow Connors-Krickstein birthday bash. But most people (except my dad) don't know that Jimbo embarrassed me in our first meeting (6-0, 6-0) in a tournament when I was just 16. I think the helicopter (with Jimbo aboard) landing right next to Center Court 10 minutes prior to our match was mentally a bit much for me. Connors was definitely the toughest competitor I ever played against.

2. Pete Sampras. I had a victory against "Pistol Pete" in Indianapolis and came, oh, so, close to beating him at the Spectrum in Philly and in Indian Wells. But Pete definitely got the best of me more times than not. In my eyes Pete had the best first and second serve EVER. He was so tough to break his serve and it seemed whenever he needed the service winner, he got it. I also thought Pete had a great volley and the best running forehand around (other than mine, of course). Certainly one of the best players of all time.

1. Ivan Lendl. I did beat "The Champion Nobody Likes" once in Tokyo when he was #1 in the world. A great win for me, indeed. But other than that victory, he beat up on me like a red-headed stepchild seven times! Big matches at the French Open, Australian Open, Key Biscayne, Forest Hills, etc, etc. We played similar styles, but he did everything just a little better. I liked to call him "The Human Ball Machine." Ivan had tremendous groundstrokes, a great first serve and was fitter than a fiddle. At least I got him once!

Note: A businessman by day and a Detroit sports fanatic by night, Jeff Moss founded of one of the area's best sports websites, DetroitSportsRag.com. Besides his affinity for Sergei Fedorov, race horses and Howard Stern, Moss feels a deep appreciation for the sports of lap and pole dancing, as well as the amazing athletes that compete in them. We'll let Moss take it from here.

"When I got the phone call from Mike Stone requesting my input into this book, I was very excited for the opportunity. Not only could this venture bring more attention to my fledgling website, DetroitSportsRag.com, I thought I could share some of my Detroit sports opinions with a different audience. And then Stoney shared with me his idea for my list: the best the Detroit area has to offer in live adult entertainment. Of course, I said, "Yes." Because what's better than telling your girlfriend that you have to go to a nudie bar to do "research" for a book? And now on with the list."

10. The Inkster Sister Clubs (Bogart's Lounge and Henry the VIII's Lounge).
As former Tigers announcer Ernie Harwell used to famously say, "Two for the price of one." And I'm sure the god-fearing, retired broadcaster is thrilled to be used as a reset for two of the more seedy clubs in the Metro area. The two Inkster bars are right around the corner from each other and if you pay the cover for one, you get a pass to get into the other. In other words, twice the amount of girls for one low cost. Unfortunately, finding a hot stripper at either place is the equivalent of locating Willy Wonka's "Golden Ticket." But if you can find a diamond in the rough (and sometimes it can get REAL ROUGH), the lap dances are top-notch. As an added bonus on Mondays and Tuesdays, the joints take turns offering $10 V.I.P. dances. Considering that most "champagne room" dances go for $25 a pop and then you mix in the current horrid economy of the Motor City, this bargain almost gets Bogart's and Henrys on the list by itself.

9. The Canadian Clubs (Jason's, The Million Dollar Saloon, Studio 4, Cheetah's on the River).
I had a very serious internal debate on whether or not the Windsor clubs should be included in a Detroit book. On one hand, you had their proximity. On the other hand, you had the increased difficulty of getting into a "foreign country" post-9/11. (I seriously didn't just mention 9/11 in a Top 10 list about strip clubs, did I? Really?) But even though you currently need a passport to get to the Windsor establishments, the fact that you can drink alcohol and see TOTALLY nude girls across the border trumped all other factors. For those of you who aren't familiar with strip club law and ordinance, Detroit clubs can't serve liquor if the chicks take off their bottoms. Call your local State Senator today if you would like to overturn this injustice!

8. The Fringe Benefit Strip Clubs (Bouzouki Club, Déjà Vu and Toy Chest Bar and Grill).
This group probably wouldn't have made my list on merit alone. But they all have something going for them beyond dining, dances and the quality of girls. Bouzouki boasts a location within walking distance of Ford Field, Comerica Park and the Greektown Casino. Now, if I was compiling a list of overrated strip clubs in Detroit, this one would be near the top because I have never been thrilled with the selection of "talent." But Opening Day at Comerica Park isn't the same without heading to this place after the game for a few drinks and dances while the crowd dissipates.

The national chain Déjà Vu doesn't serve alcohol, making it one of the few area strip joints where you get to see totally nude chicks without hearing the word "Eh" every five seconds. Finally, the Toy Chest ranks as a pretty decent bar on its own. But it mainly made this list based on some of the events they have hosted over the years. Where else can you see naked women, midget tossing, the 2 Live Crew and the Iron Sheik? Howard Stern fans, you can now put your hands down.

7. Jon-Jons Cabaret. This Warren club might be most well-known because the owner, Paul Cerrito, married Jasmine Bleeth of Baywatch fame after meeting her at a drug rehab facility a few years back. Even without that storybook romance as part of its lore, Jon-Jons has been a perennial fixture on the eastside for years. Top quality food, very nice talent and a quality V.I.P. dance area are all featured in this upscale locale. I haven't been there in a couple of years, so hopefully the girls are holding up better than Mrs. Bleeth-Cerrito.

6. Play House. Just a stone's throw away from Metro Airport, the Play House actually operates in the shadow of a different Romulus landmark, The Landing Strip (LS). As a matter of fact, the Play House has often been called a poor man's version of The Landing Strip. (Okay, actually I am probably the only degenerate to ever call it that.) But that shouldn't be seen as a knock against the Play House anymore than Nicklas Kronwall should feel insulted if someone called him a poor man's version of Nick Lidstrom. It is actually a compliment. On any given night, the girls can be just as hot as down the street and in all honesty, I have seen a lot of the same girls at both places. This place has always been my back-up airport strip club whenever LS was either too crowded or suffering an off-night with the broads. Like most clubs near an airport, it isn't cheap and the V.I.P. area leaves a lot to be desired. But you can usually find a comfortable spot to sit and the lap dances are usually well worth the cost.

5. The Chicken Shawarma Specials (Pantheon Club and BT's Lounge). Located in the most populated Arabic city outside of the Middle East (Dearborn), the Pantheon and BT's have the added attraction of being surrounded by the best Shish Tawook dinners in Metro Detroit. BT's has been a Motor City mainstay for over 25 years and is as consistent as they come. If you want the upscale Eight Mile Strip Club experience, but you don't want to go to Eight Mile, this is your place. The relatively new Pantheon Club might be the most aesthetically-pleasing strip joint in town. No expense was spared in building this club—from the plethora of plasmas to their badass bar to the luxury booths. With all of the amenities, it is a little odd that the V.I.P. area is basically located on the floor, but sometimes even that isn't a negative.

4. Flight Club. A lot of derelicts would rate the Flight Club #1 on their lists. But I just never experienced a great night at this Inkster bar. And it has all of the makings of a classic strip club. The place is first-class all the way with expensive furnishings and plenty of hi-definition TVs to watch any sporting event. The food is very good and the V.I.P. area rates five stars. And you could make a solid case that the girls working at Flight Club are the most attractive in the city. We are talking about model-level hotness for the elite girls, who are built as well as the 747s that the location used to house. It even has the added bonus of being across the street from Bogart's and Henry's, which means it has the "hot girl going out with two pigs to a dance club" angle going for it. (And trust me, there are many a night when you need to walk into this place for a few minutes after leaving the other two just to cleanse your palate.) In other words, it is the

Rasheed Wallace of Metro Detroit gentleman's clubs. It has EVERYTHING, but it still doesn't dominate on a nightly basis or live up to its incredible potential. And maybe that has a little to do with the huge crowds it usually features on a weekend or the douche-bag clientele that it seems to attract.

3. The Eight Mile Road Elite (Trumpps , Tycoons, Players Lounge, All-stars and Cheetah's on the Strip).

Before this street became infamous for lending its name to that white rapper's movie and giving Coleman Young a place to go tell muggers, pushers and rip-off artists to hit it, Eight Mile was famous for its collection of strip clubs. The street that divides Detroit and the suburbs offers a virtual smorgasbord of strip clubs featuring every experience you can imagine, including the possibility of getting raided by Detroit's finest or shot at by a member of D-12 at any given moment. With all of that said, the first name in Eight Mile Road adult entertainment is Trumpps. Take the spiral staircase to the V.I.P. room and make sure you have a lot of cash because the dances aren't cheap and you probably won't want to leave once you get up there.

2. Coliseum.

While this monstrosity is also on Eight Mile (way east of some of the other establishments previously mentioned), I felt it deserved its own ranking. While you might not know it from the outside, this huge nightclub rivals the Pantheon for interior décor. (Listen, my Grandma might read this, I have to add a little class to it and not just mention the T&A.) The Coliseum is known for its accommodations and boasts private suites and a kick-ass V.I.P area. And unlike a lot of the other sequestered areas in town, you aren't on top of another dude and stripper when shelling out 25 bucks for the two-minute-and-twenty-second lap dance version of Marilyn Manson's, "Beautiful People." There are a lot of strippers on the floor at any given time and the best of the best would probably rival Flight Club for hotness. The place is classy enough to take your girlfriend or wife to. And if you have hit the jackpot in life and your woman likes to have A LOT of FUN, the third Sunday of every month is "Swingers Night." (Umm, yeah, this list might just have gotten a little too creepy. Are you having second thoughts about asking me to do this yet, Stoney?)

1. The Landing Strip.

As you can probably tell by the name, the #1 strip club in Motown is right around the corner from the McNamara Terminal. In fact, you can sit in front of the bar at the LS and monitor your flight information while downing drinks and conversing with the best looking high-school dropouts that Downriver has to offer. It isn't the biggest club around and on weekends you sometimes have to stand for a while before a seat opens. The girls can be smoking hot, but I wouldn't say they are any better as a whole than Flight Club or Coliseum. And while there have been interior modifications in the last few years, it can't compete with places like Pantheon Club for comfort. But judging by its Wall of Fame (featuring everyone from Andre the Giant to Bob Probert), I am not the only one who enjoys the LS. It is hard for me to put into words why the Landing Strip ranks as the best strip joint in Detroit. And if I did, the Wayne County Sheriff's might storm the place the day this book is released to the public.

Without divulging too many state secrets, let's just say that the combination of attractive girls and V.I.P. lap dances is hard to beat. And with that I will wrap this up. Because I would like to continue frequenting this fine establishment and I wouldn't want to do anything to jeopardize that.

Delicious Delights: Art's Top Ten Food Products Made or Started in Detroit :: Art

With all due respect to the Big Three, the Motor City has been home base for some delicious delights that have satisfied Detroiters for generations. Many of our products have become national names, while others have just stayed local and some have closed their doors forever. These ten products represent a lot of good memories and good eats.

Honorable Mention: Velvet Peanut Butter.

10. Little Caesars Pizza. Sure they're a big national chain that, depending on the store, is hit or miss. However, back in the day nothing beat going to Little Caesars and sharing a piping hot pie and washing it down with a couple of cold ones.

9. Town Club Pop. It was cheap, loaded with sugar, came in exotic flavors and you bought it by the case, what's not too love?

8. Kowalski Meats. Say it after me, "Kowalski means Kowality," and they're right. From lunch meats to sausages to hot dogs and more! Kowalski's vast selection of marvelous morsels could whet the appetite of a vegan.

7. Vernors Ginger Ale. Vernors dates back to 1866 when a Detroit pharmacist named James Vernor invented this bubbly delight. Produced from 19 secret ingredients including ginger and vanilla and aged in oak barrels. If you drink a full glass quickly it packs a real kick and clears out your sinuses.

6. Honey Baked Ham. If you love ham, this sweet spiral splendor of salty goodness can't be beat.

5. Sanders Confections. I remember going shopping with my mom as a kid and if I behaved reasonably well, we'd cap the day off with a Sanders Hot Fudge Sundae. Sanders is responsible for me being such a well-mannered individual. Thank you, Sanders.

4. Faygo Pop. Red Pop, Grape Soda, Rock & Rye, Cream Soda, and a dozen or so other carbonated treasures. You can't get much more Detroit than Faygo.

3. Better Made Potato Chips. Always fresh, always affordable, and always exquisite!

2. Stroh's Beer. The local suds that was fire-brewed! I wish I could remember half of the good times I had drinking Stroh's, because there were many. Nothing was better than touring the brewery before a Tiger game.

1. Hygrade Ball Park Franks. They plump when you cook them! A couple of Ball Park Franks with an ice cold brew watching the Tigers in old Tiger Stadium. It was paradise!

If you are from Detroit, you understand that "Coney" means great food. If you're from the Metro Detroit area, then you also understand that the next names that go with "Coney" are "Lafayette" and "American." These two establishments are as ingrained in the downtown Detroit experience as Tiger baseball, Lions football and Red Wings hockey. Since there is no trademark on the "Coney Island" nomenclature, various families have begun similar establishments over the years to serve Coney dogs (chili dogs smothered in onions and mustard), looseys (ground beef smothered in onions and mustard) and other Coney fare. Today, one can choose from countless Coney Islands offered throughout the area from a handful of different family chains. It's a natural pass-time among Detroit's Coney connoisseurs to champion a local Coney as the true, best Coney of them all. Here are my favorites.

10. Kerby's Koney Island (various locations). They offer a nice selection of Sanders desserts, plus their Gyros are delicious.

9. Lipuma's Coney Island (Rochester). Everyone raves about the Coney dogs. The staff is extremely personable, and they really want you to get the Coneys with everything on them. Don't disappoint them!

8. Phoenix Coney Island (Sterling Heights). You may have to wait if you go at certain hours, but Phoenix is open all the time, day or night. The prices are very affordable, and the cozy space reminds people of the original downtown Coneys.

7. Downtown Leo's Coney (Inside Comerica Park, plus various other locations). If you go to a Tigers game, you have to get yourself a Coney to get the full Detroit experience. Dogs and baseball go together, but Coneys and Tiger games are divine.

6. National Coney (Roseville, various other locations). Often touted as THE best of the Coney chains, the other families will disagree, but the Nationals are great establishments. Gotta get the chili fries. Mmmmmm.

5. Ted's Coney Island (Allen Park). This is great spot to get breakfast and lunch. Like Phoenix, time your visit right if you have to eat and run. The cozy size and the pictures of yesteryear help evoke that classic Coney feel.

4. Plato's Coney Island (Garden City). This place treats you like family. Always a warm welcome here. I'm getting hungry right now for some lemon rice soup. Love this place; it loves you back.

3. Senate Coney Island (Livonia, various other locations). Another dynamo favorite of mine. Anything you order from Senate is as tasty as can be. I'm telling you, it doesn't matter if you've never been there—they are very friendly and happy to see you.

2. American Coney (114 W. Lafayette, Detroit). Flip a coin. The outcome is how often American and Lafayette switch spots. They always hold the top two spots.

1. Lafayette Coney (118 W. Lafayette, Detroit). My mouth is watery just thinking about their looseys. Never been? Go there. Now.

Note: One of the most talented and humorous people in print journalism, Schrader worked for newspapers in Missouri and Mississippi before coming to Michigan in 1985 to add to his list of "M" states. He currently serves as The Page 2 columnist for the *Free Press* sports section.

10. "I was just laughing. I thought it funny. They got excited; it's good. Sometimes you get your little brother excited when you're playing basketball and let him get the lead, then you just come back and take it back." Michigan running back Mike Hart, after the Wolverines overcame a 10-point deficit in the final 7:40 to beat Michigan State 28-24, silencing the Spartan Stadium crowd in 2007. We'll see if Hart's "little brother" has the staying power of the "arrogant asses" tag that Darryl Rogers put on Wolverine Nation.

9. "You shouldn't blame Jack McCloskey. He's not the one. It's that little con artist you've got up there. When his royal highness wants something, he gets it." Virginia Dantley, blaming the Pistons' 1989 trade of her son, Adrian, on Isiah Thomas. Whoever did it, the Pistons got Mark Aguirre from the Dallas Mavericks and went on to win their first NBA title. And maybe the "con artist" explains why Isiah lasted so long with the Knicks.

8. "Am I supposed to care what he says? I'm not his kind of guy? Why, because I was cordial in the production meeting? Because I tried to be articulate? Because I smile when I play? Because I enjoy myself out there? Because I'm not a Billy Bad-Ass? I was raised a certain way. I was raised to be polite, I was raised to look someone in the eye and when they ask you a question, you answer it." Joey Harrington, responding to Fox analyst Tony Siragusa's 2004 cryptic statement that the Lions QB was ". . . the kind of guy that's on the other side of the club than I am. He's over there with the champagne and caviar. And also the strawberries and chocolate, you know?" I like this one because it was one of the few times that this town sided with Harrington.

7. "Scotty is a great thinker, but he thinks so much that the plate in his head causes interference in our headsets during the game." Then-Colorado coach Marc Crawford, fanning the flames of the budding Red Wings-Avalanche rivalry with a tacky comment on Scotty Bowman during the 1996 Western Conference finals. (Crawford was referring to a 1951 career-ending skull injury Bowman suffered in juniors.) This was back when fans really cared about the Wings. And maybe that's what they need now—a villain like Crawford.

6. "I think Larry is a very, very good basketball player, but I have to agree with Rodman. If he were black, he'd be just another good guy." Isiah Thomas, commenting on Pistons rookie Dennis Rodman's 1987 assessment of the Boston Celtics' Larry Bird. And coincidentally, years later Bird fired Isiah as coach of the Indiana Pacers.

5. "First of all, the bar is high. The goal for this organization now is to win Super Bowls." Marty Mornhinweg when he was introduced as the new Lions coach in 2001. Forget about how high the bar is—what time did it open? And if the Lions wonder why we're all jaded and skeptical, they should take a look at quotes like this.

4."I'm ticked off! I get all the damn criticism—people hammering me! I'm a good coach! I know what the heck's supposed to be done! And I'm not going to second-guess myself one damn time! That was terrible what we did out there today! We shot ourselves in that last drive! We get two holding penalties, a motion penalty—you think I coach that stuff? I don't coach that stuff! I work on that stuff! I spend time on that stuff! And I'm getting all the damn heat! Each and every one of you is hammerin' my tail! I don't coach that way! They got to step up and start making plays! I'm tired of taking it on myself! I really am! Because I work too hard . . . for us to play like that—particularly at the end. It's embarrassing to me, and it ought to be embarrassing to them! They oughta be damn embarrassed! Questions?" Bobby Ross, imploding while facing the media following a particularly galling 10-9 loss in Philadelphia in 1998. He somehow he lasted until more than halfway through the 2000 season before "burning out."

3. "A Michigan man will coach Michigan." Bo Schembechler, who, on the eve of the 1989 NCAA Tournament, handed the reins of the basketball Wolverines to assistant coach Steve Fisher after it was revealed Bill Frieder planned to take the Arizona State job. No West Virginia jokes.

2. "I'm like that big buck that's in the field. They're trying to hunt him down, trying to shoot him. I just keep dodging those bullets. Everybody wants my rack on the wall." Lions coach Wayne Fontes, facing the media music a day after a loss to Arizona in 1995. He finished 10-6 that season and lasted one more with Detroit. And who doesn't miss him yet, when you compare quotes like that to, say, the Bobby Ross tirade? Of all the men who've had the job in recent years, the Big Buck is the only one who really got it, as in the irony of what it means to be the Lions coach.

1. "Kirk Gibson is the next Mickey Mantle."

"Barbaro Garbey is another Roberto Clemente."

"Mike Laga will make you forget about every power hitter that ever lived."

"That Jose Canseco, he's got a body like a Greek goddess."

"Torey Lovullo's going to be a star. Even the gorilla at the top of the building knows that."

"If you don't like Dave Rucker, you don't like ice cream."

"It's my way or the highway."

"Zip, zilch, nada."

Sparky Anderson. He gets the lifetime achievement award.

Note: Mitch Albom has been one of the most prominent columnists in Detroit history. Since coming to the *Free Press* in 1985, he has won numerous awards and written several best-selling books, including *Fab Five: Basketball, Trash Talk, The American Dream* and *The Five People You Meet in Heaven*. Mitch is a regular on ESPN's Sports Reporters Show and is the host of "The Mitch Albom Radio Show" on WJR. Stoney owes an eternal debt to Albom for helping launch his career on the "Sunday Sports Albom," a weekly talk show on WLLZ.

10. Jim Arnold, Lions. The punter often spoke with a wad of tobacco in his mouth, and he had a kind of large jaw and balding head and a Georgia accent and I'm really not sure what he was talking about much of the time. But when you needed a quote, you could always count on Jim. Just watch out for the tobacco juice on your notebook.

9. Bo Schembechler, Michigan football. Not at the beginning, but toward the end, when Bo had calmed down a bit, and he knew his legend was secure. Bo had a million stories, and he loved telling them. I think he actually came to have a little respect for sportswriters. Not a lot. But a little. And with him, that was plenty.

8. Wayne Fontes, Lions. He may have been the "Big Buck," the target everyone loved to shoot for. But think about the Lions coaches before him and after him and now name me the one you'd most like to listen to for an hour. You never knew where Fontes was going to go with his conversation, but you knew you were going to wind up laughing

7. Sparky Anderson, Tigers. If interviews were baseball stats, Sparky would be the all-time saves leader. I can't tell you how many of us started the day with nothing to write about and ended the day with a notebook full of stuff from Sparky on everything from baseball to meeting the Pope. The man could talk through a plate of spaghetti, while sitting in his underwear, while smoking his pipe—just a natural born communicator.

6. Brendan Shanahan, Red Wings. Still the only guy who could explain a power play goal one minute, then challenge you to name three actors who had all been in a movie with Russell Crowe the next minute. One of the smartest quotes ever in a locker room

5. Jalen Rose, Michigan basketball. Of all the Fab Fivers, Jalen was the most unpredictable. You always wanted to use a tape recorder with him, because you weren't sure, in reading your notes, if you had written it down correctly. Like the time someone asked him about trash talking and he said, "We ain't trash talking, we're conversatin'." Is that a word? It was to Jalen.

4. Lomas Brown, Lions. Another guy who always talked, no matter how awful the Lions had played. Lomas was also pretty candid. If you said, "You guys really stink," he was liable to say, "You're right."

3. Chris Spielman, Lions. He never sought attention, he spoke softly and he had no interest in being a media star. But he couldn't help fuming. He took the game so passionately that you could feel the agony in his words. And those words often summed up the Lions frustration.

2. John Salley, Pistons. We should have seen his multi-faceted career coming, even during the 80s. "Sal-Sal," as some called him back then, always understood the value of being on TV and in the newspapers—even if he only scored six points in the game. He was funny. He was irreverent. Quoting him was like taking notes during a comedy act. I'm not surprised he had the biggest media career of all the Bad Boys—and he hardly ever started.

1. Darren McCarty, Red Wings. Win or lose, rain or shine, with teeth, without teeth, you could count on Darren to sit by his locker after a game and answer every question. Sometimes, he was the only player who would come out. Sometimes, I think he actually sat there waiting, wondering when we were going to get there.

Note: John Salley was a vital member of the Bad Boys championship teams. Coming off the bench as a defensive whiz and energy guy, "The Spider" ran the floor with the best of them and was on the receiving end on many an alley-oop pass from Isiah Thomas. He was traded to Miami following the 1992 season and played three seasons for the Heat. After a cup of coffee in Toronto, he went to Chicago as a bit player on the Bulls' 72-win championship team of 1996. After a three-year layoff, he convinced Phil Jackson to bring him to the Lakers. Salley played in 43 games and L.A. won the title in 2000, with Salley retiring at the end of the year. John used his great sense of humor to make a name for himself outside of basketball. He has been in several movies, including Bad Boys I and II, as well as numerous television shows. He now serves as a panel member on FoxSports' *Best Damn Sports Show Period*.

10. Fennis Dembo, Pistons, 1988-89.

9. Alvin Robertson, Raptors, 1995-96.

8. Rick Mahorn, Pistons, 1986-1989.

7. Carlos Rogers, Raptors teammate 1995-96.

6. William Bedford, Pistons, 1987-92.

5. Shaquille O'Neal, Lakers, 1999-2000.

4. Willie Burton, Heat, 1992-94.

3. Kurt Nimphius, Pistons, 1986-87.

2. Chuck Nevitt, Pistons, 1986-88.

1. Dennis Rodman, Pistons, 1986-92, Bulls 1996.

Not all seemingly perfect pairings work out. Sometimes the imperfect ones that you think have no chance of succeeding work out beautifully. And sometimes the imperfect pairings end ugly, too. Here's a half-dozen of local sports' most unlikely partnerships, plus their good, bad or ugly outcomes.

6. Justin Fargas and Antonio Fargas. This father-son pair have both excelled in their respective fields. They're just involved in two very different fields. Father Antonio established himself as one of the leading character actors of the blaxploitation cinema in the 1970s. He co-starred in films like *Foxy Brown* and *Cleopatra* Jones as a wiry, pint-sized, quick-talking, amoral hustler. He's probably best remembered for playing Huggy Bear on the *Starsky and Hutch* TV show and the paroled pimp trying to reclaim his turf in *I'm Gonna Get You Sucka'*. He showed up in the Big House a few times to watch his son Justin, who came to play for Lloyd Carr's Wolverines in 1998. A strong, no-nonsense running back twice the size of his dad, Justin saw a lot more bad luck than playing time in Ann Arbor, breaking his leg during his freshman year (the first of several major injuries). He eventually transferred to USC and played a key role in the Trojans revival and continues to play in the NFL. Justin has dabbled in acting, but he's no Huggy Bear.

5. Dick "Night Train" Lane and Dinah Washington. Known as "The Queen of the Blues," Washington was arguably one of the top female singers of her era. The Detroit Lions' Dick "Night Train" Lane was, no debate required, the greatest NFL cornerback of his era—or any other era. The two giants in their fields headed to the altar in 1963 for what seemed like a match made in DNA heaven. Except, neither had much luck in the love match game. Lane had three wives during his life. Washington racked up nine husbands before the age of 40, not even bothering to divorce some of them before she moved on to the next. Washington, who was so fierce that she'd track down and physically assault hecklers after her concerts, may have finally found a peer and life partner in the equally ferocious Lane, who had fought his way up after being abandoned in a dumpster as a baby. But we'll never know. Washington died six months into their marriage after overdosing on diet pills.

4. Larry Brown and Rasheed Wallace. By the time Larry Brown came to coach the Pistons in 2003, Rasheed Wallace had pretty much burned every bridge he'd ever set foot on. But his fellow Tar Heel Larry Brown saw past 'Sheed's tantrums and chronic technical foul problems to the gifted, technically-proficient player underneath. Bringing in Wallace after he became the Pistons' new head coach, Brown got the iconoclastic 'Sheed to buy into his "win the right way" team philosophy. Wallace, who had led highly talented teams to underachieving results in Washington, Atlanta and Portland, become a fine, consistent player. He was a leader and then a champion in Detroit. He even cut way back on his technical fouls.

3. Larry Brown and Derrick Coleman. Derrick Coleman had pretty much napalmed every bridge he set foot on by 2004. Only Larry Brown still admired DC's skills on the court and genuinely enjoyed his company off of it. Brown brought Coleman to the Pistons for the 2004-05 season. But whatever magic Brown had worked with Rasheed Wallace fell flat on Coleman. The former Syracuse star stunk up the court and the locker room; then got cut in mid-season. So what is it with Larry Brown? Why is he attracted to players who, despite being talented and productive, move around a lot from team to team and cause trouble wherever they go—until management finally shows them the door and . . . wait, I think I just figured it out.

2. William Clay Ford and Matt Millen. Talk about a fatal attraction. The polite, aristocratic Ford was born into one of the world's richest families. The brash, often crude Millen came out of a small town in Pennsylvania's impoverished Rust Belt region. He went on to establish himself as one of the most brutal and accomplished players in the NFL. Then as one of the most grating and incompetent general managers in league history after Ford tapped him to take over the Lions in 2001. And he's still here. No one knows what keeps this partnership together. And no one wants to know. We just want it to end.

1. Lloyd Carr and Russell Crowe. The Australian Crowe was one of the world's leading movie stars at the peak of his career. Thousands of miles away, Carr was struggling as Michigan's head football coach and deflecting suggestions that it was time for him to retire. Yet they found each other. It began in 2006 when Carr showed his team scenes from the film *Cinderella Man*, starring Crowe as real-life boxer James Braddock, who fought his way back from oblivion to become world heavyweight champion and a national hero. Coming off a tough, five-loss season, Carr thought the film would offer his players some inspiration and a lesson in perseverance and courage. It worked, helping propel the Wolverines to win their first 11 games and remain in the national title picture throughout the season. When the tempestuous, controversial Crowe, who had a history of brawling and was once charged with assault for hurling a telephone at a hotel concierge, heard about Carr using his film, he gave the Michigan coach a call. They struck up a friendship. The following year, Carr returned the favor by traveling to Australia to address the players on the South Sydney Rabbitohs, a struggling rugby team owned by Crowe. The Rabbitohs went on to make the playoffs for the fist time in 17 years. Crowe and Carr remain good friends.

Note: Michigan State great Greg Kelser teamed with Magic Johnson to lead the Spartans to the 1979 National Championship. "Special K" was a first round draft choice of the Pistons, before being traded to Seattle. After his playing days ended, Kelser turned into a terrific television analyst. He currently serves as the color man on all Pistons televised games and does plenty of college games for the Big Ten Network and others. The players on his list appear in no particular order.

Honorable Mentions: I did not see the performances of the great Benny Oosterban, a two time All-American player in 1927 and 1928. But I am going to assume that Mike McGee, Juwan Howard, Tim McCormick, Rumeal Robinson, Terry Mills and Gary Grant were all a bit better.

9. Cazzie Russell. I never saw him play at UM but we all know he was the man. The stories about him are still being told today. That's why they call Crisler Arena "The House That Cazzie Built."

8. Rudy Tomjanovich. The kid from Hamtramck, Rudy T was a great player on mediocre teams. He was also one of the best shooters in Michigan history.

7. Phil Hubbard. A super player before suffering a devastating knee injury that may have stopped him from becoming UM's greatest ever. He went to the Final Four as frosh and won Olympic Gold Medal at the 1976 Games in Montreal.

6. Glen Rice. The school's all-time scoring leader. The sharpshooter from Flint was the master of the three-point shot. He was the Most Outstanding Player of the Wolverine's 1989 NCAA championship team.

5. Ricky Green. Played only two seasons, but UM was ranked in the top 10 through much of his time there from 1975-77. Maybe the fastest player ever to wear the Maize and Blue. He was one of the stars of the 1976 team that lost to Indiana in the NCAA finals.

4. Bill Buntin. An incredible performer who along with Cazzie Russell helped put Michigan back in the national basketball picture. His stats tell the story of a terrific scorer and rebounder and a model of consistency.

3. Henry Wilmore. If the tournament was a 65-team field like it is today and getting into it was not as difficult as it was in the early 1970s, more folks would have known about and celebrated Wilmore's great talents.

2. Campy Russell. I cheered for Michigan before I became a Spartan and while in high school I cheered for Campy Russell. My dad liked him as well and I remember trying to mimic his step back fadeaway jumper. Super player.

1. Jalen Rose. The heart of the Fab 5, Rose talked the talk but he could walk the walk, too. He had the swagger that the rest of the team followed. He could play any position and was an underrated defender.

Note: The pride of Clarkston High School, McCormick played three seasons at UM, leading the Wolverines to the 1984 NIT title, where he was named Most Valuable Player. The 6-foot-11 center was the 12th overall selection in the 1984 draft. McCormick played with six teams during his eight-year NBA career, then went into broadcasting. He has served as an analyst for ESPN, CBS, WDFN and the Big Ten Network.

Honorable Mentions: Terry Furlow, Sam Vincent, Julius McCoy, Ralph Simpson.

10. Mike Robinson. There were so many good players to consider for the tenth spot on my team and I hate to leave any of them off. However, Mike Robinson was an All-American in 1974, All-Big Ten three times and finished as the school's ninth all-time scorer.

9. Jay Vincent. The most underrated performer in Spartan basketball history. He won a National Championship in 1979, and developed into a scoring machine, as the school's fifth all-time leading scorer. He was the 1981 Big Ten Player of the Year and an All-American.

8. Shawn Respert. He's the best MSU shooter I've ever seen. Respert was named All-American twice and left MSU as its all-time leading scorer.

7. Scott Skiles. One of the toughest competitors that I have ever played against, Skiles was an All-American in 1986 and ranks as MSU's third all-time leading scorer.

6. Morris Peterson. He won a national championship in 2000, was an All-American and Big Ten Player of the Year. "Mo Pete" was acknowledged as the top sixth man in college basketball and is also one of the top ten scorers in the program's history. Enough said

5. Johnny Green. A two-time All-American, he led the Spartans in 1957 to the Final Four and is regarded as the best player of his era. Former Spartan coach Gus Ganakas said he belongs on my list and that is good enough for me.

4. Mateen Cleaves. A three-time All-American, he was leader of the Spartans' 2000 national title team. I'm guessing MSU's 12th all-time scorer stands at the top of Tom Izzo's list of favorite players.

3. Steve Smith. The two-time All-American won Big Ten championships in 1989 an 1990. The second all-time scorer in Spartan history also donated the Clara Bell Smith Academic Center to the school in honor of his mother.

2. Earvin "Magic" Johnson. Magic Johnson is the most recognizable name and face in MSU basketball history. He co-starred with Indiana State's Larry Bird in the most-watched game in college basketball history, the 1979 National Championship game. He was a two time All-American and is a member of the Basketball Hall of Fame

1. Greg Kelser. Gregory Kelser warrants the top selection because of his incredible, four-year run at MSU, which ended with a national championship and All-American honors in 1979. He left East Lansing as the only Spartan to record more than 2000 points and 1000 rebounds.

Note: George "The Animal" Steele worked as a top professional wrestler from 1967–1989. Born in Detroit as Jim Myers, he earned an undergrad degree from Michigan State and a master's degree from Central Michigan. Myers went on to teach at Madison Heights High School, where his legendary tenure as the school's football and amateur wrestling coach eventually gained him entry into the Michigan Coaches Hall of Fame. Myers began his Hall of Fame professional wrestling career in Detroit in the late 1960s under a mask and the stage name "The Student." His name and in-ring character changed dramatically after he was discovered by World Wide Wrestling Federation champion Bruno Sammartino in 1967. Calling himself George "The Animal" Steele, he adopted the persona of a disturbed and dangerous caveman, complete with a hairy back and bent over posture. Known for tearing apart turnbuckles with his teeth, "The Animal" grunted in lieu of speaking. Many pro wrestling fans were terrified of him, thinking him the missing link. He became a headliner and once fought the champ Sammartino to a memorable one-hour draw in Madison Square Garden. "The Animal" never won the belt, but probably didn't need it because he attracted big crowds for decades. In the mid-1980s, he turned from bad guy to fan favorite and engaged in a feud with Randy "Macho Man" Savage after "The Animal" became smitten with Savage's main squeeze "Miss Elizabeth." He is now retired and lives with his wife Pat in Cocoa Beach, Florida.

10. Freddy Blassie. The "Hollywood Fashion Plate" boasted a ring sense that was as smart as his fashion sense. "Classy" Freddie Blassie wrestled until he was 55 when he had to retire because some states wouldn't grant a license to guys that old. Then he became a top manager, coining the catchphrase "pencil-necked geek" to demean opponents and recording a song of the same name. He even helped train Muhammad Ali for his famous match in Japan against Antonio Inoki.

9. Killer Kowalski. Tested and proven over many years, Killer knew the ring and the business inside and out. He generously passed on that knowledge to several succeeding generations through his elite wrestling school.

8. Andre the Giant. He was the one and only Giant, a spectacle like no other in pro wrestling. Andre drew crowds for decades. At over seven feet tall and 400 pounds, nobody manhandled him. The only guy to ever pick him up for a slam, Hulk Hogan, suffered a permanent back injury as a result.

7. Danny Hodge. The real deal, he had incredibly strong hands and could crush an apple in one palm. A three time All-American wrestler at Oklahoma, he never lost a match in college. He was also a very good boxer. His pro wrestling opponents were always thankful that there was a script when they climbed in the ring with him.

6. Bobo Brazil. He established himself as a superstar and fan favorite back in the days when being black made you automatically unpopular in front of a lot of crowds. But Bobo had a lot of guts, talent and an amazing amount of charisma.

5. Johnny Valentine. An outstanding worker in every territory in the U.S. and in Japan, he might have gone on to be the best ever if he hadn't suffered a career-ending injury in an airplane accident. His son Greg Valentine was no slouch either

4. The Sheik. The ultimate villain, he convinced more fans to hate his guts over a longer period of time than any other pro wrestler. The Sheik was a consummate professional, never breaking out of character. He would even do his fireball trick when fans approached him on the street. A very wild wrestler, he helped establish the hardcore style carried on by others like his nephew Sabu. He also went on to be a successful promoter, starting up Big Time Wrestling in the 1960s.

3. Bruno Sammartino. He held the WWF belt for so long and was such a popular champion that when he finally lost it in 1971 to Ivan Koloff in New York, the Madison Square Garden fans were stunned into silence. Then many of them started weeping.

2. "Leaping" Larry Chene. A Detroit native and the ultimate good guy, Larry isn't well known because he stayed in one territory his whole career. But the fans that knew him loved him more than any other wrestler.

1. Hulk Hogan. The biggest money draw ever, the Hulkster changed the wrestling business. You couldn't have brought over 90,000 fans into the Silverdome for a wrestling card before Hogan. He can still pack them in on the rare occasions he wrestles these days.

Animal Kingdom Names

Some players look like they belong in a zoo. These guys' names make them sound like they belong in a zoo. Or a nest. Or an aquarium. Or at least on a leash.

14. Dale "The Moose" Alexander, Tigers, 1929-31.

13. Herman "Flea" Clifton, Tigers, 1934-37.

12. Bison Dele, Pistons, 1998-99.

11. Johann "Mule" Franzen, Red Wings, 2005-

10. Ox Emerson, Lions, 1934-37.

9. Ducky Holmes, Tigers 1901-02.

8. Harry Hopp, Lions, 1941-43.

7. Phil "The Vulture" Regan, Tigers, 1960-65.

6. Dan "The Beast" Severn, Michigan-based former UFC champion and mixed martial arts fighter 1994- .

5. Norman "Turkey" Stearnes, Detroit Stars, 1923-31, '33, '37.

4. George "The Animal" Steele, professional wrestler, 1967-89.

3. Dizzy Trout, Tigers, 1939-52.

2. Ratko Varda, Pistons, 2002.

1. Jerome "Junkyard Dog" Williams, Pistons. 1996-01.

Some players distinguish themselves in court as well as on the court.

9. Alex Karras, Lions, gambling. The former Lions standout didn't make this list for his criminal acting while playing the father of Emmanuel Lewis in the TV series, *Webster*. And Karras probably wouldn't have even have made this list if his only transgressions came during various fights he was involved in at his Lindell AC bar. But betting on NFL games? That's a serious offense, at least if you do it while you're playing in the NFL. In 1963, Karras was suspended by the league for the coming season for gambling on NFL games and associating with known gamblers.

7. (Tie) Red Berenson and Derrick Coleman, public urination. At this point, we are going to have to start grouping certain Detroit scofflaws because, well, there are just too damn many. On the evening of March 16, 1994, UM's hockey coach Berenson stumbled out of Banfield's Bar and Grill in Ann Arbor and took a leak on a library wall. He then got into his car and traveled about 20 feet before a cop arrested him for drunken driving and public urination.

In 1999, while dining at the Intermezzo Italian Ristorante, NBA power forward Derrick Coleman allegedly had his own #1 problem. Getting up from his table, he exposed, ummm, a very wet pair of pants. The restaurant staff evicted D.C. for relieving himself in the fancy joint's dining room. The former Piston pled "No Contest" while his attorney claimed Coleman had only spilled a drink on himself. The case remains the area's biggest unsolved mystery behind Jimmy Hoffa's disappearance.

6. Scott Skiles, MSU basketball, multiple offenses. The gutty point guard put up a lot of big numbers during his four years at Michigan State. But during a 16-month period starting in August of 1984, Skiles may have posted his most impressive stats: two DUI arrests, a drug possession arrest, two jail sentences and 18 days in prison. For all that, he got only a one-game suspension from Spartans coach Jud Heathcote. Opposing fans didn't let him off so easily, harassing Skiles at every opportunity. One famous spectator's sign simply read, "Mothers Against Scott Skiles."

5. Larry Harrison, UM football, public indecency. On the night of December 7, 2004, Harrison got caught masturbating in front of a house filled with female co-eds. He was suspected in 14 other similar incidents. You would have to think that the law of averages is going to catch up with you if you habitually jerk off in public. And if you're 6-foot-3 and 304 pounds, the risk increases. Harrison pled no contest and received a one-year suspended sentence, plus five years of intensive probation. He transferred to North Carolina A&T, where he miraculously kept his member in his pants while strolling around campus. We think.

4. Larry Sorenson, pitcher and announcer, multiple DUIs. You could compile an impressive list just of all the Detroit athletes pulled over for driving under the influence. But Sorenson became the local poster boy for this offense. The former UM pitcher and Tigers radio announcer has been convicted of FIVE alcohol-related driving offenses (up to the time of this writing). And that isn't even his most impressive accomplishment. On the morning of February 2, 2008, Sorenson was found passed out in the driver's seat of his car, dead drunk. Almost literally. Blood work determined that the 52-year-old retired pitcher's blood alcohol content was .48!!!! That's six times higher than Michigan's legal limit. Sports lore features a lot of famous numbers. Wayne Gretzky's 92 goals. Barry Bond's 73 home runs. Wilt Chamberlain's 100 points. But Sorenson's .48 might be more impressive than them all. Most people would die if they imbibed that much liquor.

1. (Tie) Those Crazy Football Coaches: Wayne Fontes, Joe Cullen and Gary Moeller, various offenses. Each member of this group has two things in common: they've all been employed as assistant coaches by the Detroit Lions and they've all been publicly embarrassed by a bizarre criminal scandal. On October 21, 1987, then-Lions defensive coordinator Wayne Fontes was pulled over for suspicion of drunken driving. A police officer discovered cocaine in the vehicle. Being the stand-up guy that he was, Fontes told the cop that the coke was not his, but his son's. You might think that being charged with two counts of drunken driving and throwing your own son under the bus might cause an organization to fire you. Instead, the Lions promoted Fontes to head coach the next year.

In August of 2006, Lions defensive line coach, Joe Cullen topped "Cocaine Wayne" with two incidents that drew national attention. One night during training camp, Cullen got a little hungry and drove up to a Wendy's drive-through window—NAKED. "Yes, can I get a Biggie fry, a Frosty and a pair of underwear?" But to his credit, when Cullen was pulled over a short time later, he didn't tell police that his son had taken his clothing. Just a week later, Cullen was busted for drunken driving. To the great dismay of syndicated talk show host Jim Rome, Cullen was actually dressed during the second bust. Because he was working for the Lions, Cullen kept his job.

The final debacle also involved alcohol, but unfortunately for Gary Moeller, the University of Michigan wasn't as forgiving as the Ford family. A few years after succeeding Bo Schembechler as the Wolverines' head football coach, Moeller had a few too many while dining with his wife at the ritzy Southfield restaurant, Excalibur. Moeller got a little out of control, then resisted arrest when police arrived. Audio of the event was released and played on every radio and TV program in the country, costing Moeller his job. It probably didn't help that the Wolverines were coming off an 8-4 season. The Lions, of course, weren't scared off by this blemish on Moeller's resumé and hired him to coach their linebackers in 1997. He even got elevated to Lions interim head coach for a couple games.

These guys took it to the next level.

6. Chris Webber, perjury. The former Michigan "Fab Fiver" had run-ins with the law over marijuana, resisting arrest and assault. But those were mere misdemeanors compared to the crime that landed him on this list: his key role in the Ed Martin/University of Michigan basketball program scandal. Webber lied to his coach, teammates, investigators and journalists about his relationship with Martin, a well-known Michigan booster and Detroit numbers runner who had given Webber thousands of dollars that Martin was attempting to launder while C-Webb was playing for the Wolverines. Webber's false statements continued for the better part of a decade, leading to him eventually committing perjury in front of a grand jury investigating the Martin case. Webber pled guilty to one count of criminal contempt for his big lie. The ramifications of the Martin mess included the NCAA wiping the Wolverines two Final Four appearances with Webber in 1992 and 1993 off the record books. Unfortunately for Webber, they didn't erase the memory of his infamous timeout against North Carolina in the '93 tourney final.

5. Bob Probert, various offenses. It's not easy to think on your feet, especially when you're being handcuffed. But Probert had plenty of experience in those situations. So during his 1994 arrest in West Bloomfield for crashing his motorcycle into a car while driving with a .31 blood alcohol content, the Red Wings Bob Probert was able to come up with, "Just charge me with the usual, man." And it wasn't even his best arrest line. That came in June of 2004 in Delray Beach, Florida when cops approached a drunken Probert to ask the former 29-goal scorer a few questions. Starting with, "Why are you hanging out your car window screaming at people?" Probert responded by attacking the four officers, who had to Taser him repeatedly before they could get the cuffs on the NHL's former heavyweight fighting champ. When the cops asked Probert if he had any aliases, he told them, "The Bad One."

The Bad One? Tasered repeatedly. Resisting arrest. Labeling yourself with a nickname. This is what is now known in the law enforcement community as a "Bob Probert Hat Trick." Probert had clearly earned his "Bad One" nickname during his time with the Red Wings when he was arrested several times for drunken driving and for attempting to smuggle cocaine in his undies across the Windsor-Detroit border. The border incident led to Probert's temporary banishment from the NHL. The sad thing is (actually the whole damn story is pretty depressing) the guy had a chance to be one of the best Red Wings ever. Instead, he became, "The Bad One."

4. Ron LeFlore, Tigers, armed robbery.

Long before the fictional Billy "Wild Thing" Vaughn was discovered by the Cleveland Indians in the California Penal League. The Detroit Tigers actually plucked an All-Star from prison. On the advice of another inmate in the Jackson State Penitentiary, then Tigers manager Billy Martin scouted the raw talent of centerfielder Ron LeFlore in jail. George Steinbrenner's personal human yo-yo was so impressed with LeFlore's speed that a Tigers Stadium workout was set up and LeFlore was let out of jail for a one-day tryout. LeFlore, who was doing 5-to-15 years for armed robbery, was so impressive in that workout that he eventually was paroled in 1973 with the caveat that he had to be employed by the Tigers. In his six years in Motown, LeFlore's robbery background translated well on the field as he stole 294 bases as a superior leadoff hitter. An All-Star in 1976, he led the American League in runs and swiped 68 bases two seasons later. The story was so freaking unbelievable that *CBS* made a movie about it. LeFlore returned to Tigers Stadium in 1999 for the last game ever at the ballpark. After participating in some on-field activities, LeFlore was taken into custody by the cops because there was an outstanding warrant for his arrest due to delinquent child support payments. Can you say, "full circle?"

3. Parish Hickman, Michigan State basketball, manslaughter.

While the actual crime is the most heinous on this list, Parish Hickman just wasn't a famous enough athlete to warrant higher than the #3 slot here. A Spartans forward during the 1990s, Hickman got booted off the squad for a variety of problems, including drugs. He transferred to Jerry Falwell's college, Liberty, where he finished up his collegiate career. Hickman must have missed Ten Commandments 101 at the religious school, or at least the "Thou shall not kill" part. In 2001, Hickman was charged with the murder of Gene Shelby at a Westside Detroit gas station. Eventually Hickman pled guilty to manslaughter and was sentenced to 3-to-15 years in the state pen. The former Spartan is currently serving out his sentence at the Parr Highway Correctional facility. And you thought Shawn Respert was a bust?

2. Reggie Rogers and Bruce Kimball, vehicular manslaughter.

In the summer of 1984, Bruce Kimball brought a silver medal for his efforts in the ten-meter platform dive home to Ann Arbor. Winning the medal was especially impressive because Kimball had suffered a broken leg, torn knee ligaments, a lacerated liver, a broken face and so much damage to his spleen it had to be removed after a drunk driver hit his car three years earlier. So you would think a guy who went through all of that crap, through all of the rehabilitation, through all of the pain because of a drunk driver, would never drive drunk himself. But two weeks before the U.S. diving Trials for the 1988 Olympics, Kimball drank a 12-pack of beer, got into his Mazda RX7 in the Tampa, Florida area, sped up to 90 mph and smashed into a group of teenagers, killing two and seriously injuring three others. Kimball pled guilty to two counts of manslaughter and three counts of drunken driving. A judge sentenced Kimball to 17 years in prison and permanently suspended his driver's license. The disgraced Olympic champion was released after serving five years in prison and his driver's license was reinstated in 2004.

In 1987, the Detroit Lions selected University of Washington defensive end Reggie Rogers in the first round of the NFL Draft. And while the Lions have had a lot of first round picks that have not worked out for a variety of reasons, at least Mike Williams, Joey Harrington and Charles Rogers never KILLED anyone. While on injured reserve in 1988, Rogers smashed his car into another vehicle, killing three teenagers. Rogers suffered a broken neck as well. Rogers' blood alcohol level was .15 and he was eventually convicted of negligent homicide and sentenced to the maximum of 16 to 24 months in prison.

1. Denny McClain, various offenses. Denny McClain won 31 games in 1968, along with the Cy Young and MVP awards in helping the Detroit Tigers win the World Series. But most Detroiters' gut reactions when they hear the name "Denny McClain" is, "What did that scumbag do now?" The trouble all began for McClain in 1970 when he was suspended for the first three months of the season for his participation in a bookmaking operation. After reinstatement, McClain dumped ice water over two Detroit reporters and brandished a gun in a Chicago restaurant. MLB commissioner Bowie Kuhn again suspended McClain, this time for the remainder of the 1970 season. During the offseason, McClain was dealt to the Washington Senators where he promptly lost 22 games in 1971. In just three short years, McClain had gone from a 31-game winner to a 22-game loser. But his losing ways had just begun. After retiring in 1972, McClain moved to Lakeland, Florida (the Tigers' spring training home) and became a partner in a bank called First Fidelity Financial Services, an institution that was rumored to be backed by the Mafia. In 1985, McLain was found guilty of charges that included racketeering, extortion and drugs. He was sentenced to 23 years in a federal prison. In 1987, the convictions were overturned because of procedural violations. The feds re-indicted him and he pleaded guilty. McClain received a 12-year sentence, but the government let him off with five years probation and time served.

A free man again, McCain chose to rip off some more people. McClain and a friend purchased Peet Packing Company in Chesaning, Michigan. When the company predictably went under, McClain was indicted on charges that he and his partner bilked their employees' pension fund of millions. McClain was sentenced to an eight-year prison sentence. He served six years of the sentence and eventually was released to a halfway house and worked at a local 7-Eleven selling Slurpees. There is no truth to the rumor that McClain was fired from that job for eating into the convenience store's profits by devouring all of the chain's "Mike and Ike's." After his second prison stint, McClain teamed up with Eli Zaret to write his autobiography. It was entitled, *I Told You I Wasn't Perfect*.

Ya think?

Note: Parker became the first black sports columnist for the *Detroit Free Press* in 1993 and was founding father of WDFN, where he paired with Stoney for afternoon drive time. He currently writes a column for *The Detroit News* and co-hosts "Sports Time" afternoons on NewsTalk 1200 WCHB. The controversial Parker never hesitates to ruffle feathers. But his non-media personality is best described as an old Jewish guy trapped in a black man's body—the only brother in the world addicted to both *Seinfeld* and *The Golden Girls*.

10. Ty Cobb. The only reason he isn't No. 1 is because a lot of his worst behavior was actually considered acceptable then. By all accounts, the Hall of Famer was a bad human being and infamous racist who treated most with total disregard.

9. Jack Morris. The winningest pitcher in the 1980s, never had a winning personality. The only thing worse than his skin complexion was his attitude toward the media. He was especially disrespectful toward female reporters because he didn't think they belonged.

8. Mike Vernon. The former Wings' goalie was very snippy and a bit of a hockey snob, acting as if no one else knew the game.

7. Christian Laettner. The former Duke star remains a giant in college basketball lore. But in the NBA, he was a cocky and arrogant mental midget. No wonder Jerry Stackhouse gave him a black eye.

6. Gary Ward. Talk about an angry guy. You couldn't ask him anything without him getting suspicious. Even saying "Hello" got a dirty look. This is definitely one of those guys you don't want to read a "Whatever Happened To . . ." story about.

5. Lloyd Carr. The former Michigan football coach was just plain nasty. It didn't matter if he was on TV live, in a news conference or dealing with student reporters, he always took a "chip-on-his-shoulder" approach.

4. Kirk Gibson. "Gibby" might have had two big hits in his career—home runs in two different World Series. But when it came to dealing with the masses, he struck out often. He was just rude. No wonder he got into so many fights with teammates.

3. Bobby Ross. The Lions' former head coach was another vile cat. He blamed the media for his woes and inability to win any important games. Sadly, he was nothing more than a talker with a bad brim on his cap.

2. James Toney. The Ann Arbor boxing champ might have made Michigan proud in the ring. Outside the ring, though, Toney could never say the right thing. He had no respect for anyone—fans, opponents or even his manager.

1. Bill Laimbeer. An original Bad Boy, he wasn't just bad on the court, Laimbeer also went out of his way to be rude and disrespectful to folks off the court. He also addressed many in a condescending tone as if he were too good to speak to them.

Note: Jennifer Hammond has been covering sports in Detroit since 1994 when she started doing updates at WDFN. She then moved to Fox 2 where she has been a reporter and anchor for over a decade. "The Hammer," as she is affectionately known, has covered the Lions on a daily basis longer than anyone else in the electronic media and has worked for Fox as a sideline reporter during Lions games.

8. Kevin Glover, Lions. A salt-of-the-earth guy who remains dedicated to family, friends and former teammates. The mere rumor that part of the reason Barry Sanders retired was because of the organization's porous handling of Glover's contract situation tells you a little something about how his teammates felt about him.

7. Jeff Backus, Lions. Accountable and reliable, he's started every game of the Millen era and can still manage to smile. He returns calls, talks after every loss (and there have been a lot for him) and never throws his teammates under the bus. The kind of guy you want your daughter to marry.

6. Jason Hanson, Lions. Hanson is the quintessential answer man. He's there when you need him with nothing but honesty. He treats others how he expects and deserves to be treated. From teammates, to neighbors to opponents, no one has anything but praise for this family-first man.

5. Lindsey Hunter, Pistons. If you ever want an athlete to be a role model for your son or daughter, look no further than #10 on the Pistons. Win or lose, he always steps up to the plate and gives you his time. No wonder Joe Dumars loves this guy. And so does Detroit!

3. (Tie) Kris Draper/Darren McCarty, Red Wings. Sitting side-by-side in the Red Wings dressing room for the better part of ten years, they established themselves as the go-to guys in a room. Above and beyond the personable rapport they have with the media, both showed their true character off the ice through visits to Children's Hospital, caring for terminally-ill fans and, of course, the creation of the McCarty Cancer Foundation.

2. Sean Casey, Tigers. Not only did Casey respect his obligation to the media, he seemed to enjoy it. He'd talk with writers about their families in addition to answering countless baseball questions and entertaining us with stories from the dugout. "The Mayor" was a true man of the people without all the rhetoric.

1. Lomas Brown, Lions. The kind of guy who not only stops to say "hello" whenever he sees you, but welcomes you with a hug and that ubiquitous smile. A gentleman wherever he went, Lomas never thought he was bigger than the game and, win or lose, always agreed to an interview. This is one Lion that keeps on giving by making Detroit his home and working in the local media and continuing to root for the team that gave him his start.

Note: Bob Wojnowski, better known as "Wojo" to his many fans, has worked as a sports columnist for *The Detroit News* since 1989. He also serves as the intelligent one of The Stoney and Wojo Show on Sports Radio 1130 WDFN, where he has gabbed since 1994. While not the most punctual fellow, Wojo is one of the nicest people in the media. I honestly have never heard anyone say a bad word about him. He is generous, humorous, considerate, professional, fair and, yes, portly. I can't think of a better person to work with for over 14 years.

15. The Lions defeat the Dallas Cowboys 38-6 on January 5, 1992. Why is this relevant? Well, it advanced the Lions to the NFC championship game. And the team was inspired by offensive lineman Mike Utley, who was paralyzed in a game during the regular season before flashing a "thumbs up" sign as he was wheeled off the field. Oh, right, and it remains the franchise's only playoff victory since 1957.

14. Thomas Hearns. The Hitman's rise to the status of a boxing legend brought Detroiters together, cheering a native son as they had once cheered Joe Louis. Hearns' epic bouts with Sugar Ray Leonard and Marvin Hagler were must-see TV. Leonard won the first match and the 12-round draw in the 1989 rematch stirred a controversy that simmered for years. Yes, Hearns was robbed.

13. Michigan State beats Florida, 89-76, to win the 2000 NCAA basketball championship. This was the ultimate validation for Tom Izzo's rising program, part of three consecutive Final Four appearances. It also was stirring confirmation for the Flintstones—the MSU players from Flint, led by Mateen Cleaves, who laid the foundation for a program built on toughness.

12. Michigan beats Seton Hall, 80-79, in overtime to win the 1989 NCAA basketball championship. The story had many layers, from Rumeal Robinson's clutch free throws with three seconds left to Glen Rice's magnificent shooting to Steve Fisher's ascension to the head coaching job after Bill Frieder's stunning departure for Arizona State.

11. Ernie Harwell's temporary firing. When the Tigers and radio station *WJR* fired beloved long-time broadcaster Ernie Harwell in 1991, it caused such an uproar that new owner Mike Ilitch brought Harwell back in 1993. Harwell finished out his legendary career as the team's full-time radio broadcaster in 2002, retiring as a voice for the ages, and for all ages.

10. Barry Sanders rushes into history. The Lions running back capped one of the greatest seasons in NFL history by rushing for 184 yards in the 1997 finale against the Jets to finish with 2,053 yards for the year. Sanders became the third player ever to top 2,000 yards and, in the process, led the Lions to the playoffs. He shared that season's NFL MVP award with Brett Favre.

9. The all-encompassing tale of Michigan's Fab Five. It began with their celebrated arrival in 1992 as heralded freshmen, progressed with their back-to-back NCAA championship-game losses, and continued to unfold for a decade. From their long-shorts fashion, to Chris Webber's fateful timeout that sealed the loss to North Carolina in the first title game, to the scandal that put the Wolverines on probation. Few stories resonated so long and polarized so many.

8. The Red Wings win the Stanley Cup in 2002. This was the Wings' last grab at starry glory before the NHL stumbled into a year-long lockout and a subsequent salary cap. Coached by Scotty Bowman, the cast of Steve Yzerman, Sergei Fedorov, Dominik Hasek, Brendan Shanahan, Brett Hull, Nicklas Lidstrom and others comprised a legend-laden team that had to win, and after a few bumps, it did.

7. The closing of Tiger Stadium on Sept. 27, 1999. As emotional as any event in Detroit sports history, the closure of the beloved park had fans weeping as they hugged girders on the final night. The stadium was home to the Tigers since 1912 and linked generations of baseball fans, before the Tigers moved to Comerica Park in 2000. The old ballpark's final bow was an 8-2 Tigers' victory over Kansas City, featuring a grand slam by Robert Fick that, fittingly, caromed off the fabled rightfield roof.

6. Bo Schembechler dies of heart failure. The legendary Michigan coach died on the eve of the 2006 Michigan-Ohio State game, the rivalry's biggest clash in years. The top-ranked Buckeyes beat the No. 2 Wolverines 42-39 the next day, and three days later, mourners gathered on a bitterly cold, gray day in Michigan Stadium to bid farewell to Bo. Truly, the passing of an era.

5. The Pistons stun the Lakers to win the 2004 NBA championship. The Pistons built by Joe Dumars and coached by Larry Brown were balanced and tough. But no one—NO ONE—expected them to beat the Lakers, a team whose starting line-up featured Shaquille O'Neal, Kobe Bryant, Gary Payton and Karl Malone. After losing the opener in the Finals, the Pistons dominated the next four games and proved something few in the NBA thought possible—that a true team could overcome superstars. And yes, the aura of Chauncey "Mr. Big Shot" Billups was born.

4. Michigan beats Washington State, 21-16, in the Rose Bowl. The victory capped a 12-0 season and won the Wolverines the 1997 national title, the program's first in 49 years. This was an unlikely champion, led by once-embattled quarterback Brian Griese and once-embattled coach Lloyd Carr. The title cemented Carr's standing in Michigan lore and also unveiled all the skills of Charles Woodson, who became the first predominately defensive player to win the Heisman Trophy.

3. The Pistons' win the 1989 NBA championship. The first of the team's back-to-back titles marked the culmination of a long climb past bitter rivals Boston and Los Angeles. Few teams resonated in Detroit as deeply as the Bad Boys, from Isiah Thomas to Joe Dumars to the bruising duo of Bill Laimbeer and Rick Mahorn. Their tough, no-superstar approach was a precursor to the next generation of Pistons champions.

2. The Red Wings sweep Philadelphia in 1997 Stanley Cup Finals. Long-time captain Steve Yzerman's lifting of the team's first Stanley Cup in 42 years remains one of the signature moments in Detroit sports history. What expanded the story, sadly, was the limousine accident a week after the championship that severely injured outstanding defenseman Vladmir Konstantinov and trainer Sergei Mnatsakanov. Few teams ever went from celebration to somberness so quickly. Ultimately, the tragedy helped push the Wings to repeat as champions in 1998.

1. The Tigers start the 1984 season 35-5 and go on to win the franchise's first World Series since 1968. Baseball captivates more people for a longer period of time than any other sport, and Detroiters were captivated from the opening week of the '84 season, when Jack Morris threw a no-hitter. There are few images more lasting than Kirk Gibson's home run that sealed the five-game World Series victory over San Diego. Other teams in other sports sustained more success than the Tigers' "Bless You, Boys." But this was a sorely needed celebration in the middle of a dry spell for Detroit sports, giving the city its first championship in nearly two decades.

Note: Motor City native Mort Meisner worked in journalism for 25 years, winning numerous awards and breaking a number of big stories, including the Nancy Kerrigan attack. He now heads up Meisner Associates, a company that specializes in talent representation for television and radio.

10. Tanya Harding/Nancy Kerrigan Attack. Our station won several Emmys for this, including one that I received. We broke the story and the subsequent scheme itself. WHY! WHY! WHY!

9. The 1980 Prostitute Murder Cover-up By Detroit Police Just Prior To GOP Convention. Cops were fired, demoted, and forced to retire over this one. After a lot of denial, blown leads and false accusations by police against people covering the story, plus more than a dozen deaths, all of the truths came out when we were able to obtain police documents confirming the cover-up. Funny, how things don't change in the city.

8. Kevorkian Assisted Suicides. When this broke, nobody believed it. In fact, we broke the story as Jeff Fieger called me with the tip, "Hey Mort, you won't believe this, but some old guy just offed someone."

7. Chrysler Nearly Goes Under, Iacocca and the Government Bail Them Out Saving The Day. Hey, we call it the Iacocca approach to this day. If you mess up, fess up and then dress up. Many people called for Chrysler to die a natural death and thank goodness the government and Iacocca saved the day.

6. Walter Reuther Killed In A New Year's Eve Plane Crash. The death of this labor leader was a crushing blow. He was liked by most and respected by all, and his death set back the labor movement.

5. Jimmy Hoffa Disappearance. Hey, who says he was murdered? No body after all these years. Machus stood as a landmark to the location where he disappeared in Bloomfield Township, Andiamo occupies the space today.

4. Detroit Tigers' 1968 World Series Championship. My father told me that once this miracle happened he was ready to die. He made it through the 1984 World Series, then died several months later. This 1968 Tiger team really brought an ailing city together for one summer but alas, it didn't last long, did it?

3. 1967 Riots. I was almost 14 years old when the riots broke out and all I remember was the fear that gripped the city. We stood outside of our suburban 800 square foot home watering down the roof as Lou Gordon warned that rioters were going to take to the suburbs.

2. Coleman Young Investigation including Ken Weiner, his Ann Ivory Calvert affair and the fact that Coleman had a son.

1. Kwame Kilpatrick Investigation. Talk about chutzpah? This guy is a two-bit punk by any standards. In Chicago's corrupt political system he would barely place. Maybe, he would have risen to the lofty level of an alderman!

Top Days at Michigan International Speedway
:: Rob Pascoe

Note: A long-time fan and racing expert, Rob has hosted "On The Track," a talk show dedicated to NASCAR on WDFN, for the past three years. He covered numerous events at Michigan International Speedway (MIS), the Brooklyn, Michigan site that quickly established itself as one of the most popular tracks in all of motor sports after opening in 1968. The track's wide corners feature distinct grooves that allow for some intense racing. Races often come down to fuel mileage battles, as the long green flag runs make pit strategy a top priority. Located in the Irish Hills of southeastern Michigan, MIS is also special to many motor sport fans because of its proximity to Detroit, the home of American automobile design and manufacturing. Often called the backyard of the "Big Three," the two-mile, D-shaped oval offers racing fans excellent sight lines and the guarantee of very few (if any) bad seats. I have spent many great days at the MIS, but here are my most memorable.

12. June 11, 1999. Dale Earnhardt earned an early Father's Day present by scoring a victory over his son, Dale Earnhardt, Jr., in the International Race of Champions (IROC). Senior battled Junior door-to-door coming out of the final turn, touching cars and edging out his namesake by just .007 of a second.

11. October 13, 1968. Ronnie Bucknum wins the inaugural race at MIS, a 250-mile open-wheel event. Bucknum's victory, his only win in a major racing series, came before a crowd of 55,000 fans and against an elite field that included runner-up Mario Andretti, A.J. Foyt, Johnny Rutherford, Al Unser and Bobby Unser.

10. July 26, 2003. Alex Barron beats Sam Hornish Jr. for the "spin-and-win" victory. Barron rebounded from a mid-race spinout to beat Hornish Jr. by .0121 of a second.

9. August 21, 2007. Kurt Busch wins the 3M Performance 400 NASCAR Cup race in an unprecedented Tuesday event. Originally scheduled for Sunday, the race was postponed by two days of rain. Other than a brief fog delay after the first ten laps, drivers steered clear of any more weather problems. NASCAR's top circuit had never run on a Tuesday during the modern era, which began in 1973.

8. July 18, 1976. University of Michigan grad Janet Guthrie becomes the first woman to compete in an open-wheel race at MIS. Guthrie won even wider acclaim the following year as the first woman to drive in the Indianapolis 500 and Daytona 500.

7. July 28, 1996. Andre Ribeiro won the IndyCar Marlboro 500 at MIS in a race that saw a half-dozen different leaders battle through 15 lead changes. The race also featured drivers going five-wide to make a pass. Several drivers left Brooklyn with bumps and bruises. Emerson Fittipaldi suffered a fracture of the seventh cervical vertebra and a partial collapse of the left lung. Paul Tracy came away with a chip fracture of the sixth vertebra and bruised knees. Roberto Moreno bruised his right thigh and Parker Johnstone left with black-and-blue knees.

6. August 18, 1991. In the closest margin of victory ever at MIS, Dale Jarrett edged out Davey Allison by eight inches at the Champion Spark Plug 400 for his first NASCAR Cup Series win. Adding to Jarrett's special day was *ESPN*'s live broadcast of the event with an announce team led by his dad, Ned Jarrett.

5. June 15, 1969. MIS made history by hosting the Motor State 500, its first ever NASCAR event. Cale Yarborough and Lee Roy Yarbrough (no relation) spent most of the afternoon racing door-to-door. On the last lap, they finally bumped twice upon entering Turn No. 1. Lee Roy touched the wall, spun out and crashed just 900 feet from the finish line. Meanwhile, Cale sped on to take the checkered flag in one of the most exciting finishes in Michigan International Speedway history.

4. June 15, 1997. After nearly losing his life in a Turn No. 2 crash at MIS in August of 1994, Ernie Irvan overcame the odds and some visual distractions nearly three years later to win the Miller 400. Irvan, who went on to victory after passing Bill Elliott with 20 laps remaining, said after the race, "I started getting tears in my eyes with about ten laps left. You know, it's hard to drive with tears in your eyes."

3. August 19, 2006. Dale Earnhardt, Jr. bumped Carl Edwards out of the way during the final laps of the NASCAR Busch Series Carfax 250. Earnhardt went on to win the race, inspiring Edwards to purposely ram into Jr.'s car and confront him in Gatorade Victory Lane.

2. June 15, 1986. Bill Elliott won the Miller American 400 at MIS, but Harry Gant stole the media's attention. Gant made a miraculous comeback from serious injuries, including a bruised heart, suffered in a crash only a week earlier at Pocono to finish second in his famous #33 Skoal Bandit car.

1. August 20, 1978. David Pearson took the lead from Darrell Waltrip on the final lap of the Champion Spark Plug 400 and won his record ninth NASCAR Cup event at MIS. The race featured 35 lead changes and Richard "The King" Petty driving a Chevy, instead of his trademark Dodge.

Top Ten Reasons Why the Big Ten Is the Nation's Most Overrated "Power" Football Conference :: Drew Sharp

Note: Sports columnist Sharp joined the *Detroit Free Press* after graduating from the University of Michigan in 1982. "Boodini," as he's affectionately known, also appears as a regular panelist on ESPN's *Rome Is Burning* show. Many find Drew to be overtly negative towards the Big Ten. But Sharp just thinks he's being realistic.

10. Television means more than talent. The Midwest loves its television and it's more inclined to stay home to watch. The Big Ten conference boasts the biggest concentration of large television markets among the major conferences.

9. It's become a coaching graveyard. SEC coaches leave for the NFL (Steve Spurrier, Nick Saban, etc.) while the Big Ten head coaches stick around for decades until they grow moss around themselves and their offensive play-calling (Joe Paterno, Lloyd Carr, etc.).

8. Where for art thou, Notre Dame? If the Big Ten was truly a force, it could sell Notre Dame on the concept of joining the league as a 12th team.

7. It hasn't spread the word. The Big Ten only now embraces more elements of the increasingly popular spread offense. It went from "three yards and a cloud of dust" to "three steps in the pocket and a short toss to a running back." The Big Ten remains years behind the current trends.

6. Iowa coach Kirk Ferentz is considered a genius. He's a beneficiary of Big Ten hype, always one of the five highest-paid head coaches in the country (making just under $3 million annually). But, really, what has Ferentz done to merit the occasional flirtations from the NFL and other colleges? Ferentz has taken the Hawkeyes to just one BCS bowl game.

5. It's primarily a basketball conference now. The best young athletes in the Midwest lean more toward basketball, while in the South, Texas and California, they're more likely to play football. That places the Big Ten at a logistical disadvantage.

4. Speed is considered a luxury. The Big Ten still hasn't figured out that it's the fastest, most athletic interior line that dominates. Getting equally speedy wide-outs doesn't matter when going up against the SEC when you can't keep your quarterbacks consistently upright.

3. It remains nothing more than the "Big Two." A consistent national power from "the Little Nine" has yet to emerge. It's still all about Ohio State and Michigan. Wisconsin has developed a nice little niche, but hasn't become a serious national championship contender.

2. It still can't win the big game. There should be a national movement to barricade all entrances into the state of Florida to deny the Buckeyes access into the state should they earn the privilege of having the SEC champion slap them around in next January's national championship game in Miami.

1. It still can't count. Michigan, Michigan State, Ohio State, Wisconsin, Minnesota, Penn State, Illinois, Indiana, Northwestern, Iowa, Purdue. That's 11, guys, not ten.

Michigan has won more games than any other team in the history of college football, with 869 victories spanning 128 seasons. Their winning percentage of .745 is the best in Division 1-A history. From the beginning, the Wolverines have had some of college football's greatest talents wear the Maize and Blue. When putting this list together it was apparent that Michigan has had many more than 10 great football players. However, these 10 men, each an All-American, left a legacy that will last as long as Michigan plays football.

10. Benny Friedman, quarterback, 1924-26. Friedman is regarded as one of the first great passing quarterbacks in football. He led Michigan to back-to-back Big Ten titles in 1925 and 1926 when the team posted identical 7-1 records. An All-American and Big Ten MVP in 1926, Friedman is a member of the College Football Hall of Fame and the Pro Football Hall of Fame.

9. Desmond Howard, wide receiver, 1989-91. Howard will always be remembered for doing the Heisman pose in the end zone after returning a punt for a touchdown against Ohio State in 1991. He set or tied five NCAA records and 12 single-season Michigan records during his playing days. When he won the 1991 Heisman trophy, his margin of victory was the second largest in the trophy's history. An acrobatic athlete, his most memorable catch came on fourth down against Notre Dame when he stretched out as far as he could, caught the ball on his fingertips and hauled it in for the winning touchdown.

8. Braylon Edwards, wide receiver, 2002-04. "The Bray" is Michigan's All-Time leading receiver in receptions (252), yards (3,541) and touchdowns (39). His touchdown mark is also a Big Ten record. Braylon's performance against Michigan State his senior year was remarkable. Down by 17 in the third quarter, his leaping ability and sheer talent rallied Michigan to a triple-overtime victory against the Spartans. *ff*

7. Ron Kramer, end, 1954-56. Kramer is one of the greatest athletes in Michigan history. He won nine letters in three sports (football, basketball and track). He would have won three more, but freshman weren't eligible in his era. On the gridiron, his versatility was impressive. In a single game, he'd play offensive & defensive end, running back, quarterback, kicker, and receiver. A two-time consensus All-American in 1955 and 1956, Kramer's #87, was retired by Michigan after his senior season.

6. Rick Leach, quarterback, 1975-78. Until Chad Henne's arrival, Rick Leach was the only true freshman to start at quarterback for Michigan. Known as a passer in high school, Leach completely altered his game and became a great option QB. Even though he engineered a run-dominated offense, he broke Michigan's passing, total offense and touchdown records. The lefthander set an NCAA record for most touchdowns accounted for (82) and broke Big Ten records for total offense (6,460 yards), total plays (1,034) and touchdown passes (48). A baseball-star as well, Leach was an All-American in both football and baseball, which is almost unheard of in modern college athletics.

5. Willie Heston, halfback, 1901-04. Heston was known as a speed demon and the star of Michigan's legendary "point-a-minute' teams. Michigan was 43-0-1 during Heston's career and captured four national championships. He hit the line so quickly that he was past defenders before they had a chance to react. His 170 yards rushing in the 1902 Rose Bowl stood as a record for 59 years. Willie Heston set the standard for Michigan's running backs.

4. Benny Oosterbaan, end, 1925-27. Oosterbaan was the first of only two players to be a three-time All-American at Michigan. The greatest pass receiver of his era, Benny was chosen to the All-Time All-American team in 1951. Not only a great player, he coached the Wolverines to three Big Ten titles (1948, 1949 and 1950) and the national championship in 1948.

3. Charles Woodson, cornerback, 1995-97. The only defensive player to ever win the Heisman Trophy, Woodson also played on offense and was a threat to score every time he touched the ball. The multi–dimensional talent always came up big in the big games, making spectacular plays on the both sides of the ball. Whether it was an acrobatic interception, reception, or returning a punt for a TD, Woodson did it all for the Wolverines.

2. Anthony Carter, wide receiver, 1979-82. Only the second player in Michigan history to be a three-time All-American. I could go on and on about his exploits, but to give you the proper picture of how talented a player he really was for the Wolverines, all you need to know is he FORCED Bo Schembechler to throw the football. This 5-foot-11, 160-pound wide receiver is totally responsible for Michigan's modern day passing game.

1. Tom Harmon, halfback, 1938-40. "Old 98" was Michigan's first Heisman Trophy winner. An offensive juggernaut, he dominated the game. During his three-year Michigan career, Harmon rushed for 2,143 yards, scored 33 touchdowns, kicked 33 PATs and chipped in two field goals for 237 career points. Even those savages in Columbus gave him a standing ovation after his final game against the Buckeyes. When an Ohio State crowd gives a Michigan football player a standing ovation, it means he's the best ever.

Although often overshadowed by the other Big Ten school in this state, the Spartans boast a proud football tradition of their own. Under head coach Duffy Daugherty, Michigan State remained a national powerhouse for a good portion of the 1960s. They have also turned out more than their share of great football players.

10. Dan Bass, 1976–79. The linebacker became the Spartans' top career tackler, racking up 32 in one game against Ohio State. A member of the Canadian Football Hall of Fame, Bass also had a 99-yard interception return.

9. Charles Rogers, 2001–02. The 2002 Fred Biletnikoff Award winner as the best college wide receiver in the nation, Rogers excelled in big games. He holds MSU's record for career TD receptions, snagging 27 in just 24 games. He became the second overall pick of the NFL Draft, but failed to do much in the pros due to injuries, marijuana and a bad attitude.

8. Tony Mandarich, 1986–1988. One of the greatest offensive lineman in the history of college football, the two-time All-American tackle made weak defenders cry. He also made the Green Bay Packers cry for making hin the second overall pick of the 1989 draft ahead of Barry Sanders. One of the all time NFL busts, but he was awesome at State.

7. Andre Rison, 1985–1988. The wide receiver rewrote the school's receiving records by putting up 2,992 career yards. He had 252 yards and three touchdowns in the 1989 Gator Bowl. Nicknamed "Bad Moon," Rison also played a little for the MSU basketball team.

6. Brad Van Pelt, 1970–1972. The first defensive back to win the prestigious Maxwell Award, Van Pelt was a two-time All-American who controlled games from the secondary. He switched to linebacker in the NFL and had a very good pro career, making five Pro Bowls with the Giants.

5. Bubba Smith, 1964–1966. The Hall of Fame defensive end helped hold Michigan, Ohio State and Notre Dame to minus-85 yards rushing yards one season. The two-time All-American inspired the popular "Kill Bubba Kill" slogan. The first overall pick of the NFL draft by Baltimore, he was a key member of the Colts' Super Bowl V championship team. He later became an actor, best known for his work in the *Police Academy* movies and Miller Lite commercials.

4. Percy Snow, 1986–1989. A Rose Bowl MVP linebacker and winner of the Butkus Award and Lombardi Trophy, Snow was a terrific college player who had three undistinguished years in the NFL. The older brother of NBA veteran and former Spartan Eric Snow, Percy still has to be considered as one of the best linebackers in Big Ten history.

3. Don Coleman, 1949–1951. A College Football Hall of Fame offensive tackle at 185 pounds, Coleman was an amazing blocker and tackler for Biggie Munn's teams. He was the first player named to Notre Dame's All-Opponent team for three straight years. His jersey, #78, was the first to be retired in MSU history.

2. Lorenzo White, 1984–1987. An incredibly durable and clutch runner, White twice finished fourth in the Heisman voting. In 1985, he became the first running back in Big Ten history to rush for over 2,000 yards in a season. He remains the school's leader in career rushing yardage with 4,887. A first-round pick by the Houston Oilers in 1988, White made one Pro Bowl in his eight-year pro career.

1. George Webster, 1964–1966. Duffy Daugherty's greatest player and one of the best in college football history, Webster manned a position called rover back—a combination safety/linebacker. The two-time All-American was the driving force behind the great, undefeated Spartan teams of 1965 and 1966. A member of the College Football Hall of Fame, Webster became the fifth overall pick by Houston in the 1967 AFL draft and was the league's Defensive Rookie of the Year. Webster played in three AFL All-Star games and was named to the league's All-Time team. After the AFL-NFL merger, he made three Pro Bowls. He passed away in 2007 at the age of 61.

Note: Lage covered Michigan State athletics for *The State News* from 1993-95 and the *Lansing State Journal* from 1995-2000. He has also written national columns for *Street and Smith* and *The Sporting News*.

15. 2005 Women's Final Four. The Spartans women's basketball team rallied from 16 points down in the second half to beat national powerhouse Tennessee and reach the national title game for the first time.

14. Pinning Michigan's superstar heavyweight wrestler. Jeff Smith got UM's two-time NCAA wrestling champ Dave Porter of Lansing on his back to knock off the Wolverines in a jubilant moment on Feb. 17, 1968, at Jenison Field House.

13. The Cold War, October 6, 2001. Spartan Stadium was packed with 74,554 fans—a record crowd for a hockey game—to watch Michigan State battle Michigan to a draw in what was more of an event than a game.

12. Basketbowl, December 23, 2003. Michigan State lost the game to Kentucky. But the Spartans program gained priceless exposure by surpassing a basketball world attendance record with 78,129 fans.

11. Splitting the uprights at the 1956 Rose Bowl. Dave Kaiser's field goal lifted the Spartans to a 17-14 win over UCLA, giving coach Duffy Daugherty a successful debut in Pasadena.

10. Topping Harvard for the 1986 hockey championship. Mike Donnelly led a rally with two goals to give Michigan State its second hockey title and Donnelly an NCAA-record 59 goals for that sensational season.

9. Lighting the lamp with 18.9 seconds left. Thanks to Justin Abdelkader's late, tie-breaking goal, the Spartans beat Boston College to claim the 2007 NCAA hockey title.

8. Picking Izzo. Michigan State made a brilliant decision when it elevated littleknown assistant Tom Izzo to lead its basketball program after Jud Heathcote retired in 1995. Since Izzo's hire, the Spartans have won a national championship and four straight Big Ten titles while advancing to a quartet of Final Fours.

7. Letting Saban go too soon. Saban wanted a new deal toward the end of the 1999 season, but then-president M. Peter McPherson told him to wait until after Citrus Bowl. Saban bolted for LSU, sending the MSU football program spiraling down just when it seemed to finally be set for sustained success. We all know what Saban did for LSU.

6. The 1952 football season. The Spartans went undefeated, earning their only AP national championship.

5. Cutting down the nets in 2000. Mateen Cleaves said only death could've kept him off the floor after Florida's Teddy Dupay sent the leader of the Flintstones hobbling off the court with an ankle injury. Cleaves came back to help the Spartans claim the men's NCAA men's basketball title.

4. 1988 Rose Bowl. The Spartans capped their most recent outright Big Ten championship season with a big win over the Trojans.

3. Michigan State 10, Notre Dame 10, 1966. They're still talking about this one, more than four decades after Ara Parseghian's Fighting Irish played for a tie and later beat out Michigan State for the AP national championship vote. The Spartans won, though, just by being a part of the historic game.

2. Winning the 1979 basketball championship. Earvin "Magic" Johnson, Greg Kelser and Co. beat Indiana State and Larry Bird in a transcendent event that attracted an estimated 40 million TV viewers—still a record for a college basketball game. Few games in any sport at any level have stood the test of time quite like this classic.

1. Joining the Big Ten in 1949. Michigan wanted to be the only Big Ten school in the state. But Michigan State College and its president John Hannah prevailed in a defining moment for the institution, academically and athletically. Can you imagine the Spartans in Conference USA?

The 13 Worst Days in the History of University of Michigan Athletics :: Michael Rosenberg

Note: Michael Rosenberg is a sports columnist at the *Detroit Free Press*, where he has worked since 1999 and author of numerous books, including *War As They Knew It: Woody Hayes, Bo Schembechler and America in a Time of Unrest*.

13. March 27, 1997: Boston University 3, Michigan 2, NCAA hockey semifinal. The Wolverines might have been the best team in college hockey history. They had won the national title the year before and would win it the year after. They were an astounding 35-3-4 and loaded with seniors. But the Terriers pulled off the upset, ending the career of Hobey Baker Award winner Brendan Morrison on a bitter note.

12. October 13, 1990: Michigan State 28, Michigan 27. Near the end of the fourth quarter, the top-ranked Wolverines went for two. Desmond Howard was open. MSU defensive back Eddie Brown tripped Howard, and so Elvis Grbac's pass fell incomplete. No penalty was called, and U-M lost its No. 1 ranking.

11. November 3, 2001: The "Spartan Bob Game." Michigan State quarterback Jeff Smoker hit T.J. Duckett for the game-winning touchdown on a play that UM fans will forever swear should not have taken place, because time should have expired. They will also forever swear that UM defensive end Shantee Orr was blatantly held on the play. They will forever swear, period. But they can't change the final score: Michigan State 26, Michigan 24.

10. December 9, 1997, wrestler Jeff Reese dies while training. In terms of tragedy, of course this would be No. 1. Reese was trying to cut weight and died as a result. The only reason it isn't higher on the list is that Michigan helped secure quick changes to the NCAA's weight-loss guidelines.

9. September 1, 2007: Appalachian State 34, Michigan 32. There have been bigger upsets in college football history. But none triggered such ridicule. The fifth-ranked Wolverines woke up in the morning hoping to win the national title and then lost to the I-AA national champs. UM fans will hear about this one for years.

8. January 1, 1979: USC 17, Michigan 10. Bo Schembechler was still looking for his first Rose Bowl win and felt he should have gotten it this day. USC tailback Charles White scored the decisive touchdown . . . well, no, he didn't. White fumbled at least two yards before he reached the end zone, as television replays showed. But the zebras gave White the TD, and third-ranked USC ended up with the win and a share of the national title that could have gone to the fifth-ranked Wolverines. The loss epitomized a decade worth of bowl frustrations for Michigan fans.

7. September 24, 1994: Colorado 27, Michigan 26. How brutal was this? If Michael Westbrook had just dropped Kordell Stewart's Hail Mary pass, Michigan would have been 3-0, with wins over two top-ten teams (Colorado and Notre Dame). Two days after Westbrook's catch, somebody asked UM coach Gary Moeller when he would get over it. He said it was "a lifetime thing." No kidding.

6. January 18, 2001: "And most especially. . . ." On the day Jim Tressel was hired as Ohio State's football coach, the Buckeyes happened to be hosting Michigan in basketball. Tressel addressed the crowd and promised that OSU fans would be proud of their team "in the classroom, in the community and most especially in 310 days in Ann Arbor, Michigan." UM had won 10 of 13 matchups before Tressel's hiring. Since then, Ohio State is 6-1 against Michigan.

5. November 18, 2006: Ohio State 42, Michigan 39. The day before the most hyped regular-season game in college football history, Bo Schembechler died. The second-ranked Wolverines played valiantly but lost, costing themselves a shot at the national championship. The fact that top-ranked Ohio State ended up losing to Florida in the title game made it a little more palatable for UM fans. But only a little.

4. January 1, 1970: Michigan loses the Rose Bowl—and almost loses its coach. First-year coach Bo Schembechler missed the game because of a heart attack and the Wolverines took the field without knowing if their coach was still alive. He would survive, of course, and coach for another two decades. But the Wolverines would never forget the horror of that day (and would always wonder if they would have beaten Southern California with a healthy Bo.)

3. November 25, 1973: "The Vote." Bo Schembechler arrived for the taping of his TV show in Detroit in a great mood. He left in a rage that would last for years. Michigan had tied Ohio State, 10-10, the day before, leaving both teams with no losses and one tie for the year. Since OSU had gone to the Rose Bowl the year before, both Schembechler and Woody Hayes assumed Michigan would get the nod. Big Ten athletic directors voted 6-4 to send Ohio State. Until the week he died, Schembechler said he would never forgive them.

2. January 13, 1907: Michigan withdraws from the Western Conference. Football coach Fielding Yost was scuffling with the conference that would become the Big Ten over proposed rules changes. Yost let his ego get the better of him. He thought the conference needed Michigan more than Michigan needed the conference. So the Wolverines withdrew, then struggled to find teams they could play, let alone beat. The school came crawling back to the league in 1917.

1. November 7, 2002: "A day of great shame." Those were the words of Michigan president Mary Sue Coleman when the school admitted to major violations in its men's basketball program. Most of an era was erased from the record books, banners were taken down and penalties were meted out. This, by the way, is why Chris Webber's famous timeout in the 1993 NCAA championship game is NOT on the list. In retrospect, UM was fortunate to lose the game. Otherwise, the Wolverines would have had to forfeit a national championship.

Michigan hockey is more than just "Hockeytown" and the Red Wings. The state has produced some of the top hockey players to represent the U.S. and play in the NHL. Here are the ten best.

10. Jimmy Carson (Grosse Pointe). Before being traded to Edmonton in the 1988 Wayne Gretzky deal, he established himself as a 55-goal scorer for the Los Angeles Kings. He was only 19 at the time.

9. Derian Hatcher (Sterling Heights). At 35, Hatcher is still one of the NHL's most intimidating defenseman because of his size, strength and willingness to use his 6-foot-5, 240-pound body as a weapon of mass destruction.

8. Brian Rolston (Ann Arbor). The superb defensive forward and first-rate skater has a booming shot and rink savvy that makes him one of the NHL's top penalty killers, as well as maybe the best all-around American player in the NHL today.

7. Doug Weight (Warren). A smart, gritty player known for his slick passing, Weight has been one of America's top players for the better part of two decades.

6. Brian Rafalski (Dearborn). Unwanted after a standout college career at Wisconsin, Rafalski had to take his talents to Europe. Once given a chance in the NHL, Rafalski developed into one of the league's premium defenseman,

5. Mark Howe (Detroit). The son of Gordie Howe was a U.S. Olympian at age 16, a dynamic World Hockey Association star at 18 and an NHL star in his 20s and 30s. He was a 42-goal scorer and 100-point winger before moving to defense.

4. Ken Morrow (Flint). Durable and efficient, Morrow was a rock on the 1980 U.S. Olympic gold medal team and four New York Islanders Stanley Cup teams from 1980-83. A member of the U.S. Hockey Hall of Fame, Morrow is remembered most for his technical proficiency and toughness.

3. John Vanbiesbrouck (Detroit). With 374 NHL wins, Vanbiesbrouck is generally considered one of the top American-born goalies ever to play in the NHL. "Beezer" won the Vezina Trophy as the NHL's top goalie in 1986 and his brilliant performances allowed the Florida Panthers to reach the 1996 Stanley Cup Finals. Although he played for five NHL teams, he is remembered most for his days with the New York Rangers.

2. Pat Lafontaine (Waterford). Lafontaine left home at 17 to play for Verdun of the Quebec Major Junior Hockey League. His 104 goals and 130 assists in a single season caught the attention of scouts. The flashy center went on to become star for the New York Islanders and Buffalo Sabres. A two-time 50-goal scorer, Lafontaine was usually the most dangerous player on the ice.

1. Mike Modano (Westland). One of the most magnificent skaters in NHL history, Modano has used his speed and overflowing skill to become the league's top American-born scorer. Still playing for the Dallas Stars, Modano is the face of hockey in the United States.

Note: Since he became Commissioner of the Central Collegiate Hockey Association (CCHA) in 1998, Anastos has increased the CCHA's visibility through innovative television and radio deals and by spearheading "Hockey Day in Michigan"—which evolved into "Hockey Weekend Across America." The Dearborn native was a four-year letter winner at Michigan State and is President of the Hockey Commissioners' Association and also serves on USA Hockey's board of directors.

10. Chris Kunitz, Ferris State (1999-2003). Kunitz was an offensive juggernaut for the Bulldogs. In 152 career games, he had 99 goals, 76 assists for 175 total points. Now with the Anaheim Ducks, he holds FSU's single-season scoring record with 35 goals and 44 assists for 79 points.

9. Mike Liut, Bowling Green (1973-77). Liut was the first CCHA goalie to make his mark in the NHL. A heady player, he defined the term "student athlete."

8. George McPhee, Bowling Green (1978-82). Now the GM of the Washington Capitals, he won the Hobey Baker award as college hockey's best player in 1982. Since he's become a top-flight hockey executive, his on-ice accomplishments tend to get overlooked.

7. Kip Miller, Michigan State (1986-90). Miller won the Hobey Baker in 1990 when he led the nation in scoring for the second consecutive season, tallying an astounding 101 points (48 goals and 53 assists).

6. Ryan Miller, Michigan State (1999-2002). Became only the second goalie in NCAA history to win the Hobey Baker in 2001, 11 years after his cousin Kip captured the award. Miller's 2000-01 season was the best in NCAA history, with him going 31-5-4 while posting a 1.32 GAA, a .950 save percentage and notching 10 shutouts.

5. Marty Turco, Michigan (1994-98). He backstopped Michigan to two national championships (1996 and '98). The Dallas Star netminder still holds the NCAA record for career victories with 127.

4. Rob Blake, Bowling Green (1987-90). He holds Bowling Green's single-season record for goals for a defenseman with 23. Blake became a star in the NHL and will one day be in the Hockey Hall of Fame.

3. Nelson Emerson, Bowling Green (1986-90). A great college player that had a good NHL career, Emerson remains the Falcons record holder for assists (182) and points (294).

2. Brendan Morrison, Michigan (1993-97). The first Wolverine to win the Hobey Baker, Morrison's overtime goal in the 1996 national championship game against Colorado College gave UM its first title sine 1964. He finished his career with 284 points in 155 games played.

1. Ken Morrow, Bowling Green (1975–79). A big, tough, and smart defense-man, Morrow was the anchor on a BG team that had a 23-game undefeated streak during the 1978-79 campaign. Morrow was the first All-American player for his school and for the CCHA. He also is the first player to win an Olympic gold medal and the Stanley Cup in the same year, accomplishing the feat in 1980.

Note: Since his Red Wings debut on October 15, 1993, Detroit goalie Chris Osgood has been a Motor City favorite. Second on the Wings all-time career victories list with 279, he's stopped a lot of rubber over the years. "Ozzie" split his list into wrist shots and slap shots. He explains the differences between them:

"A slapshot takes longer to get off, but given time it's a lot heavier of a shot. A wrist shot is a quicker shot that many forwards will use in close from the hash marks in, because they can get it off quicker."

Which shot is hardest to face?

"I'd say the slapshot, but a wrister is more accurate because it's less of a wind-up and usually you're closer to the net." The great and powerful OZ has spoken.

Ozzie's Top Five Slap Shots:

5. Mike Modano. He has a fast release, and he usually shoots it when he's skating in stride, which adds to its heaviness. He has a really hard shot, it's just quick and he's a big powerful guy that leans on it quite a bit. It's also very accurate and fast.

4. Adrian Aucoin. I played with him on Long Island and he has a cannon. It's more of a wicked shot, it's not as accurate as other guys but it's very heavy. If he's going to score, he's going to beat the goalie through his pads or through the arms because of the heaviness of his shot.

3. Mathieu Schneider. Schneider has a real hard shot. He kind of takes a half slapper, it's not a full shot but he gets a lot of power. It's a hard shot and he can really bring it high and hard. Out of all the slapshots, his is the most accurate.

2. Al Iafrate. He had a rocket of a shot. I remember in Toronto guys were feeding him one-timers and he just leaned into it. He's such a big guy. I think that was the main thing, Iafrate was just so big and strong that he'd fire off these rockets. Man, he could bring it too.

1. Al MacInnis. He always used a wood stick; he never changed to the newer sticks that all the young guys use nowadays. It was deadly. He could get it off in a short amount of time and it was just hard and wicked whether it rose or dropped. It was never on an even plain for a goalie, so you really had to get your entire body in front of it.

Ozzie's Top Five Wrist Shots:

5. Jaromir Jagr. He leans on his shot and he has a wicked curve on his stick. When he's coming down on the wing with his long stick he leans into his shot, which gives him a lot of whip, so it rises fast and hard.

4. Sergei Fedorov. I've never seen a guy score more from the blueline or just inside the blueline with a wrist shot than Sergei. It's as hard as some guys' slap shots. It's because he'd shoot it in full stride and he's such a great skater that when he lets it go, it's a missile.

3. Alex Kovalev. Some of the best hands in the game today. With those great hands, he sort of shoots it like Jagr does, off the toe. It's a quick, hard release. He beats a lot of goalies because they're not ready for it. He more or less snaps it by them.

2. Joe Sakic. Joe's wrist shot is great because he's very accurate. He shoots from everywhere, whereas a lot of guys will only have one or two spots where they shoot from. It's a really hard, fast, quick release. Without question, he has one of the greatest wrist-snap shots of all time.

1. Brett Hull. "Hullie" has a great wrist shot. It's unbelievable. A quick snapper. He has such big forearms and wrists. Not only is it the hardest wrist shot I've ever faced, it's also very, very, accurate. You never had to worry about him hitting you in the head, because it was going into the corners every time. He would get so much flex on his stick that he'd lean right into it and just let it whip through. It's comparable to a pitcher pitching a baseball, when his arm whips back and comes through with great velocity; Brett's the same way.

Toughest Hitters to Get Out When the Game Is on the Line :: Todd Jones

Note: Reliever Todd Jones ranks as the Detroit Tigers all-time saves leader. Jones pitched for the Tigers from 1997–2001 before rejoining the team in 2006. He has notched over 300 career saves in his Major League career. Nicknamed "The Roller Coaster" for all the scares he gives fans, Todd is one of the sports world's all-time good guys.

6. Albert Pujols. As he takes you deep, he's such a nice guy he might feel bad for you.

5. Barry Bonds. Just go ahead and walk him. Nobody can protect him in a lineup.

4. Joe Mauer. Might want to walk him to get to Justin Morneau.

3. Vladimir Guerrero. Can hit any pitch hard from shoe-level to face-high.

2. Derek Jeter. Real pro. Won't strike him out when it matters. You better get him to hit it to someone.

1. Jim Thome. His numbers speak for themselves.

Great baseball players tend to enjoy longer careers than top players in any other major team sport. But the primes of these guys didn't last long enough to extend into their time with the Tigers.

Honorable Mentions: Babe Herman, Dean Chance, Lloyd Moseby, Dwayne Murphy, Ruben Sierra, Luis Polonia and Todd Van Poppel

5. Steve Avery. The Trenton, Michigan native was a high-school phenom, earning selection as the third overall pick by the Atlanta Braves in the 1988 draft. After a 3-11 rookie campaign, the lefthander went 47-25 over the next three seasons. Avery became the youngest player to win a playoff game in 1991 and set the NLCS playoffs record of 22 1/3 scoreless innings the following year, then gained an All-Star Game selection the year after that. His career began to unravel after suffering an injury late in the 1993 season. After poor stints in Boston and Cincinnati and three years out of the Majors, Avery returned to the bigs as a member of the Tigers for the club's infamous 119-loss season of 2003. Avery pitched in 19 games that year, all out of the bullpen. But his record was a perfect 2-0, making him one of only three Tigers pitchers to post a winning record that season. And those two wins prevented the Tigers from breaking the 1962 Mets' all-time record for losses in a single season. But with a 5.63 ERA to go along with his two Ws, 2003 proved to be Avery's last year in the Major Leagues.

4. Eric Davis. The outfielder is best known for his early years with the Cincinnati Reds when he won selections to two All-Star Games, three Gold Gloves and a World Series over the A's in 1990. Davis homered off Dave Stewart in his first at–bat in that World Series, then lacerated his kidney diving for a ball in the outfield. His feud with Reds owner Marge Schott over his treatment by the team following the injury is legendary, as the Reds left him behind in Oakland. He joined the Tigers from the Dodgers on August 31, 1993. Davis did manage to hit six homers and drive in 15 runs in 23 games that September. But it wasn't enough as the Tigers finished third. The Tigers re-signed him for the following season, but Davis struggled, hitting just .183 with five home runs in 120 at-bats while battling through a disc injury in his neck. He retired after the season, but came back to rejoin the Reds in 1996, belting 26 home runs and driving in 83 while batting .287. Davis saw his following season shortened by a battle with colon cancer. Then in '98, he went to Baltimore, where he hit 28 home runs. Injuries limited his playing time in subsequent years and he retired after the 2001 season.

3. Billy Ripken. Cal's little brother enjoyed some productive years with Baltimore, leading the Orioles with a .291 batting average in 1990. He left the Orioles in '93 for Texas, went to Cleveland after a couple seasons, then back to the Orioles and back to the Rangers for brief stints. Ripken then signed as a free agent with Detroit in December of 1997. He hit .274 in 74 at-bats while serving as a utility infielder for the Tigers before being released in July, ending his Major League career

2. Fred Lynn. In 1975, Fred Lynn became the only player in baseball history to win MVP and Rookie of the Year honors in the same season. Paired with Jim Rice, Lynn also led the Boston Red Sox to the American League pennant. He played in six consecutive All-Star games and won four Gold Gloves as an outfielder for Boston, then was traded for the 1981 season to the California Angels, where he added three more All-Star appearances to his streak. His career was hampered by injuries, many of which occurred by diving for balls and crashing into walls. He signed with Baltimore in 1985 and hit 23 home runs in three consecutive seasons. The Tigers picked up Lynn for the 1988 home stretch, hoping his left-handed bat could propel them to the division title. Lynn did manage to hit seven home runs in his 27 games here, but batted just .222 and the Tigers finished one game behind Boston for the division title. He played all of the Tigers' brutal 103-loss season in 1989, hitting .241 with just 11 dingers and 46 RBI. He finished out his career with San Diego in 1990.

1. Bill Madlock. Oh, could the man nicknamed "Mad Dog" hit. Madlock won four National League batting titles, including back-to–back ones in 1975 and '76 with the Cubs. After a brief stint in San Francisco, Madlock found success in Pittsburgh as part of the "We Are Family" 1979 world champion Pirates. He won two more batting titles with the Pirates before being sent to the Dodgers during the 1985 season. Highlights of his time in L.A. included three home runs in the 1985 NLCS against the Cardinals. He was released by the Dodgers in May of 1987 and signed with the Tigers the following month. Madlock had several landmark moments during that 1987 season, including hitting back-to-back-to-back home runs with John Grubb and Matt Nokes in June and helping the Tigers wrap up the division title on the last day of the season over Toronto (where he'd received death threats after a hard slide into the Blue Jays' Tony Fernandez earlier in the month). Madlock ended up hitting .279 with 14 homers and 50 RBI that season. He was hitless in the disappointing ALCS loss to the Minnesota Twins, which marked the end of his career. Madlock did return to the Tigers as a coach during the 2000-01 seasons.

My Top Ten Broadcast Moments :: Ernie Harwell

Note: The words of Ernie Harwell, longtime Tigers broadcaster still resonate for those of us who had the privilege of hearing him. Here are the broadcast memories that still resonate loudest for Ernie.

10. My last day on the job, September 29, 2002. I closed out my career with a broadcast from Toronto. A bittersweet time for me.

9. The Tigers' 1984 World Series victory. Alan Trammel turned in a great MVP performance and Kirk Gibson climaxed the good times with his homer off Goose Gossage in the final game at Tiger Stadium.

8. My first All-Star broadcast. I worked on *NBC* radio with Bob Neal. The AL won the 1958 game on a hot, muggy day in Baltimore.

7. Milt Wilcox's near-perfecto in 1983. One of the best-pitched games I've ever seen. Wilcox was one out away from a perfect game when White Sox pinch-hitter Jerry Hairston lined a single through the box. Oh, so close.

6. My first World Series in 1964. The Dodgers, led by Sandy Koufax and Don Drysdale, swept the Yankees in four games. And I was paid on a per-game basis. My voice from that series was used in the movie, *One Flew Over the Cuckoo's Nest*.

5. Jack Morris' no-hitter. Jack's classic happened at Comiskey Park in early April of 1984. After blanking the White Sox, he came up for an interview in our radio booth, still in his spikes.

4. My first big league broadcast, August 4, 1948. It was a night game at Ebbets Field in Brooklyn. I was replacing Red Barber as Dodgers announcer in mid-season. My debut had been delayed 24 hours by rain and I was super nervous. Jackie Robinson stole home in first inning and the Dodgers beat the Cubs.

3. Bucky Dent's 1978 home run. One of the blackest moments in the history of the Red Sox nation. Bucky's fly reached the Green Monster and his three-run homer won the single-game AL East Division playoff for the Yankees.

2. Jim Northrup's triple, 1968. This was the blow that won the World Series for the Tigers. In the seventh inning of the seventh game, Jim tripled over the head of Cardinal centerfielder Curt Flood, driving home Willie Horton and Norm Cash. The hit broke up a scoreless pitching duel between Mickey Lolich and Bob Gibson and sent the Detroiters on to the championship.

1. Bob Thomson's "Shot Heard 'Round the World." I was on *NBC-TV* when Thomson hit the historic three-run homer to beat the Brooklyn Dodgers in the third and final game of the 1951 National League playoffs. My partner Russ Hodges became famous with his radio call of this home run. On TV in those days, we had no replays, no taping, and no record of my broadcast. Only my wife Lulu and I know I was broadcasting that game on TV.

Note: Samuelsen has worked at WDFN since the station first went on the air in 1994 and hosted various versions of the station's morning show since 1999. Many critics, including some who are now actually heard on the station, laughed at the suggestion that WDFN would have any staying power. Here are some highlights from the WDFN's first 14 years on the air.

10. The First Stoney and Wojo Radiothon. Stoney and Wojo (Mike Stone and Bob Wojnowski) started their annual Radiothon back in 1998. It has raised over a million dollars for the Leukemia and Lymphoma Society of America. Nobody knew what to expect the first year, but the event raised over $100,000 as they broadcast for 18 hours straight. The highlight was the on-air "tournament" to select the Greatest Bob of all-time. The winner was late WDIV reporter Bob Bennett, who came on with Stoney and Wojo the next day. He seemed truly touched by the honor.

9. Pistons win the NBA Title. For years, WDFN tried to get the broadcast rights to a major team. In 2001, the Pistons signed on. That coincided with the rebirth of Pistons basketball culminating with the title in 2004. WDFN broadcast all the games and Stoney interviewed Kid Rock in the victorious Pistons locker room, leading to Kid's memorable line, "Hey dude, I'm just trying to get laid."

8. Jim Rome Tour Stop, 2003. Rome had flirted with a tour stop in Detroit for years and finally committed to it. Nobody, not even Rome, knew what to expect. But thousands of listeners tailgated in the Palace parking lot and filed into the building for the "epic" event. A highlight was the overwhelming response for the appearance of Ernie Harwell on stage. Rome returned to the air the following Monday, his voice hoarse, and proclaimed to listeners nationwide that the Detroit tour stop ranked as one of the top three he had ever done.

7. Gregg hits Jamie with a baseball. Jamie Samuelsen and Gregg Henson (Hosts of "The "Jamie and Gregg Show") got into a debate one day on whether or not a Major League player could get out of the way of a pitch if he knew the pitcher was throwing at him. The argument escalated to the point where Gregg said he could hit Jamie with a pitch. They "took it outside" and Henson nailed him in the thigh with his second pitch. Wojo memorably called the action over the phone and it was broadcast on the station. "He hit him!" Wojo screeched.

6. "I'm shaving my P----." "The Jamie and Brady Show" (Samuelsen and Greg Brady) was playing an on-air game where a man called his wife even though she didn't know the segment was being broadcast. She was in the shower and when he asked what she was doing, she responded matter of factly, "I'm shaving my p----." For some reason, the call was left on the air, which may not have made the FCC happy, but it made for memorable radio.

5. Stoney's Cell Phone. Stoney and Wojo were having a casual conversation one day about Alex Rodriguez and Stoney gave out the number for listeners to call in: 248-860-1130. One problem. That's not the call-in line. That was Stoney's personal cell phone. Wojo realized Stoney's error first and pointed it out, but it was too late. From that point on, they kept checking the voice mail which filled up in about two minutes with listeners gleefully telling Stoney what he had done wrong. He had a new cell phone number the next day, which, as of now, remains private.

4. Wings win the Stanley Cup in 1997. Art Regner gained radio fame in Detroit for his unrelenting criticism of the Lions and his unwavering praise of the Red Wings. His "Go Wings" became a rallying cry for giddy fans who called into the "Icetime" show on WDFN throughout the Cup run. When the Wings finally finished off the Flyers, Art stayed on the air all night. He was joined by random WDFN staffers who staggered back to the studios and by such victorious Wings as Martin LaPointe, who called into the show on his way to a team party.

3. The Millen Man March. Sean Baligian orchestrated this Matt Millen protest outside of Ford Field in December of 2005. More than a thousand fans marched, carrying signs, wearing orange (in honor of the visiting Cincinnati Bengals) and screaming for the ouster of Lions' CEO Matt Millen. The protest gained national attention, but Millen somehow still survives as CEO.

2. Chris Webber calls in unannounced. After Steve Fisher was fired as Michigan's basketball coach in 1997, the calls went out to all of the Fab Five to try to get them on the air. Only Webber responded. He called in, quite unexpectedly, to "The Jamie and Gregg Show." He intended to just say his piece and defend Fisher, but got very defensive when questioned about his relationship with Michigan booster Ed Martin. Webber ripped off lines like, "You're making yourself look very asinine right now. Don't do that" and "Who are you? What are you going to do for me?" They still get played today on WDFN.

1. Battles with the Detroit Lions. Not a moment, but an ongoing theme. The Lions and *WDFN* have battled for years. Why would the Lions not like the station? Hmmmm. The great Don Swindell and his Mr. Ford impression. "The Sunday Afternoon Sit-In" hosted by Regner and Henson, which lambasted the Lions after every Sunday loss. The Millen Man March. The parody songs ("Isn't it Moronic?" and "Oh, Mister Ford"). The drops, the drops, the drops. The Lions expressed their displeasure on many occasions, even once threatening to revoke WDFN's press credentials. Former Lions wide receiver Johnnie Morton actually challenged reporter Jon Bloom to a game of "Smear the Queer" between Lions players and WDFN staffers. But cooler heads always prevailed and the two sides have maintained a (normally) professional relationship.

Over the years, the Lions have imported a number of players with great pro football resumes and turned them into roster footnotes. The list of victims is so long and impressive that narrowing it to five proved almost impossible. But we gave it our best shot.

Honorable Mentions: D.J.Dozier, Mike Bass, Eric Davis, Russel Erxleben, Rich Karlis, Dave Kopay, Brock Marion, Jim O'Brien, Pat Summerall and Gene Washington.

5. Hugh McElhenny. Equally formidable as a running back and receiver, "The King" made six Pro Bowls in 12 seasons with the 49ers, Vikings and Giants, racking up over 11,000 all-purpose yards. The future Hall of Famer didn't even get into triple figures with the Lions. After coming to Detroit in 1964, McElhenny gained just 48 yards on 22 carries and caught five balls for 16 yards. He retired rather than try a second season here.

4. Jimmie Giles. Giles established himself as one of the top tight ends of the early 1980s with the Tampa Bay Buccaneers. A terrific receiver and rugged blocker, Giles earned All-Pro and Pro Bowl selections in 1980-82 and 1985. He came to Detroit in 1986, catching just 19 passes for three touchdowns. After catching just six passes in four games the following season, he was traded to Philadelphia.

3. James Wilder. For most of the 1980s, James Wilder ran wild for Tampa Bay, eclipsing the 1000-yard rushing mark in two different seasons. In 1984, Wilder came within 16 yards of setting the record for total yards in a season. He was picked up by Washington, then traded to the Lions for the affable Eric Williams at the beginning of the 1990 season. He rushed for 51 yards on 11 carries and scored one touchdown on one of his eight receptions during his one season here. He never played again.

2. Pepper Johnson. The Detroit McKenzie High product was a great linebacker at Ohio State and enjoyed pro success in New York, making two Pro Bowls and winning the Super Bowl his 1986 rookie season and again four years later. He later played for the Cleveland Browns, before signing with the Lions for the 1996 season. He started 11 games here, but left the following year and finished his playing career back in New York with the Jets.

1. Anthony Carter. Anthony Carter left the University of Michigan as arguably its best football player ever. A three-time All-American, he was named to the College Football Hall of Fame in 2001. He joined the Michigan Panthers of the USFL in 1983 and led them to the championship. When the USFL folded, his rights were traded from Miami to Minnesota, where he made three Pro Bowls, He signed with the Lions before the 1994 season, but battled injuries and caught just eight passes, three for touchdowns. Carter played in just three games the following year and did not catch a pass, then retired.

A lot of guys who spent time on the Pistons' roster over the decades have been forgotten by most fans. You just wouldn't expect to have forgotten guys of this stature. But I bet you did.

Honorable Mentions: Lionel Hollins, Archie Clark, Stacy Augmon, Alvin Robertson, Joe Smith and Gerald Henderson.

5. Cedric Ceballos. The Pistons picked up the man who won the 1992 NBA Slam Dunk Contest blindfolded with John Wallace and Eric Murdock from Dallas in exchange for Terry Mills and Christian Laettner in August of 2000. Ceballos could have robbed banks blindfolded and it would have been a steal for the Pistons because they got rid of Laettner's contract in the deal. Ceballos averaged 20 points a game in two seasons en route to a career average of over 14 points per game. But he was a malcontent here and averaged just 5.8 points in 13 games before being dealt to Miami for a second-round pick.

4. Jeff Ruland. Ruland enjoyed four seasons of averaging a double-double with the Washington Bullets in the early 1980s, teaming with Rick Mahorn to form the original McFilthy and McNasty duo. A devastating knee injury undermined his career, which ended here in 1993 when Ruland played in 11 games, scoring five points in 55 minutes.

3. Darrell Walker. A childhood friend of Isiah Thomas from Chicago, Walker was acquired from Washington in 1991 and averaged five points per game. He played in just nine games the following year for the Pistons before leaving to finish out his career with his hometown Bulls

2. Darryl Dawkins. "Chocolate Thunder" was actually one of the Bad Boys. Well, technically, that is. Dawkins was picked up from Utah for cash and a second-round pick in November of 1987. He played in just two games that season and made it into 14 games as the Pistons won the NBA title the next season. Unfortunately, he was not around for the playoffs, so he never got a ring. Even at the end of his career, the man from the planet Lovetron could still put a smile on everyone's face. I fondly remember him joking with kids and ballboys before, after and during Pistons games.

1. Danny Manning. The man who led Larry Brown's Kansas team to the 1988 NCAA title finished out his NBA career in Detroit after the Pistons picked up the 36-year-old in February of 2003 as a frontcourt insurance policy. He averaged almost six minutes a game in the 13 he played in here. He actually got some mop-up time in four playoffs games, as well. As fate would have it, his NBA career ended when he played the last four minutes of the fourth and final game of the New Jersey Nets' sweep of the Pistons in the Eastern Conference Finals. Speaking of fate, the game was also coach Rick Carlisle's last as Piston's head coach. He was replaced by Manning's old college coach Brown, who led the Pistons to the NBA title—but without Danny Manning.

When it comes to basketball, around here it's Deeeeee-troiiiiit Baaaaaaassss-ket-ball! Like John Mason's stamp on Detroit, these players have put their stamp on the game. Here are the best players in Pistons' history.

Honorable Mentions: Grant Hill, Gene Shue, Richard Hamilton, Bailey Howell, Ben Wallace.

10. Chauncey Billups. Since signing with Detroit in the summer of 2002, "Mr. Big Shot" has become the face of the franchise, combining excellent ballhandling with clutch shooting. Chauncey was named the 2004 Finals MVP, helping win the franchise's third NBA championship. Chauncey since has earned multiple trips to the All-Star Game as well as All-NBA and All-Defense honors.

9. George Yardley. Often considered the best player on the early Pistons, "Bird" was the first player in NBA history to score 2,000 points in a season. In his first three seasons, Yardley led the Ft. Wayne Pistons into two NBA Finals, but a championship eluded him. Hall of Famer Dolph Schayes described Yardley as a scoring machine, and his NBA averages reflect that assessment. In 1996, George was inducted into the Basketball Hall of Fame.

8. Vinnie Johnson. The super-sub embodied the Pistons belief in team play over individual achievement. Danny Ainge gave him his "Microwave" nickname because Vinnie was able to heat up the game in a hurry. Vinnie was one of Detroit's most clutch shooters in the Bad Boys era. He hit the game-winning shot in Game 5 of the 1990 NBA Finals with 0.07 seconds remaining, earning him the alternate nickname of "007."

7. Dave DeBusschere. Dave was born and raised in the Detroit area, attending Austin Catholic and the University of Detroit. He was selected as a territorial pick by the Detroit Pistons prior to the 1962 NBA Draft. Dave became an instant success, earning All-Rookie honors with his tough interior defense and rebounding. He also pitched for the Chicago White Sox at this time, playing both pro basketball and baseball until 1965. Dave was also a player/coach for the Pistons from '64-67, and at the age of 24, he became the youngest head coach in NBA history. Dave was selected as one of the NBA's 50 greatest players in its first 50 years from a panel of experts in 1996 and was inducted into the Basketball Hall of Fame in 1983.

6. Dennis Rodman. If there were a statistic for energy, Dennis would have led it every year. Dennis's wriggly, energetic style quickly endeared him to Pistons fans. "The Worm" was selected out of Southwestern Oklahoma State in the second round of the 1986 NBA Draft. Chuck Daly helped shape him into one of the league's best defenders and rebounders. Dennis grabbed 11,954 rebounds and finished in the top twenty in NBA history for that statistic. Rodman earned two Defensive Player of the Year awards while with the Pistons, and over his career, Dennis earned eight All-Defense team honors.

5. Bill Laimbeer. In 1991, Hudson Soft released a video game called "Bill Laimbeer's Combat Basketball." In the game, one was encouraged to push, shove, tackle, and shoot one's way to basketball success. For many a Pistons fan, this game is a coveted treat, for it is an amusing artistic interpretation of what Bad Boys era basketball was. Bill was the consummate tough guy on the court, employing physical defense and many veteran tricks to great success. "Lambs" played 937 games and 30,602 minutes for the Pistons, ranking him third overall in both categories. Bill played 685 consecutive games before a suspension broke the streak. Laimbeer is the Pistons career offensive, defensive and total rebound leader with 9,430. His #40, is retired by the Pistons.

4. Bob Lanier. As Detroit's most dominant big man, the 6-11 Lanier had a rare combination of physical power with finesse. Detroit selected Bob with the 1st overall pick in the 1970 NBA Draft. From 1970 to 1980, Lanier played for the Pistons, averaging 22.7 points per game, 11.8 rebounds, 2.0 blocks, and 3.3 assists. Bob has the highest Pistons player efficiency rating at 22.8. In 1992, Bob was inducted into the Basketball Hall of Fame.

3. Dave Bing. The second overall pick in the 1966 NBA Draft, Dave won the NBA's Rookie of the Year honor. Over his career, Dave was selected to seven All-Star-Games. He averaged 22.6 points per game and 6.4 assists while playing over 26,052 minutes for the Pistons. In the 1971-1972 pre-season, Happy Hairston collided with Dave Bing, poking his right eye. Dave had to undergo surgery to repair a detached retina from the injury. The decrease in vision in both eyes didn't stop Dave from playing another seven seasons. In 1990, Dave was inducted into the Basketball Hall of Fame and was selected in 1996 as one of the NBA's 50 greatest players in its first 50 years.

2. Joe Dumars. Despite playing on Pistons squads known as the Bad Boys, Joe was the embodiment of sportsmanship. In 1996, an NBA Sportsmanship Award was created, and named in his honor. Joe became famous for his exceptional defense against the legendary Michael Jordan. Joe was selected by the Pistons with the 18th overall pick in the 1985 NBA Draft. He was a great player from the beginning, earning the All-Rookie NBA honor. His hard work paid off over the years and he racked up multiple All-NBA and All-Defense honors. In 14 seasons, Joe played in 1,018 games, appearing in more contests than any other Piston. Dumars scored 16,401 points, which is the second among the all-timers. Dumars was inducted into the Basketball Hall of Fame.

1. Isiah Thomas. He was the best Pistons player to play the game, and he was one of the best point guards in NBA history. With lightning-quick drives to the basket, fearless decisions in traffic, and great range on his jumper, Isiah was the leader of the Bad Boys era clubs, helping the Pistons win the franchise's first two championships in 1989 and 1990. He leads or ranks among the top Pistons in almost every statistical category. Isiah also leads the fellow all-timers with number of nicknames. He has been known as "Zeke," his most famous nickname. In addition Isiah was known by "Cuts" for the numerous cuts he would suffer while driving the lane, as well as "The Baby-Faced Assassin" for his youthful appearance and deadly shooting skill. Thomas was selected second overall by Detroit in the 1981 NBA Draft. Isiah quickly showed himself to be of superstar quality, earning All-Rookie honors and a trip to the 1982 All-Star Game. Isiah was selected to 12 consecutive All-Star Games, with the last being in 1993. Thomas was the 1990 NBA Finals MVP, averaging 27.6 points per game while dishing 7 assists and collecting 5.2 rebounds per game in that series. In 2000, Thomas was inducted into the Basketball Hall of Fame. In 1996, Isiah was selected as one of the NBA's 50 greatest players.

My Ten Favorite Magic Tricks :: Flip Saunders

Note: Saunders is what you would call a basketball lifer. After playing for the University of Minnesota, the Cleveland native began a coaching career in 1977 that took him around the Midwest and Great Plains to everywhere from Golden Valley Lutheran College in Minneapolis to the University of Tulsa to South Dakota, where he coached the CBA's Rapid City Thrillers. After winning two CBA titles, Saunders got his chance in the big time in 1995 when he was named head coach of the Minnesota Timberwolves. He led them to eight playoff berths, including a spot in the 2003–04 Western Conference Finals. The following season, he succeeded Larry Brown as the 25th head coach of the Detroit Pistons, guiding them to a franchise record 64 wins in the regular season in his first year and a trip to the Eastern Conference Finals. His Pistons posted 50-plus win regular seasons in the following two years, before he was fired after losing the Conference Finals to Boston in 2008. Saunders has been a fan of magic since childhood and here are his favorite tricks.

10. Pick a Card. A card is picked out of the deck randomly and then replaced in the deck. Then after failing to pick the right card three times, the magician pulls out a giant replica of the card originally picked.

9. Floating Dollar Bill. A dollar bill is shown and it floats around in front of the body and all around the arms and head.

8. Disappearing Card. Show a card and then throw the card into the air, where it disappears, only to be brought back.

7. Needle Thru Arm. Take a needle and push it through your forearm. Show your arm with the needle in it and a little blood oozing out. Then pull needle through and wipe the arm clean. No cuts or bruises.

6. Needle Thru Balloon. Take a giant needle and push it through a balloon. The balloon doesn't break. Then toss the balloon up in the air and touch it with the same needle, popping it.

5. One-to-100. Take a $1 bill and fold it up. Then unfold the bill and it has magically turned into a $100 dollar bill.

4. Disappearing Hanky. You show a hanky in one hand and shove it into the other hand and it vanishes and then you bring it back from an audience member's ear.

3. Self-tying Shoelace. Show your shoes with untied shoelaces, then shake your leg, with the shoelaces tying themselves right in front of everyone's eyes without you even touching them.

2. Hopping Halves. A half-dollar is shown, then it jumps from one hand to the other and at the end of the trick it turns into a Mexican peso, then back into a half-dollar.

1. Torn and Restored Newspaper. A paper is shown to the audience, then torn up into pieces. Then it reappears, fully restored.

Top Ten University of Detroit Mercy Men's Basketball Players :: Matt Dery

Note: A WDFN staple since 1996, Dery has served as the play-by-play voice of the UDM Titans for the past ten seasons.

10. Jermaine Jackson, 1996-1999. The two-time Horizon League All-Conference player and 1999 Conference Player of the Year led Titans to two NCAA tourneys, then played five years in the NBA.

9. Norm Swanson, 1950-1953. The 1952 and 1953 All-American led the team in scoring for three straight seasons and played one year in the NBA with the Rochester Royals.

8. Archie Tullos, 1985-1988. Put up four 40-plus-point games in his career, including a school record 49 vs. Bradley in 1988. The two-time All Conference player shot a ridiculous 48 percent from behind the three-point arc in 1987.

7. Terry Duerod, 1976-1979. The 1979 All-American shot over 50 percent from the field for his career and led the Titans to two NCAAs and one NIT. He played parts of four seasons in the NBA.

6. Willie Green, 2000- 2003. The 2003 Conference Player of the Year had a pair of 40- point games on his way to becoming the Titans' fourth all-time leading scorer. He led the team to two NITs, including the 2001 tourney when his 25 points paced the Titans to a huge upset of Big East powerhouse UConn. Sidelined for a year with a knee injury, he's back on track for a fine NBA career.

5. Spencer Haywood, 1969. The All-American averaged 32.1 points per game in his lone Titans season, then bolted for the ABA. He won ABA Rookie of the Year and MVP before moving to the NBA, where he played 12 years and made four All-Star teams.

4. Terry Tyler, 1975-1978. The 1978 All-American excelled in numerous areas, becoming the Titans' seventh all-time leading scorer, third all-time leader in steals and rebounds, as well as the top shot blocker in school history. He played 11 years in the NBA, including seven with the Pistons.

3. Rashad Phillips, 1998-2001. The 5-foot-9 guard ranks as the Titans all-time leader in points (2319) and treys (348). The two-time Conference Player of the Year led the Titans to two NCAAs and one NIT tourney.

2. Dave DeBusschere, 1960-1962. The three-time All-American averaged 24.8 ppg and became the Titans' all-time leading rebounder. A member of the Basketball Hall of Fame, he had a terrific NBA career with the Pistons and the Knicks, winning two titles in New York. He also played professional baseball for a couple seasons as a pitcher with the Chicago White Sox.

1. John Long, 1975-1978. The school's second all-time leading scorer led the Titans to the 1978 NCAA tourney's Sweet 16. Drafted by the Pistons in the second round, he spent over a decade in the NBA, averaging double digits per game during his first eight seasons and winning a title with the Pistons' 1989 Bad Boys team.

Top Ten Non-Detroit Sports Moments That Took Place in the Detroit Area

Over the years, the Detroit area has hosted a number of big sporting events. Stanley Cup contests featuring the Red Wings. Tigers' World Series games. NBA Finals games with the Pistons. But this list excludes all of those to showcase great sporting events that took place in Detroit, but did not feature a Detroit sports team. Also, don't look for Super Bowl XVI or Wrestlemania III because they're on Art's "Silverdome Memories" list.

10. The Northwestern State of Louisiana beats Iowa. The 14th-seeded Demons came from 17 down to upset the third-seeded Hawekeyes with a three-point buzzer beater in the first round of the 2006 NCAA Men's Basketball Tournament at the Palace.

9. Super Bowl XL on February 5, 2006 at Ford Field. A boring game, atrocious officiating and a halftime show that didn't feature original Motown sound. So how did Super Bowl XL between the Steelers and the Seahawks squeeze on to this list? Ummm, did you attend the *Playboy*, *Maxim* or *FHM* parties?

8. 2004 Ryder Cup at Oakland Hills Country Club in Bloomfield Hills. The European players signed autographs and had a good time. The U.S. team members acted like haughty douchebags and got trounced 18 1/2 to 9 1/2. Hard to believe, but many American fans were glad to see us get our asses beat.

7. The U.S Open Men's Championship at Oakland Hills Country Club in 1951. The South Course at Oakland Hills has hosted a number of big tournaments, but the 1951 Open ranks as the most memorable. Ben Hogan shot an incredible final round 67 on the treacherous track to win with a total score 287—seven over par. That's how tough Oakland Hills played that year. The win inspired Hogan to say, "I am just glad I brought this course, this monster, to its knees."

6. NHL All-Star Game in the Joe Louis Arena on February 5, 1980. The game featured the first All-Star appearance by 19-year old rookie phenom Wayne Gretzky. The opposing coaches, Scotty Bowman and Al Arbour, were absolute legends. No less than 16 future Hall of Famers took the ice that afternoon. But the game will always be remembered in Detroit for only ONE thing: the return of Gordie Howe to Detroit. The actual game was secondary to the pre-game introduction of "Mr. Hockey." Howe was representing the Wales Conference at the time for the Hartford Whalers and the NHL made sure to call Howe's name last. Well, actually, Howe's name was never uttered as the JLA crowd rose in unison to give Howe one of the most thunderous ovations in modern sports history. For four minutes, the throng chanted "Gordie! Gordie! Gordie!" while Howe tried to keep his emotions in check. At the age of 51, Howe finally got the Motor City send-off that he deserved and he had Bowman to thank for it. "When Scotty picked me to play, he really stuck his nose out because I later learned there was opposition to me playing," said Howe, who only had 11 goals at the break. "I said if Gordie didn't play, I wouldn't coach," Bowman said. "It was a natural for him to play that game in Detroit. I didn't care what anybody thought."

5. MLB All-Star Game at Briggs Stadium on July 8, 1941. Most All-Star
games are meaningless exhibitions that are forgotten moments after they end. But the dramatic way this game ended and the man who won it for the American League makes it one of the most memorable All-Star games of all-time in ANY sport. With the NL leading 5-4 in the bottom of the ninth, with two on and two out, Ted Williams came to the plate and promptly deposited a fastball in the upper-right field stands for a 7-5 American League walk-off victory.

4. USA Figure Skating Trials in Cobo Arena on January 6, 1994. If we
actually took figure skating seriously as a sport, this might have been number one. Because an incident right before this event actually transcended sports and became one of the iconic stories of its time. Following a practice session, an assailant snuck into Cobo Arena and used a baton to whack the knee of skater Nancy Kerrigan, the country's best chance at gold that year. A police investigation concluded that Jeff Gilooly, the husband of Kerrigan's rival Tonya Harding, had hired two thugs to carry out the attack, hoping to knock Kerrigan out of the competition and guarantee Harding a spot on Team USA. The injury prevented Kerrigan from participating in the Trials at Cobo, which Harding won. Since the U.S. Olympic Committee didn't have time to figure out if Harding was behind the attack on her rival—and it was terrified of a Harding lawsuit—both skaters ended up representing the U.S. in Norway. Kerrigan went on to earn a silver medal while the trailer-trash hooligan Harding finished eighth.

3. Jake LaMotta vs. Marcel Cerdan on June 16, 1949 in Briggs Stadium.
Detroit has hosted a lot of great boxing bouts. But we chose this one because events surrounding it made the Harding-Kerrigan soap opera look like a Brady Bunch rerun. Considered the greatest fighter in the history of France, Cerdan dislocated his arm and failed to answer the bell in the 10th round, LaMotta, the inspiration behind the classic Martin Scorcese film Raging Bull, was declared the victor and new champion. Here's where things get interesting. A rematch was scheduled, but never held. Right before Cerdan began training, he died in a plane crash on his way to New York to visit his mistress, the famous French singer Edith Piaf. And the FBI later discovered that LaMotta got his first match with Cerdan in the park that would eventually be known as Tiger Stadium by throwing an earlier bout against Billy Fox.

2. MLB All-Star Game, American League 6, National League 4, at Tiger
Stadium on July 13, 1971. Almost 30 years to the day that Ted Williams' home run
ended the '41 All-Star game, the Midsummer Classic returned to Detroit. Coming into the game, the AL had lost nine straight and it looked like that trend would continue when the NL opened up a 3-0 lead early in the game. Then in the bottom of the third inning, the American League took their first lead in an All-Star game in seven years! (Yes, you read that correctly.) And the Frank Robinson home run that gave the Junior Circuit a 4-3 lead wasn't even the most famous during that half-inning. It paled in comparison to the shot that Reggie Jackson hit two batters earlier. With Luis Aparicio on first base, Jackson hit a pitch from Doc Ellis over the right-field upper-deck roof. The home run ball actually struck a transformer on a light standard. And while the ball didn't cause an explosion like the climactic dinger in The Natural, the 520-foot shot remains one of the most memorable plays in All-Star history.

1. Western Conference Outdoor Track and Field meet on May 25, 1935 at Ferry Field.

In this day and age, it would be pretty difficult to imagine that an Ohio State University athlete would have the overwhelming support of an audience in an Ann Arbor stadium. But in May of 1935 that was exactly the case as Buckeye track and field phenom Jesse Owens traveled to compete on the University of Michigan campus. (For those of you wondering what the hell the "Western Conference" is, it is now known as the Big Ten Conference.) In the weeks leading up to the competition, the 21-year old Owens was nursing a back injury. What he was about to accomplish would have been unfathomable for a person in perfect health. In the span of about 45 minutes, Owens broke three WORLD RECORDS and equaled another. (Read that line again and let it sink in.)

3:15 p.m. Owens tied the World Record in winning the 100-yard dash in 9.4 seconds. 3:25 p.m. Owens set the World Record in winning the broad jump at 26 feet, 81/4 inches. 3:34 p.m. Owens set the World Record in winning the 220-yard dash in 20.3 seconds. 4:00 p.m. Owens set the World Record in winning the 220-yard low hurdles in 22.6 seconds.

We are not sure what the slacker was doing for those 26 minutes between 3:34 and 4:00 p.m. But if Owens wouldn't have been so lazy, he probably could have broken a few more world records during that time. The accomplishment by Owens was considered by many to be the greatest sporting accomplishment of the ENTIRE 20th century! While Owens would go on to win four gold medals in the 1936 Olympics in Berlin in the midst of Nazi Germany and in front of Adolph Hitler himself, that spring day in Ann Arbor went down as Owens' finest hour. Or 45 minutes if you want to be technical.

Some of the best coaches and managers in sports history have practiced their trades here. They played a big part in making Detroit the "City of Champions." So even with a Top Ten (plus four), some deserving candidates don't make the cut.

Honorable Mentions: Jim Leyland, Billy Martin, Steve O'Neil, Dutch Clark, Joe Schmidt, George Wilson, Wayne Fontes and Flip Saunders.

14. Tim Marcum, Drive (1988-89; 1991-93). Laugh if you want at Arena Football, but all the colorful Marcum did was win the Arena Bowl in three of his five years in Detroit. And in the other two years, he guided them to the title game. Few coaches in any sport can match that standard of success.

13. Bill Laimbeer, Shock (2002-). Who would have thought the original Pistons Bad Boy would do such a great job coaching, much less coaching women. Laimbeer took over a pathetic franchise six years ago and has already led them to two WNBA crowns and a conference title.

12. Mike Babcock, Detriot Red Wings (2005-). Replaced Dave Lewis after the lockout. In his first year, the Wings won the Presidents Trophy, but flamed out in the first round against Edmonton. In the second year, they were beaten by his former Anaheim team in the Western Conference Finals. In year three, they clinched another Presidents Trophy and a Stanley Cup. Demanding but fair, he could eventually turn into one of the best ever.

11. Mickey Cochrane, Tigers (1934-38). The Tigers acquired the future Hall of Fame catcher before the 1934 season from the Philadelphia A's and named him their player-manager. Cochrane led the Tigers to the American League pennant in 1934 and a World Series title the following year over the Chicago Cubs. The brash Cochrane won 348 of his 600 games as the Tigers' manager, while batting over .300 in four of his five years in Detroit.

10. Larry Brown, Pistons (2003-05). Yes, he was the ultimate drama queen. Yes, he flirted with other teams while still working as our coach. But, oh, how LB could coach. He even got Rasheed Wallace to listen to him. His "play the right way" mantra worked pretty damn well for two years, netting the franchise a championship in 2004 and a seventh-game Finals loss to the Spurs the following season. Then he drove the organization and his players nuts, forcing management to fire him in the autumn of 2005.

9. Hughie Jennings, Tigers (1907-20). The "EEE-YAH MAN" maintained his legendary grin and sense of humor despite having to deal with a toxic prima donna named Ty Cobb, whom he coaxed into a pretty good career. Jennings managed the Tigers for 14 years, guiding them to American League pennants in 1907, 1908 and 1909. He stepped down in 1920 with a record of 1131-972 and won induction into baseball's Hall of Fame in 1945.

8. Mayo Smith, Tigers (1967-70). After an undistinguished playing career and a couple of stints managing in the National League, Smith took over the Tigers' dugout in 1967. He led the surprising Tigers to a 91-71 record, losing the pennant on the final day of the season to the Boston Red Sox. The next year was magic in Detroit. Smith's Tigers won the pennant and then came back from a 3-1 deficit to beat the heavily-favored St. Louis Cardinals in the World Series. Smith may be best known for moving outfielder Mickey Stanley to shortstop in place of the light hitting Ray Oyler in the Series. The bold move enabled the Tigers to load up the starting batting order with Al Kaline, Willie Horton, Jim Northrup and Stanley. The following year, the Tigers finished second in the newly formed AL East division to the Baltimore Orioles. Smith was replaced by Billy Martin after the Tigers slumped to 79-83 in 1970. But Smith remains such a beloved figure that the biggest Tigers fan club today still calls itself The Mayo Smith Society.

7. Emanuel Steward, Kronk Gym (1971-). Steward serves as the heart, soul, brains and power behind the city's great Kronk Gym boxing machine. A former Golden Gloves champion, Steward came to national prominence by guiding Thomas Hearns to multiple world titles across a number of weight classes. Steward tutored numerous other local boxers to world titles, including Hilmer Kenty, Milton McCrory, Jimmy Paul and Steve McCrory. In all, he has trained 31 world champions, including Lennox Lewis, Evander Holyfield, Oscar De La Hoya and Michael Moorer. He was elected to the International Boxing Hall of Fame in 1997. A regular expert analyst for HBO boxing, Steward still takes the time to train the big names and the up-and-comers at Kronk.

6. Tommy Ivan, Red Wings (1947-55). Perhaps the most underrated coach in Detroit history, Ivan took over the Red Wings after coaching their minor league clubs in Indianapolis and Omaha. The eventual Hall of Famer guided the team to the best record in the league six straight seasons and Stanley Cup triumphs in 1950, 1952 and 1954. Along the way he developed young stars like Gordie Howe and Tery Sawchuk. Ivan compiled an impressive regular season record of 262-118-90 in Detroit before leaving to take over the Chicago Black Hawks in 1955.

5. Sparky Anderson, Tigers (1979-95). Many will argue that this list ranks Sparky too high; many will argue that he is ranked too low. No matter where you stand on the quality of his overall efforts here, you have to admit that Sparky made the biggest mark of any professional coach or manager in the city's history. He guided the Tigers for 17 years, taking the likes of Trammell, Whitaker, Morris, Parrish and Gibson from raw youngsters to All-stars. Getting the team off to a record 30-5 start then coasting to the World Series title in 1984 stands as his crowning Detroit moment. But perhaps Sparky's best effort came in the 1987 regular season when the team rallied to edge out Toronto to win the Eastern Division on the final day of the season. His record of 1331-1248 with the Tigers was certainly not gaudy. But his big, positive presence and charity work added so much to the city. His controversial stand not to manage replacement players during a labor lockout in spring training of 1995 did not endear him to owner Mike Ilitch and his #11 was never officially retired by the Tigers. Sparky went into Cooperstown as a Cincinnati Red.

4. Buddy Parker, Lions (1950-56). Hard as it may be to believe today, there actually was a golden age of Detroit Lions football and Buddy Parker provided the Midas touch, posting a 50-24-2 record with the Lions. Parker took over the Lions in 1950 and coached them to back-to-back championships in 1952 and 1953. Led by quarterback Bobby Layne, the Lions remained the best team in the league throughout most of the decade, reaching a third straight title game in 1954, losing to the Cleveland (imagine that). Parker stunned the sports world by leaving Detroit during training camp in 1957, saying he could no longer control his players. George Wilson took over and guided Parker's roster to the championship, the Lions' last.

3. Jack Adams, Cougars/Falcons/Red Wings (1927-47). He won just over 50 percent of his games. But Jack Adams still ranks as a coaching legend in the NHL. He took over a sad-sack Detroit team in 1927 when they were still known as the Cougars. They later became the Falcons and then the Red Wings in 1932. Adams coached the team to three Stanley Cups (1936, 1937 and 1943). He remained the coach for two decades before handing over the reins to Tommy Ivan in 1947. Adams continued as the team's General Manager until the end of the 1962 season.

2. Chuck Daly, Pistons (1983-92). Setting new standards for sideline fashion as well as on-the-court performance, "Daddy Rich" turned out to be the perfect coach for the Pistons during their Bad Boys glory days. A relative unknown when he was hired in 1983, Daly led the Pistons to nine consecutive winning seasons, never tallying less than 46 victories in the league's most competitive era. During that time, the team also bested Bird's Celtics, Dr. J's Sixers, Jordan's Bulls (hardly even a nuisance) and Magic's Lakers to claim to two consecutive NBA titles, along with three trips to the Finals and five appearances in the Eastern Conference Finals. Daly did all that by molding a roster full of role players and big talents that came with emotional baggage into perhaps the most feared team in league history. Daly was so in touch with his players that the mercurial Dennis Rodman basically considered Daly as a father.

1. Scotty Bowman, Red Wings (1993-2002). He not only ranks as the greatest coach in Detroit sports history, many consider the eight-time Stanley Cup winner as the greatest coach in any city or sport. After arriving in Detroit the previous season, Bowman guided the Wings to the 1994 Stanley Cup finals, where they lost to the New Jersey Devils. Two years later the Wings won their first Cup in 42 years, sweeping the Philadelphia Flyers. Detroit successfully defended their title in 1998 and won another Stanley Cup in 2002, Bowman's final season. Despite coaching for 35 years, the man never endured a losing season here or anywhere. Along the way Scotty Bowman established NHL coaching records with 1244 regular-season wins and 223 playoff victories.

There have been plenty of coaches that have accumulated terrible records while being the top boss for one of our professional teams. Many factors go in to the demise of a coaching career, including cheap ownership, an incompetent general manager, injuries and underachieving players. In truth, there have been more mediocre coaches than complete failures; however these individuals distinguished themselves as the worst for not being able to connect in any way with their teams.

10. (Tie) Dick Vitale and Richie Adubato, Pistons. After a successful run as head coach at the University of Detroit (where he pumped up interest in Titan basketball), the Pistons thought that bringing "Dickie V" into the fold would "reVITALEize" a so-so Detroit team. Plagued by stomach problems and poor personal decisions, "Dickie V" and the Pistons never got it together. Twelve games into the 1979-80 season, Vitale was fired after a 4-8 start. His career record is 34 and 60 for a winning percentage of .362. We all know what happened to Vitale next. He took a job with a fledging TV network, *ESPN*, and has become one of the most recognizable and imitated personalities in television history. Richie Adubato took over for Vitale and lead Detroit to a 12-58 record the rest of the way. His .171 winning percentage is the lowest in franchise history.

9. Ned Harkness, Red Wings. The "Darkness with Harkness" era ushered in the bleakest period in the history of Red Wings hockey. From the 1970-71 season through the 1982-83 campaign, the Wings made the playoffs once. A successful hockey and lacrosse coach in college, Harkness arrived in Detroit from Cornell, where he won two NCAA titles. (Ken Dryden was in net for his 1967 national champions.) Harkness lasted for 38 games behind the Detroit bench going 12-22-4, a less than stellar accomplishment, but good enough to be promoted to general manager where he proceeded to tear up the team. In fairness, Harkness saw the future of the game being a more wide-open brand of play stressing European fundamentals and tried to take a well-established group of veteran Red Wings and make them something they were not—a rah-rah bunch that would embrace a dress code and a totally foreign style. Eventually, Detroit came around to his way of thinking, but because of him it took almost 20 years.

8. Larry Wilson, Red Wings. Wilson served as interim coach of the Wings for the last 36 games of the 1976-77 season. It was total chaos. Detroit was in the process of cementing their reputation as the "Dead Things" and Wilson may have been taking one for the team, but his 3-29-4 record which was good for a .139 winning percentage, cannot be ignored.

7. Alan Trammell, Tigers. One of the greatest Tigers of all-time was a horrible manager. "Tram" was just too decent and passive, never earning the total respect of his players. Originally hired as part of the "1984 Plan" of bringing back past heroes because the team stunk, Trammell had zero managerial experience and it showed. Even with former teammates Kirk Gibson and Lance Parrish on his staff, he never grew into his role as Detroit's skipper. When it was time to take the team's talent to the next level "Tram" (2003-05) was replaced by Jim Leyland. It was a sad chapter in Tigers history and so was Trammell's 186-300 (.383) record.

6. Darryl Rogers, Lions. Delivered one of the most memorable lines in Motor City sports history, "What does a coach have to do around here to get fired?" Eventually he found out by going 18-40 (.310) during a truly forgettable run (1985-88) as the leader of the Honolulu Blue and Silver.

5. Brad Park, Red Wings. Another great player that just couldn't coach. Park replaced Harry Neale after the first 35 games of the 1985-86 season and a struggling team became worse. Under Park, the Red Wings were the NHL's version of Slapshot's Charlestown Chiefs. It wasn't aggressive hockey, it was goon hockey. An ugly period that was reflected in Park's 9-34-2 (.222) record.

4. Don Chaney, Pistons. A former NBA Coach of the Year with the Houston Rockets in 1991, something was lost in translation from Houston to Detroit because Chaney was nowhere near coach of the year caliber during his stint as the Pistons bench boss. His record of 48-116 (.297) from 1993-95 is hard to figure out. Detroit's roster was a mixture of the Bad Boys (granted, they were on the downside) and young-sters like Allan Houston, Lindsay Hunter and Grant Hill. Chaney should have done more; the potential was in place.

3. Luis Pujols, Tigers. Did he ever really want to be the Tigers manager? Evidently not. With a managerial career mark of 55-100 (.355), Pujols' tenure (2002) was marred by a divided clubhouse. It was "Insurrection City" at Comerica Park. That tumultuous 2002 season can best be summed up by Brandon Inge's response to a Pujols criticism about Inge's approach at the plate. "I don't care what he has to say," Inge said. "I don't listen to anything he tells me." In the end, it appeared that Pujols just gave up.

2. Steve Mariucci, Lions. Finally, the Lions had their coach! An offensive genius that WAS the West Coast Offense! A miracle worker with quarterbacks and Tom Izzo's best friend to boot! Mariucci's arrival in Detroit was more of a coronation. Long-suffer-ing Lion's fans were convinced that their day had come. But every day in Lion Land is like the day before, one of broken dreams and false prophets. "Mooch" was clueless. His West Coast Offense and in-game adjustments never materialized in Motown. An overall record of 15-28 (.349) from 2003-2005 was a disaster. Didn't come close to liv-ing up to his lofty reputation as one of football's most innovative minds.

1. Marty Mornhinweg, Lions. Matt Millen's first hire. Talk about foreshadowing. Marty was not ready to be an NFL head coach. That was made clear during his first training camp when he ended a practice just minutes into the session (leaving thou-sands of fans in the dust) as he rode off on his Harley. An immature move that was never addressed by the team. There are so many Mornhinweg moments that it's hard to narrow them down for this list. Of course, there's his "the bar is high" mantra of sea-son one and his "the bar is even higher" proclamation for season two; but it's that windy day in Champaign, Illinois on November 24, 2002 that will live forever! The Bears had mounted an improbable fourth-quarter comeback and tied the Lions at 17. Heading into overtime, it looked promising for Detroit since they had won the toss and Jason Hanson was sitting on their bench. Then it happened! The Lions decided to kick to Chicago to start overtime because Marty wanted to have the wind. The Bears drove into field goal range and, against the wind, kicked the game winner. Mornhinweg was 5-27 (.156) as Detroit's field general (2001-02), a dismal record of futility even for the Lions.

Note: Tom Kowalski has been covering the Detroit Lions for over 20 years, and for this he deserves our respect and deepest sympathy. His work has been featured in *The Oakland Press, Booth Newspapers* and *The Sporting News.* Tom is also a major contributor on WDFN, WRIF and WJBK–TV Fox 2.

10. Chuck Long. The 12th overall pick in the 1986 draft after finishing as runner-up to Bo Jackson in the closest Heisman Trophy voting ever (at the time), Long inspired a lot of hype and hope upon his arrival in Detroit. But he was victimized by a bad offensive line and even worse coaching. Long was 5-17 as a starter overall, finishing with 19 touchdown passes, 28 interceptions and a quarterback rating of 64.

9. Mike McMahon. While he appeared to have all the skills, including a strong arm and great running ability, Mike McMahon never put it together in Detroit or anywhere else. Playing mostly in 2001 and 2002, McMahon had 10 touchdowns and 10 interceptions, but was just 1-6 as a starter. Worse than that, McMahon's failure to show enough as a rookie in 2001 led the team to draft Joey Harrington the following year.

8. Mike Machurek. Looking like the next coming of Johnny Unitas in preseason, Machurek only appeared in four regular season games in 1984. But in that brief span, he still earned a place on this hallowed list. In those four games, Machurek completed just 14 passes in 43 attempts (32.6 percent), threw zero touchdowns and six interceptions while compiling a quarterback efficiency rating of (drum roll, please) 8.3.

7. Jeff Komlo. Komlo's five-year NFL career included three seasons in Detroit. He started all 16 games in the Lions' 2-14 season in 1979. Komlo gained notoriety for hitting tackle Keith Dorney in the head with a beer mug. Unfortunately, his accuracy in the tavern never translated onto the field. Overall in Detroit, Komlo had 12 touchdowns, 27 interceptions, a completion percentage of 49.9 and a QB rating of 50.4.

6. Stoney Case. Only with Detroit in the 2000 season, Case was 1-0 as a starter, but 0-3 in games in which he appeared as a substitute. Overall, Case had one touchdown pass, four interceptions and a passer rating of 61.7. But that isn't the worst part. Case played a key role in that infamous 2000 regular season finale loss to the Chicago Bears that knocked the Lions out of the playoffs and ushered in the Matt Millen era.

5. Ty Detmer. In the first game after the 9-11 tragedy, Detmer played error-free ball for the opening 28 minutes against Cleveland. Then he threw seven interceptions over the game's final 32 minutes. Detmer had a 1-3 record as a starter, tossing three touchdowns and 12 interceptions and had a QB rating of 56.9. (Side note: In 50 other non-Lions games in the NFL, Detmer's numbers were much better: 31 touchdowns and 23 interceptions.)

4. Jim Ninowski. A 12-year veteran who played 24 games for the Lions in 1960 and '61, Ninowski actually had a winning record in both seasons (7-5 and 8-5-1). However, he makes this list because his numbers were so horrifying that you wonder if the Lions could have contended for a title with somebody besides Nonowski at QB. In those two years in Detroit, Ninowski threw nine touchdown passes and 36 interceptions. (Side note: Ninowski rushed for 10 touchdowns with Detroit, but didn't rush for a single touchdown in any of his other ten years in the league.)

3. Joey Harrington. Another high draft pick (third overall) who lasted just four years in town, Harrington never completed more than 57 percent of his passes in a season. His passing numbers were average: 60 touchdowns and 62 interceptions. But his record as a starter was a brutal 18-37. Harrington was also one of the most polarizing figures to ever drift through Motown.

2. Andre Ware. The seventh overall pick in the 1990 draft, Ware started just five games in four years in Detroit. Despite the fact he had a 3-2 record in those five games (in 1992 and '93), Ware threw five touchdowns and eight interceptions while completing just 51.7 percent of his throws for a passer rating of 63.5. Ware never took a snap for another NFL team after that.

1. Rusty Hilger. Hilger was only with the Lions for three days in 1988 before he reluctantly took over for the injured Chuck Long against the Bears on Oct. 9. "I told Chuck before the game that if he got hurt, it better be bad enough to go to the hospital or I'd kill him after the game," Hilger said. "I want to make a public apology to the organization and to the fans of the Detroit Lions. A veteran ought to be able to come in and play a little better." Lions fans earned that apology for having to watch Hilger complete just 13 passes in 43 attempts against the Bears for one touchdown, one interception and a quarterback rating of 43.4. In his 11 games that season, his only in Detroit, the Lions went 3-8 and scored more than 20 points just once.

Detroit Lions Quarterbacks selected to the Pro Bowl Since Bobby Layne :: Stoney

Lions QB Bobby Layne made the Pro Bowl squad five times during the 1950s. Since then, mediocrity has been pretty much the best-case scenario when it came to the guy lining up under center for the Lions. How uninspiring have Lions' QBs been in recent decades? I guess you could say this list speaks for itself.

1. Greg Landry. The UMass grad's fine 1971 season culminated with a trip to the Pro Bowl. A dual threat, Landry passed for over 2200 yards and rushed for 530. Landry played 14 more seasons in the NFL, eight of them with the Lions. He won the league's Comeback Player of the Year Award in 1976, but failed to gain any more Pro Bowl selections. At 6-4, Landry stood as one of the taller QBs of his day. But at the time, no one could have imagined how tall his 1971 season would stand in comparison to those of the quarterbacks that followed him in Detroit.

Note: An award-winning sportswriter and columnist for *The Flint Journal* for 41 years, Howe covered everything from preps to Magic Johnson to the Pistons and Lions.

10. Eric Turner, Flint Central. Best high school basketball player I saw in Flint. Led Central to three straight state titles in the early 1980s. Played three years at Michigan and was drafted by the Detroit Pistons.

9. Reggie Williams, Flint Southwestern. Outstanding football player as prep and standout at Dartmouth. Played in two Super Bowls with the Cincinnati Bengals. Named NFL's Man of the Year in 1986 for his off-field contributions.

8. Jim Podoley, Mt. Morris, nearby Lakeville High School. Named greatest player in Central Michigan football history after scoring 51 career touchdowns for the Chippewas. Outstanding track star won the Kansas Relays decathlon twice. Played four seasons in the NFL with the Washington Redskins and made the 1957 Pro Bowl.

7. Glen Rice, Flint Northwestern. All State as prep, led NW to two straight Class A titles and then Michigan to 1989 NCAA title. Named NCAA tournament's Most Outstanding Player. Remains the all-time scoring leader at Michigan. Played 13 seasons in NBA with the Heat, Hornets and Lakers and was a three-time NBA All-star.

6. Mateen Cleaves, Flint Northern. Led Vikings to 1995 state Class A Basketball title. Was also a terrific quarterback in high school. A three-time All-American at Michigan State, he led Spartans to the 2000 NCAA championship. Set career records for assists at MSU. One of the greatest leaders in college basketball history. Drafted in the first round in 2000 by the Detroit Pistons.

5. Lynn Chandnois, Flint Central. All-State football halfback, became All-American at Michigan State. Player of the Year in the NFL in 1952 with Pittsburgh, where he played seven seasons. His 29.6 yards ranks second to Gale Sayers in NFL career kickoff return average.

4. Don Coleman, Flint Central. One of two football players to have his number retired at Michigan State. Runner-up for the Outland Trophy in 1951. Member of the College Football Hall of Fame.

3. Brad Van Pelt, Owosso. Standout basketball center, baseball pitcher and All-State quarterback in high school. All-American safety at Michigan State. Won Maxwell Trophy (best amateur athlete) in 1972. Played over a decade in NFL with Giants, Raiders and Browns. Named to five Pro Bowls and the College Football Hall of Fame.

2. Rick Leach, Flint Southwestern. All-State in three sports in high school. Started four straight years as quarterback at Michigan. The two-time football All-American also won All-American honors in baseball. Played 11 years in the Major Leagues with the Detroit, Toronto, Texas and San Francisco.

1. Paul Krause, Flint-Burton Bendle. Won 14 letters as a prep. Outstanding football and baseball player at the University of Iowa. Played 16 years in the NFL with Redskins and Vikings. Still holds the NFL's career interception record of 81. Was enshrined into the Pro Football Hall of Fame in 1998

Top Ten Athletes from the Grand Rapids Area
:: Greg Johnson

Note: An award-winning columnist for *The Grand Rapids Press*, Johnson has been covering sports on the local and national scene for over a quarter-century.

10. Brian Diemer. He won 1983 NCAA indoor two-mile at Michigan, then competed in three Olympics. He won the bronze in the steeplechase in the '84 Olympics and also won TAC and USATF championships in the steeplechase.

9. Bernie Jefferson. He broke the color line at Northwestern University as an African-American varsity athlete and was the top running back and defensive back for their 1936 Big Ten championship team. Later played professional football briefly in Chicago and served in the Army Air Corps as one of the famous Tuskegee airmen.

8. Loy Vaught. The leading rebounder on Michigan's 1989 NCAA championship team went on to play 10 years in the NBA, twice finishing among the top ten in rebounds.

7. Stanley Ketchel. Middleweight champ in early part of 20th century won 52 fights, 49 by KO. He once won a title in a 32-round bout, and took on the much larger heavyweight great Jack Johnson.

6. Terry Barr. Two-time Pro Bowl receiver for the Detroit Lions with 3,810 receiving yards and 35 touchdown receptions in nine seasons. Also a defensive back, he intercepted a pass and scored in the 1957 NFL Championship game.

5. Greg Meyer. The last American to win the Boston Marathon set 10 American road racing records and two world records. Also won the Detroit and Chicago marathons.

4. Mickey Stanley. Led American League outfielders with a 1.000 fielding percentage in 1968 and '70. The four-time Golf Glover is best known for switching to shortstop to help the Tigers win the 1968 World Series.

3. Jim Kaat. Ranks 31st on MLB's all-time pitching wins list with 283. Played 25 years with five different teams, and in 1966 won a career-best 25 games. Pitched for the pennant-winning 1965 Minnesota Twins and the 1982 World Champion St. Louis Cardinals.

2. George Andrie. Played defensive end next to Bob Lilly on Dallas' "Doomsday Defense." A five-time Pro Bowl selection, he returned a fumble for a TD in the famous "Ice Bowl" game. Though sacks were not official stats during his career, he is unofficially credited with 97 and a season high of 18.5 in 1966.

1. Floyd Mayweather, Jr. Since 2005, Mayweather has been considered the best pound-for-pound boxer in the world. His amateur career ended soon after he lost a controversial bout in the 1996 Olympic Games in Atlanta. But as a pro, he has won six world titles in five weight classes and is currently the WBC welterweight champion with a 39-0 record. His fights have set pay-per-view records.

Note: *Detroit News* columnist Terry Foster has been a staple on the local sports scene for over two decades. The Central Michigan graduate and Detroit native began his career in 1981 with the *Grand Rapids Press*, then moved to the *Detroit Free Press* the following year to cover anything and everything. He moved to the *News* in 1988, where he was the beat writer for the Pistons on their Bad Boys championship runs. He stayed on the Pistons beat until becoming a full-time columnist in 1993. He has since worked at both WDFN and later Detroit Sports Radio 97.1, where he has co-hosted *The Valenti and Foster Show* since 2004. Along the way, Foster has spent enough time in hundreds of establishments to qualify as an expert on the subject of this list.

Honorable Mention: Red Dog Saloon (Milford), 59 West (Highland Township), Hamlin Pub (several locations), Hockeytown Cafe (Detroit), Cecil's (Southgate), Lions, Tigers and Beers (Wyandotte), Mr. Joe's (Southfield), Mr. B's (Royal Oak).

10. Buffalo Wild Wings (several locations). I can knock down a Blue Moon, honey barbeque wings and buffalo chips a couple times a week while watching games here. The selling point for me is the Wi-Fi and late hours. I often finish stories at a BW3 after covering games during my annual high school tour.

9. Dooley's Irish Tavern (Sterling Heights). This place sells more beer than any bar in Macomb County and if the games are boring the staff will think of fun activities to make the night run smoothly. I watched the 2006 Michigan-Ohio State game and could barely breathe because of the excitement of the game and the crowd in the bar.

8. Coaches Corner (Livonia). I love simple places and Coaches Corner is a spot where you roll up your sleeves, grab a burger and brew and watch games. The decor is simple, yet comfortable. Readers of *The Detroit News* named it the area's best sports bar and they are not far off.

7. Cheli's Chili Bar (Detroit). Lions and Tigers game days here are electric. Cheli's is an errant throw away from Comerica Park and people jam the place and make the building jump. If you don't feel like being inside, Cheli's has a tent for big events and an outdoor deck on top. Load up on chili on cold days. I love it with sour cream, onions and melted cheese.

6. Mallie's (Southgate). The selling point here is Wednesday night. Women from across Down River converge on this popular sports bar. This place also features burgers as large as six pounds and they recently produced one that was close to 100 pounds. Fun is the name of the game here, and there are televisions at most booths.

5. Malarkey's (Southgate and Westland). The steak bites and bread sticks are to die for. Both locations are spacious and have televisions all over. But let's be frank. The real reason to come here is to check out the waitresses. You will not be disappointed.

4. Harry's, Detroit (Detroit). Harry, the owner, took a big gamble by placing a sports bar on the other side of the tracks. He is on the wrong side of the action by Comerica Park and Ford Field, but enough people have discovered this gem in Detroit. Things are better yet after the opening of a second-level deck. Try the crab cake sandwich and a number of other quality entrees.

3. Rosie O'Grady's (Clinton Township). This place is Detroit's version of Cheers. Everybody knows your name and if they don't then they come over and ask. There are the usual televisions but the food is better than average. Try the broasted chicken and the Rosie burger. If you have a group of six or more, ask for the Mafia table.

2. Nemo's (Detroit). It is listed as one of America's great sports bars. It does not have the usual trappings of three dozen flat screen televisions. It is just an old fashion place where folks from Detroit come to talk sports with bartenders. This was your daddy's sports bar. It is always a great spot to return and remember the past. Nemo's also has shuttle service to most sporting events downtown.

1. Lindell A.C. (Detroit). You didn't just talk about the Lions, Tigers and Red Wings here. You met them. I might be a little prejudiced because I worked at the Lindell as a fry cook and bartender along with my mother Betty who went by the name of Rosanne. There was nothing modern here. They put up a couple 25-inch color televisions. But the memories surpass any bar. And the burgers were great. The black-and-white photos and former Lions linebacker Wayne Walker's jock strap are valued at $100,000.

Top Ten Detroit Sports Clichés :: Bernie Smilovitz

Note: Bernie Smilovitz has been a Detroit television icon for over two decades. He was the first local sportscaster to inject humor and unique video into his sportscast with the "Bernies Bloopers" and "Weekend at Bernies" features. His catchphrase "We've Got Highlights" is as well-known in this town as any. He was the first to use the "roundtable" segment with newspaper writers, which was a staple of the Tigers pre-game shows. His live interviews from the Pistons champagne drenched championship locker rooms are an indelible part of the title seasons. One other note about Bernie is that he gets the blame or credit for bringing Stoney to Detroit from Washington as his producer in 1986. Stoney still holds him responsible for much of his career, teaching him two of life's most important lessons: never take yourself too seriously and always remember your family comes first.

10. "We can't look past our next opponent."

9. "Play them one game at a time."

8. "I was nowhere near the Manoogian Mansion."

7. "It's not mine . . . it's my son's (can also use "my wife's")

6. "I'd love to show you the Big House . . . if you know what I mean."

5. "Who says we can't smoke in the dugout?"

4. "Is that a toupee on the Channel 4 sports guy?"

3. "Couldn't I just take a B12 vitamin?"

2. "Yes, the big tire on 94 once belonged to Roger Clemens."

1. "Hey, this doesn't feel like an ounce."

Note: Hall of Fame defenseman Larry Murphy was once referred to by nhl.com writer John McGourty as "the most underrated star of the past 25 years in a major North American sport, a player whose on-ice skills dwarfed his need to be recognized." When he retired in 2001, the former Red Wing ranked second all-time in NHL games played (1615) and third all-time in assists (929) and points (1216) by a defenseman. During his 21-year NHL career, Murphy has heard it all from management, teammates and opposing players. He gives us his list of hockey's ten biggest lies (with a little editorial comment) reminding us that, "When you lie in hockey, you just say it and move on. There isn't a big explanation. Lies are self-explanatory and you always know that it's a lie because you hear the same ones over and over again."

10. "I was screened." (You're always screened when you're on your butt.)

9. "Next time, I will pass it to you instead of shooting it myself." (That is of course if your stick's on the ice and I can see you.)

8. "You'll be back in the lineup next game." (When our next game is in China.)

7. "You might not play a lot, but you're still an important part of this team." (Can you make another pot of coffee and bring me a cup?)

6. "I had my man." (Yeah, if your man was invisible!)

5. "Don't worry. We're not looking to move you." (We're looking to jettison you.)

4. "You can trust me. This is OFF THE RECORD." (Once I burn you, I'll deny I ever said it.)

3. "We'll look after you on your next contract." (The only problem is you won't be on the team.)

2. "An assist is as good as a goal." (Except at contract time.)

1. "You're only being sent down to the minors for two weeks." (Two weeks, two months, two years, two decades, I know that there's a two in there somewhere.)

Although none of them had quite the impact of Joe Namath's pre–Super Bowl III guarantee that his Jets would upset the Colts, Michigan sports fans have heard more than a few of our players make big promises. Some have worked very well in our favor, and then there are those that, let's just say, were not backed up. Here are the top seven guarantees, ranked from the worst failures to the biggest successes.

7. Lomas Brown guarantees a Lions playoff win.

The Lions had won seven straight games to end the 1995 regular season and were headed on the road to Philadelphia for the first round of the playoffs. On Wednesday of game week, the Lions' offensive tackle said, "There is no question in my mind, we are going to win the game. It's a matter of how much we are going to win by and how long it's going to take." The quote was in the Eagles locker room, highlighted in yellow. Whether or not it inspired the Eagles is unknown, but Philly crushed the Lions 58-37. The Eagles scored 31 straight points in the 2nd quarter, capped by a Hail Mary from former Lions quarterback Rodney Peete to Rob Carpenter. Barry Sanders was held to 40 yards and quarterback Scott Mitchell was horrible in his playoff debut. Eagles coach Ray Rhodes said of the guarantee, "If he had been a two- or three-time Super Bowl champion, I could understand it. If you haven't been there, keep your mouth shut. He's talking about walking into your house, slapping your family around and robbing you. We're not going to let anybody do that." Lomas added: "If what I said had something to do with (the defeat), then I apologize to my teammates and the city of Detroit." Certainly, Lomas Brown is not the only Lion who owes an apology to the city of Detroit.

6. Jon Kitna guarantees that the Lions will win ten.

In March of 2007, Jon Kitna was a guest on WDFN's "Jamie and Brady Show" and said the Lions would win 10 games in the upcoming regular season. It was a bold prediction, considering the team won just three in 2006, and hadn't won 10 since 1995. And, as we all know, they are the Lions. A few months later, Kitna was on the "Stoney and Wojo Show" to promote a charity event when this exchange took place.

Stoney: Now Jon, you sound less confident in this [charity event with fans] than you did talking about the season upcoming, where you said you expect this team to win at least 10 games.

Kitna: Dude, that was 10 games before I saw the schedule, too. I'll keep to myself what I think that we actually will win, but it's more than 10 games—after I saw the schedule.

Stoney: Really!? I thought the schedule was brutal.

Wojo: Wait, you're saying more than 10 games now?

Kitna: Yeah. That's what I'm saying.

Well after the Lions got off to a 6-2 start, it looked like Kitna was a prophet. But they went 1-7 the second half of the season and finished two games under .500 and three wins short of Kitna's guarantee.

5. Rasheed Wallace guarantees that the Pistons will beat Cleveland.
The Pistons won the first two games against the Cavs in the 2006 Eastern Conference Semifinals, then lost Game 3. With Game 4 set for Cleveland, Rasheed Wallace let go with one of his GUARANSHEEDS: "I know we're going to win it. Tomorrow night is the last game here in this building for this year. Y'all can quote me, put it back page, front page, whatever." That ended his streak of correct guarantees. Rasheed hurt his ankle and the Pistons were beaten by the Cavs 74-72 to even the series. Cleveland won Game 5 at the Palace, as well. But the Pistons returned to Cleveland to win Game 6 before taking Game 7 at home. But the length and difficulty of the series may have tired out the Pistons and contributed to their losing to Miami in the Eastern Conference Finals.

4. Mike Hart guarantees a Michigan win over Notre Dame. Someone needed to step up after the Wolverines began the 2007 season with two humiliating losses. In the season opener, they stunned the nation by being upset in the Big House by Division 1-AA's Appalachian State, 34-32. The following week, they were blown out at home by Oregon, 39-7. Week 3 brought the Fighting Irish to Ann Arbor and they were hurting as well. Notre Dame had just been beaten badly by Georgia Tech, 33-3, and Penn State, 31-10. The situation inspired senior running back Mike Hart to promise: "We're going to win next week. There's no question in my mind. I guarantee we will win next week. I'm going to get this team ready. Guaranteed." Well, Hart got it right and he had something to do with it, rushing for 187 yards and two scores as his Wolverines crushed Notre Dame, 38-0.

3. Rasheed Wallace GUARANSHEEDS a win against the Pacers. After losing Game 3 of the 2005 Eastern Conference Semifinals to Indiana, 79-75, and falling behind 2-1 in the series, Rasheed declared: "We're definitely going back to Detroit with this thing 2-2, no question about it." He backed up his words with 17 points, 12 boards and five blocks to lead the Pistons to an 89-75 win. Detroit went on to win the last two games of the series and advance to the Eastern Conference Finals, where they defeated Miami in six games.

2. Jim Harbaugh guarantees that Michigan will beat Ohio State in Columbus. The Wolverines were undefeated and #2 in the nation just over a week before their annual Ohio State showdown. However, they might have been looking ahead to the Buckeyes, as they were stunned by Minnesota, 20-17, in Michigan Stadium. The following Monday, Wolverines quarterback Jim Harbaugh went completely against the grain with this brash statement: "I guarantee we will beat Ohio State and go to Pasadena." Most thought head coach Bo Schembechler would be pissed off. But he was not, "Well, you know, that's not something you like to see a kid do. But if you ask our players, when we met, I said, 'Harbaugh, you keep your mouth shut from now on. But we will have to back you up on this. We'll just have to win the game, that's all.'" And they did. Harbaugh did his part, passing for 261 yards and tailback Jamie Morris rushed for 210 yards as the Wolverines rallied from a 14-3 deficit to win it, 26-24. Michigan lost to Arizona State in that 1987 Rose Bowl. One big plus did come out of the game, though. ASU's victory over Michigan impressed the folks down in Columbus so much, they hired the Sun Devils' coach to come lead their Buckeyes. His name was John Cooper. In his own way, Cooper guaranteed a lot of future Michigan victories over Ohio State.

1. Rasheed Wallace GUARANSHEEDS a win against the Pacers, the original.

The Pistons were horrible in the 2004 Eastern Conference Finals series opener against Indiana, losing 78-74 at Conseco Fieldhouse. And nobody was worse than Wallace, who shot a dreadful 1-7 and finished with just four points. After the game, he stunned Pistons fans everywhere with a vow that, at the time, sounded like a desperate guy grasping at anything. "I'm guaranteeing Game 2," said Wallace. "That's the bottom line. That's all I'm saying. They will not win Game 2. You heard that from me." After sleeping on it for a night, Wallace repeated his promise to reporters the next day.

Fortunately for Rasheed, his teammates backed up his bravado, even if he didn't. The Pistons tied the series with a 72-67 win. Rasheed was a dismal 4-19 from the field. But he did play good defense, holding Jermaine O'Neal scoreless in the second half. The win was saved by Tayshaun Prince's legendary block of a late Reggie Miller layup that would have given Indiana an amazing, come–from–behind victory. Rasheed followed up his bold prediction with another prediction that no one could argue with: "I guarantee, for Games 3 and 4, we'll go back to Detroit." The Pistons went on to beat the Pacers in six and advance to the NBA Finals and win the title.

Note: Tom McKay worked for the Greater Detroit Bowling Association for 40 years, serving as office manager from 1955-65 and Executive-Treasurer-Secretary from 1965-1995. He was also an American Bowling Congress Director for 34 years and served as President for the 1992-93 season. He notes that Michigan has more registered bowlers than any other state, and highlights the dozen best from around Detroit.

12. Therm Gibson. Won seven ABC championships with E&B/Pfeiffer team. Held record for highest triplicate (three straight 268 games) for many years. Won $75,000 on Jackpot Bowling, the TV show hosted by Milton Berle in 1961. Won 18 tournament titles.

11. Joe Joseph. Lansing-native made his name in Detroit with the outstanding Pfeiffer team. Won three ABC titles and had eight other top-ten finishes. Won first pro tournament of champions in 1962. Had smoothest delivery of anyone in the game.

10. Billy Golembiewski. "Billy G." won the ABC Masters title in 1960 and again in 1962, a feat only three other ABC Hall of Famers have accomplished.

9. Bob Strampe. Member of outstanding Stroh's Beer teams and standout on the pro tour. Won the BPAA All-star in 1963, the PBA National in 1964 and ABC Masters in 1966. Rolled perfect 300 games in five different decades.

8. Fred Bujack. Won the third most ABC titles in history (eight). Key member of E&B/Pfeiffer team that won three ABC Tournament titles and four team all-events titles between 1949-1955 and were considered top team in nation. Among Bujack's 14 other tournament championships were five more team titles in BPAA events.

7. Cheryl Daniels. One of the great African-American women bowlers of all time. Won 10 professional titles, including 1995 U.S. Open. First woman to use all boards with equal expertise. Earned over $700,000 on the circuit. Member of Michigan and Detroit Bowling Halls of Fame. Sings professionally and has backed up Motown legend Martha Reeves.

6. Tony Lindemann. On Stroh's team that won the 1951 all-events ABC title and also claimed the individual all-events title that year. Won the BPAA National Doubles in 1951, 1952 and 1954 with Buzz Fazio and team championships in 1952, 1953 and 1954.

5. George Young. E&B/Pfeiffer Team member with Bujack, Gibson and Lou Sielaff. Won six ABC titles, four with the E&B team. Rolled nine consecutive 1800 series (nine games) in ABC tournament in 1940s and 50s. His 202 lifetime ABC tournament average ranked highest in history for 20 tournaments or more. Clutch bowler always placed in team's anchor position.

4. Aleta Sill. Born Aleta Rzpecki. Sill became the first woman to win over a million dollars as a professional bowler. Won 31 titles, including two U.S. Opens. At 19, became youngest female to win a tournament. Only bowler to win each of bowling's Triple Crown events twice.

3. Ed Lubanski. Became second man to win four ABC titles in one tournament in 1959. Won BPAA National Doubles title and was member of BPAA championship teams in 1952, 1953, 1954 and 1964. Bowled back-to-back 300 games on television.

2. Buzz Fazio. Captained the Stroh's Beer team for nine seasons. Three-time ABC champion. Won seven-straight live television matches in Chicago and in Detroit rolled the first televised 800 series. Won the ABC Masters title in 1955 and was runner-up in 1968. Won BPAA National Doubles titles with Tony Lindemann in 1952, 1953 and 1954. His Stroh team won the BPAA team titles in 1952, 1953 and 1954.

1. Joe Norris. Knocked over most pins in history of ABC tournament. Organized famed Stroh's Beer team in 1933 and captained team to 1934 ABC tournament title. Won two other ABC titles and five National Match Game Championships from 1934-1945. Competed in international exhibition before the 1936 Olympics in Berlin, Germany. Known, along with Dick Weber, as the game's greatest emissary. In 1994 at age 86, he became the oldest man to bowl a 300 game.

15. Gene Achtymichuk, Red Wings, 1958-59.

14. Pete Chryplewicz, Lions, 1997-99.

13. Bill Dellastatious, Lions, 1946.

12. Bernie DeViveiros, Tigers, 1927.

11. Billy Golembiewski, local pro bowler most active in 1950s, 60s and 70s.

10. Mike Krushelnyski, Red Wings, 1994-95.

9. Ed Mioduszewski, Lions, 1953.

8. John Prchlik, 1949-53.

7. Dick Rzeszut, Lions, 1954.

6. Barry Salovaara, Red Wings, 1974-76.

5. Louis Schiappacasse, Tigers, 1902.

4. Dick Trzuskowski, Lions, 1940.

3. Alex Wojciechowicz, Lions, 1938-46.

2. Oksana Zakauluzhnaya, Shock, 2000, 2002.

1. Jerry Zawadzkas, Lions, 1967

Ten Best All-Time Athletes from Washtenaw County

Every county in Metro Detroit can lay claim to some of professional/amateur sports finest athletes. Here are Washtenaw County's 10 finest.

10. Fred Cofield (Ypsilanti). After a standout career at Ypsilanti High School, the 6-foot-3 guard was a double-figure collegiate scorer at Oregon and Eastern Michigan. He played for the Knicks and Bulls in the NBA.

9. Stan Joplin (Milan). Made a name for himself on the local playgrounds before tearing it up at Toledo University. His buzzer-beating jumper gave the Rockets their 74-72 upset over Iowa in the 1979 NCAA Tournament. A deft passer, he's among UT's career assists leaders with 428.

8. Eric Ball (Ypsilanti). Played seven NFL seasons for Cincinnati and Oakland, but he's best remembered playing for UCLA. In 1986, he tied a Rose Bowl record with four touchdowns against Iowa. He was named to the Rose Bowl Hall of Fame.

7. Mike Bass (Ypsilanti). Bass excelled in the classroom as well as on the field during high school, earning All-State honors in football and track. A member of the Wolverines 1964 Rose Bowl championship team, Bass made his mark in pro football as a defensive back for Washington. Named one of the 70 greatest Redskin players of all-time, Bass returned Garo Yepremian's errant pass attempt for a touchdown in Super Bowl VII.

6. Bob "Big Bird" Elliott (Ann Arbor Pioneer). After an outstanding prep basketball career, Elliott played college ball at Arizona and became UA's second all-time leading scorer and leading rebounder. The athletic and academic All-American is the only Wildcat to top 2,000 career points and 1,000 boards.

5. Tony Scheffler (Chelsea). Set the Chelsea record for receiving yards in a season with 1,340. He played college ball at Western Michigan where he nabbed 13 career TD passes. Drafted by Denver in the second round of the 2006 NFL Draft, Scheffler is emerging as one of the Broncos go-to guys.

4. Dan Williams (Willow Run). An elite defensive end coming out of Toledo University, he was drafted in the first round (11th overall) by Denver in the 1993 NFL draft. Williams played four seasons for the Broncos before finishing up his career in Kansas City.

3. Brian Rolston (Ann Arbor Pioneer). Considered among the NHL's top two-way forwards, Rolston is now a proven 30-goal scorer for the Minnesota Wild. He's known as a superb penalty killer and power-play performer.

2. Rodney Holman (Ypsilanti High School). He is best remembered as a tight end for the Cincinnati Bengals, even though he finished up his career with the Lions. A three-time Pro-Bowler, Holman excelled at both blocking and receiving. He played in 213 games (the second most for a tight end in NFL history) and his 318 career receptions is tops for a Bengals TE.

1. Dennis Lewis (Ypsilanti). In 1985, Lewis set the American high jump record of 7-8 1/2. An ageless wonder, he still competes today. In 2006, at age 46, Lewis set an over 45 division American high-jump record.

Top Ten Athletes from Windsor, Ontario Area
:: Bob Duff

Note: A sports columnist just across the Ambassador Bridge for the *Windsor Star*, Duff ranks as one of Canada's foremost hockey historians. The former goalie has written or collaborated on numerous hockey books, including *History of Hockeytown*.

Honorable Mentions: pro wrestling legend Killer Kowalski; harness racing driver Bill Gale; 1936 Olympic 400-meter hurdles silver medalist John Loaring; NHL player and coach Joel Quenneville; CFL Hall of Fame wide receiver Bob Simpson; five-time women's boxing world champion Margaret Sidoroff-Canty.

10. Reno Bertoia. The infielder spent 10 seasons in the American League, including two stints with the Detroit Tigers from 1953-58 and 1961-62.

9. Ed Jovanovski. The 1994 NHL draft's first-overall pick played in the 1996 Stanley Cup final as a rookie with the Florida Panthers. "Special Ed" has won Olympic gold and numerous other medals with the Canadian national team.

8. Tommy Grant. The receiver/returner played from 1956-69 in the Canadian Football League, appearing in a record nine Grey Cup games, two All-star games and winning entry into the Canadian Football Hall of Fame.

7. Nick Weslock. Considered the best amateur player in Canadian golf history, Weslock won entry into the Royal Canadian Golf Association Halls of Fame for a stellar career spanning from the 1930s to the 1980s.

6. Tony Golab. The Golden Boy of 1940s Canadian football was a five-time CFL All-Star running back and played in four Grey Cups. He suffered serious injuries while serving in World War II, but came back to play five more seasons and win entry into Canada's Sports and Football Halls of Fame,

5. Bob Probert. Arguably the toughest player and best fighter in NHL history, Probert was far more than just an enforcer. The 1987-88 All-Star scored 29 goals that season and set a Red Wings' record with 21 playoff points that postseason.

4. Rick Kehoe. He posted a 55-goal season on his way to a career total of 375 NHL goals. Kehoe won the Lady Byng Trophy in 1981 and made two All-Star games.

3. Whit Tucker. The flanker still holds the CFL career record for yards per catch (22.5). He won CFL Rookie of the Year honors in 1962 and two Grey Cups. Tucker also took home four gold medals from the Canadian Track and Field Championships in 1959.

2. Joe Krol. Formed Toronto's Gold Dust Twins backfield with Royal Copeland and won five Grey Cups from 1945-52. A four-time all-star, he was voted CFL MVP in 1946. He won election to both Canada's Football and Sports Halls of Fame.

1. Tim Kerr. Kerr holds the NHL record for most power-play goals in a season (34 in 1985-86) and most power-play goals in one period of a Stanley Cup game (three). The big, strong right wing played in two Stanley Cup finals with Philadelphia and three NHL All-Star games. He scored more than 50 goals four times in his career, finishing with 479 NHL goals.

Since baseball player Curt Flood opened the floodgates (pun intended) on free agency in professional sports in the 1970s, Detroit teams have splashed hundreds of millions of dollars to lure talent away from their rivals. Sometimes they've gotten a whole lot less than they bargained for (see the next list). But other times, they've reeled in great players at relative bargain rates (see this list).

10. Dre Bly, Lions, cornerback. With only five wins in their previous two seasons, the Lions had to overpay just for the privilege to speak with prospective free agents. And overpay they did by signing ex-St. Louis Rams corner Dre Bly to a five-year, $25 million contract. But Bly provided instant dividends, intercepting six passes and recovering five fumbles in 2003. Three of those recoveries went for touchdowns. Bly was rewarded with a Pro Bowl start that year. The North Carolina product also became a respected member of the community and the face of the organization. He even attempted to recruit other free agents to Detroit. Some will be upset that Bly's signing made this list. They will bitch that the guy took too many gambles and he was a team cancer who threw Joey Harrington under the bus during his last year in Detroit. First of all, Bly was right that Jeff Garcia was a better QB than Joey Harrington. Secondly, Bly made two Pro Bowls in Detroit and for any Matt Millen acquisition to have that kind of success constitutes a miracle. And considering that Millen eventually sent Bly to Denver for George "The Human False Start" Foster and Tatum Bell . . . well you get the point.

9. Bill Gullickson, Tigers, pitcher. Between the 1987 and 2004 seasons, the Detroit Tigers didn't do much right on the field, they didn't do much right in the draft and they sure as hell didn't do much right in free agency. But they did do right by signing free agent Bill Gullickson in 1991. With the right-handed starter coming off a 10-14 season in Houston, his addition didn't generate much enthusiasm. But during his first season wearing the Olde English D, the veteran pitcher went 20-9 with a 3.90 ERA. His 20 wins were the most of any American League pitcher that season. In four seasons with Detroit, Gullickson won 51 games before injuries ended his career.

8. Darrell Evans, Tigers, first baseman. The Detroit Tigers have never really been on the cutting edge of social advances. Whether it was their slow reaction to racial integration or their reluctance to dip into the free-agency waters, the Tigers have moved about as quickly to embrace change as Sean Casey moves on the base paths. The organization's first real venture into free agency came in 1983 when the team signed San Francisco Giants first baseman, Darrell Evans. And while Evans didn't have a real great 1984 season (.232 batting average, 16 home runs, 63 RBI), he was still a key component of that championship squad. The following year, Evans, 38, became the oldest man to ever lead the Majors in home runs with 40. In 1987, the Tigers won the AL East after an epic battle with Toronto, thanks, in large part, to Evans' 34 homers and 99 RBI. Evans might have placed even higher on this list if he didn't get picked off third base during the Tigers-Twins playoff series in 1987. Seriously, who gets picked off third base? DURING A PIVOTAL PLAYOFF GAME?? Not that we're still bitter or anything.

7. Kenny Rogers, Tigers, pitcher. GM Dave Dombrowski's signing of Kenny Rogers to a two-year, $16 million deal after the 2005 season met with a mixed reaction. The Tigers needed a reliable veteran pitcher who could eat up some innings while their young hurlers developed into front-line starters. But Rogers had assaulted two cameramen in Texas the previous season and struggled down the stretch. But the 41-year-old Rogers wasn't getting any younger—and definitely not any wiser. During the regular season, Rogers went 17-8 with a 3.84 ERA. But that was just a prelude to the show that "The Gambler" put on during the postseason, helping the Tigers reach their first World Series in over 20 years. Not only did Rogers become the oldest pitcher to win a postseason game (41 years and 330 days old), he didn't give up a run in 23 innings of playoff work. Of course, some will have you believe that the brown substance on Rogers' pitching hand had something to do with his success. We say hogwash. What's not to believe about a 40-something dude with a career 14.14 ERA in the postseason turning into the best playoff pitcher in the history of the sport? Gaylord Perry and the Easter Bunny think you're ridiculous for even bringing that up.

6. Brett Hull, Red Wings, right wing. While "The Golden Brett" had a tremendous amount of success in Dallas, the Stars declined to pick up his $7 million option after the 2000-01 season. Instead, Hull ended up signing with the Wings. The move was the last of GM Ken Holland's offseason tinkerings and the third to bring a future Hall of Famer to Detroit that summer. (The other two: Dominik Hasek and Luc Robitaille.) While there was a concern how Hull would interact with head coach Scotty Bowman, things went smoothly for the most part. During the 2001-02 season, Hull scored 39 goals and added 40 assists. The right wing added another 10 goals in the playoffs and was a key contributor on the last Red Wings Stanley Cup before 2007-08. In his four seasons in Detroit, Hull averaged 33 goals and 39 assists.

5. Pudge Rodriguez, Tigers, catcher. Because of the absolute embarrassment of a product that Tigers owner Mike Ilitch had put on the field for the better part of a decade, culminating in the 119-loss 2003 team, the "Pizza Man" was desperate enough to meet the ten-time All-Star and ten-time Gold Glove winner's demands for a $40 million contract over four years after the 2003 season in which Rodriguez had led Florida to the World Series crown. It was worth it. While Pudge's first season in Detroit was clearly his best (.334 BA, 19 HRs & 86 RBI) and it is more than a little suspicious that his offensive stats declined with the onset of steroid testing, there is no questioning the positive impact that Pudge has had in Detroit. His signing was clearly the watershed moment in the Tigers' resurgence. Free agents began to take the team seriously, a close and beneficial relationship with Pudge's superagent Scott Boras blossomed, and the catcher's top-notch defensive abilities didn't hurt either.

4. Adam Oates, Red Wings, center. Back in the 1980s, the NHL had some bizarre loophole where undrafted collegiate players were treated like free agents. And a Red Wings franchise desperate to add talent was the most active NHL team in raiding U.S. colleges for late-developing prospects. None worked out better than Rensselaer Polytechnic Institute center Adam Oates, who went on to become one of the best set-up men in NHL history. During the 1987-88 season, Oates registered 54 points in 63 games. And with Steve Yzerman out for a majority of that postseason due to a severe knee injury, Oates became the team's number one center. In 16 playoff contests in 1988, Oates compiled 20 points. The Wings top line of Oates, Petr Klima and Bob Probert carried Detroit to the Campbell Conference Finals versus the juggernaut known as the Edmonton Oilers. While Oates went onto finish his career with 1,420 career points and is a lock to make the Hall of Fame, he won't go into the Hall as a Red Wing. Why? Well, this would be a good time to look up "The 11 Worst Trades in Detroit Sports History" list.

3. Cecil Fielder, Tigers, first baseman. The rotund first baseman increased his salary by almost 10 times when he left Toronto for Japan during the 1989 season. His offensive stats increased by almost as much. After Fielder's impressive showing in Japan, the Tigers took a chance on the power-hitting food lover. The franchise was not disappointed. In 1990, Fielder hit 51 round-trippers and knocked in a whopping 132 runs, becoming the first MLB player to hit 50 home runs in a season since George Foster did it in 1977. (For you youngsters out there, hitting 50 dingers in the pre-steroid craze days of the early 90s was an actual accomplishment; the only questionable substance Fielder was putting in his body were McRib sandwiches.) During his first year in the Motor City, Fielder finished second in the American League MVP vote behind Rickey Henderson. Fielder followed-up his remarkable 1990 season with a 168 homers and 546 RBI over the next five seasons. In the process, Fielder transformed himself from a guy who had to go to Japan to make a decent living to one of the highest-paid Major Leaguers. It would serve as an inspiring tale, if we didn't later find out what a mess he was in his personal life.

2. Magglio Ordonez, Tigers, right fielder. If the baseball establishment thought Mike Ilitch was a lunatic for giving Pudge a $10 million per year deal, they must have really thought his toupee was on too tight when he signed White Sox outfielder Magglio Ordonez to a five-year, $85 million deal in 2005. Nobody else was even bidding for him. Mags was coming off a severe knee injury and two surgeries, the second performed in Austria because the procedure isn't even attempted in the U.S. He was only healthy for half his first season in Detroit. But in 2006, a fully healthy Magglio led the team to the playoffs for the first time in 19 years by hitting .298 with 24 home runs and 104 RBI. Most importantly, Ordonez's knee was stable enough for him to play in 155 games. In 2007, the $17 million per year man looked like a bargain at a Dearborn Dollar Store as Mags crushed 28 dingers, knocked in 139 runs and batted .363. His OPS of 1.029 was Bondsesque. And if it wasn't for Alex Rodriguez having an off-the-chart year (even by A-Rod standards), Ordonez would have taken down the AL MVP award. "O-E-O MAGGLIO!"

1. Chauncey Billups, Pistons, guard. In his best move as the General Manager of the Pistons (what, were you expecting the Darko pick?), Joe Dumars signed Chauncey Billups to a six-year, $35 million contract in 2002. Chauncey had spent the 2001-02 season in Minnesota playing second fiddle to Terrell Brandon. Because Brandon couldn't stay healthy, Billups had a lengthy audition that season and Joe D. liked what he saw. But Dumars still needed to get a little lucky. Billups didn't want to come off the bench any longer and the Timberwolves maintained their commitment to Brandon. Depending on whom you listen to, the choice to keep Brandon over Chauncey was either made by Kevin McHale or Flip Saunders. Obviously neither man wants to admit to that boneheaded move. In Billups' first season in Detroit, he led the team to the Eastern Conference Finals against New Jersey. And while the Pistons got swept by the Nets, the series probably would have been much closer if Billups would have been 100 percent healthy. In Chauncey's second season in Detroit, the team shocked the world by defeating the Los Angeles Lakers and winning the franchise's third championship. And in the grand tradition of Isiah Thomas and Dumars, Billups became the third Pistons guard to win the NBA Finals MVP. In addition to that MVP award, Billups has become a perennial All-Star and the anchor of a team that is now EXPECTED to win its division and get to the NBA Finals EVERY YEAR. Not bad for a guy that Rick Pitino gave up on after 51 games in Boston.

Detroit teams have had mixed results acquiring players via free agency. But with some of the General Managers that this town has seen over the last couple of decades, a lot of high-priced carnage was also inevitable. Maybe the most shocking part of this list is that Randy "The Son of Tal" Smith doesn't have one entry. Hmmm, maybe the guy wasn't so bad after all. . . . Yeah, right.

10. Michael Brooks, Lions, linebacker. In 1996, the Detroit Lions decided not to re-sign Chris Spielman. Because, you know, it is always a good idea to rid yourself of the heart and soul of your franchise while totally pissing off your entire fan base. Spielman went on to great things with the Buffalo Bills while Brooks only lasted one, lousy season in Detroit. But at least Lions head coach (and de facto General Manager) Wayne Fontes spared us the excuse that the person who REALLY made the decision to get rid of Spielman for Brooks was "Cocaine Wayne's" son.

9. Jim Pyne, Lions, center. In a move eerily similar to the Brooks-Spielman debacle, the Lions let their Pro Bowl center Kevin Glover sign with Seattle during the 1998 offseason. This actually turned out even worse than the Spielman blow off. Because while letting go of a Pro Bowler and infuriating your fan base is dumb enough, letting Glover go also pissed off the greatest player in the franchise's history. Glover was Barry Sander's best friend on the team. Who knows if #20 would have retired after the 1998 season if Glover was still in Detroit? And much like Michael Brooks, Pyne lasted one entire season in Detroit.

8. Warren Young, Red Wings, left wing. Young came out of nowhere to score 40 goals while chipping in with 32 assists as a rookie in 1984-85 for the Penguins. After that season, he became a free agent and hit pay dirt in the form of a lucrative contract with the Red Wings, who desperately needed more scoring punch. In signing Young, Detroit GM Jimmy Devellano ignored two HUMUNGOUS red flags: Red Flag #1. Young scored 40 goals for Pittsburgh playing on a line with a guy named MARIO "FREAKING" LEMIEUX. Ever hear of him? An effing Barcalounger could have scored 20 goals skating with that freak of nature.

Red Flag #2: While Young was indeed a rookie, he was 29 years old during that "magical" 1984-85 season. A 29-year-old rookie? Think that might be a little suspicious?

In his one and only season in Detroit, Young chipped in 22 goals, but he was an absolute abortion in his own end, registering a Plus/Minus of -20. At the end of the 1985-86 season, Warren "Not So" Young was sent back to Pittsburgh for cash considerations. By 1988, he was out of the NHL entirely.

7. Tim Belcher, Tigers, pitcher. The Tigers had some success with a journeyman, free-agent pitcher named Bill Gullickson, who won 20 games for the team in 1991. In 1994, they tried the same trick by signing journeyman free-agent pitcher Tim Belcher to a $3.4 million contract. While Belcher would never be considered the second coming of Tom Seaver, he was a serviceable pitcher who would eat innings and could win you 15 games in a good year. But 1994 was not a good year for Belcher. He finished with an ERA of 5.89, won only seven and lost 15 games, an American League high that year. Dude might have lost 20 if the '94 season hadn't been shortened by the August player's strike. Although some would claim that Belcher got a jump on the rest of the league and went on strike that April. When the labor strife ended, Belcher moved on to Seattle, where he, of course, rebounded to have a decent year.

6. Fernando Vina, Tigers, second baseman. After the Tigers abhorrent 119-loss season of 2003, the team had quite a few holes to fill, none bigger than at second base. So the team quickly gobbled up the St. Louis Cardinals two-time Gold Glove winner Vina. In their haste to be proactive in free agency, it's unclear whether the Tigers actually administered a physical to Vina before signing him. And if they did, the attending physician must have been Dr. Vinny Boombotz. Whatever the case may be, in 2004 Vina played only 29 games for the Tigers because of a severe leg injury. In 2005, Vina never took the field at all due to a strained right hamstring and patellar tendinitis in his left knee. To add insult to injury, Vina confirmed in 2007 on ESPN's *SportsCenter* that he used HGH to help recover from his injuries during the 2003 season. The 2003 season only. He specifically went on the record to say that he didn't take HGH in either 2004 or 2005. So Vina somehow found his conscience in 2004 after signing for the Tigers. Touching.

5. Troy Percival, Tigers, closer. During the offseason after 2005, the Tigers were in the market for a closer and Percival was coming off back-to-back 33-save seasons for the Disneyland Angels. Tigers GM Dave Dombrowski overlooked the fact that Percival's fastball velocity had plummeted during the second-half of 2004 and signed the former flamethrower to a two-year, $12 million contract. Predictably enough, Percival struggled in his 26 outings for the Tigers, posting a 5.76 ERA. He had a 1-3 record and blew three out of the eleven save chances that came his way. In July, Percival was diagnosed with a serious forearm injury and shut down for the remainder of the season. In his first spring training outing the following year, Percival experienced pain in his arm and promptly abandoned his comeback effort. In 2007, Percival's arm started to feel better and he decided to try another comeback. So did return to Detroit for a Tigers team that could have used any bullpen assistance it could find? Nope, instead he ended up in St. Louis where he went 3-0 with a 1.80 ERA.

4. Troy Crowder, Red Wings goon. In between his various incarcerations and drunken stupors, the Wings Bob Probert fought New Jersey Devils tough guy Troy Crowder early in the 1990-91 season. Probert was the undisputed heavyweight champ of the NHL. So you can imagine how shocking it was when the Devils' Crowder opened up a can of whoop ass on Probie. The Wings signed Crowder as a free agent prior to the 1991-92 season. But Crowder wasn't really a free agent. Any team signing him would have to give the Devils compensation. An independent arbitrator ruled that the Wings had to give up rugged right wing Randy McKay in exchange for the Devils' one-dimensional goon. Crowder suffered a serious back injury lifting weights over the summer and ended up playing only seven games for the Wings the next season. He sat out rehabbing all of the following season. In his seven games with the Wings, Crowder got into five fights and scored ZERO points. While Crowder was recovering from his back injury, McKay developed into a very good power forward. He would go on to score more than 15 goals for the Devils in five different seasons.

3. Damien Woody, Lions, offensive lineman. Before the 2005 season, Lions GM Matt Millen handed the Patriots' two-time Super Bowl champion a six-year, $31 million deal with a whopping $9 million signing bonus. Woody apparently celebrated by purchasing a $9 million gift certificate at Sizzler. His weight ballooned to almost 400 pounds and the Lions threatened to get rid of his fat ass if he didn't go on a diet. Woody did lose 40 pounds prior to the 2007 season and started three games early in the year at right guard. Then he was benched and kept on the inactive list for the next three games. Because of a poor play and a variety of injuries, the Lions were forced to put Woody back into the starting lineup at right tackle—a position he hadn't played since high school. In typical, ironic Lions fashion, Woody played well—so well, the Lions decided that they wanted to bring him back as their right tackle in 2008. So predictably enough, during the offseason, Woody signed a free-agent contract with the New York Jets. The effing Lions.

2. Bill Schroeder/Az-Zahir Hakim. We don't want to go all Paul Harvey on you, but if you want to know the origins of why Matt Millen thought it necessary to spend first-round after first- round pick on wide receivers, you have to know the story of Millen's abject failure trying to fill that position through free agency. Before the 2002 season, Millen signed free-agent wide receivers Az-Zahir Hakim from St. Louis and the Packers' Bill Schroeder, who'd averaged over 60 catches and almost 1000 yards in the past three seasons. Of course, those stats were put up with Brett Favre throwing him the ball and not Ty Detmer, Mike McMahon and Joey Harrington. Schroeder's stats fell in Detroit by almost half, except for his drops, which probably quadrupled. The signing of Hakim was inherently moronic. The 5-foot-10, 189-pound receiver was the perfect third option (behind Isaac Bruce and Tory Holt) for the "Greatest Show on Turf" in St. Louis. But in Detroit, Hakim didn't have the luxury of being the third wheel. It wasn't like Larry Foster and Eddie Drummond were going to divert any attention away from opposing defenses. In three, injury-plagued years with Detroit, Hakim caught an average of 39 balls for 508 yards and three TDs. The busts of Hakim and Schroeder led to the selections of Charles Rogers, Roy and Mike Williams, then Calvin Johnson. And now . . . you know . . . the rest . . . of the story.

1. Uwe Krupp, Red Wings, defenseman. In June of 1998, the Red Wings were coming off their second straight Stanley Cup championship. But due to the loss of Vladimir Konstantinov the prior year because that pothead Richard Gnida couldn't keep his limousine on Woodward Avenue and the decline of aging Slava Fetisov, the Wings needed to add a big, physical defenseman over the summer. And not only did they sign one of the top available free-agent defenseman in Uwe Krupp, they took him away from their bitter rival, the Colorado Avalanche. The Wings gave Krupp a four-year deal worth $16.4 million and the organ-EYE-zation hoped that he would be a key member of a third straight championship team. In his first season with in Detroit, Krupp was limited to only 22 games and KOed for the rest of the season in December due to a severe back injury. And if you think the Wings were frustrated that their top free-agent signing couldn't play for them, imagine how pissed they were when it turned out that Krupp suffered his injury racing sled dogs WHILE HE WAS ON INJURED RESERVE!!!!!

The Wings suspended Krupp without pay. Krupp immediately filed a grievance and the long process of arbitration began. Krupp missed the next two seasons. In 2001-2, Krupp finally returned to the Red Wings for a grand total of 10 games. Incredibly enough, Krupp played those games in Detroit while the battle over the Wings refusal to pay him $8 million in salary continued. That must have been real comfortable for everyone involved. The grievance would not be resolved until January of 2003 when the second arbitrator, Joan Scott, finally got Mike Ilitch and Krupp to agree on an undisclosed financial settlement. What can be disclosed is this free agent signing was the worst in Detroit sports history. And to make matters even worse, the Avs got the last laugh.

Here's a bunch of scores, stats and various facts that seem too good, bad, ugly or weird to be true.

1,664 weeks. Amount of time that *Sports Illustrated* was in publication before featuring a Detroit Piston on its cover.

550-0. Total by which Michigan outscored its opponents during the 1901 college football season.

198. Players selected before Michigan QB Tom Brady in the 2000 NFL draft.

Spergon Wynn. Name of last quarterback selected before Tom Brady in that draft.

186-184. Final score of the Pistons' 1983 triple overtime win over the Denver Nuggets, the highest scoring game in NBA history. (The Pistons franchise also participated in the NBA's lowest scoring game ever, a 19-18 win over the Minneapolis Lakers in 1950.)

107. Number of professional mixed martial arts bouts fought by Michigan native Dan Severn.

76. Yards gained by the Lions' Greg Landry on a quarterback sneak against the Green Bay Packers during a game in 1970.

34. Rebounds grabbed by Dennis Rodman for the Pistons in a 1992 game vs. the Pacers.

33. Points scored in one quarter by Detroit native George Gervin for the San Antonio Spurs against the Utah Jazz in 1978.

28. Years it took someone to beat Detroit native Eddie Tolan's Olympic record in the 100 meters he set at the 1932 Games.

24. Age of Dave Debusschere when he became head coach of the Detroit Pistons in 1964.

23-9 (.719). Lions all-time record vs. the Atlanta Falcons.

10-26 (.278). Lions all-time record vs. the Washington Redskins.

22. Shoe size of Pistons great Bob Lanier.

8. Yards needed by Lions QB Jon Kitna when he attempted a quarterback sneak on third down against the Packers in 2006.

1. Number of playoff games the Lions have won in the last 50 years.

.376. Pistons team shooting percentage for the 1957-58 season.

.15. Career ERA for professional women's softball pitcher Kathy Arendsen, a native of Holland, Michigan.

The Chicago Cubs. The team the Tigers lost to in their first World Series in 1907.

Some guys get christened with names that perfectly define what game they will play as adults or how they will play it. Guys like Mike Quick. Speedy Claxton. Glen Steele. And other guys get saddled with names like these.

20. Roman Colon, Tigers, 2005–06, pitcher. Not an Italian proctologist.

19. R.B. Nunnery, Lions, 1960, tackle. Not a running back or a convent.

18. Monk Meineke, Pistons, 1953–55, forward–center. Not a guy who changed mufflers at a monastery garage.

17. Dick Booth, Lions, 1941, 1945, two-way back. Not a peep show stall with a two-way mirror.

16. Cotton Price, Lions, 1940–41, 1945, two-way back. Did not trade in agricultural futures.

15. Fred Riddle, Lions, 1959, running back. Not a game show host or a supervillain.

14. Bob Dethman, Lions, 1942, running back. Not a mortician or the Grim Reaper.

13. Mike Shill, Lions, 1957, tackle. O-line draft pick who didn't make the last great Lions team—not a front office spokesman who made excuses for another crappy Lions team.

12. Phenomenal Smith, 1886, Detroit Wolverines, pitcher. Retired after seven seasons with the not-so-phenomenal record of 54-74.

11. Red Stacy, 1935–37, offensive lineman. Not a redhead cheerleader.

10. Rusty Kuntz, Tigers, 1984–85, outfielder. Not a group of washed up female porn stars.

9. Whizzer White, Lions, 1940–41, running back. Pro Bowler and future U.S. Supreme Court justice, not the guy who administered urine tests.

8. John Oldham, Pistons, 1950–51, guard. Not a cured meats salesman or a crappy, aging actor.

7. Jerry Lumpe, Tigers, 1964–67, 2B, SS, 3B. Wiry utility infielder, not a body double for William Shatner.

6. Jocelyn Borgella, Lions, 1994-96. Not a chick.

5. Liz Funk, Tigers, 1939, outfielder. Not the female keyboardist in a George Clinton band.

4. Clint Wager, Pistons, 1950, center-forward. Two-sport pro, not Alex Karras and Bobby Layne's bookie.

3. Hooks Dauss, Tigers, 1912-26, pitcher. Good starting pitcher, not the bad guy in a German slasher movie.

2. Steve Junker, Lions, 1957-60, a tight end. Didn't end up in business with Fred Sanford.

1. Don Doll, Lions, 1949-52. Not a relative of Ken doll, ex-boyfriend of the Barbie doll.

You can't go home again, as the old saying goes. But these guys probably wished they could have returned to this area when their careers took sharp turns for the worse after they left. Or that they'd never left in the first place.

10. Ben Wallace. He was beloved, a champion, a four-time All-star and four-time NBA Defensive Player of the Year award winner. Then in 2006, Big Ben reneged on a promise to re-sign with the Pistons and bolted town for Chicago. He hasn't won any awards or revisited the NBA Finals since.

9. Matin Lapointe. He jilted the Red Wings for the big money lure of free agency in 2000. The Wings won their third Stanley Cup in five years the following spring. In the six years since he left Detroit, Lapointe hasn't even won a playoff series.

8. Sergei Fedorov. Followed Lapointe's lead to career oblivion. Though his path proved even lamer with him signing with a Mickey Mouse franchise named after an Emilio Estevez movie.

7. Bill Frieder. The Saginaw native and UM business school graduate lead the Wolverines' men's basketball team to its fifth-straight NCAA tourney in 1989, But Frieder was fired by UM athletic director Bo Schembechler after announcing he would leave for Arizona State after March Madness. Frieder's assistant Steve Fisher took over and guided the Wolverines to the national championship a few weeks later. During his eight years at ASU, Frieder only won a single NCAA tournament game. He resigned in 1997 amidst point-shaving allegations against his players after a 10-20 season.

6. Barry Sanders. Who among us hasn't wanted to fax the media to announce that he couldn't take the Lions anymore? But the great running back was just a typical Barry Sanders season away from becoming the NFL's all-time leading rusher. Yet he chose to walk away. It's still sad and stunning years later.

5. Lance Parrish. During a decade in Detroit, Parrish developed into maybe the game's best catcher. A Gold Glover, he averaged almost 30 homers and 100 RBI during his last five seasons here and won a World Series in 1984. Then Lance signed a big free agent deal with Philadelphia and was never the same. Parrish's offensive numbers slumped badly, along with his spirits. A solid fan favorite in Detroit, he became a prime target for Philly's fickle bleacher lunatics. During subsequent stints with the Angels, Mariners, Indians, Blue Jays and Pirates, Parrish failed to reclaim the Detroit magic might have carried him into the Hall of Fame.

4. Dale Alexander. The first baseman averaged .331 and 120 RBI over his first three seasons in Detroit. Then he mysteriously fell out of favor with Detroit's management in 1932 and was traded him to Boston for Earl Webb. The deal didn't work out for the Tigers, who saw Webb slump the following year, then retire. The deal worked out even worse for Dale Alexander. In 1933, he sprained his knee and was treated with electric heating pads by the Red Sox trainer. The pads got too hot and gave Alexander third-degree burns, which led to gangrene in his leg. After nearly losing his leg to amputation, Alexander was barely able to run. He tried to keep playing but was sent to the minors the following season and never returned to the big leagues.

3. Larry Brown. Had he behaved himself and stayed, the Dean Smith disciple could have put questions about his mercenary tendencies behind him and cemented his status as one of the greatest basketball coaches ever. Instead, he went 23-59 with the Knicks and started flirting again with other teams on his way to another dismissal, plus a lawsuit. In the process, Brown reminded everyone of the vices he's lapsed into throughout his career and secured his legacy as his profession's biggest weasel.

2. Eddie Cicotte. The knuckleballer actually enjoyed a great career after he left the Tigers in 1905, notching 213 victories in 13 seasons for Boston and Chicago. But the Detroit native also fell into bad company. Cicotte saw his Hall of Fame-caliber career end in infamy when his White Sox turned into the Black Sox during the 1919 World Series. The right-handed pitcher was one of the Sox "eight men out" who found themselves permanently banned from the league in the wake of the game-fixing scandal.

1. Drew Henson. The nation's top QB recruit in 1997, Henson interned for two years at Michigan behind Tom Brady, then showed great promise as the Wolverine's first-string signal caller in 2000. He led UM to a share of the Big Ten title and a bowl win. His rifle arm, quick feet, 4.5 speed and improving ability to read a defense made Henson the early favorite to win the Heisman the next season and become the first overall pick in the NFL draft. But then Henson, who had been playing minor league baseball for the Yankees organization during his summers, dropped out of Michigan to dedicate himself full-time to baseball, caving to demands by Yankees owner George Steinbrenner, an Ohio State grad and big Buckeyes football supporter. Four years later, he'd made it up to the bigs for only nine-at-bats. Henson returned to football with the Dallas Cowboys in 2004. But his rust showed and the Cowboys cut him after a few dismal performances. He played in Europe for a year, then got cut by the Vikings during the 2007 preseason. A tryout with Jacksonville ended with the Jaguars opting to sign Todd Bouman instead, which is the football gods' way of telling you that it's time to retire. Had Henson stayed in Ann Arbor another year, he may well have become a Wolverine legend, a Heisman Trophy winner and national champ (Michigan was loaded that season until Henson's defection left them without an experienced QB). And he'd probably be a very wealthy young man with his choice of supermodels to date. Oh, well, at least Tom Brady accomplished most of that.

The 12 Best High School Basketball Players in Detroit Public School League History :: Perry Watson

Note: Watson served as head coach of the men's basketball team at the University of Detroit from 1993-2008. He enjoyed four straight 20-win seasons from 1998-2001 on his way to compiling a record of 258-185 to become the school's second all-time winningest coach. The Motown native previously served as head assistant coach at the University of Michigan during their Fab 5 days. His coaching legend began at Detroit Southwestern High School, where he led the Prospectors to consecutive state titles in 1990 and '91, while compiling a record of 302-34 to become the winningest coach in the history of Detroit's Public School League (PSL).

12. Johnny Davis, Murray Wright. Great athlete and scorer.

11. Bubbles Hawkins, Pershing. Prototype guard who could score, handle and pass.

10. Derrick Coleman, Northern. Tremendous rebounder, defender, scorer and could handle exceptionally well for a big man. He led the team to the 1986 City Championship on his way to being named a High School All-American.

9. Reggie Harding, Eastern. A seven-footer who could score, rebound, defend and dominate.

8. George Gervin, King. A smooth scoring machine who could handle, rebound and block shots.

7. Larry Fogle, Cooley. Great rebounder and scorer who set a PSL record with 73 points in one game.

6. Ralph Simpson, Pershing. Great shooter, rebounder and low-post scorer who led his team to the 1967 State Championship and was named a High School All-American the following year.

5. Spencer Haywood, Pershing. A powerful rebounder, defender and low-post scorer, Haywood was a man amongst boys on most nights. He carried his team to the state title in 1967 and was named an All-American.

4. Curtis Jones, Northwestern. A tremendous playmaker and floor general with a game that was way ahead of its time in the late 60s.

3. Jalen Rose, Southwestern. The 1991 High School All-American was an all-around talent who led his team to three straight City Championships and two straight State Championships.

2. Antoine Joubert, Southwestern. Named the #1 high school player in the country in 1983, Joubert was a great scorer, rebounder and floor general, He led his team to three straight City Championships and two straight State Championship runner-up finishes.

1. Clifford Williams, Southwestern. The 1963 High School All-American scored 61 points in a game against Chadsey, establishing a city record that stood until Larry Fogle broke it with 73. Williams led the PSL in scoring two straight years.

Note: Markowski has worked for *The Detroit News* since 1978. His main beat is covering high school sports. He has been inducted into the Catholic League Coaches Hall of Fame and the Basketball Coaches of Michigan (for media) Hall of Fame. His list below was compiled through personal observations, coaches' opinions, and conversations with school administrators and other sports writers.

Honorable Mentions: Randy Kinder, East Lansing; Charles Rogers, Saginaw High; Marshall Dill, Detroit Northern; Courtney Hawkins, Flint Beecher; Lamar Woodley, Saginaw High; Andre Rison, Flint Northwestern; Spencer Haywood, Detroit Pershing; Drew Henson, Brighton; Darnell Dickerson, Detroit King; Dathan Ritzenhein, Rockford; Jim Abbott, Flint Central; Pete Dawkins, Bloomfield Hills Cranbrook; Kirk Gibson, Waterford Mott; Joe DeLamielleure, Center Line St. Clement; Reggie Mackenzie, Highland Park; Ron Johnson, Detroit .Northwestern; John Rouser, Hamtramck; Earl Morrall, Muskegon; Jim Simpson, Royal Oak Shrine; Frank Tanana, Detroit Catholic Central; Bill Freehan, Royal Oak; Mateen Cleaves, Flint Northern.

Top Coach: Lofton Greene, River Rouge (basketball).

10. Bill Yearby, Detroit Eastern. Yearby was a three-sport athlete. His best sport was football and later played at the University of Michigan and for the New York Jets. He started on the basketball team and placed first in the shot put in 1962 (Class A).

9. T.J. Duckett, Kalamazoo Loy Norrix. Duckett was *The Detroit News'* No. 1 blue-chip prospect in 1998 as he played both running back and linebacker. He later played for Michigan State and in the NFL. Three times he was the shot put state champion (1997, '98, and '99). He still owns the Class A record in the shot put (64 feet, ? inch) set in '99.

8. Greg Meyer, Grand Rapids. The West Catholic grad won the 1983 Boston Marathon. He set 10 American road racing records and two world records in the (15K and the 10 Mile). He was inducted into several halls of fame including *ESPN* Road Racing and Road Runners Club of America and also won the Detroit Marathon in 1980 and Chicago Marathon in '82.

7. Ted Simmons, Southfield High. One of the best switch hitters in pro baseball history. Was one of the top running backs his senior season in the Metro Detroit area. He was selected (baseball) in the first round (10th overall) in the 1967 draft by the St. Louis Cardinals.

6. Hayes Jones, Pontiac. Jones won two state championships and set a state record during his track career at Pontiac High School (later called Pontiac Central). At Eastern Michigan University, Jones earned two NCAA hurdles championships. One of the greatest track hurdlers of all-time. Unbeaten for several years in his specialty. Won the gold medal in the high hurdles at Tokyo Olympics in 1964, and a bronze at Rome in 1960. Also a brilliant sprinter. Was part of a world record 400-meter relay team.

5. Rick Leach, Flint Southwestern. All-State in three sports (football, baseball and basketball). Leach excelled the most in football and baseball. He was named a high school All-American quarterback, and he was a Major League Baseball prospect as well. The Philadelphia Phillies reportedly offered Leach a $100,000 contract to play professional baseball right out of high school. He turned it down to play quarterback for Michigan, where her started all four years. He later played 10 seasons in the MLB.

4. Dave DeBusschere, Detroit Austin. Led Austin to the Class A state championship in 1958 and was the star hurler on an Austin baseball team that won the city championship. He also pitched a local team to a national junior championship. In '62, he received a $75,000 signing bonus from the Chicago White Sox and a $15,000 contract from the Detroit Pistons, who had claimed him as a territorial draft pick. Ended up playing both pro baseball and basketball.

3. Henry Carr, Detroit Northwestern. Sprinter in track, receiver/defensive back in football. Won the gold medal in the 200-meter dash in 1964 Olympics and anchored the winning 1,600-meter relay there. Played three seasons in the NFL as a defensive back for the New York Giants.

2. "Little" Richie Jordan, Fennville. A four-sport athlete who earned 16 varsity letters, Jordan was inducted into the National High School Sports Hall of Fame, the first athlete from Michigan to gain that honor. He had 5,132 career rushing yards (tops in the state as of 1964). He averaged 44 points as a senior. Played baseball and competed in track and field. Only 5-foot-7, Jordan could dunk the ball with both hands.

1. Tyrone Wheatley, Dearborn Heights Robichaud. As good as Wheatley was as a running back at Robichaud, he was also a fine defensive player. He dominated the game and led Robichaud to its only football title (1990). He also started on the basketball team and was a top track athlete, winning the state long jump and the 100-meter dash titles for three consecutive years. He won four individual events in the 1990 Class B finals giving Robichaud all 40 of its points as the Bulldogs won the state title. As a sophomore in 1989, he won the long jump with a jump of 23 feet, 10 3/4 inches, which is still a Class B/Division 2 record. His time of 13.7 in the 1991 high hurdles also remains a Class B/Division 2 record.

Top Ten Michigan High School Men's Basketball Players :: Keith Langlois

Note: A 27-year journalism veteran, Langlois now serves as web site editor for pistons.com and covers the team on a daily basis. He previously worked at *The Oakland Press* for 22 years as sports editor and lead sports columnist. Over the life of his career, he has won numerous awards, most recently being named the Michigan Press Association's top sports columnist in 2003, 2004 and 2006. He is also a fan and historian of Michigan high school basketball.

Honorable Mentions: Talk about a tough list to crack: Richie Jordan averaged 44.4 points a game in 1965 at Fennville, but couldn't break into the top ten; Jay Smith is Michigan's all-time leading scorer with 2,841 career points for Mio AuSable, but he didn't make the final cut, either; nor did Mark Brown of Hastings, who twice in his career averaged better than 37 points a game. A long list of Mr. Basketball winners join them on the honorable mention sidelines, including Sam Vincent, Antoine Joubert, Glen Rice, Terry Mills, Jason Richardson and Drew Neitzel. They all deserve to be in the top ten, but who gets cut to make that happen?

10. George Gervin. He wasn't widely recruited out of then-Detroit Eastern for a lot of reasons. It was shortly after the Detroit riots of 1967 and many recruiters shied away out of fear for their safety. Gervin was something of a late bloomer whose academic struggles forced him to miss half his junior season. But after sprouting to 6-foot-4 as a senior, Gervin averaged 31 points and 20 rebounds a game to carry his team to the state quarterfinals. Jerry Tarkanian, then coaching at Long Beach State, heard about him from the father of George Trapp, a former Piston who had played for Tark. Gervin never played for Tarkanian, though he signed with Long Beach. He got homesick and missed his girlfriend, transferring back home to Eastern Michigan before going on to become one of the NBA's most prolific scorers after getting his start in the ABA as a 19-year-old.

9. Dan Majerle. If "Thunder Dan" had played in Detroit, Flint or Grand Rapids, he would have been a McDonald's All-American and chased by all the national powers. Instead, he wound up playing at Central Michigan and carrying the Chippewas to the NCAA tournament, then becoming a lottery pick, booed by Phoenix Suns fans when the pick was announced. But a few months later, Majerle showed his stuff while leading the 1988 U.S. Olympic team in scoring at 14.1 a game. Majerle averaged 37 points in his senior year at Traverse City in 1982-83 and went on to a 14-year NBA career that included three All-Star appearances.

8. Shane Battier. A four-year starter at Detroit Country Day, Battier led the Yellowjackets to three state titles. He was less flashy than the more famous player who preceded him at Country Day, Chris Webber, but wound up with a remarkably similar high school resumé. Battier went on to a terrific career at Duke, where he starred as a senior on the 2001 NCAA title team while sweeping the major national Player of the Year awards. Battier also was a three-time national defensive player of the year.

7. Eric Turner. The point guard and catalyst on Flint Central's 1981 Class A state champion, Turner holds virtually every state assists record (25 in a game, 341 in a season and 726 in a career). His pro career was derailed by personal struggles, but many believe Turner to be the most dynamic player ever to come out of talent-rich Flint. He set a championship game record with 17 assists in a 108-90 Class A title win over Detroit Murray-Wright. Many consider this game to be the most entertaining in finals history.

6. Chet Walker. If Turner played in the most entertaining game in finals history, the next two entrants played in maybe the most competitively thrilling. In the 1958 Class A title game, Chet "The Jet" Walker and Benton Harbor took on Detroit Austin and Dave DeBusschere. The 6-foot-6 Walker would go on to become the best player ever at Bradley University, where he averaged 24.4 points and 12.8 rebounds a game. The master of the pump fake, Walker played 13 years in the NBA, averaging 18.2 points and 7.1 rebounds. His single-game best of 56 stood as a Chicago Bulls franchise record until some guy named Jordan came along.

5. Dave DeBusschere. DeBusschere's Detroit Austin team got the better of Walker and Benton Harbor that day, winning 71-68 with DeBusschere's big fourth quarter proving the difference. He finished with 32, Walker with 25. DeBusschere went on to the University of Detroit and played both professional basketball and baseball as a pitcher with the Chicago White Sox. DeBusschere was a player-coach with the Pistons at 24, the youngest coach in NBA history. But made his real mark with the New York Knicks, who won two NBA titles during his time there. A 12-year pro, DeBusschere played in eight All-Star games. At 6-foot-6, DeBusschere was tough as nails, a tenacious rebounder and defender who could knock down perimeter jump shots.

4. Campy Russell. Many believe the Pontiac Central teams Russell starred on in the early 70s were the best in Michigan to never win a state title. In 1970, Russell's junior year, the undefeated Chiefs were upset by Detroit Pershing in legendary coach Will Robinson's final game. The next year, in one of the most ballyhooed games in state history, Russell and Pontiac Central lost to Detroit Kettering in the state semifinals. Basketball News called Russell the best high school player in the country in 1971. Freshmen weren't yet eligible to play varsity college sports and Russell left Michigan after his junior season for a nine-year NBA career. In two years at Michigan, Russell averaged 21.2 points and 10.4 rebounds a game. He was a terrific long-range shooter who could handle the ball unusually well at 6-foot-8.

3. Chris Webber. Webber was a wunderkind who had the Detroit TV stations doing stories on him when he was in eighth grade. His enrollment at Country Day caused headlines. A man among boys even as a freshman, Webber was long and sinewy, a young James Worthy. As he grew more powerful, Webber dominated with his explosiveness. His hands were enormous. He didn't have a great shooting touch, but he jumped over everybody and created space as his body filled out. Webber carried Country Day to state championships in his last three seasons before going on to a bittersweet two-year career at Michigan that ended with two NCAA title game losses, followed by the Ed Martin recruiting scandal that found Webber to have illegally taken money and favors from the booster, resulting in NCAA sanctions for Michigan that barred Webber from an association with the school until 2013.

2. Spencer Haywood. The star of Will Robinson's 1967 state champions at Detroit Pershing, Haywood's effects on basketball were dramatic. It was Haywood who, after leading Team USA to the 1968 Olympic basketball gold medal as its 19-year-old center, successfully challenged in court the legality of the NBA's rule barring the drafting or employment of players whose college classes had yet to graduate. Before that, Haywood was a beast on a Pershing team that included future Michigan State and pro star Ralph Simpson at shooting guard and Tigers outfielder Marvin Lane, among others. When Flint Central decided to double-team Haywood in the Class A state title game, Haywood still scored 24 points but all the attention he drew allowed Simpson to break loose for 43, a finals record that stood for 14 years. Legendary Detroit Free Press sportswriter Hal Schram wrote at the time, "One superstar helped make another here Saturday night." In his one season at the University of Detroit, Haywood averaged 32.1 points and 21.5 rebounds a game. A year later, he was both the Rookie of the Year and MVP of the ABA.

1. Magic Johnson. It stands to reason that a guy in the discussion for the greatest basketball player of all-time would be No. 1 on Michigan's list. Magic was a legend in Lansing before he suited up for the first game of his freshman year at Lansing Everett. Three times an All-State player, Johnson was given his nickname by a sportswriter for the Lansing State Journal, Fred Stabley Jr., whose father was the iconic, long-time sports information director at Michigan State, where Johnson would spend two seasons, leading the Spartans to the 1979 NCAA title. Three times an All-State selection at Everett, Johnson carried the Vikings to the 1977 Class A state title in a memorable overtime win against Birmingham Brother Rice, which tied the game on a half-court shot as regulation ended. But Johnson dominated the overtime period and closed his high school career fittingly, as a champion.

Ten Best and Worst Local Sports Hairstyles

The Detroit sports scene has seen its share of good hair, bad hair, fake hair, porn hair and greasy hair. Here are the most memorable 'dos in Detroit sports history.

10. Mickey Redmond, Red Wings (player and announcer). "This entry is brought to you by Drs. Tessler and Aronovitz." Did anyone even know about hair transplants before the Red Wings' color announcer and former winger started shilling for his doctors during the team's broadcasts? Dude is like the Neil Armstrong of plugs. We must warn you, the hair transplant procedure isn't for everyone. According to the Mick, the operating room of Tessler and Aronovitz is no place for a nervous person.

9. Rob Deer, Tigers. When you're an outfielder whose career legacy is your propensity to lead the league in strikeouts and your AWFUL mullet, well let's just say you have plenty of time to do things other than write your Hall of Fame induction speech.

8. Harold Snepsts, Red Wings. During the defenseman's tenure in Detroit, Wings fans loved to chant Harold Snepsts' name while he was on the ice. "Harrrrrrrrrrrold. Harrrrrrrrrrrold. Harrrrrrrrrrrold." And it was always easy for his fans to spot him on the ice, because the glare off his bald head was about as powerful as that light outside the Luxor Hotel that can be seen in outer space. Maybe they should have changed the chant to: "Combover! Combover! Combover!"

We know that Snepsts played in the NHL when there was no rule that you had to wear a helmet, but we can't help but wonder why the guy didn't just wear one voluntarily.

7. Petr Klima, Red Wings. Did they have barbers in Czechoslavakia during the Soviet occupation? Seriously, did a Czech hockey player ever come to North America with a nicely groomed melon? Klima? Jaromir Jagr? Ziggy Palffy? We must have missed the chapter in The Communist Manifesto that referred to mandatory mullets. Oh, and did we mention that Klima had highlights? Highlights? We are talking about highlights!?! A hockey player. With highlights? In his hair?

6. Mike Ilitch, Red Wings and Tigers owner. So how much money do you need to get a really good toupee? Because you would think the man who founded Little Caesars could afford some fake hair that, you know, didn't look like fake hair. Dude, you are like a billionaire, you don't have to mail order from The Hair Club For Men. William Shatner laughs at the rug that Mr. Ilitch wears. And really, when you are mocking the guy's toupee, you really should refer to him as Mr. Ilitch. It would be disrespectful, otherwise.

5. Chuck Daly, Detroit Pistons head coach. Finally, now that is some good hair. Perfectly coifed. (Did we just say coifed?) Never a hair out of place. EVER. Seriously, John Edwards is jealous of "Big Daddy Rich's" hairdo. It really is amazing that Daly even associated himself with his assistant, Ron Rothstein's perm. When the Pistons put a banner up at the Palace to honor Daly, they shouldn't have put his name on the thing. A picture of his hair would have sufficed.

4. Kelly Tripucka, Pistons. Between that hairstyle and that moustache and those tight shorts, you weren't sure if Tripucka should have been shooting 24-foot jump shots for the Pistons or starring in the next Lady Chatterly's Lover sequel on Cinemax. If the guy was playing today, you know the Palace would play that cheesy 70s porn music every time he sank a basket.

3. Charlie Sanders, Lions. When retired tight end Charlie Sanders finally got the call from Canton that he was going to be inducted into the Pro Football Hall of Fame, he was, of course, ecstatic. So when they sat down to begin the work on Sanders' actual bust, the big question was, "How big should the Afro be?" Because when #88 played for the Lions, the damn thing was HUGE. In retirement, Sanders had his 'fro scaled down tremendously. In the end, Sanders decided to go with the smaller afro instead of the super-sized edition.

2. Ron Duguay, Red Wings. The following quote is ripped right out of the wikipedia.org entry for the former Wings forward: "In the NHL, Duguay was noted for his long curly hair, which would blow behind him as he skated without a helmet. In the 1970s he was more widely known as a pop icon and a sex symbol than for his athletic talents. He appeared in a TV commercial for Sassoon Jeans. In the 1990s, Duguay married former fashion model Kim Alexis. What can we even add to that? Vidal Sassoon Jeans? Do you realize how much confidence you must have in your own masculinity to play hockey, have that sort of hair and appear in commercials for a designer jean company when your name is pronounced, "DO-GAY"? It is really mind-boggling. Obviously, porking Kim Alexis gives you that sort of confidence.

1. Ben Wallace, Pistons. There probably isn't an athlete in all of sports who is more recognized for his hair than former Pistons center Ben Wallace. While in Detroit, Ben's 'fro was featured on billboards advertising for the team. Not a picture of Wallace, just his hair. He did a car commercial (see the "Ten Most Memorable Commercials" list) where items kept popping out of his hair. An entire advertising campaign was built around the phrase, "Fear the 'Fro." The Pistons would have giveaways at the Palace where the first 10,000 lucky fans would get a replica Ben Wallace Afro. Fans tried to determine the All-Stars mood and how he was going to play depending on the style of his afro or if he had his hair in braids. During the 2005 NBA Finals versus the San Antonio Spurs, ESPN writer Marc Stein wrote a 1,000 word piece about the importance of Ben's decision to go 'fro or cornrow.

Note: Veteran Detroit sports journalist Mike O'Hara is a graduate of Pershing High School and Wayne State University, both in Detroit. He has been writing for *The Detroit News* since 1966—with a two-year vacation, compliments of the United States Army, from 1969-71. He began covering boxing in 1967. He's also an avid runner who has completed five different marathons—Boston, Detroit (numerous times), Pittsburgh, Duluth and Big Sur. He also gained an acknowledgment on the gold-selling CD Rotting Pinata by the legendary Detroit alternative band Sponge. O'Hara is thrilled to at one time have had the home telephone numbers of Muhammad Ali, Jim Brown and Dick the Bruiser. (All three answered their own phones.)

10. Holmes, Spinks, Cooney, Cosell at the Joe Louis Arena, 1981.
Heavyweight champion Larry Holmes fought Leon Spinks with The Brown Bomber sitting at ringside. Leon knew only one way to fight—bore in and swing with everything he had. The action was furious, but Leon was overmatched. Holmes, vastly underrated because he fought in Ali's shadow, had Spinks helpless when the bout was stopped in the third round. The bout was a tune-up for a Holmes' fight with Gerry Cooney the next year in Vegas. Howard Cosell interviewed Cooney at ringside after the bout, and Holmes became enraged, thinking he'd been upstaged. A scuffle broke out, with Cosell in the middle. It was a memorable event for a lot of reasons—not the least being the presence of Joe Louis in a building named in his honor.

9. But was the blood real?
A former professional football player who turned to professional wrestling, Dick the Bruiser was a popular villain, and Detroit was one of his prime markets. In 1963, The Bruiser signed to wrestle Alex Karras, a defensive lineman for the Detroit Lions who was suspended for the year for gambling on football. A couple of nights before the bout, the two met at the Lindell A.C. Bar in downtown Detroit, and a scuffle broke out. A TV set was broken, and a Detroit cop had his hand broken. The Bruiser was arrested, but the judge put off the arraignment to let the wrestling match go on. The Bruiser pinned Karras early and left town. It was great theatre.

8. Hearns-Leonard II.
The site was the same as their first bout—Caesars Palace. But everything else had changed. By 1989, Hearns and Leonard were richer, older and slower. Hearns knocked down Leonard in the third and 11th rounds and went into the 12th round with a comfortable lead. Leonard pressed the action for part of the round and managed to pull out a draw. Most ringside observers thought Hearns had won. Hearns attended the Pistons-Lakers game the next night in Los Angeles. He had a courtside seat. Interviewed on national TV, Hearns said: "For the first time in my life, I can say I was robbed."

7. Kronk Crown. Hilmer Kenty was a tall, slender lightweight who moved to Detroit to join the Kronk Boxing Team. On March 2, 1980, he fought WBA lightweight champ Ernesto Espana and was a heavy underdog. It looked like Kenty was overmatched when he went down on a flash knockdown in the first round. But Kenty got up, regained his senses and carried the fight to Espana. The bout was stopped in the ninth round, and Kronk had its first world champion—Hilmer James Kenty.

6. Ali Shuffle in Motown. Muhammad Ali was heavyweight champ, but his title was stripped when he refused induction into the Army. In 1967, former Pistons player and coach Ray Scott promoted a fight card in Detroit that included two three-round exhibitions by Ali. One opponent was Alvin "Blue" Lewis, a charismatic Detroit heavyweight. They were only exhibitions, but nobody put on a better show than Ali. He did not get back in the ring until 1970.

5. Robinson–LaMotta, the series. The Detroit native's given name was Walker Smith. But everyone knew him as Sugar Ray—the original, and pound-for-pound, the best fighter of all time. Robinson's five bouts with Jake LaMotta were legendary. "We were married," LaMotta once told me in an interview decades later. Robinson was 40-0 when he met LaMotta for the first time on February 5, 1943 at the old Olympia Stadium in Detroit. LaMotta won a unanimous decision—the only time he beat Robinson. Robinson won the rematch 21 days later, also at Olympia. Robinson got his first title shot in 1946, with a record of 73-1 and one draw. Robinson beat Tommy Bell on a unanimous decision in New York to win the welterweight crown.

4. Hearns–Leonard I, 1981. Hearns and Sugar Ray Leonard were on a collision course since the day both turned pro. Leonard, with his gold medal from the 1976 Olympics and Hollywood smile, was a man of the world. Hearns was a man of the ring, and he craved Leonard's stature. They met on September 16 at Caesars Palace in Vegas. Hearns dominated the early going until Leonard exploded a right uppercut on his jaw, almost ending the bout. Hearns survived—barely—and turned boxer, piling up points. Hearns was comfortably ahead when Leonard landed a long right that stunned him in the 13th round. Leonard almost raced from his stool when the 14th round began. Hearns was helpless on the ropes when the bout was stopped.

3. Hearns–Hagler. For sheer furry, Hearns' bout with middleweight champ Marvelous Marvin Hagler in Las Vegas in 1985 was the best short fight in history. Neither fighter backed up, which was not a good strategy for Hearns. They went toe-to-toe. Hagler hurt Hearns badly in the second round and finished him off in the third. A group of us were talking about the fight later that night. Somebody asked Larry Merchant, the HBO boxing commentator, how he had scored the first round.

"I gave them both 11," Merchant said.

2. Hearns-Cuevas. Thomas "Hit Man" Hearns turned pro in 1977 and was climbing the welterweight ladder, with a sizzling left hook and straight right that kept him undefeated. All that was missing was a world title. Hearns met WBA welterweight champion Pipino Cuevas on August 2, 1980 at Cobo Arena in Detroit. Cuevas had made a show of ripping the supports off the wall when he hit the speed bag at the end of his workouts. Emanuel Steward, Hearns' manager and trainer, wasn't impressed. "Tommy's not going to stand there so he can hit him," Steward said. And he didn't. Hearns finished the first round with a flurry and went after Cuevas in the second, knocking him out to win his first world title.

1. Joe Louis-Max Schmeling rematch. Detroiters listened to The Brown Bomber's fights on the radio, and when he won—which was most of the time—they ran into the streets of neighborhoods like Black Bottom and Paradise Valley to celebrate. When Louis and Schmeling met in their historic rematch on June 22, 1938, all of America was listening and ready to celebrate. America had not yet entered World War II, but the bout had stunning international ramifications. Schmeling was seen as the representative of Hitler's Nazi regime. Louis symbolized America as the keeper of freedom. Schmeling, the former heavyweight champ, had KOed Louis in the 12th round in 1936. President Franklin D. Roosevelt visited Louis at his training camp and told him: "Joe, we need muscles like yours to beat Germany." Just a fight? Hardly.

By now, Louis had won the title, and he wouldn't let Schmeling take it. Louis swarmed on Schmeling from the opening bell. Schmeling crumpled to the canvas and went down early. Three more power punches resulted in clean knockdowns. On the third, Schmeling screamed in pain. Back in Germany, Hitler turned off the radio. Referee Art Donovan stopped the bout at 2:04 of the first round. "I got what people call revenge," Louis said after the fight. "I can go back to Detroit smiling again."

A Dozen Amazing Things about Joe Louis

The heavyweight champ ranks as one of the greatest boxers of all time and probably the greatest athlete in any sport to come out of the city of Detroit. But those aren't the only extraordinary things about Joe Louis. Here are a few more.

12. "Louis" was his middle name. His real last name was "Barrow." The form he filled out for his first amateur fight didn't have enough room for him to complete his full name, so he became known as just "Joe Louis."

11. He was a shy kid. Joe was so withdrawn and unassertive during his early youth, many people thought he was developmentally disabled.

10. He chose boxing over music. Joe began boxing at age 16 in Detroit's Brewster Recreation Center, paying his trainers with money his mother had given him for violin lessons.

9. He owed his knockout power to ice cream. After school during his teens, Louis worked at the Detroit ice cream maker Pickman and Dean, carrying huge blocks of ice, a task he later claimed helped him develop the extraordinary upper body strength that made the all-time hardest puncher in a 2003 Ring Magazine poll.

8. He celebrated his honeymoon in the ring. Louis married his first wife, Marva Trotter, two hours before climbing into the ring to beat former champ Max Baer in 1935.

7. He repaid Detroit. After he became successful, Louis repaid the city of Detroit $250 in welfare benefits it granted his family during his youth when his stepfather was badly injured in a car crash.

6. He went broke. Lewis found himself nearly penniless later in life, having given away most of the millions he made in the ring and from other projects.

5. He broke the PGA color barrier. An avid golfer, Louis became the first black to ever play in a PGA Tour event when he was granted a special exemption to enter the 1952 San Diego Open.

4. He gained a CFL Tribute. The Winnipeg Blue Bombers of the Canadian Football League were named in honor of Louis and his nickname, "The Brown Bomber."

3. Military service. During World War II, he served four years in the army, where he met a young Jackie Robinson. The future baseball Hall of Famer credited Louis with helping embolden him to become the first African-American to enter the Major Leagues a few years later.

2. He played a big role in helping ease racial tensions in America. Louis served as the nation's standard bearer against Nazi notions of Aryan racial superiority with his 1938 KO of German Max Schmeling, then later worked as a spokesman promoting the contributions of blacks to the war effort during World War II.

1. He's buried at Arlington. President Ronald Reagan brushed aside the usual requirements to gain burial at Arlington National Cemetery so Louis could be interned there after he died in 1981.

We really don't like these guys. The reasons may be legitimate or they may be childish. But it doesn't matter. We still wish ill on them.

Dishonorable Mentions: Emmitt Smith (Barry was better); Brett Favre (never lost to Lions at Lambeau); Jerry Sloan and Norm Van Lier (dirty scoundrel Bulls who beat up the Pistons); Dwyane Wade (diva wimp who gets every call); Lebron James (48 in 2007 Game 5 at Palace will make you a villain); Tie Domi (proclaimed himself new NHL fighting champ after getting slapped around by Bob Probert, then proved how tough he was by challenging a hemophiliac to a fight during an exhibition game).

10. Jim Palmer. One could admire the Baltimore Orioles' players of the 1960s, 1970s and 1980s who so often frustrated the Tigers with their skill and teamwork. Except for Jim Palmer. The future Hall of Fame pitcher and male underwear model was an arrogant, hypercritical pretty-boy. He blistered teammates in the media for minor lapses and blamed his losses on everyone but himself. Which made it all the sweeter to beat him. But he was also a helluva pitcher, so that was hard to do.

9. Fran Tarkenton. He might have achieved infamy just through his post-playing career, hosting infomercials and bellowing "That's Incredible!" on network TV. But this spiritual godfather of Joe Theisman and Don Lupree earned our eternal contempt years before that as quarterback of the Minnesota Vikings in the 1960s and 1970s. Tarkenton always seemed to elude the grasp of Lions pass rushers just as they were about to pulverize the little twit into purple vapor. Then he'd head off on a 25-yard scramble or hurl a 40-yard TD pass. The fact that Fran got embarrassed in four Super Bowl losses, then turned into a bizarre old coot on TV in bad need of a haircut and some career counseling, helps a little. But not enough.

8. Maurice "Rocket" Richard. The Canadian great challenged Gordie Howe with a shove during Howe's rookie year and got knocked out with one punch. Still, Montreal usually got the better of the Wings in those days. Red Wings fans hated Richard, and he hated us back.

7. Sugar Ray Leonard. While the world loved Sugar Ray Leonard, many Detroiters despised him. Leonard was the glib pretty boy and his Motor City rival Thomas Hearns was just the opposite. Hearns was ahead on all cards when they first fought in 1981. But Tommy got tired and was beaten in the 14th round. The rematch in 1989 was a travesty. Hearns won the fight, knocking Leonard down twice, but somehow it was ruled a draw. Giving us all the more reason to hate Leonard.

6. Karl Malone. He played dirty as a matter of habit, kicking his feet out on his jump shots to kneecap any defender who got too close. In 1991, Malone delivered one of the most despicable cheap shots in NBA history when he elbowed Isiah Thomas in the face as the Pistons guard drove through the lane. The elbow cut Isiah so badly he needed 40 stitches. Piston fans got revenge some 13 years later, when Detroit denied Malone, by then with the Lakers, his last chance at an NBA title. His daughter Cheryl Ford of the Detroit Shock has two rings. Maybe she can let her daddy wear one on his pinky.

5. Patrick Roy. He was a great goalie who often stymied the Wings. But his brash personality and showboat antics, like his infamous Statue of Liberty maneuver, often backfired. The great Red Wings-Avalanche rivalry may have become more violent due to Claude Lemieux. But Roy made it more fun.

4. Max Schmeling. The German heavyweight played an all-too-willing role in the Nazi government's racist buildup to his 1938 rematch with champ Joe Louis. Americans, especially African-Americans—and particularly those in Louis' hometown of Detroit—were outraged and disgusted. "The Brown Bomber" blitzkrieged Schmeling with a first-round KO. But afterwards, Schmeling claimed Louis cheated by hitting him with a kidney punch. He went on to serve as a Nazi paratrooper in World War II. In later years, he reached out to Louis and tried to play down the racial tensions generated by the fight and his role in the hype. But it was too late by then. The damage had been done to race relations and international relations. Few, if any, athletes ever did more to stir up hatred than Max Schmeling.

3. Ron Artest. Get in line, because a lot of fans and players around the league despise Artest. But after the 2004 "Malice in the Palace" brawl, Detroit got moved to the front of the line. Artest should probably be forced to get in line at a pharmacy for an anti-psychotic medication before being allowed to play, or even walk the streets, again.

2. Michael Jordan. It will probably hurt his feelings that he's not #1, because anything less than the top spot feels like failure to His Airness. But, truth is, the Pistons owned Jordan and the Bulls for five years before he got his act together—and the Bad Boys declined enough for the Bulls to finally beat them. Still, Jordan spent the rest of his career trying to gain vengeance for those early blows to his ego in any way he could. Plus the NBA changed the rules and pussified the sport to help Jordan and his Bulls win six titles.

1. Claude Lemieux. A vile cheap shot artist and a coward, Lemieux showed no remorse for his 1996 face-breaking check from behind on the Red Wings' Kris Draper. Confronted the following season by Draper's teammate Darren McCarty, Lemieux fell to his knees and curled up like a turtle in the center of the ice. It was enough to make you gain a little respect for Patrick Roy.

Jordan always wants to come out on top in every contest. And much as we dislike him, he will always win the hate-off with Detroit sports fans. Here's why.

16. The Pistons made "The Shot" pointless. Jordan's jumper over Craig Ehlo to beat the Cavs as time expired in their 1989 first-round playoff series remains his most iconic moment. But it turned out to be an act of irrelevance. Because a couple weeks later in the Eastern Conference Finals, the Pistons eliminated the Bulls.

10. (Tie) The final NBA Regular Season standings, 1984-90. The Pistons finished ahead of the Bulls in the Central Division for Jordan's first six seasons in the league.

9. 5 >1. The Pistons showed Jordan that five players are greater than one, a huge blow to his young ego. While Jordan obsessed over his individual stats during his early NBA years, the Pistons just focused on winning. His Airness didn't discover team play until after the Pistons rubbed his face in it for a half-dozen years.

6. (Tie) The NBA Playoffs, 1988-90. The Pistons eliminated Jordan and the Bulls from the playoffs in all three seasons. He wasn't happy about it then, he's not happy about it now.

5. Joe Dumars. Despite giving up four inches in height and about a foot of vertical jump, the Bad Boys resident good guy proved one of the most effective defenders against Jordan. And after he retired, Dumars succeeded spectacularly doing something at which Jordan failed miserably: rebuilding a franchise from the front office.

4. Rip Hamilton. Jordan was part of the Wizards personnel "brain trust" when they dealt Rip to Detroit in 2002. The Pistons won a title in large part due to Hamilton and also dumped Jerry Stackhouse's contract in the deal. Remember to thank Mike for that next time you see him.

3. Dave Debusschere. The Detroit native established himself as a legitimate two-sport player back in the early 1960s when he pitched a couple seasons for the White Sox while also playing with the Pistons. Remember Michael Jordan's attempt to play pro baseball? He's probably hoping you forgot.

2. We brought out the worst in him. His rivalry with the Pistons betrayed the first cracks in Jordan's obsessively crafted public image as a smiling, good guy. He turned surly when up against Detroit and publicly belittled the Pistons' style of play (then why couldn't you find a way to beat it earlier, Mike?). Then he waged a petty, behind-the- scenes campaign to ban his nemesis Isiah Thomas from the 1992 Olympic Dream Team. In the process, he showed that to "Be Like Mike" required some ugly behavior.

1. We made him wait seven years for a ring. A guy that obsessed with winning, and he had to wait seven effing years for an NBA title. Must have damn near killed him. The Detroit Pistons were the biggest reason that he had to wait that long, of course. And that remains the biggest reason Jordan still hates Detroit.

Some guys don't need to make the game-winning play against a local team to gain our dislike. Some guys can just do it by standing on the sidelines.

10. Bo Ryan. It isn't just his 11-3 record vs. MSU that irks Spartan fans. His Wisconsin teams run up scores and his smugness rubs people the wrong way.

9. Bobby Knight. You tend to root for sport's elder statesman to go out on top—or at least with dignity, even if they coach a rival. But dignity was never an option for Bobby Knight. And seeing him get outclassed by Tom Izzo in every way during the late 90s to lose his status as the Big Ten's top basketball coach—and then his job—felt like overdue justice.

8. Urban Meyer. It takes a lot for a guy to earn your contempt when he coaches at a school that's not even in your conference—a team that UM has beaten in its last two match-ups. But Urban Meyer is That Kind of Guy.

7. Phil Fulmer. That Kind of Guy, Part II. Make that times two.

6. The Notre Dame Leprechaun. The Domers should stop misappropriating the name and symbolism of the good people of Ireland. They need to get a mascot more in keeping with their bloated, overrated, arrogant, has-been, bad joke of a football program: Roseanne Barr. Or maybe they should just make Charlie Weis their new mascot.

5. Phil Jackson. All the alleged spiritual wisdom of the Zen Master hasn't spared his Bulls and Lakers teams from suffering some of the ugliest internal blowups in recent sports memory. Or kept them from coming off like arrogant jackasses. Or kept Phil from resorting to stirring up racial hatreds to motivate his team. Hey, Phil, Buddah thinks you're a dick.

4. Jim Tressel. Just go away already.

3. Marc Crawford. Epitomized the Avalanche's vile lack of class and ethics. Yeah, Scotty Bowman has a metal plate in his head, Marc. But it beats the hell out of the three pounds of excrement you're storing inside your cranium, pal.

2. George Steinbrenner. He's the most consistently selfish, meddling and dislikable owner in all sports. And to make it worse, he owns the Yankees. "The Boss" is also an Ohio State grad and lured UM quarterback Drew Henson away from UM. And, well, he's George Steinbrenner. Come to think of it, you really don't have to say much more than that.

1. Woody Hayes. Decades have passed since the Ohio State football coach got whisked off to retirement in a strait jacket. The intense emotions have faded that he generated through his feud with Bo Schembechler and all things related to the state of Michigan. It's possible now to take a more objective, levelheaded look at the college football legend, his impressive record, his legacy and his leading role in creating the rivalry between Ohio State and Michigan—the greatest in American sport. And, you know, it's still impossible not to conclude that Woody Hayes was a complete asshole.

You can't win 'em all. But Detroit and Michigan fans and teams really want to win when they play these teams.

13. (Tie) Cleveland Teams. The Cavs, Browns and Tribe have offered a lot more comic relief than competition over most of the last four decades. But they are from northern Ohio, which counts for a lot.

12. Minnesota Vikings. The mind-boggling, all-time series record: Minnesota 61-Detroit 30, with a couple ties. A small-market franchise that has played its home games in an icebox and giant hefty bag shouldn't be that tough to beat, even for the Lions.

10. (Tie) Toronto Maple Leafs and Montreal Canadiens. Back during the quarter-century (1942-67) when the NHL consisted of only six franchises, it was hard for teams not to develop a healthy contempt for one another. But the Maple Leafs and Canadiens were particularly unlikable. The Red Wings won five Stanley Cups during that period. But the Canadiens and Maple Leafs won the Cup every other season except one. Neither club has troubled the Wings much in recent decades. But try walking through a senior center lunch room around here wearing a Canadiens or Maple Leafs jersey and see how far you get before somebody hip checks you with his Segway or hurls a tapioca pudding at you.

9. Indiana Pacers. The brawl to end all brawls (or so we can hope) between the Pacers, Pistons and a bunch of Palace fans turned up the flame on an already heated rivalry. And should keep it hot for years to come.

5. (Tie) Any team from Chicago. Except for the Cubs, of course. They get a pass because they compete (to use the term loosely) in a different league than the Tigers and because they are the Cubs.

4. New York Yankees. It's just so much fun to hate them. Who can resist? And why should you?

3. Colorado Avalanche. The rivalry has faded a bit in recent years as the Avs slumped from Cup contention. But the nasty, classic playoff series between the Wings and Avs in the late 90s when they were battling for NHL dominance along with the Western Conference title still boil the blood.

2. Notre Dame. The vaunted Fighting Irish football team hasn't been very good for a couple decades. But they're still arrogant and get a ridiculous amount of national media attention. The Domers also play the Spartans and Wolverines each season in games that still mean a lot to all three programs, no matter how Charlie Weis tries to discount them.

1. Ohio State. Just hearing the name is enough to put most Michiganders in a foul, fighting mood. MSU and OSU have had more than their share of nasty encounters. But that cold afternoon in November each year when the Wolverines and Buckeyes meet still ranks as the greatest rivalry event in American sports.

Rivalries are born out of some of the best and worst moments a sport has to offer. Whether it was a play, a call or an on-field incident, most fans can recall when a rather ho-hum game/event turned into a full-fledged blood feud. Detroiters have witnessed many great rivalries over the last several decades, however there's only one that has captivated two nations as well as two cities over the last dozen years: Detroit vs. Colorado. The Red Wings and the Avalanche hate each other, or at least at one time they did. Maybe too many of the original participants have mellowed, moved on or retired, but the rivalry still remains strong. Today, it's based more on the actual competition than the blood lust of the early years. These are my top five games that I believe turned Detroit/Colorado into one of sport's most celebrated rivalries.

5. Game 6, Western Conference Finals, May 29, 1996. This game started it all. The Avs beat the Wings, 4-1, to capture the Western Conference championship. In the Stanley Cup Final, they swept Florida to win their first Cup. What's significant about this game is: Claude Lemieux blindsided Kris Draper and rearranged his face. There isn't a Wings fan around that doesn't have the distorted image of Draper's face burned into their memory bank. If it wasn't for this incident, the rivalry would have never gotten off the ground.

4. Game 3, Western Conference Semifinals, May 11, 1999. In Games 1 and 2 in Denver, the Red Wings had beaten the Avs and everyone, including the Colorado media, was handing the series to Detroit. The Wings had loaded up at the trade deadline, picking up Chris Chelios, Wendel Clark, Ulf Samuelsson, and Bill Ranford. It appeared to be paying off as the Wings took an early 2-0 lead in this game. Steve Yzerman clanged a shot off the crossbar that would have given Detroit a three-goal lead. After that it was all downhill, Ranford lost his playoff magic, the Avs beat Detroit, 5-3, and won the next three games to eliminate the Wings from the playoffs.

3. Game 6, Western Conference Finals, May 29, 2002. Detroit was down in the series 3-2 and faced elimination heading back to Denver for game six. The Wings had lost in overtime in Game 5 and I can remember traveling to Colorado with the team and how focused the Red Wings were. They weren't uptight; they just had a resolve that transcended into confidence. I didn't know if they would win or not; I did know that they wouldn't go down without a fight. This game stands out for two reasons: Patrick Roy's "Statue of Liberty" non-save and Dominik Hasek's stick measurement. Each incident favored the Wings. Roy for being a show-off resulted in a Detroit goal by Brendan Shanahan and Hasek being tipped off that the Avs would call for a stick measurement, which nullified a Colorado power play with the Wings clinging to a 2-0 lead. Darren McCarty scored the insurance goal and the Wings stayed alive with a 2-0 victory.

2. Game 7, Western Conference Finals, May 31, 2002. This game may be the contest Detroit fans will remember forever! With the right to play for the Stanley Cup riding on the outcome, the Wings stormed the Avalanche and never let up. Patrick Roy was lifted in the second period after surrendering six goals and in the third period with the Wings in command, 7-0, the fans chanted, "We want Roy! We want Roy!" Detroit blew out Colorado. In the two games versus their archrival when they faced elimination, the Wings won by a combined 9-0 score. This game was also a testament to the balance of the Detroit team. The line of Tomas Holmstrom, Igor Larionov, and Luc Robitaille accounted for three of Detroit's first four goals. They stepped it up and allowed the Wings to pummel Colorado.

1. March 26, 1997. Not only did this game pave the way for Detroit's first Stanley Cup in 42 years, it created the modern day Red Wings team. Until March 26, Detroit was a good team with a bunch of great players. After March 26, the Red Wings became a team, a great team. It was a game of redemption for Kris Draper as Claude Lemieux was pounded by Darren McCarty. Brendan Shanahan first took on a fired up Patrick Roy and then slugged it out with Adam Foote after Mike Vernon wanted a piece of St. Patrick. The goalies fought, the tough guys fought, and Igor Larionov and Peter Forsberg got it all-started. Not only did Detroit win all the battles, they also won the game in overtime on a goal by McCarty. Talk about adding insult to injury. March 26 is one of the most significant days in the history of the Detroit Red Wings. It brought a team and city together. Once that game was over you knew that something was unleashed. It was the defining moment for this core group of players. After March 26, Detroit became a team of destiny. They rallied around each other and finally embraced the team concept. By standing up for one another, they realized that if they stuck together and did whatever it took for the team to succeed, they were unbeatable.

My Ten Favorite Detroit Teams and Players of All Time
:: Sonny Eliot

Note: Born and raised in Detroit, Sonny Eliot is a Motor City icon. For more years than he cares to admit, Sonny has been entertaining the Metro Area with his offbeat antics and rapid-fire sense of humor that has endeared him to our community. Whether he's doing the weather, hosting a TV show, the Thanksgiving Day Parade or acting as an umpire for the ceremonial first pitch on Opening Day, you can't get any more Detroit than Sonny. For over 80 years, Sonny has been a passionate supporter of Detroit's teams and athletes. He shares his ten all-time favorites in each category.

Favorite Teams

10. The 1988 and 1989 Detroit Pistons. Okay, they're really two teams, but they won back-to-back championships. It's like picking your favorite child, you just can't. I love both teams equally.

9. The 2006 Detroit Tigers. Man, what a year! They came out of nowhere and rekindled Detroit's love of Tiger Baseball.

8. Detroit Red Wings of 1997 and 1998. Again, it's two teams, but, like the Pistons, they won back-to-back championships. The '97 team won our first Stanley Cup in 42 years and the guys in '98 won it again even with the tragic memory of the limo accident still fresh in their minds.

7. Michigan's Fab Five basketball team. We tend to forget that they were just kids and all that improper stuff occurred off the court. I remember what they did together on the court and it will never, ever and I mean NEVER be done again. Five freshmen starting the National Championship game . . . unbelievable and fantastic!

6. The 1973-74 Detroit Pistons. The first real good Pistons team since they moved here from Fort Wayne. They won 50 games for the first time, had a great coach in Ray Scott and two of the greatest players not only in Pistons history but, in NBA history, with Dave Bing and Bob Lanier. They were a classy group.

5. The 1984 Detroit Tigers. Wow, a 35-5 start! They led from day one of the season to the last day of the season and they crushed the opposition in the playoffs and World Series. What's not to like?

4. The 1955 Detroit Red Wings. Detroit's best hockey team ever! They were loaded with Gordie, Ted Lindsay, Red Kelly, and Sawchuk in goal. What a group of players, they made it look easy and they were a tough bunch of SOB's.

3. The 1957 Detroit Lions. It's hard to believe that this is the Lions' last championship team, 1957 was a long time ago. This team was full of leaders with Bobby Layne, Joe Schmidt, Lou Creekmur, Terry Barr, Jack Christensen, Roger Zatkoff, Yale Lary, and Jim David. I could name the whole team! If Detroit never wins another pro football championship, take pride in knowing that our last championship team was a great group of guys that represented us well.

2. The 1968 Detroit Tigers. This team was full of characters with Norm Cash, Gates Brown, and Denny McLain. They were also a great ball club! Al Kaline, Bill Freehan, Willie Horton, and Mickey Lolich were fantastic players. For as good as they were on the field, I'll always remember what they accomplished off the field. They healed our city after the 1967 riots and I'm forever grateful.

1. The 1934 Detroit Tigers. Hey, they were the team of my childhood. You always remember your first one of anything during your life and they were my first team. Always have been and always will be!

Favorite Athletes

10. Carl Brettschneider, Lions, linebacker (1960-63). A hell of a player and a great guy, he was mean, smart, and not a bad actor in Paper Lion. A good friend that left it all on the field.

9. Tommy Bridges, Tigers, pitcher (1930-43, 1945-46). A forgotten talent in Detroit Tigers' history, Bridges was a dominant force in the league, but was never the same after he lost two years because of service during World War II. I always looked forward to watching him pitch.

8. Alex Karras, Lions, defensive lineman (1958-62, 64-70). Football-star, wrestling star, and acting star, Alex was terrific at everything he put his mind to. Only trouble was he wanted to do it all and looking back I guess he did!

7. Dave Bing, Pistons, guard (1966-75). I'm not sure we will ever see an athlete as smooth and determined as Dave Bing. He may be better known now as being a major player in Detroit's business community, but he was first a player on the court and the Pistons best ever.

6. Norm Cash, Tigers, first baseman (1960-74). Stormin' Norman was a fierce competitor with a heart of gold. He was po/werful and b/right . . . he was po/right. Sorry, I couldn't pass it up.

5. Joe Schmidt, Lions, linebacker (1953-65). Joe Schmidt was the best player the Lions had until Barry Sanders. There wasn't anything he couldn't do on defense. With Schmidt out there, I was always confident that the Lions had a chance.

4. Charlie Gehringer, Tigers, second baseman (1924–42). A Michigan native, "The Mechanical Man" could do it all: field, hit for average and hit for power. Even old, miserable Ty Cobb was impressed.

3. Hank Greenberg, Tigers, first baseman (1930-46). "Hammerin Hank" was a gifted slugger. He was also a hero serving his country for four years during the Second World War, a tremendous player.

2. Al Kaline, Tigers, rightfielder (1953–74). From the moment he hit Detroit, he's conducted himself with dignified grace. He's as humble of a man as I have ever met.

1. Gordie Howe, Red Wings, right wing (1946–71). Mr. Hockey, that's all you need to know.

Note: Dave Bergman was acquired with Willie Hernandez by the Tigers the final week of spring training in 1984. The left-handed-hitting first baseman became a key role player for the team that went on to win the World Series. Bergman played another eight seasons for the Tigers before retiring in 1992. He currently works as a successful financial planner and investor. He also runs baseball showcases around the Michigan area. Always a class act, "Bergy" wins gratitude from Stoney for being one of the first guys to show him respect when he was a behind-the-scenes sports producer at WDIV-TV.

10. My home run against Toronto!!! What a night! June 4, 1984 and Toronto was still in our sights. Boom, game over and I was lucky to connect off of Roy Lee Jackson. This may have been a pivotal game that season because Toronto was playing extremely well and we couldn't put much ground between them and us. Well, we did after this game.

9. Larry Herndon catching the last out of the World Series at Tiger Stadium. I shared this as one of my fondest memories because Larry Herndon was one of our quiet warriors. He was actually playing with some pain that year, but never complained and the boys really respected him. The fact that he caught the last out in the World Series was a beautiful, final touch on a magical season.

8. The pitching staff. Every one of our starters and bullpen guys did his job all season long. Bair and Berenguer were rubber arms out of the bullpen. They always took the ball and they battled their butts off all season long.

7. The bench players. Barbaro Garbey, Rusty Kuntz, Tom Brookens, Marty Castillo,,John Grubb—all filled in and carried the load while the starters either got a rest or were injured.

6. Tom Brookens. Steady, a great teammate and a great piece to the world championship puzzle.

5. Willie Hernandez. Game over! What a year he had. Mr. Automatic for the entire year. Won the Cy Young and the MVP.

4. Aurelio Lopez. Willie got most of the accolades, and rightfully so. But Lopey was the backbone of our bullpen. We all new that if our starters could get us to the seventh inning with a lead, the game was over because Lopey would hand over the keys to Willie in the ninth and he would drive us home.

3. Sparky Anderson's speech before Opening Day. We had a meeting before the season's first game in Minnesota. Sparky, who wasn't keen on meetings, took the "podium" and proceeded to say that he felt we had a very special team. He proved his point by asking everyone in the room to look to their left, then to their right and then across the room. He said, "Boys, I bet there isn't one person in this room that you wouldn't crawl into a foxhole with." He was right! He said that is why we are going to be special this year!

2. Alan Trammell's MVP play during the playoffs. Alan Trammell had a very good regular season, hitting .314 with 14 home runs, His post season was more than very good—it was great! He started us off in the first inning of the first playoff game with a triple that scored Lou. He homered in that game, as well. We won the series in three straight, with Alan hitting .363. The World Series was even better for Tram. He drove in our first run in the top of the first of the first game and did not stop. He hit two homers in Game 3 and drove in four in the clincher. He was the well-deserved World Series MVP.

1. Kirk Gibson's home run against Goose Gossage in the fifth and final game of the World Series. Padres manager Dick Williams went to the mound and told Goose that he wanted to walk Gibson. Goose responded by saying he didn't! Goose won the argument, and Gibby won the battle.

Top 13 Teams in Michigan in the Last 50 Years

Not all title teams are created equal. Though area teams have won numerous championships in the last half-century, only 13 made this list. Why did some title teams make the cut, while others did not? Read on.

Honorable Mentions: 2006 Detroit Tigers; 1992 Michigan Men's Basketball Team (Fab Five); 1997-98 Detroit Red Wings.

13. 2003 Detroit Shock. The ultimate worst-to-first story. New coach Bill Laimbeer used his Bad Boys' mentality to rebuild the WNBA's last-place team into the toughest bunch of chicks you ever saw. Led by Swin Cash, Cheryl Ford and Deanna Nolan, the Shock breezed to the Finals to meet the two-time defending champion Los Angeles Sparks. In the opening game of the best-of-three Finals series, the Shock were drilled (can that be said about women?). But they came back to win Game 2, then win the title in front of a big, raucous crowd at the Palace.

12. 1966 Michigan State Football. Coached by Duffy Daugherty and with a roster featuring the likes of Bubba Smith, George Webster and George Washington, the '66 Spartans established themselves as one of the great college football teams of all time. They went undefeated and played in one of the most storied contests of all time, the Game of the Century against Notre Dame on November 19, 1966 at Spartan Stadium. It ended in a 10-10 tie, meaning Michigan State had to share the national title with the Irish.

11. 1983 Michigan Panthers. Some readers of this book will be infuriated that we picked a USFL championship squad over some of the other title teams listed above as honorable mentions. But considering that the only professional football success that multiple generations of Detroit sports fans have witnessed firsthand is the Michigan Panthers title in 1983, we felt the Albert Taubman/Max Fisher team deserved inclusion. In the USFL's inaugural season, the Panthers fired up local football fans desperate for success during their march to the title game against the Philadelphia Stars. Panthers QB and league MVP Bobby Hebert hooked up with former UM standout Anthony Carter on a 48-yard touchdown in the fourth quarter to help give Michigan a 24-22 victory. For many Detroiters it was the first (and probably last) professional football championship they will ever get to celebrate.

10. 2000 Michigan State Basketball. In 1999, Tom Izzo's Michigan State Spartans lost in the Final Four to the Duke Blue Devils. Feeling that they still had something left to prove, guards Mateen Cleaves and Morris Peterson decided to return to East Lansing for their senior years of eligibility. And the decision to return to school and forego the NBA worked out just the way the Flintstones had planned. In front of a capacity crowd at the RCA Dome in Indianapolis, the Spartans defeated the Florida Gators 89-76 to win the school's first national championship since 1979. A resilient Cleaves rebounded from a sprained ankle that he suffered early in the second half to lead the Spartans to a 16-6 run that iced the game and secured the title.

9. 1989 Michigan Men's Basketball. "A Michigan man is going to coach a Michigan team." (Michigan athletic director Bo Schembechler).

The most ironic thing about the late Bo Schembechler's life is that even though he became a legend for coaching the Wolverines football team, the most famous words that he ever uttered were about UM's basketball team. After Bill Frieder took a gig at Arizona State, Bo promptly canned his ass and promoted assistant coach Steve Fischer. Because of the turmoil, many pundits figured Michigan wouldn't make it out of the first weekend. But behind the deadly shooting of Glen Rice, the Wolverines got all the way to the Final Four. In their first game at the Kingdome in Seattle, U of M defeated fellow Big Ten rival Illinois in a nail-biter, 83-81. The title game was even closer as Seton Hall and the Wolverines could not settle the championship in 40 minutes. The game went to overtime and Rumeal Robinson's two clutch free throws with three seconds remaining gave Michigan an 80-79 victory. Rice ended up scoring a record 184 points in the '89 tourney and was honored with the Most Outstanding Player award. That record still stands to this day. The interim label was removed from Fischer's job title after the championship and Bo went back to focusing on football.

8. 2001-02 Detroit Red Wings. It had been a few years since the Wings had won a Stanley Cup and the fans and owner Mike Ilitch were getting a little impatient. So in the offseason before the 2001-02 year, GM Kenny Holland went out and added three Hall of Famers: Dominik Hasek, Brett Hull and Luc Robitaille. The team cruised through the regular season per usual and won another President's Trophy. Although there were some bumps in the road (going down 2-0 to Vancouver in Round 1 and trailing Colorado 3-2 in the Western Conference Finals), the Hall of Fame-laden squad dispatched of the Carolina Hurricanes in the Finals fairly easily to give the Wings their third Cup in six years.

7. 2003-04 Detroit Pistons. The 2003-04 Los Angeles Lakers were very similar in nature to the 2001-02 Red Wings. They had already won multiple titles in preceeding years and when they added Karl Malone and Gary Payton to the mix, it became a foregone conclusion that they would add another championship banner. Even when the Pistons added Rasheed Wallace at the trade deadline, most experts figured that Detroit might get to the Finals, but there was still no way they could win it all. The absolute defensive slopfest that was on display in the Eastern Conference Finals between the Pistons and Pacers did not add much credence that either team would give the Lakers any challenge in the Finals. And all of the experts were right. It wasn't much of a series AT ALL. The Pistons crushed L.A. in all of their home games and won the series 4-1. Many still call the series a five-game sweep because the Lakers had no business winning Game 2 in overtime. The 2004 Pistons Chauncey Billups, Rip Hamilton, Ben Wallace, Rasheed Wallace and Tayshuan Prince were also considered the first NBA champion without a true superstar. Amazingly enough we just got through a recap of the 2004 Pistons without saying, "Doing things the right way." Well, we almost did. Damn.

6. 1997 Michigan Football. In 1997, the Michigan football team did something that they could not accomplish under Bo. They won the mythical national championship. Well, actually they won a share of that title. Led by a stifling defense and an economical offense, the Wolverines posted a perfect 12-0 record that culminated with a 21-16 victory over Ryan Leaf's Washington State squad in the Rose Bowl. Heisman Trophy winner Charles Woodson anchored a defense that only gave up more than 17 points once all season long and Brian Griese managed the offense while trying not to do anything stupid after replacing Scott Dreisbach under center. (Something that didn't come naturally for Bob's son.) Lloyd Carr's team ended up sharing the championship with Nebraska as UM was #1 in the AP Poll while the Coach's place Tom Osborne's last Cornhusker team #1 in their poll.

5. 1979 Michigan State Basketball. If you don't like Bracketology. If you don't like Dick Vitale screaming at you through your TV every March. If you don't like the song "One Shining Moment." Then you can probably blame it on the 1979 Michigan State basketball team led by Magic Johnson. Because most college basketball experts would claim that "March Madness" didn't really take off until the '79 title game between Magic's Spartans and Larry Bird's Indiana State Sycamores, still the highest-rated collegiate basketball game ever. And that large audience witnessed the Spartans defeat Bird's squad 75-64. In his sophomore season, Magic won the Most Outstanding Player honor and the championship with the help of Greg Kelser and Jay Vincent. To this day, Jud Heathcoate thanks his lucky starts that Earvin Johnson's parents decided to live in Lansing, Michigan.

3. (Tie) 1989-90 Detroit Pistons. If the criteria for this list was which "Bad Boys" championship was more fulfilling, you would have to go with their first title. After the grueling battles with the Celtics, the Isiah Thomas inbounds pass to Larry Bird that led to a Dennis Johnson basket, the phantom foul on Bill Laimbeer in Game 6 of the 1988 NBA Finals, there was nothing more satisfying than the Pistons winning the franchise's first Larry O'Brien trophy in 1989. The Pistons sweep of the Lakers that year was the NBA equivalent of climbing Mt. Everest. But if you were to base this category on who was the better team between the '89 and '90 title teams, you would probably have to give a slight nod to the second championship squad. While the nucleus of both teams was basically the same (Zeke, Joe Dumars, Laimbeer, Dennis Rodman, John Salley, Mark Aguirre, James Edwards, etc.), the '90 team had a swagger about them that was more imposing than the '89 team. Who can forget Clyde Drexler proclaiming "we wont be coming back here" after Portland tied the finals series at 1-1. He was right they didn't. The Pistons won the next three in Portland to win the championship as Vinnie Johnsons shot with 0:07 left sealed it. On the other hand, the 1989 team only lost two games during their postseason run while the 1990 squad lost five games. Wait a second, are we actually debating this nonsense? Let's just group the two teams together and move on.

3. (Tie) 1996-07 Detroit Red Wings. There is no Pistonsesque debate about which Red Wings back-to-back title team should be on this list. The 1996-7 Wings team had Vladimir Konstantinov on it. The 1997-8 Wings team did not. End of debate. After a 42-year drought between drinks out of the Stanley Cup, the Wings finally won the NHL championship after many near misses. When Steve Yzerman lifted that Cup at center ice in Joe Louis Arena, all of the memories of the Dead Wings, Goose Loonies, the Game 7 overtime loss to the Leafs on Nikolai Borschevsky's goal, the monumental upset at the hands of the San Jose Sharks, the Avalanche knocking the Wings out of the playoffs on the same night that Claude Lemeiux rearranged Kris Drapers' face went right out the window. The Wings had finally got the 800-pound gorilla off of their back and the celebration felt like it would last forever. Well, the party lasted for exactly six days. On Friday June 13, 1997, a limousine transporting Konstantinov, Slava Fetisov and team masseur Sergei Mnatsakanov crashed into a tree on Woodward Avenue, with Vladdy and Mnatsakanov suffering life-threatening injuries. While both survived the crash, their severe close-head injuries ended their careers and changed their lives forever.

2. 1984 Detroit Tigers. As great as all of the other Detroit championships were, there is really nothing like your baseball team winning the World Series to bring a city together. (Well, maybe a Super Bowl victory would be similar, but we wouldn't have any clue around here. And for those of you counting, that would be the 3,533rd rip on the Lions in this book.) There is just something about following a team night-after-night for seven months and then having it culminate in a world championship. And the 1984 Tigers got everyone in the area hooked real early that season by starting out with a 35-5 record and cruising through the rest of the season. After winning 104 games, the team easily dispatched of the San Diego Padres in the Fall Classic. The other thing that made the 1984 team special is that we got to see the team develop through the farm system. Alan Trammell, Lou Whitaker, Jack Morris and Kirk Gibson all came through the Tigers minor leagues. The only reason the 1984 team got edged out by the 1968 squad in a photo finish was. . . .

1. 1968 Detroit Tigers. The riots of 1967. As great a team as the 1968 Tigers happened to be, the fact that the city NEEDED a championship squad to unite the city after the divisive civil unrest the year before played a HUGE part in this team being selected number one. The 1968 Tigers weren't only exceptional (they won 103 games), but they also never quit. They could have made excuses when Al Kaline broke his arm after being hit by a pitch in May and missed significant time. Instead, they won the American League pennant by 12 games. The team could have laid down when the St. Louis Cardinals jumped out to a 3-1 series lead in the World Series. Instead they fought back behind Mickey Lolich's pitching to win the final three games of the Series. In Game 7, Lolich started on TWO DAYS REST and once again shut down the St. Louis lineup. By the time Curt Flood misread Jim Northrup's fly ball in the seventh inning and broke up a scoreless tie, the Cardinals didn't know what had hit them. Lolich had outpitched Bob Gibson (a man whose ERA was so low, 1.12, that the league had to change the pitching mound height becase of him) in the deciding game and the Tigers had won their first World Series title in 23 years. The following letter was sent from Michigan Governor George Romney to Tigers owner John Fetzer after the Series victory:

"The deepest meaning of this victory extends beyond the sports pages, radio broadcasts, and the telecasts that have consumed our attention for several months. This championship occurred when all of us in Detroit and Michigan needed a great lift. At a time of unusual tensions, when many good men lost their perspective toward others, the Tigers set an example of what human relations should really be."

The 12 Best Sports Movies of All Time
:: Art and Stoney

The criteria to make this list are very basic. One, the movie must have been released in an actual movie theatre. So, unfortunately, the TV movie that made it acceptable for men to cry, Brian's Song, does not appear. Two, sports has to be the major theme of the movie. So films with classic sports scenes like *The Big Lebowski*, *M*A*S*H* and *Horse Feathers* didn't qualify. Here are the best of the ones that did.

12. *Bull Durham* (1988). This comedic yet somewhat realistic look at minor league baseball-starred Susan Sarandon, Tim Robbins and Kevin Costner, who's actually pretty good as minor league legend Crash Davis. The players want to make it to the "show" but very few do.

11. *Million Dollar Baby* (2004). Excellent film, but do not watch this if you're feeling blue. It's a film about the American Dream, as well as a female counterpart to Rocky.

10. *Field of Dreams* (1989). "If you build it, he will come." The final scenes of the film tend to give people tears of joy, no matter how tough they are.

9. *Hoop Dreams* (1994). The superb documentary followed the life and times of two young Chicago basketball players, trying to make the grade in the classroom and on the court so they can make it to the next level to play big-time college ball. This remains a must-see film, even almost 15 years after it came out.

8. *The Natural* (1984). This baseball film set in the 1930's had it all: a handsome hero, a beautiful woman, gunfire, suspense and a magnificent ending, great acting, beautiful cinematography and a fine Randy Newman score. A terrific movie, even if you don't like baseball.

7. *The Hustler* (1961). If you consider pool a sport, then this has to make the list. Paul Newman plays "Fast Eddie" Felson, a pool hustler who tries to take on the legendary Minnesota Fats, played to perfection by Jackie Gleason. My favorite line from the movie is when Eddie's former manager (George C. Scott) yells at the top of his lungs, "EDDIE, YOU OWE ME MONEY!" Eddie came back 25 years later to teach his protégé Vincent Lauria (Tom Cruise) in *The Color of Money*.

6. *The Longest Yard* (1974). Burt Reynolds plays Paul Crewe, a convict and former pro quarterback thrust into a vicious prison football contest between the inmates and guards. Ironically, it's what it feels like to attend the average Lions game. So wrong, but so right! With all due respect to Adam Sandler, the 2005 remake sucked.

5. *Caddyshack* (1980). This spoof of country club life may be the funniest movie ever. I don't think there has been a movie with more lines quoted by men of all ages. "Cinderella story." "Naked lady tees" "Noonan." "You will have nothing and like it." "Hey, but it looks good on you." "Billy, Billy, Billy." "So I have that going for me, which is nice," "Mrs. Green, you're a monkey woman." The cast of Bill Murray, Ted Knight, Chevy Chase and Rodney Dangerfield is one of the best in comedy history. We should also never forget the hot Lacy Underall. Like in most sports movies, the good guys win at the end.

4. *Slap Shot* (1977). A classic movie that is revered by hockey fans and players of all ages. In fact, this movie is played by numerous hockey teams on bus trips through-out North America. You are not a hockey player or fan if you don't like *Slap Shot*. The minor league Charlestown Chiefs are floundering in the standings and in the stands until the arrival of the Hanson brothers. The spectacled triplet goons who play with toy cars steal the movie with their thuggery and stupidity. Paul Newman plays coach Reggie Dunlop and his boys run amok over the league. The cast of characters in this movie is hysterical as they personify the stereotypical minor league hockey team. They fight, they ride buses, and they make you laugh. Who can ever forget the names Ogie Ogilthorpe, Dr.Hook McCracken and Morris Wanchuk, just to name a few. I wonder how many times a forward will tell the opposing player that "your wife is a dyke" Red Wing scout Danny Belisle actually played one of the Syracuse Bulldogs.

3. *Hoosiers* (1986). Based on a true story, this film tells the ultimate underdog tale of the Milan Indians, a tiny, rural high school team that beat all the state's powerhous-es to win the 1954 Indiana high school basketball title. Gene Hackman's portrayal of coach Norman Dale is one of his best performances in his storied career and Dennis Hopper was amazing as the alcoholic assistant coach. Watching Hopper and others listen to the games on the radio brought back memories for many. It's hard to believe that Hopper was the film's only major Oscar nominee.

2. *Rocky* (1976). If Hoosiers is the underdog movie that did not win anything, Rocky was the underdog that did. It introduced the world to both Sylvester Stallone and his character Rocky Balboa, the barely literate club fighter who was given a chance to fight for the heavyweight title. Filmed on a shoestring budged, the movie overcame long odds itself to win the Best Picture Oscar and become a huge hit.

1. *Raging Bull* (1980). Don't even try to argue. This is the best sports movie ever. Robert DeNiro won the Oscar for Best Actor for his portrayal of real-life ex-heavyweight champ Jake LaMotta. He somehow played the troubled fighter at every adult age at multiple weights. Joe Pesci was incredible as Jake's brother and how about Jake's wife Vicki? How fricking hot was Cathy Moriarity? Some of the incredible fight scenes were supposed to be at Tiger Stadium, so there was a Detroit angle as well. It's hard to believe that this was beaten out by *Ordinary People* for the Best Picture Oscar.

Note: Detroit native Michael Regan has reviewed movies for numerous publications across the country and is a recovering late-night TV addict. Over the years, he's seen some good movies and a lot of really, really bad ones. He urges you not to think of what follows as a list, so much as a series of warnings.

13. *Dreamer* (1979). We saw how good a bowling movie could be in the hands of great filmmakers like the Farrelly Brothers with their 1996 masterpiece *Kingpin*. But we first saw just how bad a bowling movie could be a couple decades earlier with *Dreamer*. You could call it a cinematic gutter ball. But you'd better not—gutter balls come rolling back to you after a few seconds.

12. *Bobby Deerfield* (1977). If only Warren Wallace had been around at the time. He might have driven onto the set early in the filming of this car racing melodrama and put the title character "into the wall." Warren's violent intervention would have spared Al Pacino from giving a performance so embarrassing, it sent his status as a top movie star in for a decade-long pit stop.

11. *Amazing Grace and Chuck* (1987). Before *Hoop Dreams*, there was this *Hoop Nightmare* starring then-Nuggets forward Alex English and Gregory Peck. Actually, calling it a nightmare makes this movie seem too interesting and potentially rewarding. Maybe *Hoop Coma*. Peck sure seems like he's drifting in and out of one during the film.

10. *Rocky IV* (1985). Sylvester Stallone gave a great, funny, inspiring and humble performance in the original *Rocky* as a guy who gets a one-way ticket back from Palookaville. By *Rocky IV*, the 'roids had apparently leeched from Sly's pecs into his ego and brain. The result: a two-hour infomercial for megalomania.

9. *The Replacements* (2000). A movie celebrating the scabs who crossed picket lines to take the jobs of striking NFL players in 1987? Uh, maybe not such a winning concept in a union town like Detroit. Or anywhere populated by people with a conscience or a vague notion of what makes for a watchable movie. Would have placed lower if it didn't remind us that, for a few games one season, the NFL fielded some teams that the regular Detroit Lions could have actually routed.

8. *D2: Mighty Ducks* (1994). Having wiped the ice with everything American youth hockey had to offer in their first film, the Ducks migrated to an international tournament for *D2*. But with the Soviet Union no longer around to provide reliable hockey villains, the film resorted to pitting the Ducks against a group of evil Icelanders (no, that's not a typo—"evil Icelanders.") When I saw this in the movie theater, a group of bored little kids ran up halfway through the film and tried to attack the screen. They got the biggest cheer of the night.

6. (Tie) *The Babe* (1992) and *The Babe Ruth Story* (1948). The Hollywood people responsible for these two biopics must have been big Dodgers fans out to beanball the legacy of the Yankee great. They succeed, at least for a couple of hours—or however long you last before walking away from these films, muttering under your breath.

5. *Mad Bull* (1977). Don't get me wrong: "sports entertainment" can be great stuff. But by the time this came out, every American over the age of 11 or an IQ of 12 had figured out that pro wrestling was as scripted and premeditated as the Ice Capades. Except, apparently, the producers of this film. They really want us to believe that the main character can redeem himself personally and professionally by winning a climactic steel cage match. Gets docked a few notches down the list for throwing a crazed assassin into its plot mix and embarrassing star Alex Karras, a former Detroit Lions great.

4. *Body and Soul* (1981). Robert Rossen's 1947 original starring John Garfield was a terrific drama about a charismatic boxing champ who loses his way. But this remake starring Leon Issac Kennedy as a Sugar Ray Leonard-like champ facing a Roberto Duran-type challenger had audiences begging *"no mas"* soon after the opening credits. Leon proved so uncharismatic that the filmmakers had to manipulate us into rooting for him by calling his rival "Animal." Then having "Animal" hurl a baby off his lap during a pre-fight photo op. The audience I saw it with was still 80-20 for "Animal."

3. *The Legend of Bagger Vance* (2002). A sort of *Fairway of Dreams*, this Robert Redford film aims for a combo of folksy wisdom, myth and spirituality on the golf course. But it ends up shanking into the gallery and smacking upside the heads of its poor audience. Almost unimaginably awful.

2. *Slap Shot II: Breaking the Ice* (2002). The original *Slap Shot* ranks as one of the great sports films of all time. But ten minutes into this sequel, you start hoping the Charlestown Chiefs accidentally sign *Friday the 13th*'s Jason as their new goalie so he can turn it into a slasher movie.

1. *No Retreat, No Surrender* (1986). With so much unworthy competition, it might be impossible to designate any one film as the worst sports movie of all time. If it wasn't for *No Retreat, No Surrender*. Hell, *NRNS* may well be the worst movie of any type of all time. It definitely features the worst metaphor in the history of cinema: its martial arts master compares the film's naive young hero to an empty glass; then he symbolizes his own vast experience and wisdom by filling the glass with a Diet Coke. By the time the karate tournament finale rolls around—pitting the hero against an evil Russian played by Jean Claude van Damme—you may want to eject the DVD and beat it up yourself. A couple other films, for some strange reason, borrowed the title *No Retreat, No Surrender*. Accept no substitutes. Or rather, accept only substitutes. They couldn't possibly be any worse than this.

My Ten Favorite Things Heard on a Movie Set
:: Jeff Daniels

Note: Actor Jeff Daniels grew up in Chelsea, Michigan as a Red Wings and Tigers fan. He dropped out of Central Michigan his junior year and moved to New York City to pursue his acting dream. Within a few years, he established himself as a major stage actor, appearing in numerous plays and winning an Obie and a Drama Desk award. His work caught the eye of the film industry and Daniels began appearing in a number of movies, working with such top directors as Woody Allen, Milos Forman, James Brooks and Mike Nichols. His résumé quickly filled up with extraordinary performances in over 40 films, including *Something Wild, Arachnaphobia, Terms of Endearment, Dumb and Dumber, Pleasantville, The Purple Rose of Cairo,* and *Gettysburg*. His film work led to three Golden Globe nominations. Daniels also founded The Purple Rose Theatre in his hometown of Chelsea as a showcase for his plays (he has written 11 stage plays to date) and as a place for aspiring actors to develop their craft. He established himself in the music world by producing three excellent CDs of his own songs, which include the terrific "Lifelong Tiger Fan Blues." Despite achieving international film stardom, Daniels remains true to his Midwestern roots. Even after decades as one of the world's top actors, Jeff Daniels insists of being just a regular Michigan guy with his feet firmly planted with his family in his hometown of Chelsea.

10. "We got Jack Nicholson!" Director Jim Brooks to me after stopping in the middle of a rehearsal for *Terms of Endearment* to take a phone call.

9. ". . . and then turn and put two into him." Clint Eastwood to me while directing a gunfight scene in *Bloodwork*.

8. "Did the check not clear?" Director Barry Sonnenfeld, calling out after a particularly bad take on *RV*.

7. "Do you think you could memorize this?" Woody Allen to me on the set of *The Purple Rose of Cairo* as he handed me a scrap of paper with the handwritten rewrite, "Twenty-four hours ago, I was in an Egyptian tomb and here I am now on the verge of a madcap, Manhattan weekend!" That scrap of paper has been framed.

6. "If they don't like this speed, they're gonna hate my other one." A New York Teamster after being told to hurry up on the set of *Heartburn*.

5. "You won't die." The spider wrangler on the set of *Arachnophobia* after I inquired what would happen if his big-as-my-hand spider bit me.

4. "I ate a cat for breakfast." Michael Richards when I asked him how he was one morning on the set of *Trial and Error*.

3. "You want to know how to cure the spread of AIDS? Let MGM distribute it." A bitter producer on the set of *State of Play* telling me how badly that studio had handled his last film.

2. "Can I get some powder, please?" Jim Carrey, in mock anger and naked from the waist down as he turned to face the whole crew during filming of one of the deleted scenes from *Dumb and Dumber* when Harry and Lloyd were standing at two urinals with our pants around our ankles.

1. "Of course." Me, telling a bald-faced lie when asked if I could ride a horse before playing George Washington in *The Crossing*.

In the big moments in the big games, a team's big stars are supposed to step up and deliver. But sometimes in those situations, a different kind of hero emerges, someone unexpected. And sometimes those overlooked players make their own big moments.

7. Gabe Alvarez. In 1988, the Tigers rookie third baseman hit two homers in his second MLB game, inspiring the headline "Gabe Ruth" in the *Detroit Free Press*. He only managed to hit four more homers the rest of his career.

6. Joey Harrington. It's hard to remember now, but Joey Harrington did flash greatness in Detroit. Well, maybe not greatness, but at least competence. And it was for only one game—a Lions rout, which should have clued us in right away that it was just a freakish fluke. In the 2003 regular season opener against Arizona, Joey tossed four touchdown passes with no interceptions to guide Detroit to a 42-24 win over Arizona. He made you think his disastrous rookie season had just been a learning experience and he was ready to shine. But the next week, he went out and tossed three interceptions and let us know what we were really in for.

5. Milt Wilcox. A career journeyman (119-113, 4.07 ERA), Wilcox tossed one of the best games anyone ever pitched in 1983, stopping the first 26 White Sox batters from reaching base. A two-out single in the ninth by Jerry Hairston prevented Wilcox from becoming only the 11th MLB pitcher to post a perfect game.

4. Levi Jackson. The Spartans sophomore running back went on to have a decent career in East Lansing, gaining over 2000 yards. But he was having a rough day against Ohio State in 1974, getting repeatedly stuffed on running plays between the tackles. With just over three minutes remaining and the Spartans down four points with the ball on their own 12-yard line, Spartans QB Charlie Baggett inexlicably handed the ball to Jackson for another running play into the teeth of the Buckeyes' fearsome defense. Only this time, Jackson busted free and sprinted to a stunning 88-yard TD run, the winning score in a shocking upset of the top-ranked Buckeyes.

3. Cesar Guiterrez. You'd be hard-pressed to find too many Detroit fans who remember Guiterrez, a shortstop for the Tigers from 1969-71. But on June 21, 1970, the native Venezuelan carved his name into the record books by going 7-for-7 in to lead the Tigers to a 9-8 win over the Indians. He was the first player since the 19th century to collect seven hits in a game without making an out. The feat would not be matched until the 21st century when Pirates Rennie Stennet did it in 2004. Guiterrez improved his batting average that day by over 30 points, but still hit only .241 for the season. He finished the following season with a .189 average and retired.

2. Phillip Brabbs. August 31, 2002 was the best of days and the worst of days for Phillip Brabbs. In a hotly-contested season opener in the Big House against the Washington Huskies, the Wolverines new starting kicker badly missed field goals of 36 and 42 yards. Then he was replaced with only 90 seconds left by Troy Nienberg, who missed a chip shot FG to win the game and get Brabbs off the hook. The Wolverines somehow got the ball back and to the Huskies 27-yard line with just five seconds left. But instead of calling for a pass play into the end zone, coach Lloyd Carr decided to try another field goal. By Brabbs. With groans sounding all around him, Brabbs trotted out and drilled a 44-yarder for the 31-29 win, setting off a raucous celebration. The following week against Western Michigan, Brabbs missed his only two-field goal attempts. He went 1-3 two weeks later against Utah and was never called upon again. But his game-winner against Washington still resonates. Mention Brabbs to a Wolverines fan and you'll invariably get a story about where he was when he saw "The Kick." One of the top posters on UM's "Stadium and Main" fan forum goes by the handle "brabbsfrom44." UM fan polls still rank Brabbs' unlikely field goal as one of the greatest plays in Michigan's storied football history. Not bad for a field goal kicker who played in just three games and went two-for-eight.

1. Jaimie "Shoes" Huffman. Michigan State's third-string guard realized the dream of every kid shooting at a hoop in his driveway when he got sent into an NCAA tournament game late in the second half. Okay, it was garbage time in the opening-round game against Lamar, with the eventual champ Spartans up by over 30 points. But Huffman still seized the moment and established himself as one of the most talked about players in the tournament. And he did it by losing a shoe.

Shortly after Huffman entered the game, a Lamar player accidentally stepped on the back of his low-top sneaker, flat-tiring him. With the game continuing around him, Huffman spent almost a minute getting his shoe back on. When he finally did, a Spartan teammate immediately passed him the ball and Huffman drained a long jumper for his first basket of the season. *NBC* commentator Al McGuire rechristened him "Shoes" Huffman on the spot. When Huffman went to the foul line in the game's final seconds, the TV camera zoomed in for a close-up of his suddenly famous shoes. Upon returning to East Lansing, Huffman found that he had become a national media sensation on par with teammate Magic Johnson and that the MSU bookstore was selling "Shoes" Huffman souvenirs. Two weeks later after Michigan State routed Penn in the Final Four, Huffman was granted a personal live interview by McGuire and Dick Enberg on national TV. It would be his last. Huffman was dropped from the Spartans team before the following season and transferred to Ferris State, where he closed out his playing career by scoring five points in three games during the 1981-82 season.

The world does not live—and play—by baseball, football, basketball and hockey alone. Dozens of other sports allow great athletes to strut their stuff. Michigan has produced some of the greatest of these major players in minor sports. Here's six area athletes who haven't turned up in other lists, but still deserve a spot in this book.

6. Dawn Riley. If it's possible to blaze new trails on the water, Michigander Dawn Riley has done it again and again. In 1989, she was part of the first all-female crew to participate in the Whitbread Round the World Race. Three years later, the Macomb County product served as the first active female crew member to win an America's Cup when she helped the America 3 team get across the finish line first in the world's most prestigious yachting race. Three years after that, the L'Anse Creuse High and Michigan State grad captained the first all-female crew in the America's Cup.

4. (Tie) Dell and Connie Sweeris. Has any husband and wife ever accomplished this much in a single sport? The Grand Rapids couple won 25 table tennis championships between them in the 1960s and 1970s. Not surprisingly, both gained induction into the United States Table Tennis Hall of Fame. Connie joined the historic trip to China by the U.S. Table Tennis Team in 1971, a key event in leading to the normalization of relations between the two nations.

3. Terry McDermott. The shy barber from Essexville pulled off an Olympic upset comparable to the 1980 U.S. Men's Hockey team triumph. At the 1964 Winter Games, McDermott beat the Soviet Union's four-time Olympic gold medal winner and massive favorite Yevgeny Grishin to win the 500-meter speed skating race. And he did it wearing borrowed skates. McDermott, who won silver in the event at the following Olympics, set a record that day that would stand for eight years. He was later inducted into the National Speed Skating Hall of Fame.

2. Kathy Arendsen. Sometimes stats can be deceiving. And sometimes they shout out the full-on, no arguments allowed truth. As in: KATHY ARENDSEN WAS ONE OF THE GREATEST FASTPITCH SOFTBALL PITCHERS OF ALL TIME. Her stats: a 338-26 record and an 0.15 ERA with 79 no-hitters and 42 perfect games from 1978-93. During that time, Arendsen led the Raybestos Brakettes to nine American Softball Association titles. The Zeeland native gained All-American status 13 times and a spot in the International Softball Federation Hall of Fame.

1. Marion Ladewig, The Gordie Howe of female bowling won the Women's Bowler of the Year award and the Women's All-Star Tournament nine times between 1950-63. Her 247 average at the 1951 All-Star Tournament would have won her the men's title as well. The Grand Rapids native added five World Invitational titles on her way to being named the greatest female bowler of all time in a 1973 poll. Call her "Queenpin."

Note: Saginaw native Stewart Francke has quietly created a body of work both spiritual in tone and remarkable in its emotional breadth. His seven albums have generated a number of hits, including Kiss, Kiss, Bang, Bang. He's performed around the world on bills with the likes of Sheryl Crow, Steve Earle, Hootie & The Blowfish, and Chuck Berry. But Stewart regards the night he was invited to perform his own compositions with the Saginaw Symphony in his hometown as his biggest thrill. Stewart has won numerous Detroit Music Awards, including Best Artist, Best Songwriter, Best Album and a Special Achievement Award for his leukemia foundation. For three years running he was voted Most Popular Musician in the Best of Detroit poll in Hour magazine. In 2005 Stewart released *Between the Ground & God*, a collection of his lyrics and writing on music, life and Detroit on Ridgeway Press. His 2006 CD *Motor City Serenade*, features the lyrics "Stoney and Wojo on the radio," so it has to be great song. On a personal note, I find Stewart as one of those great performers who obviously did not kiss enough ass to get national commercial recognition. When you see The Stewart Francke Band play, you are treated to a night of thoughtful music and great rock and roll. He is a great guy and a great talent, but don't just take my word for it. According to *Playboy* music critic Dave Marsh, "Stewart Francke's *What We Talk Of . . . When We Talk* is the most important blue-eyed soul record in a musical generation." Bruce Springsteen says simply, "Stewart Francke makes beautiful music." Stewart excluded Motown vocal acts like the Temptations, Supremes, Miracles, and the Four Tops from his list of top Detroit bands.

10. Nolan Strong & The Diablos. Fusing the whispered surrenders of Sonny Til (The Orioles), the sincerity of Clyde McPhatter (The Drifters, solo) and the gospel styling of the church, Strong and the Diablos created a sound first recognized consistently as a "Detroit" sound. Formed in 1950 at Central High in Detroit, Strong and the Diablos produced the finest music on the legendary Detroit music label Fortune, including great singles like "The Wind," "The Way You Dog Me Around," "I Wanna Know," "Is This Really Real?" and "Mind Over Matter."

9. Bob Seger & Silver Bullet Band. I saw the original great Silver Bullet Band with Charlie Martin on drums in 1973 when I was 15. They were a steamroller of a rock act, doing 40 minutes opening for REO Speedwagon without stopping but once for a brief introduction. Seger was, and is, the great Midwestern lion-hearted rocker—friend of the everyman and voice of the economic fringe. But it's this first band I'm thinking of as one of Detroit's ten best. Listen to *Live Bullet* (Martin's last record before tragically being paralyzed in a car accident) and then go on to subsequent live and studio albums; the edge is polished off and a lot of the excitement is gone. But rock 'n' roll is about the moment. On those Cobo Hall nights when *Live Bullet* was recorded, the moment was sublime.

8. Was (Not Was). The creation of producer/bassist Don Was and lyricist/conceptualist David Was, W(NW) came out of Oak Park in the early 80s and hit internationally with "Walk the Dinosaur," a George Clintonesque funk groove and sentiment. Diverse and soulful, W(NW) found its real groove with the shared vocals of Sweet Pea Atkinson and Sir Harry Bowens. The horn section was comprised of Detroit mainstays David McMurray and Raicey Biggs. A party band that made you think and smile, W(NW) became an international touring draw.

7. The Stooges. If you want the full story of Iggy & The Stooges' impact on punk and rock culture, read Legs McNeil's *Please Kill Me: The Oral History of Punk*. With his dadaist stage performance and the band's raw minimalism, they were every kid's (and every rock critic's) dream, the real, uncensored explosion of rock's fury. The two solo records that Iggy made with David Bowie (*The Idiot* and *Lust for Life*) have had the most longevity. If you listen to his most ardent fans, Iggy possibly invented: stagediving, garage rock, punk, self mutilation, exposing one's self on stage, cutting one's self with glass, vomiting on stage, heroin addiction, Ann Arbor, Blondie, and much more.

6. The Romantics. Vastly overlooked and underrated as songwriters. Fantastic live band. The Romantics chose to play short, high-energy explosions of post-punk pop, but in actuality they could play anything. It's hard to capture humor in a short rock single, and they did it. No Romantics, no Green Day. They looked great, they moved great, they sang great. Whaddya' want?

5. Marshall Crenshaw Trio. This was his touring band while promoting the classic first record, with brother Robert on drums. I saw this band at the Royal Oak Music Theater in the spring of 1982 and quit my job at a printing plant the next morning, knowing I had to make music. That was the power suggested by Marshall's beautiful miniatures and the promise inherent in the band's playing. There could be more. Period. The band played Marshall's songs with the joyful innocence found in Buddy Holly and the early Beatles. However, there was a knowing exclusionary vibe to it all—Marshall and the boys had obviously worked through other classic forms—funk, soul, country, rockabilly—because it was all there in the performance. And the listener was the beneficiary of this unpretentious musical knowledge. A life-changing experience, for me at least.

4. Mitch Ryder & The Detroit Wheels/Detroit. Maybe the best soul singer ever out of this town, or maybe the best soul singer out of any town, Mitch Ryder's two early career high points were with his first band, the Wheels, and his third, simply called Detroit. In between was a Vegas-style show band, a career choice foisted on the young Ryder that killed his early success with "Devil With A Blue Dress"/"Jenny Take A Ride" and other late-60s radio hits. Detroit was a biker band, a tough group of musicians who walked it like they talked it. It's no coincidence that both bands featured the great Johnny Bee on drums and impulse direction. Highlights from the lone Detroit album include Lou Reed's "Rock And Roll" and a heart-ripping rendition of Wilson Pickett & the Falcons' "I Found A Love."

3. MC5. So much has been written about the MC5 being the proto-punk, proto-metal, proto-political band that it's easy to lose sight of their essence. It was pure rock and roll energy, burning from note one to the ending amp ringing. Rob Tyner is rarely mentioned as one of rock's great all-time voices, but that's exactly what he was. I don't think the band members themselves ever cared all that much for the attendant political drama that surrounded them; they wanted to jam and be the biggest rock band in the land. Period. Although the sound on the Jon Landau-produced *Back in the USA* is thin, it's easily their best album, chock full of their best performances. Landau got it right: it was about the twin-guitar attack and Tyner's high watt voice. Both are celebrated on *Back in the USA*.

2. Parliament-Funkadelic. They invented funk's extreme geography. And they defined the battle between fun, intelligence, sex, honesty, open expression and freedom versus boredom, the status quo, oppression, stupidity, constriction, frigidity and falsehoods. Built around George Clinton's endless tribe of players, writers and singers, P-Funk created a completely new way for African Americans (or anyone who wanted to be aboard) to view the world. It was a reaction to the pressures of the white world while simultaneously being a musical/cultural/religious expression of funk love. Funk was all about feeling good, and to achieve that state, you had to dance. P-Funk was the endless dance party. The world would be a much bleaker place without the contributions of P-Funk. That's not hype or catchy kitsch. I believe it as strongly as I believe anything. Listen to "Flash Light" or "Bop Gun" every morning and it'll be a long time before another bad day visits your visage.

1. The Funk Brothers. Their influence will end well after our generation, if ever. Essentially jazz players who coalesced as a studio rhythm section, the Funks played on more Top 40 tracks than the Beatles, Beach Boys and Elvis combined. Often taking little more than loosely voiced riffs from Smokey or the Holland Brothers, the Funk Brothers made ornate, beautiful and funky radio singles. Their names should be voiced for years to come: Earl Van Dyke, Joe Messina, Eddie Willis, Joe Hunter, Benny Benjamin, Uriel Jones, Jack Ashton, Bob Babbitt, Robert White and the incredible James Jamerson.

Note: Founder and proprietor of the website DetroitSportsRag.com, Jeff Moss sifts through all the MVPs, Hart Trophies, Heisman statues, Cy Young Awards and other individual season award winners to determine which area players actually had the greatest seasons of all-time.

Honorable Mentions: Magglio Ordonez, 2007 Tigers (hit .363 to win batting title along with 28 HR's and 139 RBI); Curtis Granderson, 2007 Tigers (became only second player in MLB history to record over 30 doubles, 20 triples, 20 homers and 20 stolen bases); Desmond Howard, 1991 UM football (Heisman Trophy); Norm Cash, 1961 Tigers, 1961 (hit .361 to win batting title, along with 41 HRs and 132 RBI); Mickey Lolich, 1971 Tigers (25-14, 2.92 ERA, 308 Ks); George Yardley, 1957-58 Pistons (became first NBA player to score 2,000 points in a season); Cecil Fielder, 1990 Tigers (led league with 51 Homers and 132 RBI); Al Kaline, 1963 Tigers (hit .340 to win batting title, along with 27 HRs and 102 RBI); Gordie Howe, 1952-53 Red Wings (47 goals and 39 assists).

9. (Tie) Steve Yzerman, Red Wings, 1988-89 and Sergei Fedorov, Red Wings, 1993-94.

Coming off a severe knee injury, Stevie Y came back stronger than ever with a ridiculous 65 goals and 90 assists for 155 points. If a guy named Mario Lemiuex and another dude named Wayne Gretzky hadn't put up video game stats the same season, Yzerman might have won the MVP. While Sergei Fedorov's stats five years later (56 goals and 65 assists for 121 points) weren't nearly as gaudy as Yzerman's, he had more luck. While Gretzky had an "off year" ("only" scoring 38 goals and chipping in 92 assists), Lemieux missed most of the season with a back injury. So Fedorov's points total along with his ludicrous plus/minus of +48 was good enough to net him the Hart Trophy as the NHL MVP. Not only did Sergei take home the Hart, he also won the Selke Award for best defensive forward.

8. Alan Trammell, 1987 Tigers.

Let's get this straight right off the bat. Retired Tigers shortstop Alan Trammell should be in the Baseball Hall of Fame. The fact that Tram hasn't even gotten within sniffing distance of Cooperstown is a travesty. That Ozzie Smith (who wasn't nearly the all-around player that Tram was) is in the HOF and Trammell is not, is a total, unmitigated abomination. But the Hall issue isn't the first time that Trammell has been screwed over by a moronic electorate. In 1987, Trammell led the Tigers on a late run to overtake Toronto to win the AL East title in the season's final week. He batted .343, with 28 home runs and 105 RBI while scoring 109 runs and stealing 21 bases. MVP winner George (Jorge) Bell of Toronto did have a fine season himself in '87, but don't the victors get the spoils? After the final regular-season win against Toronto, Trammel's double-play partner Lou Whitaker handed Tram second base, which he'd inscribed with: "To Alan Trammell, 1987 AL MVP."

7. Charles Woodson, 1997 Michigan football. In its almost three-quarter century history, the Heisman Trophy has only been claimed once by a guy who played primarily on the defensive side of the ball. That guy was Wolverines cornerback Charles Woodson. Based on that distinction alone, Woodson made this list. That he kept Peyton Manning from winning a Heisman and pissed off the entire state of Tennessee in the process was just an added bonus. Thanks, in large part, to Woodson's efforts, the Wolverines went undefeated, won the Rose Bowl, and claimed a share of the national championship with Nebraska. But Woodson didn't have to share the Heisman with anyone. It was all his.

6. Terry Sawchuk, 1951-52 Red Wings. With all apologies to Tim Cheveldae, Vincent Riendeau, Bob Essesna and Corrado Micalef, the best goalie the Detroit Red Wings ever employed was Manitoba native Terry Sawchuk. And while Sawchuk had an incredible Hall of Fame career that included 447 wins, 103 shutouts and a 2.52 GAA, 1951-52 remains his defining season. In his second full year in the NHL, Sawchuk posted a 44-14-12 record with a 1.90 GAA and 12 shutouts. Imagine what kind of numbers the dude could have put up if they gave him a damn mask.

5. Willie Hernandez, 1984 Tigers. Hernandez had been a pretty good pitcher throughout his career. But Tigers GM Jim Campbell couldn't have imagined the type of season the Tigers would get out of the left-handed reliever when they acquired him just before the '84 season. The Tigers 35-5 start, the AL pennant, their first World Series in 16 years—none of it could ever have happened without Hernandez. During the regular season, Hernandez posted a 9-3 record with an ERA of 1.92. He closed out 32 of 33 save ops. He not only won the Cy Young, he also accomplished the rare double of winning the MVP award, too. To put that into context, the best New York Yankees closer Mariano Rivera ever finished in the MVP ballot was ninth.

4. Ty Cobb, 1911 Tigers. In 1909, Ty Cobb won the American League Triple Crown. And that's not even the season that got him on this list. Because in 1911, "The Georgia Peach" posted these numbers: .420 batting average, 8 HRs (a lot in those dead-ball days), 127 RBI, 83 stolen bases, 147 runs, 248 hits. Those numbers are just ridiculous and if Cobb actually had to play (and his racist beliefs didn't cause him to quit the game) against some of the great Negro League players who weren't allowed in the MLB at the time, he might have been even higher on this list.

3. Hank Greenberg, 1935, '38 and '40 Tigers. Hank Greenburg was guaranteed a place on this list. The only question was which of his three most remarkable seasons to highlight. Take a look at the numbers and you'll understand the dilemma:

1935 – .328 BA, 36 HR, 170 RBI, 121 Runs, 203 Hits, AL MVP.

1938 - .315 BA, 58 HR, 183 RBI, 144 Runs, 175 Hits.

1940 - .340 BA, 41 HR, 150 RBI, 129 Runs, 195 Hits, AL MVP.

How the hell do you pick one of those over the others? It is like the "Sophie's Choice" of this book. (Is it poor taste to make a reference to a Nazi movie when discussing the best Jewish hitter in baseball history? Probably.) At first blush we picked the 1938 season. Seriously, the guy came within two home runs of tying Babe Ruth's home run record. But '38 was the only year in which Greenberg DIDN'T win the AL MVP! Aww, the hell with it. We don't have a sadistic Auschwitz physician forcing us to make a decision. We are just going to include all three seasons on this list.

2. Barry Sanders, 1997 Lions. After starting out the season with a pair of games that were crappy even by Lamont Warren's standards (53 yards on 25 carries), Barry Sanders closed out 1997 with a tear that was impressive even by Barry Sanders' standards. In the next 14 games, Sanders ran for 2,000 yards, becoming only the third back to break the 2,000-yard barrier. Barry would share the NFL MVP award with Brett Favre that year. Now, let's hear from the loquacious Barry Sanders on his amazing accomplishment:

(*Cricket's Chirping*)

Umm, thanks Barry.

1. Denny McClain, 1968 Tigers. This is the chapter where we have to say good things about career criminal Denny McClain. Because in 1968, McClain became the last MLB pitcher to win at least 30 games, finishing the year with a 31-6 record and a 1.90 ERA, plus 280 Ks. The incredible regular season earned McClain the Cy Young Award and the AL MVP. Because the game has changed so much since then, it is unlikely that a pitcher will ever again win 30 games in a single regular season. In fact, nobody has seriously threatened the 30-win barrier since McClain. That's a nice legacy for Denny, and it sure beats being known as the most famous 7-Eleven employee of all-time. Uh, wait. We're not supposed to get into that here. See the list on Detroit Athletes who had brushes with the law for all that.

They say IF is the biggest word in the English language. Thus, the phrase "what if" becomes huge and always debatable. Here are some of the best "what if" conundrums of the last 25 years.

10. "What if" the Pistons lose Game 5 to the Washington Bullets in the 1988 playoffs?

The Pistons had come off the devastating seven-game Eastern Conference Finals loss to the Celtics in 1987. The next year they were supposed to take the next step. In the first round of the 1988 best-of-five series with Washington, the Pistons won the first two at the Silverdome. However, the Bullets, led by Jeff and Moses Malone, tied the series with two wins at the Cap Centre. The deciding Game 5 at the Dome was no contest. The Pistons won it 99-78 and went on to beat Boston and eventually lose to the Lakers in the Finals. If they had not won that series with Washington, Chuck Daly and/or some key players might have been gone and we might not have had back-to-back titles.

9. "What if" Juan Gonzalez agrees to THE contract?

After being acquired by Texas in the multi-player trade, Mike Ilitch allegedly offered Gonzalez an eight-year, $140 million contract. He turned it down and left after one uninspired season. If he did agree to the deal, would he have continued to be a great player and lead the Tigers out from the doldrums? Or would he have been the malingering lout he always was and cost the Tigers tons of money? If the answer was the later, who knows whether Ilitch would have done the things needed to bring the Tigers back to respectability.

8. "What if" the Quebec Nordiques did not move to Colorado in 1995?

The Nordiques moved to Denver and became the Colorado Avalanche after the 1994-95 season. How did this affect us? Well, first of all the Nordique franchise would have stayed in the Eastern Conference, so the Wings would have never had to play them in the conference playoffs. However more importantly, it would be highly doubtful that the Montreal Canadiens would have traded Patrick Roy to their provincial rival, Quebec. But since there was no Quebec, they traded him to Colorado and one of the key ingredients of the Wings-Avs rivalry was now an Av. For better or worse, if Quebec had not moved to Colorado, the greatest hockey rivalry in the last 20 years would never have happened.

7. "What if" Chris Webber does not call timeout?

Trailing the 1993 NCAA championship game to North Carolina 73-71, Webber grabs a rebound off a missed free throw with 19 seconds left. He brings the ball upcourt, gets away with a travel and calls a timeout that Michigan does not have. North Carolina goes on to make four more free throws and wins the game 77-71. If Webber does not have his brain cramp, does Michigan get the tying basket, or does Webber pass the ball to Rob Pelinka for an open 3 to win the game? Well, we will never know.

6. "What if" Kenyon Martin does not break his leg? The University of Cincinnati star broke his leg on March 9, 2000. Due to his injury, the Bearcats lost their first game in the Conference USA tournament. That combination led the selection committee to drop Cincinnati to a second seed in the NCAA tournament, which allowed Michigan State to get the top seed in the Midwest. The reason that was so big was that the Midwest Regional was at the Palace of Auburn Hills. The Spartans used the home crowd to spark come-from-behind wins over Syracuse and Iowa State to reach the Final Four and eventually win the NCAA Championship. If Martin does not get injured, Cincy gets the one seed in the Midwest and who knows how far the Spartans would have gone.

5. "What if" Gary Moeller never gets arrested for his night of drunkenness? One drunken April night in 1995 changed the football landscape around here. The Michigan football coach gets so drunk he can't even be allowed to stay in jail. They have to send him to the hospital. Tapes are released of Moeller being belligerent to the police. He danced on tables and cursed out his wife. An embarrassed University of Michigan fires Moeller and replaces him with defensive coordinator Lloyd Carr. Three seasons later, Michigan goes undefeated, shares a national title and Lloyd Carr stays the head coach for 13 seasons. Would they have won a title under Moeller? Would they have won more with Moeller's less conservative approach? Would Rich Rodriguez be the coach now? Who would have taken over the Lions for Bobby Ross? We will never know because of one wild night at the Excalibur restaurant.

4. "What if" the Pistons drafted Carmelo Anthony? With the second pick in the 2003 draft, the Pistons selected 6-foot-11 Darko Milicic. We know the history of how he never came close to being a player here. However, if they had taken Carmelo Anthony would they have won a title? Would Larry Brown have ruined Anthony's early years? Would Tayshaun Prince have developed? Would they have been able to make the Rasheed Wallace trade that put them over the top? Would Anthony have thrived in this environment? We have no way of knowing. We do know that Anthony went on to play in All-Star games and the Olympics, while Darko became a joke. We also know the Pistons won a title, went to Game 7 of another Finals and have been in the Eastern Conference Finals every year since 2003. We also know that Darko was sent to Orlando and the Pistons got a number one, which turned out to be Rodney Stuckey. Maybe the Pistons did the right thing by doing the wrong thing.

3. "What if" there was never a limousine accident involving Vladimir Konstantinov?

On June 13, 1997, Red Wings defensemen Vladimir Konstantinov and Slava Fetisov, along with masseuse Sergei Mnatsakonov, were in a limousine coming home from a Stanley Cup celebratory golf outing. Limousine driver Richard Gnida fell asleep at the wheel and crashed the limo into a tree, seriously injuring Konstantinov and Mnatsakonov. As we know, the accident unfortunately ended Konstantinov's All-Star career. If the accident never would have taken place, would the Wings have had the inspiration they used to win it again in 1998? Would they have won more than the three they have? We never would have heard the plea for acquiring a tough defenseman. Chris Chelios would have never been traded here and we would not have Cheli's Chili Bar. Would the Wings been able to keep Vlade and Lidstrom under the salary cap?

2. "What if" Maurice Taylor did not total his Ford Explorer?

On February 17, 1996, Michgan basketball forward Maurice Taylor crashed his leased Ford Explorer on M-14 around 5 a.m. In the car were teammates Robert Traylor (who broke an arm) Louis Bullock, Willie Mitchell and Ron Oliver. Also in the car was recruit Mateen Cleaves. As a result of the crash, the NCAA and Big 10 investigated how Taylor and other basketball players received cars. This investigation led to the Ed Martin investigation which led to the firing of head basketball coach Steve Fisher and then the self-imposed sanctions in 2002 which banned the basketball team from postseason play in 2002-03, forfeited 113 victories from the 1990s and repaid the NCAA more than $450,000 for money earned during Final Four appearances. Michigan also took down four banners including ones from the 1992 and 93 Final Fours. In 2003, the NCAA Infractions Committee called the cash scandal the largest in NCAA history, and handed out additional sanctions, including a second year's postseason ban, four years of probation and reduction of one scholarship for each of four years. Oh yes, that passenger named Mateen Cleaves. He decided not to attend Michigan and go to Michigan State, where he led the Spartans to the NCAA title. Would MSU have a title and would Michigan be one of the biggest jokes in college basketball without the crash? We will never know.

1. "What if" Paul Edinger missed the 54-yard field goal?

Christmas Eve, 2000. The Lions at 9-6 need to beat the Chicago Bears to make the playoffs. After blowing leads of 10-0 and 17-13, the Lions had come back to tie the Bears at 20. After getting the ball back and moving into Bears' territory, Lions QB Stoney Case was hit by R.W. McQuarters who fumbled. Chicago recovered and a couple of plays later Paul Edinger drilled a 54-yard field goal, giving the Bears a 23-20 win and knocking the Lions out of the playoffs. If Edinger misses the field goal, who knows what happens in overtime. But more important than that, if the Lions win that game, they finish 10-6 and chances are Matt Millen is not hired. We need no further comment.

Top Ten Major League Players I Saw or Interviewed :: Ernie Harwell

Note: How great of an announcer was longtime Detroit Tigers play-by-play man Ernie Harwell? Early in his career, the Dodgers traded a promising young catcher in exchange for Harwell moving from Atlanta to Brooklyn to call their games. Ernie is best known for his 42 years as the Voice of the Tigers and would make any top ten list of all-time greatest baseball announcers. Here's his top ten of all-time greatest baseball players.

10. Walter Johnson. Although he pitched for a bad team, the Washington Senators, he won 417 games, second only to Cy Young. His lifetime strikeout record lasted 62 years.

9. Jackie Robinson. Most exciting player I ever saw. Stole home in first inning of my first Brooklyn broadcast. His breaking of the color line is the most significant event in sports history.

8. Ted Williams. A personal favorite. Best pure hitter. Interviewed him in 1942, after he hit .406 the previous season.

7. Joe DiMaggio. Grace personified. His 56-game hit streak is still one of baseball's most sacred records. He was introverted, but was an interesting conversationalist once you earned his trust.

6. Roberto Clemente. Terrific all-around star. His humanity cost him his life when his plane delivering food and medical supplies to earthquake victims in Nicaragua crashed into the ocean.

5. Barry Bonds. Despite the steroid issue, which has clouded his reputation, he was a great hitter. No other player had more influence in a single game. His imposing presence in the batting order forced opposing managers to switch their strategies.

4. Hank Aaron. The underrated superstar. He could do it all. Home runs and RBI were his specialties. When he served on the Hall of Fame Veterans' committee with me, I was impressed by his insights about the candidates.

3. Willie Mays. Best player I ever saw. He played the game with a verve no other player could match. I was fortunate to broadcast his big league debut in 1951.

2. Ty Cobb. He was Mr. Baseball of the early 1900s. A cerebral standout. He could outplay and outthink the opposition. Never saw him in action, but interviewed him in my first year in radio, 1940. Despite his reputation as the meanest man in baseball, he was very warm and friendly to me.

1. Babe Ruth. The biggest name in the history of Baseball. He was larger than life. The first celebrity athlete known around the world by first name only. The first Major League game I saw featured Ruth's final American league appearance in Chicago. In that 1934 game at Comiskey Park, he made a fine running catch of a foul fly to left field.

The Wings postseason drive to the 2008 Stanley Cup took place after the rest of this book was written. So while the franchise's latest, great achievement may not receive its proper due in other lists, we wanted to commemorate it with a list of its own.

Honorable Mentions: Wings fined 10 grand for Al Sabotka swinging an octopus on the ice; Nicklas Kronwall's numerous, jarring body checks throughout the playoffs.

10. The Stuart hit, Game 6, Cup Finals. Just as he was getting up off the ice, Penguins captain Sidney Crosby was leveled against the boards by the Wings' Brad Stuart. The Penguins most potent scorer, Crosby was not the same for the rest of the game.

9. Draper goal off face, Game 6, Western Conference Finals. The Wings had seen a 3-0 series lead shrunk to 3-2. But fears of a collapse were eased just 3:45 into the first period when Kris Draper bounced a puck off his face into the Dallas net past Marty Turco for a 1-0 lead. The Wings went on to win the game 4-1 and secure a trip to the Finals.

8. LIdstrom's bounce goal, Game 6, first round. The Wings and Nashville were locked in a scoreless second period when Nicklas Lidstrom took an easy slap shot from center ice. The puck took a big bounce past Predators goaltender Dan Ellis into the net for a short-handed goal. The Wings went on to win the game, 3-0, and eliminate Nashville.

7. Zetterberg backhander, Game 4, second round. Henrik Zetterberg has scored some beautiful goals in his career. But his spinning backhander to beat Colorado's Jose Theodore up top was one of his best.

6. Goaltender interference. A series of strange goaltender interference calls proved to be the biggest controversy of the playoffs. In Game 4 vs. Dallas, a Pavel Datsuyk goal was waved off because Thomas Holmstrom's ass was ruled to have interfered with Stars goalie Marty Turco, perhaps preventing the Wings from sweeping the series. Then in Game 5 of the Stanley Cup Finals, Henrik Zetterberg was sent off for goalie interference in the first overtime and Dan Cleary for the same infraction in the second overtime. Neither call was even close to correct.

5. Schedule screws fans. Detroit sports fans were furious as the first three games of the Stanley Cup Finals were held on the same night as Games 3, 4 and 5 of the Pistons-Celtics Eastern Conference Finals NBA series. To make matters worse, both the Wings and Pistons were home for the first two conflicted games.

4. The emergence of The Mule. Johan Franzen turned into a scoring machine during the 2008 playoffs. He netted the overtime winner in Game 5 vs. Nashville and scored nine times in the sweep of Colorado. Franzen lit the lamp 12 times in just 11 games and would have probably scored more, if concussion symptoms didn't keep him from playing the last five games vs. Dallas and the first game with Pittsburgh.

3. Temporary heartbreak. The Wings looked set to clinch the Stanley Cup at home in Game 5 in front of almost 20,000 fans. But Pittsburgh's Maxime Talbot pushed in a rebound with just 35 seconds left to tie the game at 3-3 and send it into extra time, where Peter Sykora won it for the Penguins with a goal in the third OT.

2. Five-on-three, no problem. The Wings faced a pair of crucial five-on-three disadvantages, one in the third period of Game 4 against Pittsburgh while clinging to a one-goal lead. The lead held, thanks to a great shift by Henrik Zetterberg, who was all over the ice and lifted Sidney Crosby's stick just as he was about to score the equalizer. Then in the first period of Game 6, the Wings once again killed a five-on-three, limiting Pittsburgh to just two shots over the 93 seconds of the two-man disadvantage.

1. Ozzie! Ozzie! It was Game 4 of the first round in Nashville when the complexion of the Red Wings team and the playoffs changed dramatically. Dominik Hasek had just let up a soft goal by Greg Devries that put Nashville ahead 3-1. Coach Mike Babcock had seen enough. He pulled Hasek for Chris Osgood and the Wings never looked back. Detroit lost that game 3-2, but Osgood played the rest of the way. The Red Wings seemed to play with a calm confidence that they did not have when Hasek was in net. Ozzie won nine straight games at one point, then shutout Pittsburgh the first two games of the Finals. He ended the playoffs with a record of 14-4 with a 1.55 goals against average and a 93 percent save percentage. There is little doubt that the much-maligned Osgood was the key to the 2008 Stanley Cup Title.

All fans think their teams have lost games because of the referees, and most of the time they are wrong. However, there have been times when we were screwed like a $5,000-an-hour hooker on a big-time governor. Are we bitter? Damn right we are! If we weren't, we wouldn't be fans.

10. 2007 NHL Western Conference Finals, Game 5—Anaheim Ducks 2, Detroit Red Wings 1 (May 20, 2007 at Joe Louis Arena)

In an extremely tight (and sometimes dirty) series, Detroit and Anaheim entered Game Five at Joe Louis Arena tied at two games apiece. The Wings led the crucial matchup 1-0, thanks to a second-period goal by defenseman Andreas Lilja. It was late in the third period when the referees decided to intervene. With just more than four minutes remaining in the game, the Ducks' Joe Motzko was whistled for holding Henrik Zetterberg. When the Wings failed to score on that power play, everyone at the JLA knew that the refs might even things up (as they are prone to do) if given a chance. And just like clockwork, referees Paul Devorski and Don "Eat another Doughnut" Koharski called an interference penalty on Pavel Datsyuk with 1:47 left. (The same Pavel Datsyuk who would win the Lady Byng Trophy a few weeks later. You know, the award the NHL annually hands out to the guy who AVOIDS taking penalties.)

While Wings fans were trying to figure out who Datsyuk interfered with, the Ducks pulled their goalie (Jean-Sebastien Giguere) for a 6-on-4 advantage. After Zetterberg missed an empty net that would have clinched the victory, Scott Neidermayer tied the score with a shot that deflected off of Nicklas Lidstrom's stick with 48 seconds remaining. The game went into overtime and the man who stood to be the Wings hero earlier in the day, Lilja, thought it would be a good idea to hand the puck over to one of the most prolific scoring right wingers of all-time, Teemu Selanne. The Finnish sniper made no mistake as he buried the puck behind Dominik Hasek, thus giving the Ducks a 3-2 series lead. The Ducks would go on to finish the Wings off 4-3 in Game Six and proceed to win their first Cup at the expense of the Ottawa Senators a couple weeks later.

9. Tommy Hearns vs. "Sugar" Ray Leonard II (June 12, 1989 at Caesar's Palace)

On September 16, 1981, one of Detroit's favorite sons, boxer Thomas "The Hitman" Hearns, lost a classic "Super Bout" versus "Sugar" Ray Leonard. After leading most of the match-up to unify the World Welterweight division, Hearns tired badly in the later rounds and suffered his first career defeat by technical knockout in the 14th. But as if losing wasn't bad enough for the "Motor City Cobra," Hearns had to deal with the reality that he probably would have won the fight if he could just have stayed on his feet for another round and a half. Detroiters and Hearns himself had to wait a LONG eight years for a shot at a rematch. While Leonard won the first bout, he suffered a detached retina at the expense of Tommy's fists and "Sugar" Ray really wanted no part of a second match.

But in June of '89, the two met again in the twilight of their respective careers at Caesar's Palace in Las Vegas. This time the fight was only scheduled for 12 rounds, and it went the distance. Despite the fact that Hearns knocked Leonard down in Rounds 3 and 11, the always pro-Leonard Vegas judges scored the bout a draw.

In 2006, ESPN.com detailed the top 10 most controversial boxing decisions of all-time. Hearns-Leonard II topped the list. The author of that list, Kieran Mulvaney, wrote, "[Leonard was awarded the draw] despite the belief of most ringsiders—and, reportedly, even Leonard—that Hearns had won."

8. Michigan State 28 Michigan 27 (October 13, 1990 at Michigan Stadium)

7. Michigan State 26 Michigan 24 (November 3, 2001 at Spartan Stadium)
The next two "Screw Jobs" are tied together, and are a little difficult to write about because half the readers of this book are probably U of M fans and the other half supporters of MSU. So while Wolverine fans are probably satisfied that these two games are included in this category, just remember, Spartan fans: you WON both of these matchups.

In 1990 the Wolverines entered their annual in-state rivalry game at home with Michigan State ranked as the number one team in the nation. With the Spartans leading late in the game, Michigan scored a TD on a reception by Derrick Alexander to close the gap to 28-27 with only six seconds remaining. Because U of M had already lost a game to Notre Dame earlier in the year, the Maize and Blue couldn't afford another defeat and expected to contend for the Mythical National Championship. So the choice was made by head coach Gary Moeller to go for the two-point conversion and the win. (The "Big House" crowd of 106,188 might have swayed the coach's decision as well.)

Future Heisman Trophy-winning split end Desmond Howard lined up to the left and cut to the end zone and achieved separation from the State secondary. Quarterback Elvis Grbac delivered a pass that surely looked like it would give the Wolverines the victory, but. . . .

Burned Spartan cornerback Eddie Brown, in an act of desperation, grabbed at Howard's left shoe and tripped the receiver up just as Desmond got his hands on the ball. The officials ruled that Howard didn't maintain possession of the pigskin when crashing to the turf and the game ended with State springing the huge upset. (At least, that is the 1991 *U of M Media Guide* version of the incident.)

Brown maintained that Howard pushed off to gain the separation, but never really denied that he took a swipe at Howard's leg. As a matter of fact, Brown figured a pass-interference penalty was going to be called. When he looked at the field and saw no flag (just a maize pom-pon), Brown celebrated one of the biggest Michigan State victories in the rivalry with the rest of his Spartan teammates.

In the 2001 rivalry game at Spartan Stadium, the Wolverines and Spartans celebrated the near one-year anniversary of the 2000 Presidential Election debacle with a controversy of their own. Jeff Smoker connected on a touchdown pass to T.J. Duckett with no time remaining on the clock, thus giving the Spartans a 26-24 victory over their bigger brother™ (Mike Hart). The debate over this ending centered on the Michigan State timekeeper who later would be nicknamed "Spartan Bob." Now, if you listen to Wolverine fans, they will tell you that Smoker failed to spike the ball before the game clock ran out on the penultimate play. If you listen to Spartan fans, they will explain that Michigan State was unfairly charged a timeout earlier during the game-winning drive and the clock issue should have been moot anyhow.

And just like that George W. Bush vs. Al Gore election, the debate regarding the time clock still goes on to this day. And while the Big Ten always denied that "Spartan Bob" cheated, this game did lead the conference to changing its timekeeping process. It is still a mystery why it took almost 100 years to place the time clock in the hands of a *neutral* party.

6. NCAA Tounament, Sweet Sixteen—Kansas 96, Michigan State 86 (March 21, 1986 at the Kemper Arena)
There aren't many stadiums or arena names that can be mentioned to an entire fan base that will elicit a horrified universal response. But if you ever want to ruin a Michigan State fan's day, go up to said Sparty and mention the words "Kemper Arena."

In the Midwest bracket (there weren't pods in the 80s), the #5 seed Spartans, led by gritty, gutty Scott Skiles, faced off against the #1 seed, Kansas, in the semifinals. With 2:21 left in the game, MSU scored and went ahead by four points. On the next possession Kansas's Ron Kellogg grabbed an offensive rebound, made a two-point shot and cut the State lead to two. The only problem was after that possession ended, the game clock showed 2:20 to play. It was estimated that about 15 seconds elapsed during the Kansas possession, but a clock malfunction led to only one second running off. State head coach Jud Heathcoate noticed the problem and calmly alerted the officials (Read: pounded his fists on the scoring table), but there was nothing the refs could do to correct the error. It turned out that even though the NCAA has a 563,035-page rulebook, it didn't say *anything* about being able to correct a clock error. Would the 15-second deduction from the clock have meant that State would have won the game? Well, it couldn't have hurt. It also wouldn't have damaged State's chances if they would have made the front-end of *any* of the three one-and-one free-throw situations they had in the last two minutes of the game. Kansas coach Larry Brown actually thinks the Jayhawks were hurt by the stoppage, because he got a technical foul and MSU converted..

After 22 years we have yet to determine if Brown diabolically froze time in an effort to:

A) Have his team catch-up to MSU.

B) Give him 15 extra seconds to contemplate his next coaching gig.

5. 1966 NHL Finals, Game 3—Montreal Canadiens 3, Detroit Red Wings 2 (April 22, 1966 at Olympia Stadium)
It is bad enough to lose a playoff game on a controversial play. It is even worse when you lose a playoff game on a goal scored by a dude whose nickname sounds like a female sex toy.

After dispatching the Chicago Blackhawks in the first round in six games, the Wings met the Habs in the Stanley Cup Finals. The series opened in the historic Montreal

Forum and Detroit won both games up north to take a commanding 2-0 series lead as they headed back to the Olympia. With the Wings up in Game Three, the series took a dramatic turn for the worse on a heavily disputed goal. Here is how Wings center Norm Ullman described the goal scored by Henri "The Pocket Rocket" Richard on Wings goalie Roger Crozier:

"We beat Montreal in the first two games of the 1966 Finals and were leading in Game Three when Henri Richard slid about 15 or 20 feet into our net with the puck. They went on to win that game and sweep the rest of the series."

The Wings ended up losing that game 4-2 and the series by the same margin. In the deciding Game Six, the Canadiens won in overtime by a score of 3-2. Even though he was on the losing side of the series, Crozier STILL won the Conn Smythe Trophy as the postseason MVP. Imagine how impressive Crozier would have been if the officials wouldn't have allowed players to score goals by catapulting themselves into the net.

4. Big Ten Rose Bowl Telephone Conference Call (November 25, 1973)

On November 23, 1973, the #4-ranked Michigan Wolverines hosted the #1-ranked Ohio State Buckeyes at Michigan Stadium. The game was to decide the Big Ten Championship and one of the two undefeated teams would represent the conference in the Rose Bowl. The only problem was that the teams played to a 10-10 tie at "The Big House" and there was no such thing as overtime in the collegiate ranks during the early 70s.

And the lack of overtime wasn't the only difference between the college game in1973 and the present. This wasn't an issue of one team going to the Rose Bowl and the other going to the BCS Championship. No, one team was going to the Rose Bowl and the other squad was going to spend New Year's Day watching TV because the Big 10 had a rule that only *one* school was allowed to go bowling. So, the day after the Michigan-OSU game, the Big Ten had a conference call and it was announced that the Buckeyes would head to Pasadena. U of M head coach Bo Schembechler called the decision an "embarrassment" and claimed "petty jealousies" were involved. Although it was never confirmed, many Maize and Blue supporters accused Michigan State of voting for OSU during that conference call.

3. NCAA Tournament, Sweet Sixteen—Georgia Tech 81, Michigan State 80 (March 24, 1990 at the Superdome) If there was any ambiguity regarding

how badly State got *effed* at Kemper Arena in '86, there was no such confusion about this atrocious result. The Steve Smith Spartans entered the 1990 Tournament as a #1 seed and faced Georgia Tech in a Sweet 16 matchup. With five seconds left in regulation, Smith was on the foul line and MSU ahead 75-73. Smith, who lit up G-Tech for 32 points in this game, missed the front end of a one-and-one. The Yellow Jackets' Dennis Scott snatched the miss and tossed the ball to super freshman Kenny Anderson who flew up the court and jacked up a three-pointer that hit nothing but net. The last-second shot appeared to give Tech a berth in the Elite Eight. But immediately there was a disagreement over the play. One ref called the shot a three and another signaled for a two-pointer. After a three-minute debate at the scorer's table, the latter official won the argument and the game entered OT tied at 75-75. So, how did the Spartans get screwed™ (Briana Banks)? Well, it wasn't a deuce or a trey. If you watch the replay (youtube.com has it), it clearly appears that the FREAKING BALL WAS STILL IN

ANDERSON'S HAND when the clock struck zero. Unfortunately, 18 years ago there was no instant replay rule, or even a tenth-of-a-second display on the time clock.

"You've got an awful lot at stake here, for them, for the schools, for the conferences," State coach Jud Heathcote said. "There should not be a mistake by the officials on whether a shot beat the buzzer or didn't beat the buzzer."

And you wonder why the dude used to beat himself over the head?

Predictably the Spartans lost in the five-minute extra period while Tech eventually got to the Final Four before losing to eventual champ, UNLV. Between Kemper and New Orleans, I am amazed that Heathcoate can even keep a clock on his bedroom nightstand.

2. Rose Bowl—Southern Cal 17, Michigan 10 (January 1, 1979 at the Rose Bowl) If Jud Heathcoate's proverbial Moby Dick was the time clock, in the late 70s Bo Schembechler's white whale was the Rose Bowl.

Entering the game against USC, Bo's Michigan teams were on a four-game losing streak in Pasadena. This particular game was decided by seven points, and one touchdown scored in the second quarter will go down in Michigan football infamy forever. With the ball on U of M's three-yard line, Trojans RB Charles White took the handoff and approached the end zone. Just as White got within sniffing distance of the goal line, Wolverines defender Ron Simkins stripped the ball out of White's hands and the rock was recovered by cornerback Mark Braman at the one-yard line. Although it was evident that White never crossed the plain of the end zone on the play, the officials awarded the Trojans a touchdown anyhow.

When ESPN.com published their list of worst calls in sports history, the White "touchdown" was listed as the TENTH WORST EVER.

Not in Michigan sports history. . . .

Not in college football history. . . .

No, in the HISTORY OF SPORTS . . . PERIOD!!!!

It is no wonder that Schembechler didn't have the first of his 57 heart attacks on New Year's Day in '79.

1. NBA Finals, Game 6—Los Angeles Lakers 103, Detroit Pistons 102 (June 19, 1988 at the Forum) In all honesty, not only was this game the biggest screw job in Detroit/Michigan sports history; there really isn't a close second. And it wasn't just the dubious call itself that makes this such an easy choice, it was *everything* that led up to Hugh Evans blowing his whistle and sending the pilot from *Airplane* to the free-throw line in Game Six.

For years the Pistons had fought like hell to win the franchise's first NBA title. The battles with the great Boston Celtics teams alone could fill a book. And after finally vanquishing the Celtics in 1988 (only one year after the infamous Isiah Thomas inbound pass to Larry Bird), the Bad Boys only had one more mountain to climb: Magic Johnson and the Los Angeles Lakers. The first five games of the Finals were hard-fought back-and-forth affairs as both teams stole a victory on the other's court. In Game Five at the Silverdome, shooting guard Joe Dumars (and contributor to this book) scored 19 points by going 9-for-13 from the floor and led Detroit to a 104-94 victory and a 3-2 series lead. Unfortunately, the series was heading back to the Left Coast for the final two games.

And Game Six was an NBA Classic from the beginning. With the Lakers up 56-48 in the third quarter, Isiah went on a ridiculous run: Zeke scored the game's next 14 points before rolling his ankle over Michael Cooper's foot. Thomas suffered a severe ankle sprain and was forced to sit out the next 35 seconds of action. When the banged-up point guard returned, he continued his torrid run, eventually scoring 25 points in the third quarter!

NBA.com labeled Isiah's performance the third best in Finals history. His 25 points are an NBA Finals record for one quarter. At the end of that insane third quarter, the Pistons had an 81-79 lead. The fourth quarter remained close with Detroit nursing a one-point lead in the dying seconds. With the game hanging in the balance and the Lakers on offense, they turned to their aging Hall of Famer center, Kareem Abdul-Jabbar. And as if he was on cue, Kareem attempted his patented skyhook . . . and missed. It was at that moment that Evans stepped in and called what is now known in the Motor City as the "phantom foul" against Bill Laimbeer. Most Pistons fans have reviewed the tape of this call repeatedly like it was the Zapruder film (or, for the younger generation, *One Night in Paris*) and have come to one conclusion: If anyone fouled the former Lew Alcindor, it was Laimbeer's reputation, not his body.

"Look at the tape," fellow Bad Boy Rick Mahorn said. "Maybe the air got him. None of us did."

The career 74-percent free-throw shooter made both free-throws and gave the Lakers the one-point victory.

Game Seven was another epic battle, but with Isiah hampered by the ankle sprain, Detroit lost 108-105.

In another controversy, the Pistons inbounded the ball with two seconds left in Game Seven and down by three points. With half of Hollywood on the court ready to celebrate the Lakers' second straight championship, Thomas couldn't get a decent shot off to tie the game. And even though the Pistons finally broke through the next two years and won back-to-back titles of their own, the sting of Evans' bullshit call in Game Six still hurts to this day. If that bogus call is never made, maybe Detroit wins three titles in a row instead of two and they are considered one of the best teams of all-time instead of just a great team. In 2001, Evans retired from the NBA and gave an interview to *USA Today*. In that article he was asked who was the most controversial team he ever refereed. His answer?

"The Bad Boys days. They brought the best out of you or scared you to death."

Well, in the dying seconds of Game Six of the 1988 Finals, the Pistons sure didn't bring the best out of you, Hugh. Unfortunately, they didn't scare you to death either.

Trading is not exactly a science. The cliché is that the best trades are the ones that help both teams. Here in Detroit we have had our fair share that have only helped the other team. I must admit I had a hard time narrowing the field to 10, so I narrowed them to 11 and surprisingly enough Matt Millen was not involved in any of them. Yes his trading a fourth-round pick for Ty Detmer was a doozy, but the entries below are much worse than that one. This list does not include the Red Wings sending Marcel Dionne to the Kings for Dan Maloney and Terry Harper. That deal was forced to be made because Dionne signed with the Kings as a free agent and the league demanded some type of compensation.

Honorable Mentions: Tigers deal Travis Fryman for Gabe Alvarez, Joe Randa, and Matt Drews; Red Wings trade Ted Lindsay and Glenn Hall for Hank Bassen, Forbes Kennedy, and Johnny Wilson; Pistons trade Bob Lanier to Milwaukee for Kent Benson and 1980 first-round pick; Lions trade Al "Bubba" Baker for third- and eighth-round picks.

Special Honorable Mention: Tigers trade John Smoltz for Doyle Alexander. Many people think this could be one of the worst trades in history, but I disagree. The Tigers were in the 1987 Eastern Divisional race and Alexander went 7 and 0 as the Tigers won the division, which they would not have done without the trade. Yes, Smoltz has gone on to a probable Hall-of-Fame career, but I contend he would never have done it here.

11. Red Wings send Joe Murphy, Adam Graves, Petr Klima and Jeff Sharples to Edmonton for Jimmy Carson and Kevin McClelland, 1989.

Maybe the Wings felt guilty about passing on Grosse Pointe's Carson for Murphy in the 1986 draft, but by the time the Wings brought him home he was not the sniper he was for Los Angeles or Edmonton. He did score 100 goals in his three-plus years in Detroit but he never equaled his 55- or 49-goal years he had before coming to Detroit, and was kind of a wussy as well. He was eventually sent to Los Angeles in the deal that sent Paul Coffey to Detroit. McClelland was a tough guy, accumulating 183 penalty minutes in his one full year with the Wings. Graves was a gritty role player in Edmonton, winning the Stanley Cup in 1990, but truly blossomed into a star when he went to New York. He scored 52 goals in the Rangers' Stanley Cup-winning year of 1994. He ended up with 329 goals, with only seven as a Red Wing. Klima meanwhile could score goals with any team. He scored 129 with the Wings and kept it up with Edmonton, scoring 118 goals in four years. He ended his career with 313 career goals. Murphy did not do anything for the Wings, but had 62 goals in his second and third years as an Oiler. He ended up playing on five other teams before retiring in 2001 with 233 goals. Sharples did not play in the NHL after the trade. Basically the Wings got a one-way player in Carson and a physical player who played one year for three productive players. This certainly was a bad trade.

10. Tigers send Justin Thompson, Gabe Kapler, Francisco Cordero, Frank Catalanatto, Bill Hasselman and Alan Webb to Texas for Juan Gonzalez, Danny Patterson, and Gregg Zaun, 1999.

Who can forget where they were when the Tigers announced they were getting two-time MVP Juan Gonzalez? Most Tiger fans were excited with the thought of a legitimate All-Star on their team. The critics said they were mortgaging the future giving away valuable young players for a guy who had been called a lazy ass throughout much of his career. Both sides were correct. Gonzalez was a far cry from an MVP, but he was not a complete bust, hitting .289 with 22 home runs. The problem was he only played 115 games and turned down an alleged eight-year $140 million contract. He hated the dimensions of Comerica Park and could not wait to leave. In fact, at his welcoming press conference he was asked about buying a house in Detroit. His answer was an instant classic, mocked for years on sports radio. "APARTMENT. APARTMENT." Many of his teammates thought he was a pussy for milking his many nagging injuries. He signed with the Indians the following season. Much of the youth the Tigers gave up did not do that much. Thompson never recovered from an injured left arm and pitched just two games for the Rangers. Kapler, a female favorite, was a serviceable major leaguer hitting .270 in his nine-year career. "The Cat" as he was called is still a very good reserve who has hit for a career .294 average. Cordero was the one piece that really got away. A very good closer, Cordero has saved 177 games in his career.

9. Tigers send Billy Pierce to Chicago White Sox for Aaron Robinson, 1948.

At 21 years of age Billy Pierce was coming off a 3-0 record for the Tigers. He started five of the 22 games he pitched in, but for some reason the Tigers never had faith in the Detroit-born lefty. He was sent to Chicago after the 1948 season for Aaron Robinson, a 33-year-old catcher who was selected to one All-Star Game with the Yankees in 1947. Robinson played two years and part of a third. He made little impact although he did hit 13 homers in 1949. Pierce on the other hand was terrific, as he was selected to seven All-Star games. He led the American League with a 1.97 ERA in 1955. He won 20 games in '56 and '57 and finished his career with San Francisco. Pierce ended up with a career record of 211-169. Making the trade even worse, the Tigers actually had to throw in $10 grand to Chicago to complete the deal.

8. Tigers send Jim Bunning and Gus Triandos to Philadelphia for Don Demeter and Jack Hamilton, 1963.

Bunning was coming off a sub-par 1963 season with just a 12-13 record. At age 31 the righthander might have showed signs of slowing down, but he would prove the Tigers wrong. In fact Bunning would regain the form that made him a six-time All-Star Game selectee with the Tigers. He won 20 games in 1957 and was 90-73 for the Tigers in the next six years. Not bad, but Bunning became a star in Philadelphia, winning 19 games in '64 and pitching a Perfect Game against the Mets on Fathers Day. (He became the first pitcher to have no-hitters in both leagues, having pitched a no-no for the Tigers in 1958). He almost led the '64 Phillies to the World Series, but they blew a six-and-a-half-game lead with 12 to play. His next three years in Philadelphia were also stellar with 19, 19, and 17 wins. His highest ERA as a Phillie was 2.63. He finished up with a record of 224-184 and was elected to the Hall of Fame in 1996 and is currently a senator from Kentucky. Demeter did hit 22 home runs and drive in 68 runs in 1964, but he drove in just 58 the following year and was sent to Boston in a trade that brought the Tigers Earl Wilson. Hamilton did nothing here pitching in just nine games in two years. His claim to fame came years later when he hit Tony Conigliaro in the eye with a pitch. Triandos, who once hit 30 home runs for Baltimore in 1958, could not even come close to his 14 with the Tigers.

7. Red Wings send Garry Unger and Wayne Connelly to St. Louis for Red Berenson and Tim Ecclestone, 1971. Allegedly this one had to do with hair. Garry Unger was a popular young star for the Red Wings. He scored 42 goals as a 23 year-old in the 1969-70 season and was projected to be a superstar for years to come. But there was this hair thing. Unger had long blonde hair and he liked to keep it long, but Wings head coach Ned Harkness was an old-school former college coach and he wanted Unger's hair cut. Well, in what Ted Montgomery of *USA Today* called "among the worst trades in NHL history," Unger was shipped to St. Louis for Berenson. The "Red Baron" was the first expansion star, as he led the Blues to the Stanley Cup Finals in their first three years. The problem was Berenson's age started to catch up with him. He was 32 when the trade took place. He did have 3 decent years and scored 73 goals in almost four full seasons before being sent back to the Blues. Unger, on the other hand, became a star in St. Louis, scoring at least 30 goals or more in each of his eight years as a Blue.

6. Pistons send Dave DeBusschere to New York for Howie "Butch" Komives and Walt Bellamy, 1969. All you need to know about this trade is this quote from Knicks Center Willis Reed: "It only took getting one trade, getting DeBusschere, to turn them into champions." It's hard to believe that the Pistons actually traded DeBusschere. Not only was he a three-time All-Star who averaged 16 points and over 10 rebounds a game, but he was a hometown boy. A star at the Univerity of Detroit, he was even the Pistons player-coach for a few seasons. But they did. By doing so they set the Pistons back and helped make the Knicks into two-time NBA champions. By moving Bellamy, New York was able to move Reed to center and have DeBusscherre and Bill Bradley play together as forwards. The Knicks would turn into one of the least selfish teams in history. DeBusschere had good years as a Piston, but as a Knick he was selected to both the All-Star Game and all-defensive team in all five years in New York. He retired as a Knick at age 33 after the 1974 season, a season where he averaged over 18 points per game, which was his best offensive season as a Knick. Bellamy did his job averaging over 14 points and 10 rebounds a game in his 109 games as a Piston, before being sent to Atlanta in a multi-team deal where a guy named John Arthurs ended up in Detroit from Milwaukee. Arthurs never played for the Pistons or anyone after that deal. Komives was a decent guard who averaged just under 10 points a game in his three-plus years here. "Butch" as he was known was sent to Buffalo for a second-round pick in 1972.

5. Tigers send Luis Gonzalez to the Arizona Diamondbacks for Karim Garcia, 1998. In fairness, when the Tigers announced they had sent the 30-year-old lefthanded hitter to the National League, Tiger fans and media barely made a ripple of protest. But as I told Randy Smith a fews year later, it's his job to be right—not the fans or media. Gonzalez had a decent year as a Tiger hitting 23 homers with a .267 average and 71 RBIs. He wanted to play every day and not be a designated hitter, which was not going to happen. The Tigers had signed free agent Gregg Jeffries and planned to play young phenom Juan Encarnacion; the Tigers had to actually entice Arizona by paying $500 thousand of his $2 million dollar salary. Garcia hit .222 in his one full season with Arizona. He did improve with the Tigers, hitting a robust .240 with 14 dingers. He struck out about one out of every four-and-a-half at bats and was sent to Baltimore after just eight games in 2000. Gonzalez, as you know, went on to stardom. He hit .336 in his first year with the D'backs, finishing second for the batting title. In 2001 he hit 57 home runs while driving in 142 as the Diamondbacks went to the postseason. And it was in the postseason where Gonzalez had his most famous moment, with his blooper off Mariano Rivera to win the World Series in the bottom of the ninth of Game 7. He never hit close to 57 home runs again (hmmm, stopped juicing maybe?) but did hit over 25 a couple of times. I think it's obvious that this seemingly insignificant move became the worst trade in the history of the Detroit Tigers.

4. Lions send Bobby Layne to the Pittsburgh Steelers for draft choices, 1958.
Bobby Layne was the catalyst of the Lions' three championships in the 1950s. His exploits have been chronicled for years. When Tobin Rote took over for the injured Layne and was still able to lead the Lions to the '57 title, some thought Layne might be expendable. Former coach Buddy Parker took over the Steelers' gig in 1957 and then traded for his former quarterback after the 1958 season. Layne and the city who loved him were pissed, to say the least. Layne vowed to take the Steelers to a title and, although he did make the Pro Bowl in 1959, he never got the Steelers that championship. He retired in 1962 at age 36. The actual trade may not have been that bad, however the after-effects makes this trade one of the worst. You see, as legend has it, Layne put a curse on the Lions after the trade. He allegedly said the Lions would not win a championship in 50 years. As we speak, it is late in 2008 and the Lions boast one playoff win in 50 years. Do you believe in curses?

3. Lions acquire Pat Swilling from New Orleans for first-round (8th overall) and fourth-round (89th overall) picks, 1993.
The Lions signed the restricted All Pro free agent linebacker to an offer sheet after the 1991 season only to have the Saints match the offer. But these Lions were relentless—if they wanted someone they got him, no matter what the cost. Lions head coach Wayne Fontes always wanted someone to create havoc on the quarterback, so it was no surprise that Swilling was coveted by Fontes. On the Saints, Swilling was part of one of the best linebacking corps in history with Ricky Jackson, Vaughn Johnson, and Sam Mills. Swilling made four Pro Bowls and was considered a star. But the Lions perhaps wanted him a bit too much as they gave up the 8th and 89th picks in the draft. Swilling did make the Pro Bowl for the Lions in 1993, but it was more a reputation pick as he had his lowest sack total since his rookie season of 1986 with 6.5. The following year he recorded just 3.5. His work habits and selfishness were often questioned, and what he did before he played one game with the Lions was even worse. He asked Hall of Fame linebacker Joe Schmidt if he could wear his retired number 56. Schmidt could not say no, but I am sure he would have if he would have known how disappointing Swilling's two years in Detroit would be. Oh yes, and who did the Saints pick with those picks that makes this one of the worst trades in Detroit history? The Saints selected Louisiana Tech offensive tackle Willie Roaf with the 8th pick and fullback Lorenzo Neal with the 89th. All Roaf did was become one of the best offensive tackles in history, making 11 Pro Bowls and being named All Pro 10 times. The only Pro Bowl he was not named to was due to a season-long injury. Do you think Barry Sanders would have had a few more yards running behind Roaf, especially after Lomas Brown left? And do you think Sanders would have enjoyed having a fullback the caliber of Neal as well? He is only one of the best blocking fullbacks ever. We better stop dreaming—these are, after all, the Lions.

2. Red Wings trade Adam Oates and Paul MacLean to St. Louis for Bernie Federko and Tony Mckegney, 1989. The Red Wings appeared stacked at center for years to come. Steve Yzerman was the main man and captain of the team, and behind him was Adam Oates who was coming off a terrific fourth season with 78 points in 69 games. Both players were under 30, so it was an unbelievable shock when the Wings sent Oates to St. Louis with MacLean for Federko and Mckegny. Federko was a good player and coach Jacques Demers loved him when he coached him with the Blues. But at the time of the trade, his career was on the downside. Oates went on to a spectacular career with four seasons of over 100 points. He teamed with Brett Hull in St. Louis and the tandem of Hull and Oates was one of the best 1-2 combos in the league for a few years. He actually played the bulk of his career with the Bruins and Capitals. Oates finished with 341 goals and 1,420 points. MacLean, who had 36 goals in his one year with Detroit, scored 34 with the Blues before retiring the following season. Federko was decent in his one year here with 17 goals, but retired after that season at age 34. McKegney played 14 games as a Wing before being sent to Quebec.

1. Pistons trade M. L. Carr and two 1980 first-round picks to the Boston Celtics for Bob McAdoo, 1979. Not only was this the worst trade in Detroit sports history, it turned out to be one of the most lopsided in NBA history. The Celtics had signed M. L. Carr as a restricted free agent. The Celtics convinced the Pistons to take McAdoo as compensation as long as the Pistons threw in a couple of first-rounders as well. God only knows what then Pistons coach and GM Dick Vitale saw with his one eye in that trade. McAdoo could score, that's for sure, but he was known as a malingerer who rarely played defense. He averaged 21 points a game in his first year as a Piston. The next season he played in just six games for Detroit due to various injuries. The Pistons waived him after he filed a grievance with the players association. He was eventually picked up by New Jersey. His career was reborn when he was traded to the Lakers with whom he played four years and won a title. He finished his NBA career with Philadelphia before going overseas to play in Italy. The reason the trade is considered so bad has more to do with what Boston did with those picks. First, they traded those two picks, which included the first overall, to Golden State for Robert Parish and the third pick overall. With that third pick, the Celtics selected some lanky forward from Minnesota named Kevin McHale. Knowing the Pistons at the time, they probably would not have been suave enough to pull off the same trade that Red Auerbach did. But it is true, they gave up a chance to have a Parrish and McHale frontcourt for Bob McAdoo. And now you know why Dick Vitale is now doing television.

Narrowing all the trades down to 15 was a laborious task, especially considering some of the ones before World War II. These are the ones that had both the biggest impact and seemed to be the most one-sided.

Honorable Mention: Syd Howe and Scotty Bowman (a different Scotty Bowman) for 50,000 dollars and Ted Graham, Dino Cicarelli for Kevin Miller, Earl Wilson for Don Demeter, Brett Perriman for a fifth round pick, Rick Mahorn for Dan Roundfield, Tony Leswick for Gaye Stewart, and Mark Aguirre for Adrian Dantley.

15. James Edwards from Phoenix Suns for Ron Moore and a number one. February 1988. An underrated but vital member of the 1989 and 1990 NBA Championship teams. He assimilated into the lineup when he came to Detroit in 1988 as the Pistons made it to the finals. His minutes and production picked up in the 1989 season as he averaged over seven points a game. In 1990, Edwards came into his own as a Piston. With Rick Mahorn lost in the expansion draft, Edwards started 76 games and averaged over 14 points a game in both the regular season and in the play-offs. Nicknamed Buddah due to his fu manchu, the Pistons rode the Buddah train early and often in the first quarter. He scored over 13 and a half points a game in the 1990-1991 season. He was sent to the Clippers before the 1992 season and eventually picked up another ring with Chicago in 1996. As for Ron Moore, he played 14 games in his NBA career, the last five after the trade.

14. Kris Draper from Winnipeg Jets for 1 Dollar June 1993. Hard to believe but true, The Red Wings acquired Draper for a dollar. Draper was quoted as saying "it was a Canadian dollar so it only cost them 60 cents." All the Wings got for their "big investment" was a guy who has played for 14 years in Detroit. He was a member of the "Grind Line" with Darren McCarty and Kirk Maltby that wrecked havoc with their fast and reckless play. Draper unfortunately is best remembered for being on the wrong end of the dirty hit from Claude Lemiuex in the 1996 Conference finale in Denver that basically broke his face. He scored a huge goal in game two of the 1998 finals against Washington. He also won the Selke Trophy for best defensive forward in 2004. Definitely one of the best guys off the ice to ever wear the winged wheel.

13. Vinnie Johnson from Seattle for Greg Kelser. November 1981. A popular player who grew up in Detroit and starred at MSU, Kelser did average almost 13 points a game in a little over two years here in Detroit, but he never made the impact that Johnson did. The microwave was a scoring machine when he came off the bench. He averaged over 13 points a game in a ten year stint with the Pistons. He was part of arguably the greatest three guard rotation in NBA history with Joe Dumars and Isiah Thomas. He hit the winning shot in Portland to give the Pistons the 1990 NBA title with less than a second to play. Kelser meanwhile never came close to his numbers as a Piston, playing with Seattle, San Diego and Indiana. Ironically Kelser is the analyst on Pistons television games, while Johnson used to fill that role on radio.

12. Richard Hamilton, Bobby Simmons, and Hubert Davis from Washington for Jerry Stackhouse, Ratko Varda and Brian Cardinal, September 2002. Perhaps the gutsiest trade Joe Dumars had to make. Stackhouse became the face of the franchise, once Grant Hill left. A great guy, he was a pillar in the community and he was a tough player who embodied the mentality of Detroit. He wanted the ball at the end of games, but was not always successful. Stackhouse even toned down his offense to play in Rick Carlisle's defensive style game. His willingness to adapt was one reason the Pistons made the playoffs in the 2001-2002 season. But he shot a dismal 32 percent in those playoffs and Dumars knew the team needed more and that's what they got from Hamilton. Rip was coming off a season averaging 20 points a game, but obviously Michael Jordan did not want him anymore. All Hamilton has done is team with Chauncey Billups to be the best backcourt in the league, make five consecutive conference finals, one championship and three all-star games. He has expanded his game each year. The other players in the deal were insignificant. Stackhouse did ok for the Wizards before being sent to Dallas where he is a very valuable sixth man. However it is safe to say the Pistons got the best of the trade and would not have won a title without Richard Hamilton.

11. Ebbie Goodfellow and Bob Connors from New York Americans for John Shepard. 1928. We go way back to find a trade that helped the Red Wings win three Stanley Cups John Shepard was a pretty good player who was coming off 13 and 10 goal seasons, but he could not compare to Ebbie Goodfellow. He scored double digit goals in 6 straight seasons as both a forward and defenseman. He was a first team all star at defense in 1936, 77, and 1940. Goodfellow won the Hart Trophy (NHL MVP) in 1940 and led the team to the Stanley Cup title in 1936, 37 and 43. He is currently the 24th leading scorer in Red Wings history with 134 goals and 190 assists and was inducted into the Hockey Hall of Fame in 1963. Shepard finished his career in 1934 with 68 career goals.

10. Brendan Shanahan and Brian Glynn from Hartford for Keith Primeau, Paul Coffey, and first round draft pick, October 1996. Coming off a record regular season which ended in a disappointing loss in the semis to Colorado, the Wings finally pulled the trigger on getting the power forward they were missing. Brendan Shanahan wanted to be traded from a hopeless situation in Hartford and the Wings had finally run out of patience with former first round pick Keith Primeau. The deal was one that had Wings fans doing cartwheels. Shanahan became a fan favorite instantly, getting into a fight in his first game as a Red Wing with Greg DeVries of Edmonton. He scored 46 goals in the 96-97 season and nine more in the playoffs as the Wings won their first Stanley Cup in 42 years. In his nine years as a Wing, Shanny never scored less than 25 goals and three times scored 40 or more. He was physically dominant player through most of his Wing career, before going to a more finesse game in the last couple of years. Primeau became a good player with Carolina after the Whalers moved there and then in Philadelphia he was transformed into a leader before he had to retire due to concussion. Primeau will always be looked on by Wings fans as the guy the Wings drafted instead of Jaromir Jagr. Coffey played well here for three and a half seasons but was never a Scotty Bowman favorite. Coincidentally he was traded from Hartford to Philadelphia in the middle of the 97 season and met the Wings in the 1997 Cup finals. Glynn, by the way, never played a game for the Wings.

9. Ben Wallace and Chucky Atkins from Orlando for Grant Hill, August 2000.
They could have lost Hill for nothing, but Joe Dumars would not let that happen. Hill was the best player the Pistons had since the Bad Boys, but they could never get past the first round if they managed to even make the playoffs. Hill seemed like he would stay, but bolted for Orlando with Tracy McGrady. Dumars was able to get Atkins and Wallace in a sign and trade. Atkins was a shoot first point guard who averaged 12 a game his first two years here before the arrival of Chauncey Billups. His playing time diminished and was involved in another trade to be discussed later. Wallace became the face of the franchise. His big hair became the most popular hair style to watch in Detroit. All Wallace did was epitomize the Going to Work slogan of the team. He was a great rebounder and an amazing defensive player. He won the defensive player of the year award four times in a five year stretch. With the exception of his first season in Detroit, the Pistons appeared in the Eastern Conference Finals every season and of course won the 2004 NBA title. He did grow frustrated with his fourth Piston coach Flip Saunders and left to Chicago as a free agent following the 2006 season. Hill meanwhile had a nightmare with injuries in Orlando and never became the superstar many thought he would be. He left the Magic for Phoenix before the 2007-2008 season.

8. Placido Polanco from Philadlephia for Ugeth Urbina, June 2005.
Many players were pissed off with Dave Dombrowski when he traded the right handed reliever for Polanco. And while Urbina was popular with some players he was despised by others, getting in fights on planes while intoxicated. The Phillies needed him badly and he was a huge bust, saving just one game in 56 appearances. Polanco meanwhile was a godsend. He hit .338 the rest of 2005 and finished 2006 with a 285 average. His shoulder injury coincided with the Tigers divisional collapse at the end of the season as he missed a month. He did recover and had a great playoff, hitting over .400 against the Yankees and won the ALCS MVP by hitting 529 in the sweep of Oakland. He did go hitless in the World Series. 2007 was spectacular for the guy with the biggest head in the majors. He was third in the American League with a 341 average and did not commit an error. In fact he has not committed an error since July 1st of 2006. His 181 consecutive games without an error is a major league record for second basemen. Oh yes about Urbina. Well his career ended after the 2005 season, after he was jailed for 14 years for attempted murder. And this was not your ordinary murder attempt. He attacked and injured workers at his family ranch with machetes and then poured gasoline on them. Hey, anytime you can trade a guy who uses a machete and gasoline for an all-star, I'd say it's a good one.

7. Carlos Guillen from Seattle for Ramon Santiago and Juan Gonzalez, January 2004.
Sometimes you get lucky, and sometimes you are smart. Dave Dombrowski knows this trade was a little of both. The Tigers needed a shortstop badly after the Deivi Cruz era thankfully ended. They wanted free agent shortstop Rich Aurelia, but that fell through after he signed with Seattle. The only reason he signed with Seattle was because the Mariners tried to send Guillen to Cleveland for Omar Vizquel, but Vizquel flunked the physical. So, the Tigers dealt young fielding wiz Ramon Santiago and prospect Juan Gonzalez (not the other one) to Seattle for Guillen, Talk about a fleecing, Guillen never hit more than 276 for Seattle and he never had double digit home run totals. Given a chance to play everyday, the Venezuelan flourished. He hit 318 with 20 homers and 97 RBI's his first year. He batted 320 the next 2 seasons including the pennant winning year of 2006 in which he hit 571 in the

ALDS and 353 in the World Series. He was selected to the all star game in 2004 and 2007. He moved to first base for the 2008 season. Santiago meanwhile had just 48 major league at-bats in his two seasons with the Mariners. He was released and then signed by the Tigers in 2006. Gonzalez has been with five organizations since the trade and finally Double A in 2007.

6. Bill Laimbeer and Kenny Carr from Cleveland for Paul Mokeski. Phil

Hubbard, a first round and second round pick, February 1982. There probably would not have been the Bad Boys if this deal did not occur at the trading deadline. Laimbeer wanted out of the awful situation in Cleveland badly, he practically begged to be traded. Ironically his coach in Cleveland was Chuck Daly, who did not want to trade Laimbeer. Carr was traded that summer for a first round pick after he averaged just over seven points a game. Hubbard was the Pistons first round pick out of Michigan in 1979. He was a solid, productive player who averaged double digits almost every season for both Detroit and Cleveland. Mokeski, a member of the all ugly team played a year and half with the Pistons and was traded to Milwaukee by the Cavs in 1983. The lumbering seven-footer averaged four points and three rebounds in a hard to believe 12 year career. Laimbeer was the one who made this the lopsided deal it was. He was the villain of the NBA, a role he cherished. He never considered himself dirty. He once told me he was "chippy" like Bobby Clarke of the NHL's Philadelphia Flyers. He agitated everyone from players to refs to fans all over the NBA. Even many of his teammates thought he was a prick, but he was their prick and they went to war with him. Laimbeer was more than a thug, although you would never get Michael Jordan, Larry Bird, or others to see differently. The guy could rebound and shoot the lights out from the outside. He is the Pistons fifth all time leading scorer with 12, 664 points and its all-time leading rebounder with nine, 430. The four time all-star is one of the few players to finish his career with over 13, 000 points and 10, 000 rebounds. He retired at age 36, 11 games into the 1994 season because he could not get motivated anymore. He is currently the head coach of the WNBA's Detroit Shock, whom he has guided to two titles.

5. Joe Coleman, Aurelio Rodriguez, Ed Brinkman, and Jim Hannan from Washington for Denny McLain, Don Wert, Elliott Maddox, and Norm McRae, October 1970. This was both one of the biggest heists and biggest trades

ever. McLain, who won 31 games in 1968 and 24 in 1969, was coming off a 1970 campaign where he went just 3-5 in a season where he was suspended three times for various illegal activity. He was 10-22 in his only year for the Senators and finished his career at age 28 with the A's and Braves in 1972. The light hitting Wert ended his career with the Senators playing just 20 games. Maddox was a journeyman outfielder who hit 261 during an 11 year major league career. McRae never played in the majors after the trade. Coleman was a stud, going 88-73 with the Tigers including consecutive seasons with 20, 19, and 23 wins. He was an all star selection in 1972 and threw a seven hit, 14 strikeout shutout in the 72 ALCS. He was sold to the Cubs during the 76 season. Rodriguez was a steady fixture at third base most of the 1970's. He was a great fielder who won the gold glove in 1976 and would have won more if there had not been a guy named Brooks Robinson around at the time. He was sold to San Diego for $200,000 in December of 1980. Brinkman was not much of a hitter, but he could field. He won the Gold Glove in 1972

4. Rasheed Wallace and Mike James from Atlanta and Boston for Zelkjo Rebracca, Chucky Atkins, Bob Sura and Lindsey Hunter, February 2004. One of the biggest thefts in NBA history. The Pistons, who had made the Eastern Conference finals the year before, were basically just a good team with no edge under first year coach Larry Brown. At 34-22, and riding a six game losing streak they needed something to put them over the top and Rasheed was just that something. He had been traded from Portland to Atlanta, but everyone knew Atlanta could not or would not want to keep the impending free agent. Brown lobbied publicly to get the immensely talented and controversial Wallace. It did not look like it could happen and then Danny Ainge stepped in. In order to make the trade work, salary cap wise Joe Dumars had to find someone to take Chucky Atkins and his contract, Ainge obliged and voila. Rebracca and Sura went to Atlanta along with a first round pick that originally belonged to Milwaukee Atkins and Hunter ended up in Boston along with a 2004 first round Cleveland head coach Paul Silas blamed Atlanta saying "I don't know what some teams are thinking about" Wallace delivered what was promised. He and Ben Wallace became a dynamic defensive duo. Wallace X2 they were called and oh did they play defense. In one stretch the Pistons held their opponents to under 70 points for six straight games. The Pistons finished the season as the third seed. They beat Milwaukee, came from 3-2 down to beat New Jersey, before losing the first game of the Eastern Conference finals at Indiana. After that game Rasheed guaranteed a game two win saying "they will not win game two, they will not win game two". He did not play well, but his teammates had his back. They won game two and went on to win the series in six games and the championship over the Lakers in five. Mike James was more than just a throw in. He and Hunter (he was released by Boston and re-signed with the Pistons) formed the pit bulls. A defensive duo that made life miserable for their opponents. James signed with Milwaukee as a free agent and now plays for the Hornets. Rebracca played just briefly for the Hawks and then two years for the Clippers, he is now out of the NBA as is Sura who played one year with Houston after his sentence in Atlanta. Wallace meanwhile is still confounding as ever. When he is focused he is awesome, but when he is not it's a different story. He still regrets his brain fart, by trapping Manu Gnobli during the final seconds in game five of the 2005 NBA finals. He left Robert Horry wide open for a three pointer that gave the Spurs a 3-2 series edge, which they won in seven. In 2007 he was the Pistons best player in the playoffs, but blew a gasket and was ejected in the sixth and final game in Cleveland when the game was still in doubt. He would be on the all-dichotomy team.

3. Willie Hernandez and Dave Bergman from Philadelphia for Glenn Wilson and John Wockenfuss, March 1984.

Late in Spring Training the Tigers decided they needed a closer. Aurelio Lopez was fine but Sparky Anderson thought he was better as a setup man. Nobody knew that the acquisition of Hernandez would be one of the best in the teams history. Hernandez and the rest of the team got off to the amazing 35-5 start. With a lights out screwball Hernandez was practically unhittable all season. When Hernandez would enter the game, fans knew the game was basically over. He saved 32 of 33 attempts. His ERA was a stellar 1.92. He won both the Cy Young and MVP, which was unheard of for a reliever. He gave up two runs and seven hits in nine post season innings as the Tigers won the World Series. He was selected to the all-star game the following two seasons as well. His effectiveness started to go away during the 1987 season and retired from baseball after the 1989 season in Detroit or so we thought. He tried to come back with the Yankees AAA team in Syracuse during the 1991 season and yes he was a replacement player for the Yankees during spring training of 1995. Bergman played nine seasons for the Tigers. The part time first baseman made a huge impact in 1984 especially in two games against Toronto. On June 4th, he fouled off seven three and two pitches before pounding a three run homer off of Roy Lee Jackson to win a ten inning game 6-3. Sparky Anderson called that the "best at bat in his life" He hit another three run tenth inning home run against Toronto on September seven to put the Tigers nine and a half games ahead of Toronto. He finished his major league career with a 258 average. Wockenfuss was a reserve player who had been with the Tigers since 1974 and hit 80 home runs as a Tiger. His southern down to earth style made him a fan favorite. And who can forget his unorthodox batting stance where held the bat completely over his head with his right elbow sticking out? Wilson was a former number one draft choice whose second year with the Tigers in 1983 showed some promise with 11 homers and 65 RBI's. He was looked on as a future star, and after a dismal 1984, started wearing glasses, Lo and behold he made his lone all star appearance in 1985. He did have a very good arm and led the National League in assists in 1985 and 1986. The Phillies traded him to Seattle after the 1987 season. He also played for Pittsburgh and Houston.

2. Norm Cash from Cleveland for Steve Demeter, April 1960.

Perhaps the most underrated and lopsided trade in Detroit history, the Tigers gave up a guy who ended up batting .087 in just 15 major league games for a 4 time all star. Stormin' Norman owned first base for the Tigers for 15 seasons. While the baseball world was swooning over Mantle and Maris in 1961, Cash won the batting title hitting 361 with 41 homers and 132 RBI's. He later admitted he used an illegal bat in that year and his numbers were never the same. But, he was still productive hitting over 30 home runs four times. He hit 385 in the 1968 World Series victory over St. Louis. Cash was also one of the great characters of the game. In 1972 during Nolan Ryan's second no-hitter, he came to bat with a chair leg as his bat.

1. Bobby Layne from the New York Bulldogs for Bob Mann 1950. Maybe it's because they have not a great quarterback since, or maybe they have only won one playoff game since he left, but the trade for the best quarterback in Lions history should be number one. Bob Mann was no slouch, he played on Michigan's 1947 undefeated championship team before being joining the Lions in 1948. He was one of the first African-Americans to play for the Lions and led the league in receiving yardage in 1949. Mann never played for New York. He played five years for Green Bay, his best year being 1951 when he had 50 receptions. He retired after the 1954 season. Layne was the real deal, although his stats were not overwhelming. He led the Lions to three championships in 1952, 1953, and 1957. In the 1952 title game he scored two touchdowns. The following year, down 16-10, Layne led the Lions down the field by completing 4 of 6 passes, the last a 33 yarder to Jim Doran for the winning score as the Lions beat Cleveland 17-16, He broke his leg during the 57 season and had to watch as Tobin Rote led them to their last championship. He made four Pro Bowls on his way to the hall of fame. But it was his style that made him what he was, both on and off the field. He could run and pass, make the key play when they needed it the most. Off the field, the tales of his nightlife are legendary in the Motor City. Legend has it he would be hung over for games, but he always came to play on Sunday. In a historic look back at Layne, the *Detroit News* quoted both Layne and linebacker Joe Schmidt. "Joe Schmidt, the old middle linebacker and later coach of the Lions, remembers one night he went out with Layne and running back Gene Gedman to Charlie Costello's, a popular watering hole on East Jefferson. Unable to find a parking space, Bobby left his car on the sidewalk. When the cops showed up a few minutes later Schmidt and Gedman hid under the table while Layne got up to talk to the officers. Next thing he knew, Schmidt said, Layne was driving off behind a police car with its siren blaring. Layne had talked the cops into providing a police escort to the next watering hole. "I'm just a born night owl," Bobby once said of his Detroit playing days. "Maybe I'm a better player because I start having fun at midnight, get to bed when everybody else is waking and sleep all morning. Makes me fresh as a daisy for the game." Layne was traded to Pittsburgh early in the 1958 season. Legend has it he said the Lions would not win a championship in 50 years. The wait continues.

Selfishly Stoney had to find the best Mikes or Michaels in the history of Detroit sports. Unfortunately there were not tons of great ones, but here are the best. . . .

Honorable Mention. Mike Compton, Mike Blaisdell, Mike Kenn, Mike Utley, Mike Brkovich, Mike Hammerstein, and Michael Curry.

12. Mike Foligno—Red Wings. The third overall pick of the 1979 draft,Foligno was a terrific player for the Wings, scoring 77 goals in his two and a half seasons, including 36 in his rookie year. He was traded to Buffalo during the 81-82 season with Dale McCourt and Brent Peterson for Danny Gare, Jim Schoenfeld, and Derek Smith.

11. Mike Abdenour—Detroit Pistons. We know he is not a player, but Abdenour has been a fixture on the Pistons bench for 29 of his 32 years as an NBA trainer. He has patched up injured players since 1975. His shouting of "go to it" as the shot clock ran down was synonymous with the Pistons during the Bad Boys era.

10. Mike Peplowski—MSU basketball.
The Warren DeLasalle graduate was first team All Big 10 in 1992. His best statistical year was 1992-1993 when he averaged 14.5 points and ten rebounds per game. The 6-10 big man played 55 of his 68 NBA games with the Sacramento Kings.

9. Mike Weger—Lions. A solid member of the secondary, Weger played for the Lions from 1967-75. He had 17 interceptions and also played himself in the movie *Paper Lion*.

8. Mike Cofer—Lions. A solid line-backer, with a chiseled body, Cofer was one of the bright spots during one of the many poor eras of Lion football. He played ten years and made the Pro Bowl in 1988 when he had 12 sacks.

7. Mike Henneman—Tigers. He came on to the scene out of nowhere during the 1987 season and was a key ingredient to the Tigers divisional title. The rookie reliever went 11-3 with 7 saves in that magical regular season. The righty side-armer was also accidentally shown naked during a locker room report on Channel 2 that season. He pitched eight and a half seasons for the Tigers and is second to Todd Jones on the Tigers all time save list with 154.

6. Mike McGee—Michigan basketball. He did not play organized basketball until his sophomore year in high school, but this Omaha Nebraska native never let you know it. He is second on the Wolverine all time scoring list with 2439 points, trailing Glen Rice by just three. McGee was not shy, he is the all-time leader in field goal attempts. He was an All American in 1981 and he was an all Big 10 first team selection twice and second team his other two seasons. A first round pick of the Lakers in 1981, he played nine years in the NBA and won rings with the Lakers.

5. Mike Vernon—Red Wings. The goalie who some say was the missing link came to Detroit in the 1994 off season from Calgary in a deal for defenseman Steve Chiasson. All Vernon did was lead the Wings to the Stanley Cup finals, before getting swept by New Jersey. He was not spectacular in the finals, which did not make him a fan favorite. The following year he shared the Jennings Trophy with Chris Osgood, but played in just four playoff games. In 1997 he became a hero for life for taking on Patrick Roy in the infamous March 26 brawl with Colorado. He then ended his Red Wing career in style, capturing the Conn Smythe Trophy as the Wings won their first Stanley Cup in 42 years.

4. Mike Babcock—Red Wings. All this guy has done in three years is improve every season. A Presidents Trophy in his first year was tarnished by a first-round play-off loss to Edmonton. In year two the Wings lost in the Western Conference Finals to Stanley Cup Champion Anaheim in six grueling games. And then in 2007-08, the Wings won another Presidents Trophy and this thing called the Stanley Cup. He may be a tough SOB, but man can he coach. He was awarded with a three-year extension in June of 2008.

3. Mike Hart—Michigan Football. At 5-foot-9 inches, not many people figured Mike Hart would become the Wolverines all time leading rusher, but that's what he did. He burst out his freshman year with a tremendous 1,455 yards and nine touchdowns in becoming the Big 10 freshman of the year. He gained 662 yards in an injury plagued 2005, in which he missed four games and parts of three others. He came back from injury to have a sensational junior year, leading Michigan to the great 11-0 start. His 1,562 yards and 14 touchdowns helped him get many All-American honors. He became the schools all time leading rusher with a 218 yard performance against Eastern Michigan on October 6, 2007. His senior year was a mixed bag of brilliance and injury. He missed three full games and parts of three others, but still managed 1,361 yards and 14 touchdowns. The lone blemish on his career is his 0-4 record against Ohio State.

2. Mike Lucci—Lions. From 1965-1973, Mike Lucci was a defensive force for the Lions. The linebacker was both mean and agile. He had an uncanny ability to play through injury. Lucci was part of a great line-backing trio that included Wayne Walker and Paul Naumoff. He made the Pro Bowl in 1971, a season in which he had five interceptions and two of them he returned for scores. He also had a role in "Paper Lion".

1. Mike Ilitch. His contributions to sports in the city are legendary. He bought the Red Wings in 1982 and in his 25 years of ownership oversaw three Stanley Cups and turning the team into the best franchise in the United States. He purchased the Tigers ten years later and after 14 years of the worst baseball we had ever seen, the Tigers went to the World Series in 2006. He helped rejuvenate downtown with the building of Comerica Park (with help from the public) and was championship owner with the Arena Football League's Detroit Drive. His Little Caesars youth hockey program has been one of the best in the country for 30 years and he is a member of the NHL Hall of Fame.

Top 10 Reasons the Lions Are Cursed

When you have only won one playoff game in over forty years, when you have NEVER, even been to a Super Bowl and most of your fan-base wasn't alive for your last championship, something must be to blame. And of course it couldn't be the most inept ownership to blame. Nope, a lot of Detroit Lions fans think that the team must be cursed. After all Bobby Layne allegedly was so pissed off after he was traded to Pittsburgh in 1958 that he said the Lions would not win a championship for 50 years. It's now 2008 so Layne's alleged curse is alive but should die soon right? And unlike the Curse of the Bambino (the Boston Red Sox) or the Curse of the Billy Goat (the Chicago Cubs), the Lions don't really have a smoking gun moment that you can hang your hat on. So the following are 10 incidents that might prove the Detroit Lions are cursed.

10. The Lions finally get a good coach . . . and he drops dead. The Lions have not had a wonderful history of head coaches in their history under owner William Clay Ford, Sr. So it was quite a coup when the team landed Super Bowl winning coach Don McCafferty during the 1973 off season. It was hoped that McCafferty would translate his success in Baltimore (where he won Super Bowl V) to the woeful Lions franchise. Unfortunately, McCafferty only lasted one season in which the team posted a record of 6-7-1. On July 28, 1974, McCafferty suffered a heart attack while cutting his lawn in Bloomfield Hills and died. Unbelievably enough, McCafferty won't be the only person on this list to die while cutting his lawn.

9. The Lions only win when they shouldn't. During the 2005 season, the Lions were sitting at 3-12 heading into the last two games of the year. In their 15th game, they traveled to New Orleans to play an equally awful Saints team. (Of course, the Saints had an excuse for being atrocious. They had been uprooted from their home by Hurricane Katrina.) In a game they shouldn't have wanted to win because of draft position, the Lions eeked out a 13-12 victory. So instead of selecting second in the draft, they picked ninth. Of course, Matt Millen was making the pick anyway so curse or no curse, it probably didn't matter anyway.

8. Expansion screws the Lions. Coming off a 2-14 season, the Lions didn't have the first pick overall in the 2002 NFL Draft. Because of the expansion Houston Texans entering the league, they didn't even have the number two pick. With the third pick that year, the Lions selected Joey Harrington. And who went with the second selection? A player Detroit could have theoretically drafted if it wasn't for the league's decision to expand? Pro-Bowl stud defensive end, Julius Peppers out of North Carolina.

7. A 5-0 Playoff Game? We have seen plenty of 5-0 baseball games. We have even seen some 5-0 hockey scores. But a 5-0 football game? And a playoff match-up at that? On December 26, 1970, the Lions traveled to Dallas where they failed to score a single point. We are guessing that going into the game, the team PROBABLY felt they would have a decent chance to win if they held the Cowboys to five freaking points. Instead, the Lions ended up losing the lowest scoring game in NFL postseason history. And it wouldn't be surprising if that is a record that will stand for a very, very long time.

6. Barry Sanders Heads to Great Britain. For all of the misery suffered during William Clay Ford, Sr.'s ownership of the team, at least we had one of the greatest running backs of all-time to watch during the nineties. For years, Lions fans had one thing to look forward to and that was the day that Barry would eventually break Walter Payton's all-time rushing record. At the age of 29, Sanders was only 1,457 yards behind Payton's all-time record. And not only was a healthy Sanders expected to break Payton's record, it was almost a certainty that he would obliterate the mark. But instead of breaking Sweetness's record in 1999, Barry decided to retire on the eve of Training Camp without giving the team. To add insult to injury, Lions fans had to watch Emmitt Smith break Payton's record a few years later.

5. Reggie Brown's Career Ends. On what should have been one of the greatest days in the history of the franchise, the team instead suffered another tragic event. During the last game of the 1997 season, Barry Sanders surpassed the 2,000 yard barrier for the season. The team also beat the Jets in a must-win game that earned the team a playoff berth. Sounds like a banner day for the moribund organization, right? Well, it would have been if one of the better players on the team didn't almost die in front of a sold-out crowd. Before Sanders went over the 2,000 yard marker, Brown suffered an injury tackling the Jets Adrian Murrell. Brown lay motionless on the Silverdome artificial turf for 17 minutes while medical staff applied CPR to the up and coming defensive star. And while the doctors saved Brown's life, the linebacker suffered a spinal cord contusion injury that ended his career. At the time of his injury it appeared that Brown was on his way to a Pro-Bowl career, but the injury forced the former Texas A & M standout into selling cars in Dallas.

4. One-Footed Kicker Beats the Lions. It would be bad enough to lose a game on a 63-yard field goal. But only the Lions could lose a game on a 63-yard field goal...to a stump-footed place-kicker. On November 8, 1970, the Saints trailed the Lions 17-16 in the dying seconds of a game in New Orleans. As the time kicker Tom Dempsey ran onto the field, the NFL's longest field goal to date was 56-yards. The kicker with a specially designed shoe knocked the ball through the uprights to give the Saints a 19-17 victory. So not only did the Lions get beat by a kicker with half a foot, they got beat by a kicker with a half a foot WHO ALSO HAPPENED TO BREAK THE NFL FIELD GOAL DISTANCE RECORD BY A WHOPPING SEVEN YARDS!!!! Jason Elam (with a whole foot in the altitude of Denver) would later tie Dempsey's record in 1998.

3. Mike Utley Gives the Thumps Up. In his first three seasons as a Detroit Lions offensive lineman, Mike Utley suffered a crushed right leg, broken ribs, injury to his right shoulder and another to his right hip. But that was all child's play compared to what occurred during Utley's fourth season. On November 17, 1991, the Detroit Lions were hosting the Los Angeles Rams in a game at the Silverdome. On a freakish play, Utley would suffer an injury to his sixth and seventh cervical vertebrae. The injuries would cause permanent paralysis from his waist down. If it weren't for Utley's unbelievable attitude, this might be even higher on the list. But since the injury occurred, Utley has turned the horrific event into a positive. He started the Mike Utley Foundation— Finding a Cure for Paralysis. Utley also hasn't let his paralysis from doing things like skydiving out of an airplane. (Of course, when you aren't afraid of paralysis, it is probably easier to work up the nerve to jump from a plane.)

2. Eric Andolsek Dies While Mowing His Grass. After losing Utley to his injury, the Lions were inspired by his up-beat attitude which was personified by the famous "thumbs-up" he gave while being carted off the Silverdome turf. That season culminated with an appearance in the NFC Championship game in which the Lions were thrashed by the Washington Redskins. But even with the loss of Utley, it appeared that the team had a quality offensive line that included Eric Andolsek. Unfortunately, Andolsek's last game ever would be that NFC title match-up. On June 23, 1992, while cutting his lawn at his home in Thibodaux, Louisiana, Andolsek was struck by a semi-trailer truck while cutting his lawn. So in the span of a few months, the Lions lost two quality members of their offensive line to tragedy. Between the Andolsek incident and the death of McCafferty, if any members of the Lions organization are reading this chapter, maybe you should think about hiring a lawn service.

1. Chuck Hughes Dies on the Field. Over the last few years, the Lions have had some serious issues with the wide receiver position. But as bad an experience the team has had, at least Charles Rogers or Mike Williams never dropped dead on the field. The same couldn't be said of Lions WR Chuck Hughes. On October 24, 1971, the Lions were hosting the Chicago Bears at Tiger Stadium. In the dying moments of the game (no pun intended), Hughes ran a pass-route in which he wasn't part of the play. On an incomplete pass to Charlie Sanders, Hughes collapsed to the grass of Tiger Stadium. After a few seconds in which the two teams didn't know what the hell was going on, the Bears Dick Butkus discovered something wasn't right and started frantically waiving for medical assistance. Attempts to resuscitate Hughes failed and the receiver died at the age of 28. As bad as things have gotten for the Lions and their fans, Hughes is the only member of the organization whoever croaked during a game. We can't be sure how many of the team's fans have suffered a similar fate putting up with the organization's antics though. For losing his life in the line of duty, the team retired Hughes' #85 jersey.

The Top 13 Michigan Team Championships in the Last 50 Years

The following list details the great Detroit area sports teams since 1950. As you are about to find out, not all championship teams are created equally. Thankfully this book isn't being published in Cleveland, because that would be one really short chapter.

Honorable Mention: 2006 Detroit Tigers, 1992 Michigan Men's Basketball Team (Fab Five), 1997-98 Detroit Red Wings.

13. 2003 Detroit Shock. The ultimate worst to first story The WNBA Shock was the worst team in the league the year before. But, Coach Bill Laimbeer used his NBA mentality and built the toughest bunch of chicks you could ever want. Led by Swin Cash, Cheryl Ford (Karl Malone's daughter, [gee Dad, nice of you be around when I was growing up]) and Deanna Nolan, the Shock finished with wins and breezed to the finals against the two time defending champion Los Angeles Sparks. The best of three series opened in LA and the Shock were drilled. Detroit squeaked a one-point victory to tie the series. The winner takes it all game three was played in front of a legitimate 22,076 at the Palace. (And no you can stop with the 'I bet they thought it was a Lillith Fair concert' jokes) It was a terrific athletic event and the place was as loud as hell. The game was a physical dogfight, which the Shock pulled out 83-78. Ruth Riley led the Shock with 27 points. Two Championship Drive was changed to Three Championship Drive, which does not seem right. Not to be politically incorrect but shouldn't WNBA titles count as only half of a men's title?

(Staff note: We feel very dirty including a women's basketball team on this list. At least we didn't include the Detroit Demolition [women's football].)

12. 1966 Michigan State Football. The 1966 Spartans football team shared the mythical National Championship with Notre Dame because on November 19, 1966 in what was dubbed as "The Game of the Century", the two teams tied 10-10 at Spartan Stadium. The MSU squad, led by Bubba Smith, actually shared a National Championship, but didn't go to a bowl game. The Big Ten had a moronic rule that a team could not go to the Rose Bowl in back-to-back years (and State played in Pasadena the previous season). The conference also had a rule that only one team could go to a bowl. So, the 9-0-1 Spartans got to celebrate their title on New Year's Day in the comfort of their own homes. It is really amazing that the college football system was more effed up 40 years ago then it is today.

11. 1983 Michigan Panthers. Some readers of this book will be infuriated that we picked a USFL championship over some of the Red other titles that are listed above as honorable mentions. But considering that the only professional football success that multiple generations of Detroit sports fans have witnessed firsthand is the Michigan Panthers title in 1983, we felt the Albert Taubman/Max Fisher team deserved inclusion. In the inaugural season of the USFL (a league that was trying to take a bite out of the NFL's market), the Panthers made it to the championship game against the Philadelphia Stars. Led by University of Michigan standout flanker Anthony Carter, future New Orleans Saints QB Bobby Hebert and defensive stud John Corker, the Panthers in their first season won as many home playoff games at the Silverdome as their fellow tenant, the Lions, did in 26 years. In front of a crowd of 60,237 excited football fans desperate for any modicrum of success, the Panthers thrashed the Oakland Invaders 37-21 to gain entrance into the USFL Championship game. In the title game, Hebert threw for 319 yards and 3 TDs to lead the team to the championship. The Northwestern State Louisiana product took home the MVP title with the performance that was highlighted with a 48-yard touchdown pass to A.C. in the fourth quarter that helped give Michigan a 24-22 victory. For many Detroiters it was the first (and probably last) professional football championship they will ever get to celebrate.

10. 2000 Michigan State Basketball. In 1999, the Tom Izzo coached Michigan State Spartans lost in the Final Four to the Duke Blue Devils. Feeling that they still had something left to prove, guards Mateen Cleaves and Morris Peterson decided to return to East Lansing for their senior years of eligibility. And the decision to return to school and forego the NBA worked out just the way the Flintstones had planned. In front of a capacity crowd at the RCA Dome in Indianapolis, the Spartans defeated the Florida Gators 89-76 to win the school's first national championship since 1979. A resilient Cleaves rebounded from a sprained ankle early that he suffered early in the second half to lead the Spartans to a 16-6 run that iced the game and secured the title. Cleaves was awarded the Most Outstanding Player while Peterson led the tournament with a total of 105 points. "Oh my god, this is what I came back for," said Cleaves. "This was a total group effort." And after his professional career (and it is very liberal of us to call it a career), Cleaves' decision to stay at MSU for his senior season looked even better. He might want to check and see if he has any eligibility left, actually.

9. 1989 Michigan Basketball. *"A Michigan man is going to coach a Michigan team." – Michigan athletic director Bo Schembechler.* The most ironic thing about the late Bo Schembechler's life is that even though he became a legend for coaching the Wolverines football team, the most famous words that he ever uttered were about U of M's basketball team. After Bill Frieder took a gig at Arizona State, Bo promptly canned his ass and promoted assistant coach Steve Fischer. The third seeded Wolverines were considered a contender for the title, but with the turmoil that Frieder created by abandoning the team, many pundits figured Michigan wouldn't make it out of the first weekend. But behind the deadly shooting of Glen Rice, the Wolverines got all the way to the Final Four. In their first game at the Kingdome in Seattle, U of M defeated fellow Big Ten rival Illinois in a nail-biter, 83-81. The title game was even closer as Seton Hall and the Wolverines could not settle the championship in 40 minutes. The game went to overtime and Rumeal Robinson's two clutch free-throws with three seconds remaining gave Michigan an 80-79 victory. Rice ended up scoring a record 184 points in the 1989 tourney and was honored with the Most Outstanding Player award. That record still stands to this day. The interim label was removed from Fischer's job title after the championship and Bo went back to focusing on football.

8. 2001-2 Detroit Red Wings. It had been a few years since the Wings had won a Stanley Cup and the fans and owner (Mike Ilitch) were getting a little impatient. So in the off season before the 2001-2 year, GM Kenny Holland went out and added three Hall of Famers to the lineup. Slava Kozlov was shipped to Buffalo in exchange for one of the greatest goalies to ever live in Dominik Hasek. One of the most prolific scoring right wingers in the history of the league, Brett Hull, was added via free-agency. Left winger Luc Robitaille was also acquired because the team obviously didn't have enough 500 goal scorers. The team cruised through the regular season per usual and won another President's Trophy. Although there were some bumps in the road (going down 2-0 to Vancouver in Round 1 and trailing Colorado 3-2 in the Western Conference Finals), the Hall of Fame laden squad dispatched of the Carolina Hurricanes in the Finals fairly easily. Thanks to a Nicklas Lidstrom goal from outside the blueline in Vancouver and the Patrick Roy Statue of Liberty goal, the Wings lived up to the expectations and won their third Cup in six years.

7. 2004 Detroit Pistons. The 2003-2004 Los Angeles Lakers were very similar in nature to the 2001-2 Red Wings. They had already won multiple titles in previous years and when they added Karl Malone and Gary Payton to the mix, it became a foregone conclusion that they would add another championship banner. If you believed the media, the best the Pistons could have hoped for was an Eastern Conference title and the right to get their asses spanked by the Laker juggernaut. Even when the Pistons added Rasheed Wallace at the trade deadline, most experts figured that Detroit might get to the Finals, but there was still no way they could win it all. The absolute defensive slopfest that was on display in the Eastern Conference Finals between the Pistons and Pacers did not add much credence that either team would give the Lakers any challenge in the Finals. When the Larry Brown coached Pistons vanquished their ex-coach's Pacers in six games, both the national and local media predicted the Pistons would get promptly swept by Shaq and Kobe. Colin Cowherd told his ESPN Radio audience that the Pistons didn't even belong on the same floor as the Lakers. Drew Sharp predicted the Pistons would lose to L.A. in the first three game sweep in the history of the best-of-seven format. And all of the experts were right. It wasn't much of a series AT ALL. The Pistons shocked the world and the Lakers in Game 1 at the Staples Center. And if it wasn't for a late collapse in Game 2 by Detroit, the Pistons would have been the team sporting a broom. As it was, the Pistons crushed L.A. in all of their home games and won the series 4-1. Many still call the series a five game sweep because the Lakers had no business winning game two in overtime. The embarrassment for Los Angeles led to a tumultuous off-season in which Shaq was dealt to Miami and Phil Jackson temporarily retired. The 2004 Pistons of Chauncey Billups, Rip Hamilton, Ben Wallace, Rasheed Wallace and Tayshuan Prince were also considered the first NBA champion without a true superstar. (Amazingly enough we just got through a recap of the 2004 Pistons without saying, "Doing things the right way." Well, we almost did. Damn.)

6. 1997 Michigan Football. In 1997, the Michigan football team did something that they could not accomplish under Bo. They won the mythical national championship. Well, actually they won a share of that title. Led by a stifling defense and an economical offense, the Wolverines posted a perfect 12-0 record that culminated with a 21-16 victory over Ryan Leaf's Washington State squad in the Rose Bowl. Heisman Trophy winner Charles Woodson anchored a defense that only gave up more than 17 points once all season long and Brian Griese managed the offense while trying not to do anything stupid after replacing Scott Dreisbach under center. (Something that didn't come naturally for Bob's son.) Lloyd Carr's team ended up sharing the championship with Nebraska as U of M was #1 in the AP Poll while the Coach's place Tom Osborne's last Cornhusker team #1 in their poll.

5. 1979 Michigan State Basketball. If you don't like Bracketology. If you don't like Dick Vitale screaming at you through your TV every March. If you don't like the song "One Shining Moment". Then you can probably blame it on the 1979 Michigan State basketball team led by Magic Johnson. Because most college basketball experts would claim that "March Madness" didn't really take off until the 1979 title game between Magic's Spartans and Larry Bird's Indiana State Sycamores. The title game between two of the greatest basketball players to ever live is still the highest rated collegiate basketball game ever. And that large audience witnessed the Spartans defeat Bird's squad 75-64. In his sophomore season, Magic won the Most Outstanding Player honor and the championship with the help of Greg Kelser and Jay Vincent. To this day, Jud Heathcoate thanks his lucky starts that Earvin Johnson's parents decided to live in Lansing, Michigan.

3. Tie: 1989-1990 Detroit Pistons. If the criteria for this list was "which 'Bad Boys' championship was more fulfilling", you would have to go with their first title. After the grueling battles with the Celtics, the Isiah Thomas inbound pass to Larry Bird that led to a Dennis Johnson basket, the phantom foul on Bill Laimbeerin Game six of the 1988 NBA Finals, there was nothing more satisfying than the Pistons winning the franchise's first Larry O'Brien trophy in 1989. The Pistons sweep of the Lakers that year was the NBA equivalent of climbing Mt. Everest. But if you were to base this category on who was the better team between the 1989 and 1990 title teams, you would probably have to give a slight nod to the second championship squad. While the nucleus of both teams was basically the same (Zeke, Joe Dumars, Laimbeer, Dennis Rodman, John Salley, Mark Aguirre, James Edwards, etc.), the 1990 team had a swagger about them that was more imposing than the 1989 team. Who can forget Clyde Drexler proclaiming "we won't be coming back here" after Portland tied the finals series at 1-1. He was right they didn't. The Pistons won the next three in Portland to win the championship as Vinnie Johnsons shot with 0:07 left sealed it. On the other hand, the 1989 team only lost two games during their entire postseason run while the 1990 squad lost five games. Wait a second, are we actually debating this nonsense? Let's just group the two teams together and move on.

3. Tie: 1996-1997 Detroit Red Wings. There is no Pistons-esque debate about which Red Wings back-to-back title team should be on this list. The 1996-1997 Wings team had Vladimir Konstantinov on it. The 1997-1998 Wings team did not. End of debate. After a 42 year drought between drinks out of the Stanley Cup, the Wings finally won the NHL championship after many near misses. When Steve Yzerman lifted that Cup at center ice in Joe Louis Arena, all of the memories of the Dead Wings, Goose Loonies, the Game seven overtime loss to the Leafs on Nikolai Borschevsky's goal, the monumental upset at the hands of the San Jose Sharks, the Avalanche knocking the Wings out of the playoffs on the same night that Claude Lemeiux rearranged Kris Drapers' face went right out the window. The Wings had finally got the 800-pound gorilla off of their back and the celebration felt like it would last forever. Well, the party lasted for exactly six days. On Friday June 13, 1997, a limousine transporting Konstantinov, Slava Fetisov and team masseur Sergei Mnatsakanov crashed into a tree on Woodward Avenue. While Fetisov would escape with relatively minor injuries, Vladdy and Mnatsakanov would suffer life-threatening injuries. While both survived the crash, their severe close-head injuries ended their careers and changed their lives forever.

2. 1984 Detroit Tigers. As great as all of the other Detroit championships were, there is really nothing like your baseball team winning the World Series to bring a city together. (Well, maybe a Super Bowl victory would be similar, but we wouldn't have any clue around here. And for those of you counting, that would be the 3,533rd rip on the Lions in this book.) There is just something about following a team night-after-night for seven months and then having it culminate in a world championship. And the 1984 Tigers got everyone in the area hooked real early that season. The team went gate-to-wire by starting out with a 35-5 record and cruised through the rest of the season. After winning 104 games, the team easily dispatched of the San Diego Padres in the Fall Classic. The other thing that made the 1984 team special is that we got to see the team develop through the farm system. Alan Trammell, Lou Whitaker, Jack Morris and Kirk Gibson all came through the Tigers minor leagues and Tigers fans got to witness first-hand their development. By the time Goose Gossage insisted on pitching to Gibby in Game Five on the Series and the Michigan State star took him deep into the Upper-Deck, the Tigers felt like family with Sparky Anderson playing the role of the insane uncle that everyone tries to avoid at Thanksgiving dinner. The only reason the 1984 team got edged out by the 1968 squad in a photo finish was …

1. 1968 Detroit Tigers. The riots of 1967. As great a team as the 1968 Tigers happened to be, the fact that the city NEEDED a championship squad to unite the city after the divisive civil unrest the year before played a HUGE part in this team being selected number one. The 1968 Tigers weren't only exceptional (they won 103 games), but they also never quit. They could have made excuses when Al Kaline broke his arm after being hit by a pitch in May and missed significant time. Instead, they put their superstar's injury out of their mind and won the American League by 12 games anyhow. The team could have laid down when the St. Louis Cardinals jumped out to a 3-1 series lead in the World Series. Instead they fought back behind Mickey Lolich's pitching and stormed back to win the final three games of the series. In Game Seven, Lolich started on TWO DAYS REST and once again shut-down the St. Louis lineup. By the time Curt Flood misread Jim Northrup's flyball in the seventh inning and broke up a scoreless tie, the Cardinals didn't know what had hit them. Lolich had out-pitched Bob Gibson (a man whose ERA was so low, 1.12, that the league had to change the pitching mound height becase of him) in the deciding game and the Tigers had won their first World Series title in 23 years. The following letter was sent from Michigan Governor George Romney to Tigers owner Jim Fetzer after the Series victory: "The deepest meaning of this victory extends beyond the sports pages, radio broadcasts, and the telecasts that have consumed our attention for several months. This championship occurred when all of us in Detroit and Michigan needed a great lift. At a time of unusual tensions, when many good men lost their perspective toward others, the Tigers set an example of what human relations should really be."

A tough loss is defined by a fan as one you can't get over. You know, the one that keeps you up at night for months. The one that years, even decades after it occurs, pops into your head for some damn reason while you are sleeping. The one that you swear you were going to win the big one and it just got away. Yes, these are those games that make you want to cry.

Honorable Mention: Pistons vs. Celtics Game seven, 1987 Eastern Conference Finals. Adrian Dantley and Vinnie Johnson bang heads on the Boston Garden floor as the Pistons lose the series. Michigan 45 vs. Michigan State 37, October 30, 2004. Spartans blow 17 point fourth quarter lead as Braylon Edwards puts on a one man show to beat MSU in overtime.

10. Well there is always next year—Detroit Tigers vs. California Angels, October 1, 1967. The American League pennant race was wild (to put it mildly). After splitting a doubleheader with the Angels on Saturday, the Tigers enter Sunday a half game behind Minnesota and Boston who will play the regular season finale at Fenway. The loser will be eliminated and the winner will remain a half game ahead of the Tigers if the Tigers can win the first of two. Boston eliminates Minnesota and the Tigers beat the Angels 6-4. The Tigers can force a playoff with the Red Sox if they can complete the sweep. In game one, Willie Horton homered and Eddie Matthews drove in a pair of runs as the Tigers beat the Angels 6-4. Joe Sparma got the win and Fred Gladding pitched two innings of one hit ball to preserve the victory. So it all came down to the second game. The Tigers sent one seven game winner Denny McLain on the Tiger Stadium mound to face one two game winner and Mt. Clemens native Rickey Clark. Rick Reichardt homered off McLain in the second , but the Tigers knocked out Clark with three of their own on a two run Jim Northrup home run and an RBI triple by Dick McAuliffe. McLain gave up three hits in the third before being pulled by Mayo Smith in favor of John Hiller. The first batter Hiller faced was Don Mincher who promptly hit his 2fifth homer of the season and suddenly it was 4-3 Angels. The Angels added three more in the fourth as Hiller walked two guys before Mike Marshall came in and was shelled for a single and a Roger Repoz triple. The possibility of a playoff looked bleak as the Tigers trailed 7-3. It was 8-3 until the home seventh, when McAuliffe singled home Don Wert and Bill Freehan. Down 8-5 heading into the ninth, the Tigers showed some life as Freehan doubled and Wert walked to lead off the inning. The tying runner came to the plate in the person of pinch hitter Jim Price. He flied out. McAuliffe was the next guy to keep the pennant hopes alive. But he hit into a season ending 4-6-3 double play and the Tigers were Division One for the year. Boston completed their Impossible Dream and won the pennant. That loss was thought about all winter. Little did anyone know that the starting pitcher that game would win three one games the next season and the Tigers would win the World Series.

9. Spartan Bob stole the game—The 2001 Michigan vs. Michigan State game. Known to Michigan fans as the game the Spartans stole. MSU trailed 24-20 late in the game when they forced Michigan to punt. The Spartans took over on the Michigan 44. After a sack of quarterback Jeff Smoker and two incompletes, that's when the fun began. The Spartans faced fourth-and-16 with just 1:25 left in regulation. On fourth down, Smoker's pass fell incomplete, but Michigan defensive back Jeremy

LeSueur was flagged for grabbing the facemask of receiver Charles Rogers, giving the Spartans fifteen yards and an automatic first down. Two plays later, wide receiver Herb Haygood caught a 13 yard pass and another first down. On first down Smoker was sacked again, but as the players turned to walk off the field, a flag was thrown against the Wolverines for too many men on the field. With 36 seconds remaining, the penalty resulted in half the distance to the goal being marked off. The clock should have stopped, but continued to run. A second -and-4, pass was incomplete bringing up third-and-4. After an incompletion in the back of the end zone one, Smoker completed a pass to T. J. Duckett for first and goal on the three-yard line. MSU rushed to spike the ball to stop the clock at 0: 17, one second and goal, Smoker rolled to the right and ran the ball down to the one-yard line, but stayed inbounds. With time running out, the Spartans frantically lined up to spike the ball; when they did so, the stadium clock showed one second remaining. Michigan coaches and players argued that the clock should have expired on the play, but game officials did not agree. Replays showed the ball was snapped on the spike play at 0:0 1. Michigan broadcaster Frank Beckmann speculated that State had benefited from its home field advantage, though Big Ten officials would not agree. On the ensuing play, Smoker lobbed a pass into the back of the end z1 where it was caught by Duckett, giving the Spartans a 26-24 victory. Michigan State has not beaten Michigan since then. Debates on the last remaining second continue to this day. Some Michigan fans contend that clock operator Bob Stehlin, known colloquially as "Spartan Bob," stopped the clock before the spike play had actually concluded, to give the Spartans one more chance. Others have countered by arguing that the game clock in Spartan Stadium could only show the time to the nearest second, leaving open the possibility that a fraction of a second was left. One thing we do know, Michigan fans believe they got screwed and they might be right. But being Michigan fans, they think they are right, no matter if they are or not. Remember, Michigan never loses. They are either screwed or they run out of time.

8. Time Out—Michigan vs. North Carolina, NCAA 1993 Championship Game. This would be the last game the Fab Five would play together. This was a great game. Michigan saw a four point lead with less than five minutes to play turn into a five point deficit with a minute left. But the Wolverines scratched and clawed their way to cut it to 72-71 with 35 seconds left. UM fouled Par Sullivan with 20 seconds left. He made one and it was 73-71. He missed the second and the rest is history. Webber rebounded the ball, got away with a travel and then called timeout with 11 seconds left. Unfortunately Webber had a brain fart. Michigan had no time outs left. They had to give the ball back. Donald Williams the games Most Outstanding Player made the two technical fouls and then two more to make the final 77-71. Webber actually had a great game with 23 points 11 rebounds and 3 blocks, but he will always be remembered for the time out they didn't have. This might have been ranked higher, but even without the timeout they needed a two to tie and a three to win. So the bonehead play probably only cost them a chance of winning a title. Webber left for the NBA that summer where he did not get that elusive title.

7. Big Shot Bob—Pistons vs. Spurs, game five NBA Finals. This one still haunts us. The Pistons were beaten badly the first two games of the series in San Antonio and then blew out the Spurs in the next two games at the Palace to even the series. Game five was a doozy. Neither team led by more than four points after the third quarter. Robert Horry was the story of the game. He was scoreless until he hit a three with one second left in the third quarter. But in regulation and in overtime he added 18 more including the dagger. With the Pistons leading 95-93, Chauncey Billups missed a lay-up with nine seconds left. Tim Duncan rebounded the ball and the Spurs called time out, Horry in-bounded the ball to Maun Gnobli in the corner. For some g-d da**ed reason that only he knows Rasheed Wallace left Horry to trap Gnobli. He promptly passed the ball back to the wide open Will Smith lookalike who buried the three to silence the Palace with 5.8 seconds left. Richard Hamilton's chance to win it was way off and the Spurs escaped with the win and a 3-2 series lead. The Pistons won game six and then lost a nine point second half lead and the title in game seven. Sometimes when I shower I still see that bonehead play that cost the Pistons a title. I guess seeing Rasheed Wallace and Robert Horry while I shower is a whole other issue.

6. Don't cry for me Chris Osgood. The top seeded Red Wings had the Cup on their mind as they took on the eighth seeded San Jose Sharks in the first round of the playoffs. It was Scotty Bowman's first season and this series would be as weird as their head coach. San Jose stunned the Wings in the first game at Joe Louis Arena. The series went back to San Jose tied, but arena issues forced this series to have the next three games in California. The Wings won game three, but blew a 3-1 lead in game four and then were beaten 6-4 in game five. Facing elimination back home the Wings killed San Jose 7-1, forcing a game seven. A Saturday night at home. Game seven. One year earlier Toronto beat the Wings in overtime in an identical scenario. But this was going to be different. This was San Jose. But with the score tied at two, Chris Osgood left his net and his clearing pass was intercepted by Jamie Baker who blasted it into the half empty net giving San Jose a 3-2 lead midway through the third period. The Wings could not get any good chances on Arturs Irbe and lost the series to an eighth seed who had a losing record in their first ever playoff appearance. Not many of us who were in that locker room could forget the site of a 21-year-old Osgood answering question after question through a river of tears.

5. He was wide open—Lions vs. Packers, Divisional Playoff game, January 7, 1994. The Lions beat the Packers the week before to win the division and get a home playoff game. This game was a classic that the Lions did dominate. Barry Sanders came back from a Thanksgiving injury that forced him to miss the previous five games with a vengeance. He gained 169 yards on 27 carries. Brett Perriman had ten catches for 150 yards. With the Lions leading 17-14 late in the third, Erik Kramer drove the Lions deep into Packer territory, but his pass in the end zone one intended for the incredibly mediocre Ty Hallock was picked off by George Teague and returned 101 yards for a score and a 21-17 Green Bay lead. Why the hell did he try to squeeze the ball to Ty Hallock?? I mean come on it was Ty F***ing Hallock, not Jerry Rice or even Herman Moore for that matter. I am convinced that if the Lions get a touchdown there, they win it. Give them credit they did recover and go ahead on a Derrick Moore touchdown, making it 24-17 with 8:27 left. The Lions got the ball back and seemed in control but had to punt it away. The Packers took over on their own 29 with just under two and a half to play. Favre marched them down to the Lions 40 when on second and four Favre got away from pressure, scrambled and hurled the ball downfield to a wide open Sterling Sharpe, who walked in for the winning score with 55 seconds left in the game. Sharpe, who had three scores got behind Kevin Scott who thought he had help after he bumped Sharpe and let him go. The miscommunication excommunicated the season and gave birth to another heartbreaking Lion loss. That is the last home playoff game the Lions have played.

4. That was not a foul—Pistons vs. Lakers, game six NBA Finals. The underdog Pistons won game 1 at the Forum, the Lakers evened the series in game 2 before the series moved to the Silverdome for three games. The Lakers took game 3 before the Pistons won the next 2 games by a combined total of 25 points. Back in LA, the Pistons were down 56-48 in the third when Isiah scored the next 14 points to put the Pistons up six. He then sprained his ankle, but continued a Herculean performance scoring a record 25 in the third quarter. It looked like the Pistons were going to pull the upset, they led 102-99 with a minute left. Byron Scotts jumper cut it to 1. Isiah, who ended up with 43 missed on their next possession. The Lakers got the rebound and called timeout. They got the ball to Kareem Abdul Jabbar who turned to let go his vintage sky hook with 17 seconds left. The shot was no good, but Bill Laimbeer was called for a foul by Hugh Evans. Laimbeer barely breathed on him. A horrible call…To make that call in that situation was heinous. Jabbar made both free throws. Joe Dumars missed a shot off the glass and the Lakers ended up with a cheap 3 point win. They won the title in game 7.

3. New Years Eve prayer not answered—Lions vs. 49ers. Divisional Playoff game, December 31, 1983. The Lions, winner of the Central Division were at Candlestick taking on the Niners. The Lions trailed 14-3 in the second quarter before kicker Eddie Murray booted his third field goal of the game to make it 14-9 at the half. It was 17-9 after three quarters and then the Lions rallied. Billy Sims scored two touchdowns to give the Lions a 23-17 lead with five minutes to play. The Niners, behind Joe Montana got it back. Montana completed six straight passes including a 14-yarder to Freddie Solomon for a touchdown and a 24-23 lead. But, the Lions did not quit. Gary Danielson, who was intercepted five times, drove the Lions downfield, completing four passes to set up the winning field goal attempt with five seconds left from 43 yards out. Murray who had kicked four previously was ready to put the Lions into the NFC title game. But, Murray "babied" the kick and pushed it right and the Lions lose again. Most die-hard Lions fans had a premonition when they saw Head Coach Monte Clark praying on the sidelines. Coaches of great teams don't pray. The Lions were not a great team. After all, they are the Lions.

2. The miracle at Michigan—Michigan vs. Colorado, September 24, 1994. The fourth ranked Wolverines led 7th ranked Colorado at the Big House by 12 points with two and a half minutes left. Colorado closed to 26-21 and then with six seconds left Kordell Stewart on a play called Rocket Left, took advantage of Michigan only rushing three guys by heaving the ball over 70 yards towards the end zone. The ball was tipped by receiver Blake Anderson into the outstretched arms of Detroit's own Michael Westbrook for a touchdown and a Colorado 27-26 victory. The defeat was also the beginning of the end for Head Coach Gary Moeller. He would never recover from the defeat and eventually led to a sub-par season and his drunken episode at the Excalibur Restaurant in Southfield for which he was terminated.

1. Bird stole the ball—Pistons vs. Celtics, game five, 1987 Eastern Conference Finals. Series tied 2-2. This was the most painful loss ever. Earlier in the game Robert Parrish punched Bill Laimbeer to the ground, but Parrish was not ejected. Who knows why, maybe Jack Madden or Jess Kersey were actually blind. Anyway, the game was back and forth. Isiah Thomas hit a jumper with 17 seconds left to put the Pistons up 107-106 with 17 seconds left. After a timeout, Larry Bird's shot was blocked by Dennis Rodman. The Pistons had possession with five seconds left. They were going home with a 3-2 lead, but didn't. Isaiah did not see Chuck Daly signal for a timeout, and hurriedly passed the ball to Laimbeer. All of a sudden, Bird cuts in front of Laimbeer, steals the ball and finds a streaking Dennis Johnson who gets past Joe Dumars for the lay-up and a 108-107 win. I think all of Detroit basically crapped their pants. How could this happen? Just when the f***in Celtics appeared dead, they weren't. Isiah said it was the toughest loss of his life. The Pistons did win game six, but lost game seven and the series a few days later.

How do you make a list of the top 100 in a state as rich in athletic accomplishment as Michigan? The answer is simple: you make rules. Here are our rules. To be considered, you had to have either played for a pro or college team in the state. Or if you were an individual athlete, you had to grow up in Michigan or be known to be from Michigan. For example, Sugar Ray Robinson was born in Detroit, but is known as a boxer from New York. Conversely, Joe Louis was born in Alabama, but grew up in Detroit and is known as a Detroiter. Jerome Bettis is from here, but did not play college or professional football here. Also, only a player's career during his or her days in Michigan is considered. For instance, you won't find Tom Brady on this list. And "Magic" Johnson qualifies for his high school and college career here, but his professional career in L.A. does not count toward his ranking.

Above all, remember: there is no right or wrong with a list like this. Yes, there will be some who rank higher than you think they should. And there will be some omissions and others who you think don't belong. But just have fun with it and let the debate begin.

100. Bobo Brazil. Benton Harbor's native son was known as the "Jackie Robinson of professional wrestling." On October 18th in 1962, Bobo used his devastating "coco butt" to defeat Buddy "Nature Boy" Rogers to win the NWA World Heavyweight Title. It was the first time an African-American had won a pro wrestling world title. A fan favorite throughout his long career, Brazil's showmanship and athletic ability blazed a trail for blacks to excel in the arena of "sports entertainment." A true pioneer.

99. Mary Jo Sanders. The daughter of football Hall of Famer Charlie Sanders, Mary Jo is currently considered the top female boxer in the world. A former body-building and toughwoman champion, Sanders has won titles in three different weight classes and currently has a record of 25-1, with eight KOs. Mary Jo also works as a personal trainer and tried to whip one of the co-authors into shape. It was probably the only thing she ever failed at (way to go Stoney).

98. Jalen Rose. Son of former Detroit Piston Jimmy Walker, Rose was a prep star at Detroit Southwestern before becoming part of Michigan's legendary "Fab Five." Rose was the group's leader, playing point guard with an icy coolness. He set Michigan's freshman scoring record with 597 points and accumulated over 1700 points, 400 rebounds, 400 assists and 100 steals during his Wolverine career.

97. Marty Turco. Arguably the best hockey player in University of Michigan history, Turco is, without a doubt, the best goaltender to ever wear the Maize and Blue. The four-year starter led the Wolverines to the 1996 and 1998 NCAA titles and holds the NCAA record for most career wins by a goalie with 127.

96. Billy Sims. Would have rated much higher on the list, if a knee injury didn't cut short his NFL career. A three time Pro Bowler with the Lions, Sims was a powerful runner and terrific receiver who amassed 5,106 yards rushing, 2,072 receiving yards and scored 42 touchdowns during his sensational but brief 60-game NFL career.

95. Rasheed Wallace. A model citizen since the Pistons acquired him from the Atlanta Hawks in 2004, 'Sheed is Detroit's main vibe on the hardwood. As Sheed goes, so go the Pistons. Wallace can dominate a game at both ends of the court and the Pistons would not have won their third NBA title without him in 2004. He also made the phrase "Ball Don't Lie" a part of Detroit basketball culture.

94. Norman "Turkey" Stearnes. The greatest black baseball player in Detroit sports history, Stearnes has largely gone unnoticed because of his unassuming nature and the league and era he played in. Stearnes hit for average and power, winning or sharing six home run titles and three batting crowns for the Detroit Stars in the Negro Leagues during the 1920s and 30s. "He was as good as anybody who ever played baseball," according to pitching great Satchel Page. Stearnes was inducted into the Baseball Hall of Fame in 2000.

93. Kip Miller. The Lansing native is probably the best college hockey player from the famed Miller family and possibly from the state of Michigan. The Spartan great led the nation in scoring two straight years on his way to 116 college goals and a Hobey Baker Award in 1990. His brothers Kevin and Kelly had more success in the NHL, where Kip played for eight teams while accumulating 74 goals in 449 games.

92. Jane "Peaches" Bartkowicz. A premier junior tennis player, Hamtramck's Bartkowicz won 17 junior titles including the 1964 women's singles title at Wimbledon. At the 1968 Olympics in Mexico City, she won the silver medal in women's singles and bronze medals in women's doubles and mixed doubles. As a pro she won 14 tournaments reaching a world ranking of eighth in 1969.

91. Deanna Nolan. While teammates Swin Cash and Cheryl Ford got most of the publicity, the sharpshooter from Flint grew into the best player in Detroit Shock history. A "Miss Basketball" for the state of Michigan in 1995, she led Flint Northern to back-to-back state titles. Nolan became a college star at Georgia, leading the Lady Bulldogs to the 1999 Final Four. "Tweety" took the Finals MVP trophy when the Shock won the 2006 WNBA title. She is so clutch that she should be called "Miss Big Shot."

90. Andre Rison. Long before his girlfriend Lisa "Left Eye" Lopes of the R&B group TLC burned down his Atlanta mansion in 1994, Rison was a star at Flint Northwestern and Michigan State. In high school, Rison was an All-State point guard, an All-State punter and played eight different positions on the football team. As a Spartan, he became MSU's all-time leading receiver, with 146 catches for 2,292 yards and 20 TDs. "Bad Moon" also played basketball and was on the track and field team at Michigan State.

89. Percy Snow. A great linebacker, Snow was a vital member of the Michigan State defense that won the 1988 Rose Bowl over USC. Snow won the game's MVP award with 17 unassisted tackles. Snow claimed both the Butkus and Lombardi Awards in 1989 while piling up 163 tackles, one short of the school record he'd set the previous season.

88. Trevor Francis. One of the greatest soccer players in the world, the Brit played two seasons for the NASL's Detroit Express, scoring 36 goals and adding 18 assists in 33 games while wowing crowds at the Silverdome. He was an All-star in both his seasons here and finished with more NASL points than Pele, despite playing 23 fewer games than the man considered by many as the greatest soccer player ever.

87. James Toney. Born in Grand Rapids and raised in Ann Arbor, Toney was a very good high school football player, but turned to boxing after he allegedly got into a fight with Deion Sanders at the University of Michigan football camp. Nicknamed "Lights Out" due to his punching power, Toney became IBF middleweight champion in 1991 and claimed the super middleweight crown in '93. He later became a cruiserweight champ and defeated Evander Holyfield in a heavyweight fight. Toney defeated John Ruiz for the heavyweight title, but the bout was declared a "no contest" after Toney tested positive for steroids. His career record was 70-6-3, with 43 KOs.

86. Bill Buntin. Teaming with Cazzie Russell, the native Detroiter led Michigan to national prominence and consecutive Final Fours in 1964 and '65. He averaged over 21 points a game in his three years and is the Wolverines eighth all-time leading scorer. Buntin played for the Pistons in the 1965-66 season, but died two years later of a heart attack while playing pick-up basketball.

85. Spencer Haywood. One of the greatest high school players in the city, Haywood took Pershing to the State championship in 1967, then the following summer led the United States to a gold medal in the Olympics. He transferred to the University of Detroit after the Olympics and had an amazing season for the Titans, scoring 32 points per game and leading the country in rebounding with 21.5 boards per contest. He then turned pro and played the following season for the Denver Rockets of the ABA, where he was both MVP and Rookie of the Year. He went on to the NBA, where he played in four All-Star games.

84. Eddie Tolan. A Cass Tech and Michigan graduate, Tolan was a world-class sprinter who won gold medals in the 100 & 200 meters at the 1932 Summer Olympics. At UM, he set the world record in the 100-yard dash at 9.5 seconds and equaled the world record in the 100 meters on several occasions.

83. Herman Moore. Selected to the Pro Bowl four times as a Lion, Moore set the NFL record for receptions in a single season with 123 in 1995. Moore toiled for 12 years as a Lion, retiring in 2001 with 670 receptions for 9,174 yards and 62 TDs, all franchise records.

82. Pavel Datsyuk. Experts thought he was too small for the NHL, but, oh, how they were wrong. Datsyuk was a key role player his rookie year as the Wings won the 2002 Stanley Cup. His point production increased each year from 35 in 2002 to 97 in 2008, as he became the most exciting Wings player since the departure of Sergei Fedorov. He won the Lady Byng Trophy in both 2006 and 2007.

81. Richard Hamilton. Six years with the Pistons, six trips to the Eastern Conference finals. Rip's tenure in Detroit has been amazing. A fearless competitor, Rip passed Isiah Thomas in 2008 to become the Pistons all-time leading playoff scorer. Who will ever forget Hamilton during the Championship celebration screaming "YESSIR! YESSIR!"?

80. Stanley Ketchell. Born Stainislaus Kiecal in Grand Rapids in 1886, Stanley Ketchell became a legendary boxer and lethal slugger. What he lacked in technique, he made up for with sheer heart and determination. Although he never received proper training, Ketchell compiled a record of 52-4-4 with 49 KO's. He became middleweight champ in 1908 and the following year took on legendary heavyweight champion Jack Johnson, knocking him down in the 12th round despite giving up 35 pounds, though Johnson would recover to beat him. Ketchel would have accomplished even more if he hadn't been killed by robbers when he was only 24.

79. Henrik Zetterberg. Hank has rapidly turned into one of the elite players in the NHLA. A master with the puck, he frequently dazzles with his acrobatic moves and goals However it was his all around play in the 2008 Stanley Cup Finals that earned him worldwide raves. He not only led the NHL in playoff scoring with 13 goals and 14 assists, he was a defensive monster, keeping Sidney Crosby in check during the Stanley Cup Finals. His goal and probable game saving play on Crosby during a 5 on 3 in game 4 was a key in the Wings title. He was awarded the Conn Symthe Trophy as 2008 playoff MVP.

78. Mike Hart. Michigan football's all-time leading rusher (5,040 yards) Hart was an energetic leader that didn't mind verbally sparing with the opposition. He fumbled only three times, despite starting nearly every game during his four-year Wolverine career.

77. Dutch Clark. Talk about a guy who did everything. Clark passed, ran, caught, kicked and even coached for the Detroit Lions from 1934-38. One of the last drop-kick specialists, Dutch led the league in scoring three times and the Lions were 39-18-2 in the five seasons he played in Detroit, including the championship season of 1935. He took over as player-head coach for his final two seasons here. In 1963, Clark became the first Lion inducted into the Pro Football Hall of Fame.

76. Brad Van Pelt. Born and raised in Owosso, Michigan, Van Pelt was an All-State quarterback in 1969, then a two-time All-American for Michigan State at safety. In 1972, Van Pelt became the first defensive player to win the Maxwell Award as the nation's best player. During his college career, the multi-talented Van Pelt won nine letters, three each in football, basketball and baseball.

75. Desmond Howard. Perhaps the most exciting player in Michigan football history, Howard was a runaway winner of the 1991 Heisman Trophy. He punctuated the season with an electrifying 93-yard punt return for a TD against Ohio State, striking the Heisman pose as he waltzed into the end zone. He played 11 seasons in the NFL, winning the Super Bowl XXXI MVP with 244 total return yards (including a 99-yard kickoff return) and gaining selection to the 2000 Pro Bowl as a Lion with 1858 yards in combined kickoff and punt returns.

74. Meg Mallon. A graduate of Mercy High School in Farmington Hills, Mallon won the Michigan Amateur Championship in 1983 and turned pro in 1986. She has won 18 LPGA tournaments, including four major championships, and became the first LPGA member to shoot a round of 60 in competition.

73. Brendan Shanahan. The prototypical power forward turned out to be the missing ingredient the Red Wings needed to get over the hump. An immediate fan favorite, he scored 46 goals his first season and helped the Wings get the Stanley Cup in 1997. He never equaled his goal or point total in subsequent years, but was still an excellent player, helping the Wings win Stanley Cups in 1998 and 2002.

72. Greg Kelser. "Special K" was an All-American and Academic All-American at Michigan State where he and Magic Johnson led the Spartans to their first NCAA Basketball Championship in 1979. The Detroit Henry Ford High School star is the only Spartan and the first Big Ten player to score over 2000 points and grab over 1000 rebounds during his college career. Kelser will always be remembered as being on the receiving end of Magic's alley-oop passes; it was a sight to behold.

71. Ben Wallace. The most surprising face of a franchise in history, Wallace became a four-time NBA Defensive Player of the Year and All-star, as well as the team's most popular player during his six years in Detroit. He left for "greener pastures" in 2006, but remains one of the most important players in Pistons' history.

70. Braylon Edwards. "The Bray" is Michigan's all-time leading receiver with 252 career receptions for 3,541 yards and 39 TDs. Gained the coveted #1 jersey his junior year, then during his senior season of 2004, he became an All-American, the Big Ten Offensive Player of the Year and the Fred Biletnikoff Award winner as the nation's best pass catcher.

69. Shawn Respert. The Detroit Bishop Borgess product used one of the sweetest shots you've ever seen to become Michigan State's all-time leading scorer with 2,531 points. He was named as *The Sporting News* College Basketball Player of the year in 1995 and was selected eighth overall in the 1995 NBA Draft. Stomach cancer undermined his pro career.

68. Steve Smith. One of the true class individuals to ever grace our state, the 6-foot-7 Michigan State guard was a two time All-American (1990-91), the Big Ten MVP (1990) and the Big Ten scoring champ (1991). The Detroiter was also MSU's all-time career scoring leader with 2,263 points when his Spartan career concluded. With all his hardwood heroics, Smith's most lasting contribution is the $2.5 million he gave to MSU to help fund the Clara Bell Smith Athletic Center. Named after his mother, Smith's gift is one of the largest single donations ever given by a pro athlete to his alma mater.

67. George Kell. Many remember the guy with the Arkansas twang more for his years as a Detroit Tiger broadcaster, but George Kell was a great player before that. In seven seasons with the Tigers, Kell never hit below 300. The ten-time All-star won the AL batting title in 1949 with a .343 average and was elected to Cooperstown in 1983.

66. Ron Kramer. If freshman had been eligible during Kramer's playing days at Michigan he would have won 12 varsity letters. He was a star on the football field, the basketball court and in track and field. A two-time All-American as an offensive end (1955-56), Kramer led the Big Ten in punting in 1954, and played defensive end, running back, receiver, and quarterback as a Wolverine. One of the greatest all-around athletes in Michigan history, the East Detroit high school star had his number retired by the Maize and Blue.

65. Todd Martin. The East Lansing native ranks as one of the best tennis players in the state's history. He made it to two grand slam finals in 1994 and 1999. Martin won eight singles and five doubles titles in his career and won 11 Davis Cup matches. He was ranked as high as fourth in the world in 1999.

64. Marcel Pronovost. One of the best defenseman ever, Pronovost was a member of the three Stanley Cup Red Wings teams in the 1950s. He was known for his steady play and ability to deliver the big hit at the right time. His physical play led to his nose being broken at least 14 times. He was a four-time All-star and played 13 seasons for the Red Wings. Pronovost was inducted into the Hockey Hall of Fame in 1968

63. Dave Hill. The top born-and-bred Michigan golfer, the Jackson native accumulated 13 victories on the PGA tour. He probably should be given the key to Memphis, since he won the tour stop there four times. He was a member of three Ryder Cup squads and went undefeated in singles matches. Hill also picked up six wins on the Seniors Tour. His younger brother Mike Hill won three PGA events and 16 senior tournaments.

62. Aaron Krickstein. A world-class tennis player as a teenager, Krickstein became the youngest player to ever win an ATP singles title at age 16 in 1983. He's also the youngest player ever to crack the ATP top ten at age 17. Nicknamed "The Marathon Man" for his ability to stage comebacks during his matches, Krickstein won nine tournaments during his career and defeated many of the game's best, including the world's number one Ivan Lendl. Born in Ann Arbor, he attended University Liggett School where he set the Michigan high school record for most consecutive match wins at 56.

61. Grant Hill. Yes, he was not the clutchest player, but many forget how good Grant Hill was as a Piston. Had the best first step in Piston history until he was injured. He shared the 1995 Rookie of the Year award with Jason Kidd. Made five All-Star games as a Piston and averaged 21.6 a game here, including almost 26 per his last year. He was called soft by some, but played in the playoffs with what was later diagnosed as a broken ankle. His departure to Orlando seemed devious, which pissed people off. But he was still one great Piston.

60. Julie Krone. She is not only the greatest female jockey of all time, Krone is one of horse racing's best riders, period. Born in Benton Harbor and raised on a Michigan farm, she remains the only woman to win a Breeders' Cup race and became the first women to post a Triple Crown victory at the 1993 Belmont Stakes atop Colonial Affair. The winningest female jockey in history, Krone was elected in to the Racing Hall of Fame in 2000 and in 2004 *USA Today* named her one of the country's 10 toughest athletes for battling back from devastating injuries. When she retired, she had amassed 3,704 wins and her purse earnings were a staggering $90,125,088.

59. Chauncey Billups. The former third overall draft pick had a nomadic career until he was signed as a free agent in 2002 by the Pistons, his sixth NBA team. "Mr. Big Shot" became an elite level player for the Pistons. His clutch shooting, accuracy at the free throw line, and his defensive prowess have earned him many individual awards including the 2004 NBA Finals MVP and All-Star Game status in 2006, '07 and '08.

58. Hal Newhouser. "Prince Hal" is the only American League pitcher to win back-to-back MVP awards (1944 & '45) and picked up a World Series title in '45. The workhorse of the Tigers pitching staff, Newhouser had more victories before his 30th birthday (188) than any other pitcher in the live-ball era. A seven-time All-Star, the Detroit native was elected to the Baseball Hall of Fame.

57. Bernie Oosterbaan. An amazing athlete from Muskegon, Oosterbaan was Michigan's first three-time All-American football player (1925-27). He was the receiver in the great Bennie combination of Friedman-to-Oosterbaan. A basketball All-American, he also rates as one of the greatest athletes in Big Ten history, The National Football Hall of Famer also coached the Maize and Blue from 1948-58, leading Michigan to the national championship his first season.

56. Chris Webber. A well-known hoop star long before his days as a member of Michigan's Fab Five, C-Webb was a basketball standout at Detroit Country Day School, leading DCDS to three state championships. He was named Michigan's "Mr. Basketball" as a senior and National High School Player of the Year for 1990-91. The Ed Martin scandal erased his Michigan b-ball career, but it was a memorable two-year run. Webber's Fab Five revolutionized college basketball with their fashion sense and play, reaching the NCAA Final in their freshman and sophomore seasons. A 1993 first-team All-American, Webber became the first overall pick in that year's NBA Draft and went on to play 16 seasons in the league, averaging 20 points and 10 rebounds per game.

55. Norbert Schemansky. An icon in the world of weightlifting, Schemansky won the 1952 Olympic gold medal in the middle heavyweight division and three more Olympic medals (silver in 1948 and two bronze in 1960 and 1964) making him the only weightlifter to win four medals in Olympic competition. The Detroit native achieved 26 World Records, nine national titles and three world titles in various weight divisions during his storied career.

54. Sam Crawford. "Wahoo Sam" was a terrific baseball player whose brilliance was overshadowed by teammate and rival Ty Cobb. When he retired in 1917, Crawford ranked as the American League career leader in RBI, home runs, extra-base hits, total bases and triples. He still holds the MLB career record for triples (309) and inside-the-park home runs (51). Elected to the Hall of Fame in 1957, Crawford didn't find out until Cobb died four years later that his old rival's influence got him enshrined at Cooperstown.

53. Shelia Young-Ochowicz. Born in Birmingham but raised in Detroit, Sheila Young was one of the greatest female athlete's in Michigan history. A world champion speed skater, she became the first American to win three medals in one winter Olympiad when she took bronze, silver and gold in 1976. She also won the world sprint championships in 1973, '75 and '76. She was also a great cycler, winning world championships in 1973, '76, and '81. If cycling had been an Olympic sport in 1976, she probably would have won medals in both the Summer and Winter Olympics in the same year.

52. Mickey Lolich. A hero to potbellied men everywhere, Lolich never looked like an elite athlete, but he sure could pitch. When he retired in 1979, he had 2,832 strikeouts, the most by a left-hander in baseball history at that time. His 2,679 K's as a Tiger are still the American League record for a lefty. After a motorcycle fell on him as a child, breaking his left collarbone, he became a southpaw due to a rehab program designed to strengthen his left arm. Lolich will always be remembered for his exploits during the 1968 World Series, when he won three complete games while giving up only five runs. He outdueled the Cardinals' Bob Gibson on only two days rest in Game 7 to clinch Detroit's third World Championship. His 3-0 record earned him the series MVP and he also clubbed a homer (the only one of his career) on his first at-bat during Game 2. His World Series performance ranks as one of the greatest in baseball history.

51. Lorenzo White. The most prolific rusher in Michigan State history, White holds the MSU record for career rushing yards with 4,887 and for total yards in a season with 2,006 during his amazing 1985 sophomore season. Spartan fans will always remember his 56 carry, 292-yard game against Indiana to clinch the 1987 Big Ten title and MSU's first Rose Bowl appearance in 22 years. In the subsequent 20-17 Rose Bowl win over USC, White scored two touchdowns. He was a first-round draft pick and played seven years in the NFL.

50. Willie Horton. A real hometown hero, Willie grew up as one of 21 children in Detroit. Horton led Detroit Northwestern to the city title in 1959 and signed with the Tigers in 1961. Horton had tremendous power, both on and off the field. During the riots of 1967, he stood on a car in his Tigers uniform to calm a riotous crowd. Horton hit 36 home runs for the 1968 World Series title team that helped unify the city and stop the violence. The four-time All-star played parts of 15 seasons with the Tigers, who retired his #23 and erected a statue of him outside Comerica Park.

49. Sid Abel. He centered Ted Lindsay and Gordie Howe on the Wings' famed "Production Line" and produce he did. A great leader and one of the best captains of his time, Abel helped the Detroit win three Stanley Cups. A hard-nosed player, he won the Hart Trophy in 1949. He also coached the Wings and was a legendary broadcaster. Abel was named to the Hockey Hall of Fame in 1969 and his # 12 jersey hangs from the rafters of Joe Louis Arena.

48. Doak Walker. A close friend of Bobby Layne, Walker came to the Lions from Southern Methodist where he won the 1948 Heisman Trophy. As a Lion, he was named 1950 Rookie of the Year, a five-time All Pro and won two NFL titles in 1952 and 1953. The versatile Walker played at running back, flanker, defensive back, return man, kicker and field goal specialist. Elected to the Hall of Fame in 1986, Walker is the Honolulu Blue and Silver's best all-around, all-time player.

47. Red Kelly. Kelly was Bobby Orr before Bobby Orr. During his 12-year Red Wings career, Detroit won four Stanley Cups and eight regular season championships. Kelly was an All-Star for eight consecutive seasons and he won the first Norris Trophy (as the NHL's best defenseman) in 1954. A superstar on a team of many stars, Kelly's versatility allowed the Wings to establish a 1950's dynasty that historians rate as one of the greatest in NHL history.

46. Jack Morris. The right-handed starter led the Tigers in victories a team-record 11 seasons during his 14 years in Detroit on his way to 198 wins with the team. His 162 victories during the 1980s were the most by a pitcher during that decade and Morris holds the MLB record for most consecutive opening-day starts with 14. An intense man, Morris was as nasty off the field as he was on it, something he tearfully apologized for when he was inducted in the Michigan Sports Hall of Fame in 2001. His personality notwithstanding, Morris was one of the dominant pitchers of his era and belongs in the Hall of Fame.

45. Rudy Tomjanovich. He may be best known for being punched by Kermit Washington, but around southeastern Michigan, basketball fans remember Tomjanovich for his sweet jump shot and great career. He was a legend in Hamtrammack before starring at the University of Michigan, where he averaged 25 points per game and still holds the school record for career rebounds with 1044. The second overall pick in the 1970 NBA draft, Rudy T. played in five NBA All–Star games and won two NBA titles as a coach with Houston in the 1990s.

44. Charlie Sanders. An acrobat in cleats, Sanders caught anything thrown in his vicinity. Elected to the Pro Football Hall of Fame in 2007, the 6-foot-4 225 pound tight end was named All-Pro six times and appeared in seven Pro Bowls. A Lion for 10 seasons, Sanders became Detroit's go-to receiver in an era when a tight end was utilized more as a blocker. Sanders retired as the Lions all-time leading receiver in 1977 with 336 receptions.

43. Micki King. The Pontiac native became the dominant female diver in the world from 1965-72. At the 1968 Olympics in Mexico City she led late in the three-meter springboard event, but broke her arm on her second-to-last dive. She battled back and won the Olympic gold four years later in Munich. She was inducted into the International Women's, International Swimming and Michigan Sports Halls of Fame.

42. Mateen Cleaves. The leader of Michigan State's "Flintstones," the Flint native made up for a lack of God-given talent with God-given heart and desire. His sheer determination led the Spartans to their second NCAA Basketball national championship in 2000. Cleaves was named the Most Outstanding Player of the Final Four to cap a college career where he was a three time All-American and two-time Big Ten Player of the Year. A three-time Spartans captain, Cleaves led the Spartans men's basketball program back to elite status.

41. Dick "Night Train" Lane. Considered one of the greatest defensive backs of all time, Lane patrolled the secondary for the Lions from 1960-65. At 6-foot-2, 220 pounds, he was one of the biggest defensive backs in his day and also one of the most vicious hitters. A star before he was traded here from L.A., Lane made All Pro with the Lions from 1960-63. He was named to the Pro Football Hall of Fame in 1974

40. Glen Rice. Without his sharpshooting, Michigan never would have won the 1989 NCAA Basketball National Championship. Rice still holds the record for most points in the NCAA Tournament (184). A second team All-American, the Flint native put the Wolverines on his jumping shooting back after Bill Frieder was replaced by Steve Fisher just two days before the start of 1989 NCAA Tournament, unleashing what is considered one of the greatest individual performances in NCAA Tournament history. Drafted by the Miami Heat with the fourth overall pick in the 1989 NBA Draft, Rice played 15 years in the NBA, making three All–Star squads and winning an NBA title.

39. Floyd Mayweather. The current best pound-for-pound fighter in the world, Mayweather boasts an amazing 39-0 record with 25 KOs. The Grand Rapids native has been world champion in four weight classes and beaten the likes of Ricky Hatton, Arturo Gatti, Zab Judah and Oscar De La Hoya. A sports superstar, Mayweather has also appeared on *Dancing with the Stars* and "defeated" the 7-foot, 450-pound Big Show in one of the main events at Wrestlemania XXIV.

38. Lou Whitaker. It's an injustice that "Sweet Lou" isn't even on the ballot for the Baseball Hall of Fame anymore. A Tiger for 19 seasons, Whitaker played every inning of his career at second base, forming the longest-running double-play duo in MLB history with shortstop Alan Trammell. The 1978 AL Rookie of the Year, Whitaker is the only second basemen to club 200 home runs, knock in 1000 runs, score 1000 runs, and record 2000 hits besides Joe Morgan and Rogers Hornsby. Did we mention that he's no longer eligible for the Hall of Fame?

37. Alan Trammell. The Tigers shortstop could do it all: hit, field and run the basepaths with guile and deceptive speed. The 20-year Tiger was selected to six All-Star Games, won four Gold Gloves and was MVP of the 1984 World Series. He should have won the AL MVP award in 1987, when he hit .343 with 28 homers and 105 RBI to lead the Tigers past Toronto to win the AL East.

36. Dennis Rodman. If you can get past his tattoos, piercings, multi-colored hair and provocative behavior, Rodman ranks among the very best Pistons of all-time. A raw and immature talent when the Pistons drafted him in the second round in 1986, "The Worm" became an instant hit because of his frantic style of basketball. He won a pair of NBA Defensive Player of the Year awards and two rebounding titles in Detroit. He also won two NBA titles here, providing the missing piece (some may say link) that put the Pistons over the top during their "Bad Boys" championship runs. He should be in the Hall of Fame.

35. Rick Leach. Leach was a three-sport star at Flint Southwestern and given the starting quarterback job at Michigan before he even showed up on campus, which was unheard of for Bo Schembechler. He was all Big Ten quarterback three times, breaking the conference record for TD passes. Leach also rushed for almost 2200 yards at UM. A great baseball player as well, Leach won the Big Ten batting title as a junior and went on to play a decade in the MLB.

34. Alex Delvecchio. When "Fats" Delvecchio retired from the Red Wings after a 24-year career, he was second only to Gordie Howe in goals (456), assists (825) and points (1281). A winner of three Stanley Cups with the Wings, Delvecchio served as Detroit's captain for 12 seasons and still holds the NHL record for playing the most games and seasons for only one team. Admired for the way he handled himself on and off the ice, Delvecchio won the Lady Byng Trophy three times and participated in 13 All-Star games. His #10 sweater hangs in the rafters at Joe Louis Arena.

33. Charles Woodson. The only defensive player to win the Heisman Trophy, Woodson was so dominant that teams would refrain from passing the ball his way. His one-hand interception against MSU in 1997 rates as one of the greatest plays in Michigan history. He was also used as a wide receiver at times and returned punts. Besides the Heisman, Woodson took home the Bednarik, Nagurski, Thorpe and Camp trophies. The main reason the Wolverines won the 1997 national title was this guy, the best defensive player in Michigan history.

32. Bubba Smith. Standing 6-foot-7 and weighting over 280 pounds, the Texas native was considered a behemoth when he played defensive end for MSU in the mid-1960s. A two-time All-American in 1965 and 1966, Smith along with George Webster anchored a Spartans defense that shared the 1965 National Championship with Alabama. The College Football Hall of Famer had his #95 retired in 2006 by the Spartans before they played Notre Dame on the 40th anniversary of "The Game of the Century," which ended in that infamous 10–10 tie between the Spartans and Fighting Irish. Smith went on to become the first pick overall in the 1967 NFL Draft.

31. Jack Christiansen. This does not happen very often. The Lions draft a guy in the sixth round and he becomes a six-time All Pro, a Hall of Famer and helps lead the team to three NFL titles. Jack Christiansen is that guy. He was an incredible defensive back for the Lions of the 1950s, heading up their famous "Chris's Crew" secondary. Christiansen led the league with 10 interceptions in 1953 and 12 in 1957. He was not too shabby as a return specialist either, with eight punt returns for touchdowns and an average of over 22 yards a return.

30. Bill Laimbeer. The rough-and-tumble center and teammate Rick Mahorn became the poster boys of the Pistons' "Bad Boys" era. A tough, no nonsense player, Laimbeer not only loved to frustrate opponents, he enjoyed inciting the fans ire when he played on the road. What gets lost in all the anger and histrionics is the fact that he was a tremendous basketball player. "Lambs" is the Pistons career rebound leader with 9,430 boards and ranks third in Detroit history in games played (937) and minutes (30,602). Currently he's the head coach of the WNBA's Detroit Shock and has won two WNBA titles.

29. Sergei Fedorov. After bolting from his Russian team during the 1990 Goodwill Games, #91 became the most enigmatic Detroit player in recent memory. In his 13 seasons with the Red Wings, Fedorov electrified the fans with his speed and his skill. He could do it all, as his MVP season of 1994 and great playoff performances confirm. But for many, he never did enough. The MVP season was almost a curse, as fans thought he should score 50 goals every year. A great two-way player, Fedorov won two Selke Trophies. But his holdout in 1998 pissed off many locals. He certainly made up for it with a 20-point playoff and by helping Detroit secure its second consecutive Stanley Cup. He left the team after the 2003 season for less money but more responsibility with Anaheim. The fans never forgave him and still boo Fedorov.

28. Kirk Gibson. "Gibby" was a high school star at Waterford Kettering, a college football All-American at MSU and one of the best clutch hitters in the history of Major League Baseball. He'll be the first to tell you that he didn't post Hall of Fame career numbers. But that doesn't really matter. Gibson was a player that lived for the moment and when the moment called for it, he delivered. Drafted by the Tigers and the NFL's St. Louis Cardinals coming out of Michigan State in 1978, "Gibby" chose baseball and became an integral piece to Detroit's 1984 World Series club. Nationally, he'll be remembered for his World Series-winning home run against Dennis Eckersley in 1988 for the Dodgers. In Detroit, Gibby is remembered for another World Series-winning home run, this one off of Goose Gossage in 1984.

27. Bill Freehan. Born in Detroit, Freehan probably lived every Michigander's childhood dream (unless you were a Maize and Blue hater). Freehan played both football and baseball at the University of Michigan. He proved better at baseball, setting a Big Ten record by hitting .581 in 1961. He signed with the Tigers that year and went on to play 15 years behind the plate for Detroit while establishing himself as the top catcher in the American League of his era. He was selected to every All-Star game but one between the years 1964-1975. He won five Gold Gloves and his block of home plate on Lou Brock in the fifth game of the 1968 World Series helped turn the series around for the Tigers.

26. Lem Barney. A multi-talented athlete during his college days at Jackson State, Barney got drafted by the Lions in the second round of the 1967 NFL Draft. Barney snagged 10 interceptions as a rookie and was named Associated Press Defensive Rookie of the Year. Barney finished his 11-year Lions career with 56 interceptions. The seven-time All Pro was also named to the NFL's 1960's All-Decade Team and elected to Pro Football's Hall of Fame in 1992.

25. Anthony Carter. A.C. was arguably the best receiver in Michigan football history. A three-time All-American and Big Ten MVP in 1982, he held numerous Michigan and NCAA receiving and return records by the time his college career ended. Carter stayed in the state and played for the USFL's Michigan Panthers, helping lead them to the league's inaugural championship game, where he caught nine passes, including the winning, 48-yard score. After the USFL folded in 1985 season, Carter joined the Minnesota Vikings, where he gained three Pro Bowl selections.

24. Bob Lanier. The Pistons drafted him first overall in 1970 and his 22.6 points per game average remains the highest in Pistons history. A gigantic man (6-foot-11 265lbs.) with mammoth feet (size 22), Lanier was a physical force with a dead-on hook shot, a decent outside game and incredible rebounding skill. Often plagued by injuries, especially gimpy knees, he never reached his goal of winning an NBA championship. But he made the All-Rookie team in 1971, was the MVP of the 1974 All-Star game, and got elected to the Hall of Fame in 1992. "The Dobber" ranks second in career rebounds (8,063) and third in career points (15,488) for the Pistons and was named one of the 50 Greatest Players of All Time by the NBA.

23. Gordon Johncock. The Coldwater native was a fixture at the Indianpolis 500, winning the race in 1973 and 1982. Both wins were notable for different reasons. The 1973 race featured a fiery crash on the 58th lap which caused the death of Johncock's teammate Swede Savage. The 1982 win was one of Indy's most exciting finishes, as Johncock held off Rick Mears to win by 0.16 of a second. He also won the Michigan 500 in 1982 and he was the USAC champion in 1976. He dabbled in NASCAR, gaining seven top 10 finishes in his 21 races. At just 5-foot-7, Johncock stood as a giant in the sport and is a member of both the Motor Sports and Michigan Sports Halls of Fame.

22. Cazzie Russell. Russell laid the foundation for the modern era of Michigan basketball. During Cazzie's three-year career (freshman weren't eligible back then), Michigan captured three Big Ten titles (1964-66), went to three NCAAs and made two Final Fours. He generated so much interest in the program that he's credited with the construction of Crisler Arena, still referred to as "The House That Cazzie Built." Listed as a guard, Russell's all around ability allowed him to excel at any position on the hardwood and become a three-time All-American, two-time Big Ten MVP and the 1966 College Basketball Player of the Year. He averaged 27.1 points per game over the course of his college career, still a Michigan record.

21. Joe Schmidt. The seventh-round draft pick hit hard and he was smart as hell and revolutionized the middle linebacker position. A mainstay of the Lions defense that won three championships in the 1950's, Schmidt made 10 Pro Bowls and was a co-MVP in 1960. Others in his era may have gained more fame, but #56 was one of the best ever.

20. Ted Lindsay. Pound-for-pound the toughest player in Detroit's sports history, Lindsay stood only 5-foot-8 and weighed just 160 lbs. But "Terrible Ted" would take on anybody to ensure a Red Wing victory. His bellicose nature sometimes overshadowed his extraordinary talent as a hockey player. Playing on Detroit's famed "Production Line," Lindsay blossomed into one of the greatest scoring left wings in NHL history. A leader on and off the ice, he was instrumental in forming the player's union, which resulted in him being exiled (traded) to Chicago in 1957. After spending three seasons with the Blackhawks, he retired in 1960 only to come back for one more season in Detroit (1964-1965) so he could retire as a Red Wing. Detroit finished atop their division that season for the first time since they had traded Lindsay seven years earlier. During his 14-year Red Wings career, the Hall of Famer scored 335 goals and had 393 assists, was named a first-team All-Star eight times and won four Stanley Cups.

19. Joe Dumars. A mixture of grace, greatness, mental toughness and humility, Dumars ranks as the classiest Detroit athlete ever. Since coming here as an unheralded draft pick in 1985, Dumars has been a fixture in Detroit and a standout, winning the 1989 Finals MVP, two titles, plus selections to six All-Star Games and four NBA All-Defensive Teams. He ranks second on the Pistons in career points and assists and first in treys with 990. The guy is so cool, the NBA renamed its annual Sportsmanship Award after him. He also did a helluva job rebuilding the team as its GM. Though just his 14-year Piston playing career was enough to get him elected into the Basketball Hall of Fame in 2006.

18. George Webster. "George was the greatest football player I ever coached," said legendary Michigan State coach Duffy Daugherty. Daugherty created the position of roverback for the 6-foot-4, 218-pound Webster because he could cover a speedy receiver and take down a bruising running back one-on-one. A team captain and a two-time consensus All-American (1965-66), Webster led the Spartans of 1965 and 1966 as they complied a 19-1-1 record, won back-to-back Big Ten titles and shared two national championships. Elected to the College Football Hall of Fame in 1987; Webster also had his #90 retired by MSU in 1967, becoming only the second athlete to be bestowed that honor by Michigan State.

17. Thomas Hearns. Hearns was Detroit boxing in the 1980s. Helmer Kenty was Kronk Gyms first champion, but Hearns was the best. He won his first major title by knocking out Pipino Cuevas with a single, devastating right hand at Joe Louis Arena for the WBA welterweight title in 1980 and went on to win belts in five other weight classes. Still, Hearns is best known for his spectacular losses to Sugar Ray Leonard and Marvin Hagler (in what many consider the best three rounds of boxing ever). He did whip Leonard in their rematch, no matter what the judges said. His career record was an impressive 61-5-1. He remains a beloved fixture at Pistons games (always showing up late) and will always be a Detroit legend.

16. Dave DeBusscherre. Perhaps the best all-around athlete to ever come from Detroit, DeBusschere was a prep standout in basketball and baseball for Detroit Austin. During his high school days, Austin would win the Class A basketball title, the baseball city championship, and he pitched a local baseball team to a junior national championship. DeBusschere attended the University of Detroit, then signed with both the Detroit Pistons and Chicago White Sox in 1962. He's one of only 11 to play Major League Baseball and in the NBA, where he made a bigger mark. Known as a tremendous defensive player with a gift for rebounding, DeBusschere was named to the NBA All-Rookie team (1962-1963) and at age 24 became the Pistons head coach and the youngest coach in NBA history. In December of 1968, Detroit traded their native son to New York, where DeBusschere would reach superstardom with the Knicks. An eight-time NBA All-Star, DeBusschere, was named to the NBA's 50th Anniversary All-Time Team and was elected to the Basketball Hall of Fame in 1983.

15. Terry Sawchuk. Maybe the best goaltender of all-time and definitely the best in Red Wing history, Sawchuk minded the Red Wings net for 12 years over two different stints with the club. He still holds NHL records for regular season shutouts with 103 and regular season games played with 971. He was Rookie of the Year in 1951, won two of his three Vezina Trophies with Detroit and guided the Wings to two Stanley Cups.

14. Al Kaline. The greatest Tiger of the modern era, Kaline never played a day in the minors, joining the Tigers right out of high school. A tremendous all-around player, Kaline was the picture of consistency during his 22 year Tiger career. In 1953, the 21-year-old Kaline won the AL batting title with a .340 average becoming the youngest player in baseball history to win a batting crown. He could do it all: hit, field, run and throw and established himself as one of the game's greatest clutch performers. Kaline was a 15-time All-star, won 10 Gold Gloves, clubbed 399 home runs (the most in Detroit history), collected 3,007 hits, and finished with a .297 career batting average. Appearing in only one World Series (1968), Kaline hit an impressive .379 with two home runs and eight RBI. Respected by his peers and loved by Tiger fans, Kaline turned down the Tigers first $100,000-a-year contract in 1971 because he felt that he didn't deserve the money after a sub-par season. Elected to the Hall of Fame in 1980, he was, at the time, only the tenth player to ever be elected on the first ballot. Known as "Mr. Tiger," Al Kaline is one of the most popular athletes in Detroit sports history.

13. Dave Bing. Strange how things work out. UM's Cazzie Rusell was the first overall pick of the 1966 draft and the Pistons used the second pick to take Syracuse's Bing, who went on to win NBA Rookie of the Year honors. Overshadowed by contemporaries Oscar Robertson and Jerry West, Bing flourished under the radar, gaining seven All-Star Game selections and a spot in Basketball Hall of Fame and on the NBA's All-Time 50 Greatest team.

12. Earvin "Magic" Johnson. A high school basketball legend during his days at Lansing Everett, "Magic" Johnson is the greatest basketball player to ever come out of Michigan, and arguably the greatest basketball player ever. A 6-foot-9 point guard, Johnson's uptempo style revolutionized basketball. As a high school senior, the McDonald's All-American averaged 28.8 points per game and 16.8 rebounds as Lansing Everett won the state title with an astounding 27-1 record. When he became a Spartan, he took a mediocre program and turned it into a powerhouse. During Johnson's freshman season (1978), the Spartans won the Big Ten Title and advanced to the Elite Eight of the NCAA Tournament, losing to eventual champ Kentucky. In his sophomore season, MSU won the national title and "Magic" became a household name. His final college game (the NCAA final showdown with Larry Bird's Indiana State) remains the highest-rated college basketball game on TV ever. The pure joy he exuded while he played and his career-long rivalry Bird revived basketball. After his sophomore year, Johnson would leave Michigan State and reach superstardom with the Lakers, claiming the NBA title and Finals MVP his rookie season. Magic was later named the greatest Laker of All-Time, but will always be a Michigander and a Spartan.

11. Bobby Layne. Let's see. He led the Lions to three NFL titles (although he was hurt for the 1957 title game), made the Hall of Fame, was the most popular NFL player of his era, became notorious for drinking and carousing, even on the nights before games, established himself as the best quarterback in the history of the team and, oh, yes, allegedly put a curse on the team after he was traded that has so far lasted a half-century. Do you think Bobby Layne had an impact here?

10. Tom Harmon. Michigan's first Heisman Trophy winner in 1940, Harmon is the most talented and versatile athlete to ever play football for the Maize and Blue. Harmon was a star at running back and also shined at quarterback and kicker. Scholarships weren't available when he played, so Harmon spent his summers working in a steel mill and during the school year he held down two jobs at a college bookstore and washing dishes at the Michigan Union to pay for his education. He dominated college football in 1939 and 1940, leading the nation in scoring both seasons and establishing a record that still stands today. He finished his Wolverine career with 2,134 rushing yards, 33 rushing TDs, over 100 pass completions, 16 TD passes, eight interceptions as a defender and two INTs returned for touchdowns, plus a 29.9 yard average on kickoff returns, a 12.5 yard average on punt returns and 237 career points. Harmon saved his best for last, leading Michigan to a 40-0 drubbing of Ohio State in the 1940 clash at Columbus. He rushed for three TDs, tossed two TD passes, kicked four extra points and averaged 50 yards per on three punt returns. When he left the field for the final time as a Wolverine, even the Ohio State crowd gave him a standing ovation.

9. Hank Greenberg. Many of the Hall of Famer's season numbers are staggering: 170 RBI in 1935; 183 RBI in 1937; 58 home runs with 146 RBI in 1938; 41 homers and 150 RBI in 1940. Greenberg was the Tigers slugging star and the idol of every Jewish kid in the United States. He was a two-time MVP who ended up his career with 331 homers and 1276 RBI, despite missing four seasons when he went into the military.

8. Niklas Lidstrom. Red Wing hockey changed the day Detroit drafted Nick Lidstrom in 1989. The Wings best player over the last decade, many of his teammates will tell you that he has never made a mistake on the ice. A six-time winner of the Norris Trophy, Lidstrom was the first European to be awarded the Conn Smythe Trophy (play-offs MVP). He has appeared in 10 NHL All-Star games and won three Stanley Cups. A magician with his stick, Lidstrom takes away the puck from opponents without them realizing that the play is moving up ice. In 1,252 games played for the Wings, Lidstrom has 938 points, a Red Wing record for defenseman. Always among the NHL leaders in ice time, Lidstrom actually gets stronger as a game wears on. Already considered the best defenseman of his generation and one of the best Red Wings of All-Time; when he finally hangs up the blades Nicklas Lidstrom will be regarded as one of the greatest players in NHL history.

7. Charlie Gehringer. One of the greatest second baseman in baseball history, the "Mechanical Man" played all of his 19 MLB seasons with the Tigers. He was MVP in 1937, when he won the batting title with a .371 average and had a career batting average of .320. The Hall of Famer batted .375 in the Tigers 1935 World Series victory over the Cubs. Born in Fowlerville, he attended the University of Michigan and played his whole career in Detroit and he passed away in Bloomfield Hills at the age of 89 in 1993.

6. Steve Yzerman. No athlete in the modern era of Detroit sports has had the impact of Steve Yzerman. He played 22 years with the Red Wings and became the longest-serving captain in NHL history (19 seasons). His 1983 arrival marked the beginning of a glorious era of Red Wings hockey. Second only to Gordie Howe in career points (1755) and goals (692), Yzerman is Detroit's career leader in assists (1,063) and holds the single season Red Wing record for points (155), goals (65), and assists (90). When he retired in July of 2006, he was the NHL's sixth All-Time leading scorer and winner of numerous awards including the Conn Smythe, Selke, Masterton, and Lester Patrick trophies. The three-time Stanley Cup champion was one of the toughest players to ever don the winged-wheel, as his tolerance for pain and playing hurt are unmatched by any athlete in Detroit history. A model of class, grace, and dignity, Yzerman never craved the spotlight. "The Captain," represented Detroit and the state of Michigan the only way he knew how: by playing tremendous hockey with as little fanfare as possible.

5. Isiah Thomas. Forget about what' he's done since retiring, Isiah Lord Thomas is the greatest Piston ever and maybe the greatest little guy to ever play the game. His toughness was legendary, scoring an unbelievable 25 points in the third quarter of Game 6 in the 1988 NBA Finals on a sprained ankle. He ranks as Detroit's all-time leader in points, assists and steals. He led the Pistons to back-to-back titles and was named the 1990 finals MVP, an All-star 12 times and one of the NBA's 50 Greatest All-Time players. He was elected to the Basketball Hall of Fame in 2000.

4. Barry Sanders. The Lions' greatest player, Sanders is also their most enigmatic. An unassuming superstar, the former Heisman Trophy winner hit Detroit in 1989 and didn't stop running until his stunning retirement a decade later. Sanders was a 10-time All-Pro and Pro Bowl selection, NFL Offensive Player of the Year twice and the league's co-MVP in 1997 when he rushed for 2,053 yards and set an NFL record by rushing for 100 yards in 14 consecutive games. When he abruptly ended his career in July of 1999, he had rushed for 15,269 yards and was within easy reach of Walter Payton's then all-time NFL rushing record of 16,726 yards. Several years later, Sanders revealed that the Lions losing ways had destroyed his competitive drive, an explanation that made perfect sense to any Detroit fan.

3. Ty Cobb. The greatest Tiger played 22 seasons in Detoit. How good was Cobb? His career batting average was .366. He won the batting title 11 times and the Triple Crown twice and hit over .400 twice and collected over 4000 hits. Cobb would do anything to win, including sliding with spikes up, and was, by all accounts, a horrible person. But he was also one of the greatest players ever in any sport.

2. Gordie Howe. Without question, Gordie Howe is not only the greatest hockey player of all time, he's the greatest player in the history of team sports. No one can match his combination of offense, toughness, strength, and longevity. Howe retired as the NHL all-time leading scorer and still holds many NHL records. Howe played professional hockey in six decades and holds the NHL record for most seasons (26) and games (1,767) played. "Number 9" remains the Red Wings' all-time leader in goals (786) and points (1,809). He is the Wings' and the NHL's record holder with 21 All-Star selections. Six times in his Detroit career he led the league in scoring and six times he was named the NHL's MVP. A four-time Stanley Cup champion, Howe was among the NHL's top five scorers for twenty consecutive seasons, also an NHL record. A modest and quiet man, Gordie asked only for a Red Wings jacket as his first signing bonus. "Mr. Hockey" is universally recognized as an athlete of supreme ability and unrivaled character.

1. Joe Louis. Perhaps the greatest heavyweight of all time, "The Brown Bomber" moved to Detroit when he was ten years old. He was a great amateur fighter, winning the Michigan Golden Gloves title. He won the world heavyweight title in 1937 and became a national hero with his 1938 first-round KO of German Nazi poster-boy Max Schmelling. Probably the first African-American athlete to be loved by all races, Louis successfully defended his title 25 times before losing to Ezzard Charles in 1950. He retired with a record of 69-3 with 55 KOs. Joe Louis was not only Detroit's favorite son, but America's as well.

X